Fine WoodWorking

ROUTER

THE COMPLETE GUIDE TO THE MOST

BANDSAW

ESSENTIAL POWER TOOLS

TABLESAW

Fine WoodWorking

ROUTER

THE COMPLETE GUIDE TO THE MOST

BANDSAW

ESSENTIAL POWER TOOLS

TABLESAW

PAT WARNER / LONNIE BIRD / KELLY MEHLER

The Taunton Press

The Taunton Press, Inc., 63 South Main Street, PO Box 5506, Newtown, CT 06470-5506
e-mail: tp@taunton.com

JACKET/COVER DESIGN: Giulio Turturro
ILLUSTRATORS: Vince Babak, Ron Carboni, and Rosalie Vaccaro
PHOTOGRAPHERS: Lon Atkinson (pp. 2–125), Terry Nelson (pp. 126–258),
Lonnie Bird (pp. 259–377, except where noted)
FRONT COVER PHOTOGRAPHERS: (clockwise from top) Scott Phillips, Terry Nelson, Lonnie Bird
BACK COVER PHOTOGRAPHERS: (top to bottom) Lon Atkinson, Terry Nelson, Lonnie Bird

LIBRARY OF CONGRESS CATALOGING-IN-PUBLICATION DATA
Bird, Lonnie.
  Router, bandsaw, and tablesaw : Fine woodworking's complete guide to the most essential power tools / Lonnie Bird, Kelly
Mehler, and Pat Warner.
     p. cm.
  Includes index.
  ISBN-13: 978-1-56158-928-9
  ISBN-10: 1-56158-928-4
  1. Routers (Tools) 2. Band saws. 3. Circular saws. 4. Woodwork. I. Mehler, Kelly. II. Warner, Pat, 1943- III. Fine woodwork-
ing. IV. Title.
  TT203.5.B445 2006
  684'.083--dc22
                          2006011278

Printed in China
10 9 8 7 6 5 4 3 2 1

Working wood is inherently dangerous. Using hand or power tools improperly or ignoring safety practices can lead to permanent injury or even death. Don't try to perform operations you learn about here (or elsewhere) unless you're certain they are safe for you. If something about an operation doesn't feel right, don't do it. Look for another way. We want you to enjoy the craft, so please keep safety foremost in your mind whenever you're in the shop.

Contents

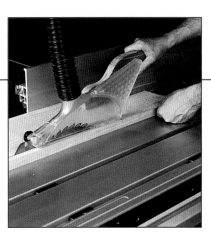

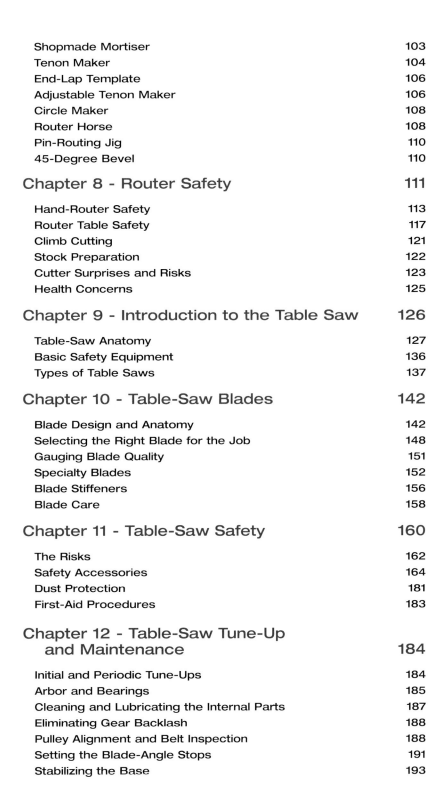

Introduction to Routing

R outers have worked themselves into the premiere spot among
woodworking power tools—only drills outsell them among portable
power tools. It's even fairly common for woodworkers to own a
small family of routers in different sizes and shapes. But the sheer size of the
router field can make the job of choosing the right tool seem daunting. And
the vast number of accessories on the market offers a feast of choices that
provides another challenge. To navigate this sea of choices, and find a
sound strategy to incorporate this tool in our shops, we might think about
why we use these tools to begin with and what makes them so special.

This pair of experimental round tenons demonstrates the measured and precise removal of
material. The tenons are part of the stock; they are not dowels.

The author's mortising jig uses a pair of edge guides and a pair of jig stops so it can be adjusted to rout virtually any mortise.

Routing is basically the high-speed removal of stock from a workpiece; think of it as the measured wasting of material. All sorts of materials can be routed, but solid wood may be the most common. And while the tool has many uses other than woodworking, most router bits are designed primarily for use with wood and plywood. However, medium-density fiberboard (MDF), plastic, solid-surface material—even rock or metal—can be routed given enough power, the right setup, and appropriate tooling. But the majority of us work with wood most often.

Many woodworking processes, including routing, are subtractive. I can't think of an example where routing adds anything to a workpiece. In many forms of art, such as ceramics and goldsmithing, the material is reformed and added to the whole, thus conserving materials. Not so with wood: We chop, saw, sand, drill, plane, joint, and rout most of our resource away. And routers are the preeminent stock removers. They can remove stock on the edge, on the ends of a workpiece, or anywhere in the middle. And they can remove stock in nearly any profile, from a thin slice along the edge for jointing, to complex shapes for raised panels, cope-and-stick joinery, or decorative details. Depending on the power and size, they can remove the tiny burr of plastic laminate while trimming a countertop or hog out a mortise in hard maple. So as we investigate router choices in subsequent chapters, a major consideration will always be the scope of the work and the power requirements.

Routing is rarely done to rough stock. Routers normally are used after the jointer, planer, and table saw operations. That is one of their distinctions. They can't—or shouldn't—compete with tools that prepare stock. They are intended for precision work. This will be taken into account as we discuss the various choices.

But routers, unlike many hand tools, need jigs, fixtures, fences, and holders to apply themselves. Edge and collar guides, custom subbases and various kinds of templates are very useful. But even more important are the jigs, fixtures, and platforms that provide a way to do precise joinery. The router is seriously handicapped without its accessories. You can rout with bearing-guided profile cutters without much ado, but virtually any

This ensemble is not cheap, by any stretch, but for a lifetime woodworker they will cover most routing challenges. From left: DeWalt 621 plunge router, PC-690 mid-range fixed base router, 310-PC trim router, PC-7518 fixed base router.

Fluting, whether on flat stock or mounted on a lathe, is one of the router's important uses.

Finish carpenters typically use routers to mortise for hinges on custom door installations.

Trim routers may get their heaviest use in countertop fabrication. Here, plastic laminate is being flush-trimmed after being glued down on the particleboard substrate.

other cut (without bearings) will require some jig, fixture or external guide. Another consideration, then, is the router's ability to work well with a variety of jigs and fixtures.

Because of their great and vast potential, routers are major woodworking problem solvers. No other tool finds its way into so many facets of woodworking. Routers apply themselves well in the joinery and decoration of your work, excel in making jigs, fixtures and templates, and—even better—they can usually help you out of a jam. They are, it's true, dependent on a massive array of potential jigs, fixtures, holders and cutters but they also help solve nearly every woodworking problem. No other tool offers so many cutting and shaping possibilities. And no other tool provides quite the same challenge when it comes to sorting through all the choices to get the right tooling to match your particular needs.

Applications

So far we've talked about the router's use for a variety of woodworking tasks, its relationship to other tools, its array of accessories, and the way it can reach any part of the workpiece. Let's take a minute and talk about the most important criterion of them all, the router's specific applications. The router has three major areas of application: decoration, joinery, and millwork.

TYPES OF ROUTING

Type	Description	Duty Cycle	Power Demand (hp)	Router
Light-trim	Flush trim laminate/veneer. Shallow, small cutter routing	Short	< 1	Trim router
Decorative trim, light-duty edge	Shallow edge cuts up to ⅜ in. x ⅜ in. Volume, ogees, bevels, ball bearing decorator and template cuts.	0–60 minutes	1½–2 router	Medium fixed-base
Plunge	Inside multistage work, large excavations; casting must be supported for plunge. Mortises, circles and laps.	Can be long	1½–3 will be acceptable for most work	Plunge router
Table	All stationary work.	No time limit	3+	Fixed-base or plunge router (more common)
Heavy-duty hand router	Edge and template full-thickness cuts.	All day	3+	Big fixed-base
Template	Pattern work; line, fractional or full thickness cuts.	No time limit	1–3	All routers and tables

DECORATION

Categorically, the greatest number of router bits are for trim and decoration. Catalog inventories usually exceed 50 percent in decorator cutters. This is strange in a way, because decoration has so little to do with practicality; your desk, jewelry box, or bed will survive just as well without decoration. Nevertheless, finishing and decoration are two of the most important criteria in which woodwork is judged. It would indeed be a mistake to overlook them.

JOINERY

The power of the router is in its joint-making capability. Nearly all of Western joinery is possible with a router, with the addition of its cutters, jigs and you. It has its limitations, like bridle joints and deep skinny dovetails, but it can address an enormous number of both ordinary and special joints. But the router isn't perfect, and there are many occasions, due to fixturing, cutter design and so on that a joint is compromised. You may not exceed or even meet the capacities of a hand joiner, but do expect to make mortises and tenons; tongues and grooves; laps; glue joints; through, blind, and sliding dovetails; splines; lock miters; cope and stick; box joints; and various combinations.

This screw-driven router fence employs a dial indicator to achieve accuracy in the thousandths of an inch range.

This platform jig uses an oversized base and a ball bearing rabbeting bit to form a square tenon on the end of a workpiece.

Routing lends itself well to a wide range of joinery challenges.

MILLWORK

Router work that doesn't fall into the decoration or joinery genres I call millwork. This is not the millwork associated with shapers and molders. Rather, it is work like trimming panels to length, jointing, dimensioning, and squaring stock. I also use the router to make jigs, and I frequently make short runs of jigs and fixtures for those of you who'd rather woodwork. The platforms and their windows are usually template routed. The squared fences, adjustable slots, and rabbeted stops are also routed.

Wide glue-ups pose serious dimensioning problems. A jigsaw, router, and template can be used to square off the ends.

The fence on the work holder can be adjusted parallel to its work edge. With the cutter surrounded by an MDF straight fence, you can joint and machine to width in one operation.

Inexpensive router bits can reproduce a variety of traditional profiles.

Types of Routing

It would be a mistake to think that all of this application can be enjoyed with just one router. It can't be done. There are some cuttings that, if done to full depth, will break the cutter; sometimes the router is just too small and underpowered for the job. Certain cuts put the work or the operator at risk with the wrong router. There are problems of scale that may require the router table. Small jobs may be better suited for a trim router, and multistage work should be done with a plunge router. However, routing is versatile and there are distinctions you should know about.

LIGHT TRIM

Frequently, trade work calls for very light and shallow cuts in wood, metal, or plastic. These cuts are of short duration, and require little power or set-up complexity. You may not need a full-size router for these cuts. Examples include the mortising of hinges, chamfering, and small roundovers. But mostly I'm talking about the cutting and trimming of plastic laminate (Formica), wood veneers, fiberglass and thin aluminum. This work is always light duty, shallow, done with only ¼-in. tool shanks, and only with trim routers.

The PC-310 trimmer and offset subbase are a good match to trim (bevel) these edges. The work can be seen through the plastic base while the router is kept flat on the work.

Sliding dovetails are great for locking legs and rails. Sockets are made on the router table and the tenons with the hand router.

Bread and butter trim (cove) cuts require about 1.5 hp, a sharp cutter, and a medium-weight fixed base.

DECORATIVE TRIM

The next level of complexity I call decorative trim. Work is of medium duration (up to 30 minutes or so) along the edge of stock or template, and the fixed single-depth cuts are less than the equivalent of a ⅜-in. by ⅜-in. groove. These cuts are too demanding for a trim router and not enough for an industrial-strength tool. Some fixturing may be required, but most of the work is decorative, using bearing-guided trim cutters like ogees, roundovers, rabbets, and bevels. This work is best done with midrange fixed-base routers typically of 1 hp to 2 hp. The fixed base is low-centered, close-handled, and has a small casting designed for this kind of work.

A big cut like a slice off the face of this tenon requires a lot of power. The weight of this tool may be a safety factor rather than a control problem.

HEAVY-DUTY HAND ROUTING

The cuttings in this category are often all-day, fixed-depth cuts like big single-pass roundovers, dovetails, dadoes, and full-thickness template cuts for sink cutouts or furniture parts. These cuts are also along the edge of the stock or template. This is hand routing at its finest. Midsized routers "stumble" when called for this duty. Big cutters are common, ¾ in. to 1½ in. in diameter and up to 1¾ in. long. Fixtures, templates, and jigs are more common than ball-bearing profile bits. The cuts are often more than ⅜ in. by ⅜ in. or as deep as the design of the cutter and power will permit. Again, this is the domain of the fixed-base router, not for stability but because these cuts are essentially single pass-single depth and do not use the multistage capability of the plunge router. In this case, the cutter is set to depth and not changed. Some shops buy dedicated single-cut routers for this work.

PLUNGE ROUTING

Routers designed to allow changes in depth without shutting off the machine have come to be called plunge routers. The base incorporates a mechanism with a series of stops so that the router can be lowered incrementally. The design allows you, for example, to quickly rout a deep mortise in a number of smaller steps that only remove ¼ in. or so of material at a time. It also allows you to start a cut anywhere in the middle of a workpiece—and it is especially useful when routing on panels.

Although it's possible to "plunge" a fixed-base router into the work, it's an inherently unsafe operation because the base isn't supported during the operation. Plunging is simply not safe with a fixed-base router. The plunge

Mortises and tenons require fixtures for quality and repeatability. A good fit like this imposes a lot of demands on the jigs.

Half-laps are shallow and large in area, perfect for the plunge router. These are made in a template jig (under the work).

router is expressly designed to function in your hands with the aid of gravity. Its spring-load motor head, turret stops, upstop, handle grips, motor lock and switch are all situated for you to slide the tool to its destination with the cutter retracted and motor on. Now, with you at the controls, you can safely change the depth under power and waste wood in stages.

The plunge router does its best work "plunging." Plunging is best carried out and sometimes only possible when the router is completely sur-

Tongues and grooves of all sorts can be made on the router table with straight bits.

Stopped open mortises are safely done on the router table.

rounded by substrate. Plunging with only half of the casting on the work can tip the router over or, in some cases, arrest the plunge action altogether. The safest arena for plunging then is on inside cuts like mortises. That is not to say that plunge routing cannot be along the edges and ends of the workpiece. It just means that the base casting has to be on solid ground to support its plunging function and relative top heaviness. Cuttings that are deep and wide or otherwise impossible with a single-depth setting should be done with a plunge router. Plunge cuts too dangerous for a fixed-base router also include inside blind excavations where the cutter must be under power and extended to begin the pass.

TABLE ROUTING

Table routing essentially turns the tool into a stationary machine with a fence that wraps around the cutter and supports the workpiece. Unlike portable routing operations, the workpiece moves past the cutter, instead of the reverse. More than 80 percent of all routing can be done on the router table. There are restrictions to its use (such as very large work and long sticks on end) but the majority of routing is on individual workpieces and quite manageable on the table.

Router table work, more often than not, demands a lot of power. There is no single router tailored exclusively for the router table. Big motors, resistant to changes in momentum and load, are required here. Long-grain, cross-grain, end-cutting, and some inside cuts are possible on the table. Joinery and template work are also common. (Only use very long cutters over 1¾ in. These cutters require at least a 3-hp motor and work best with variable speed control.)

Complementary template joinery is about the only way to join wood along curvy lines. One sample is a lap, left, one is glue jointed, middle, and the other is tongue and groove, top.

I use these templates to make the platform for the tenon-maker. Since the instructions are already "carved" into the template, you can't make a mistake.

TEMPLATE ROUTING

Template routing allows you to rout multiples of nearly any shape by using a pattern that's attached to the workpiece and rides against a guide pin or other reference surface. Templates can be used for joinery, making copies, mortising, shaping, and making parts for jigs. Most repetitive routing jobs can be expedited by a template.

By far, the most popular type of cutter in my router locker is the pattern bit with a bearing on top. These come in many diameters and lengths for use in a variety of situations. The art of template routing demands an

Common Accessories

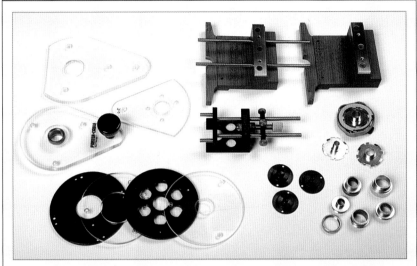

THERE ARE A HOST OF ACCESSORIES available to extend the capabilities of your router. There are, for example, aftermarket subbases made from clear plastic (at lower left above) that will allow greater visibility as you're making a pass with the router. Also available are subbases with an offset design (upper left) that provide greater control because more of the base is on the workpiece as you work.

Another category of accessories is the edge guide, which acts much like the fence of a table saw and rides along the edge of workpiece (upper right). The two at top are shop-made edge guides; the black guide in the middle is an aftermarket edge guide made by Micro Fence (see Resources on p. 180).

There are also a variety of collar guides (lower right) to fit most popular routers. The collar guides fit into the subbase and surround the bit, providing a way for the cut to follow a template.

understanding of all forms of routing, guide systems, clamping procedures, jig making, and basic woodworking. Template routing can be done on the table or on the bench with plunge or fixed base. It is the essence of routing.

Just as no single knife will work in the kitchen, no single router will suffice for all routing applications. Trying to cover all bases with one router will have you overpowered in one situation and at risk in another—or perhaps empty-handed if the router is tied up in the router table. Just as the jigsaw, radial saw, table saw, and bandsaw address your sawing needs, so do the trim, plunge, medium and heavy fixed-base router cover your routing needs.

Fixed-Base Routers

I n the United States, the fixed-base router has been the dominant
router design for over half a century. The tool is simple, with few
moving parts, and in my view is safer than a plunge router for most
operations. The motor, clamped firmly (fixed) in its base casting, has a
simple depth adjustment, but it must be stopped and reset between cuts.
The plunge router overcomes this disadvantage, and is the tool of choice
for deep mortises that must be cut in several passes.

This 1960s-vintage
Black & Decker model
442 is still running.

A fixed-base router, left, is best applied in single-depth edge cuttings. The plunge router,
right, is designed for successive depth changes under power and is best for multistage
inside excavations like mortises.

Fixed-Base Router

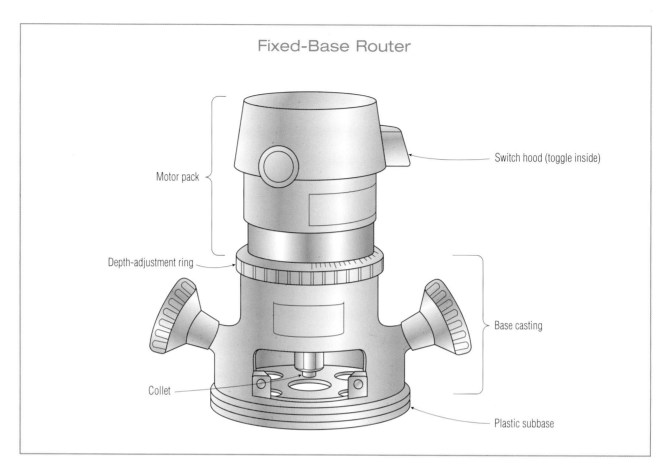

Motor pack

Switch hood (toggle inside)

Depth-adjustment ring

Base casting

Collet

Plastic subbase

Cross grain dadoes and dovetails are easily cut with a fixed-base router and collar guide.

The plunge router allows you to change its cutter depth because a trigger or latch releases the locking mechanism to lower the cutter into the workpiece with the base fully supported. This is risky if these same maneuvers are tried with the fixed-base tool: Because it must be tipped, the base won't be fully supported as the cutter enters the work. But the additional weight and overall awkwardness of the plunge router make it unsuitable for a lot of the general routing we do along edges and against templates.

Router Basics

The anatomy of the fixed-base router is quite simple and has remained essentially the same since it first came on the scene. The motor is packaged in a precision-ground cylinder that fits precisely in a matching aluminum base casting. All of the motors have bearings on either end of their armatures, a pair of carbon brushes that transmit electrical current to the armature, and a collet (see the sidebar below) fixed to the business end of the tool. The positioning of the motors in the base castings varies from manufacturer to manufacturer, as well as the knob assemblies, castings, switches, wire sets, and collets.

Router Collets

ALL COLLETS MADE TODAY are multislotted except the short ones in trimmers, and the fixed-base DeWalt 610. They are connected to their collet nuts and as such pull themselves out of the router when unwound from the armature. Cutters sticking in the router are a thing of the past.

There is still a lot of design variation, however. The slotting varies. The slots originate from one or both ends of the collet. Some have three, six, or eight slots. The components vary in length, wall thickness, and materials—though all are steel. The nuts can be square, hexagonal, or octagonal. One thing is constant: They all hold the cutter and hold it well if you apply 15 or so pounds of squeeze to a 10-in. set of wrenches.

Use no abrasives to keep them clean. They are made to very tight tolerances. Clean the dust out of them and the collet seat if they get dirty. If a cutter slips in a collet, you should probably scrap it, especially if it is scratched or burred. Worn collets don't hold the cutter well and out-of-balance tool bits will vibrate more in a worn collet. Keep at least ¾ in. of shank in the collet and whenever possible use the

entire length of the collet for maximum holding power. Do not use any of the shank in the collet where the flute fades away from grinding, because the holding power will be compromised.

Knocking Off the Sharp Edges

Base and motor castings can be a bit rough, and sharp enough in some places to cut you. An accidental quick grab for a cutter change, storage, installation of a guide collar, or router control can result in injury. I spend 10 minutes with a deburring tool on any new casting. You can also use a file and a wire brush.

Many router castings can use some deburring to get rid of jagged edges. A deburring tool like this one is a $10 purchase.

The underside of motor caps can be sharp. I dropped this router, saving it from a crash, but then cut myself on the cap reaching for it.

CASTINGS, HANDLES, AND SWITCHES

Base castings vary and are quite distinguishable. All have windows for good cutter visibility, though most base plates are black and hide the work surface. DeWalt and Porter-Cable will supply accessory transparent subbase replacements. A router that can readily stand upside down for bit changes is a nice convenience. Porter-Cable, DeWalt, and Milwaukee have accounted for this. The Bosch model has a radius on the motor cap for comfort, but at some expense for upside down stability.

The knob or handle assemblies of most fixed-base routers are placed low on the machine and provide stability. Plastic, wood, and metal are the typical materials, and most people will have their own opinions on which are most comfortable. I use an offset subbase on all of my fixed-base routers, and I control the tool with one hand on the base casting and the other on the offset base. This configuration allows maximum control especially around the corners and along the edges of the work. However, you should be aware that the position of the two casting knobs supplied with a router is well thought out. So give them a good try before considering any changes.

Wire sets are either two- or three-conductor depending on how the tool is insulated. Double-insulated tools will have two-prong plugs without the ground. All commercial routers use rubber jacketed wire sets but most are different lengths. I am 6 ft. tall and I always use an extension cord, but I would like the plug to remain on the ground and for me that means a 10-ft. wire set.

The DeWalt 610 shown here can be supplied with a clear plastic, round replacement subbase for collar guide use. The flat head provides a stable base for turning it upside down for bit changes.

The maple knobs on the Bosch subbase get you as close to the work as any router.

The Porter-Cable model 690 base casting is the perfect size for my hand. I've got the same control on this router as the quarterback has on the football.

Switches are slide, toggle, rocker or trigger, and their locations vary. I would not select a router based on the switch; it's a good idea to clarify the off position so you know the tool is off when you plug it in 10 ft. away. Also, prepare yourself for a quick stop and keep your hands in a conven-

For added safety, the author highlights the off direction on the switch.

ient location for hitting the off button easily. You never know when a clamp may slip or something else go awry.

POWER

Fixed-base routers in the commercial class range from about 1 to 3 hp. Weight and appropriate applications scale up with the power; expect about 7 or 8 pounds difference within this power range. More power also means more metal and consequently the capacity to soak up heat. A router in heavy use can heat up, and if the heat exceeds the cooling fan's capacity, then the router gets hot to the touch. However, the longer it takes to heat up, the less likely it will break down from overload. So if your router is consistently hot, reduce the load or get a bigger router.

Porter-Cable has every power range covered—from ⅞ hp to 3¼ hp. DeWalt's only entry is 1.5 hp; Bosch has models in 1¾ hp and 2 hp; and Milwaukee in 1½ hp and 2 hp Ryobi, Makita, and Sears/Craftsman also have fixed-base entrants of various strengths, but Makita is the only commercial-grade tool with two entries at 1 hp and 1⅞ hp. Porter-Cable has an exclusive in the sustained all-day power class (7518), and there are no other fixed-base routers of its size (3 hp).

D-HANDLED ROUTERS

The D-handled router is the least popular fixed-base design and the most costly. It does enjoy a limited niche market, however. Its advocates claim safety and control because a pistol-style switch is gripped to start the router. To stop, you just release. With the switch in hand, you can shut down quickly, but in my view that safety margin is more than offset by a loss of control. A D-handled router is always held the same way and has less stability as you finish a pass at the end of the workpiece. Moreover, the obligatory D-handle in line with the travel of the router interferes with cuts made with edge guides and collar guides.

The D-handled style of router provides one-handed control, which is often convenient for repetitive work.

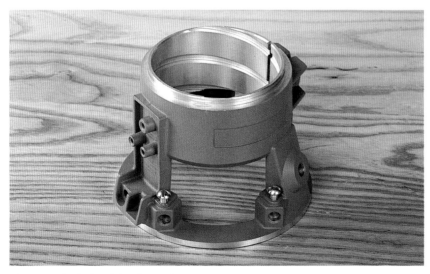

The Porter-Cable 691 D-handle casting.

The Industry Standard

THE PORTER-CABLE 690 IS THE most popular commercial-grade medium weight fixed-base router in North America. The motor is trapped in its base casting with four pins, which allows it to turn and move easily up and down when you release the clamp. It's a simple but effective method of raising and lowering the cutter.

Porter-Cable 690

One side of the base casting has been actually sawn in half so the motor clamp will evenly squeeze down on the motor for a firm grip. However, for me, its base-tightening thumbscrew is too small, and I have replaced mine with a lever. The motor travel in its base is about 1¾ in. with all four pins engaged. (It is not advisable to operate the tool without all of its pins engaged in the base casting.)

This 8-lb., 1.5-hp, single-speed, hard-start router has the smallest base casting in its class. But the weight and balance of the 690 is about right for most cutters less than 1⅝ in. long and 1⅝ in. diameter. The 690 sits easily upside down on its flat motor cap for bit changes. Two wrenches of the same size are required to change cutters. Its collet design is self-releasing and very effective. There are six sizes: ¼ in., ⅜ in., ½ in., 8mm, 10mm, and 12mm.

The Porter-Cable enjoys popularity like no other router. Many accessories, jigs and fixtures are designed around the 690. It has a low center of gravity and is comfortable to use. The 690 applies itself best to fixed-depth edge and template cuts. I would not have the 690 serve as the only router in a shop, but I would consider it as a first purchase. As a bonus, its base casting also accepts the smaller ⅞-hp motor for light work.

Porter-Cable 690	
Weight	8 lbs.
Speed	Single, 23,000 rpm
Amps	10
Soft start	no
Horsepower	1.5
Height adjuster/mechanism	Continuous, motor twist
Collets	¼ in., ½ in., ⅜ in., & metrics option
Baseplate diameter	5¾ in.

The squat casting, shown with upgraded lock lever and accessory offset base provides so much control that it can feel like an extension of your hands.

Leading Fixed-Base Routers

There is no single perfect router. Most have some excellent features, but make compromises in other important areas. Some are old designs that still work well; others offer new solutions to some sticky problems. The DeWalt 610, for example, is a quality tool that's been in production virtually unchanged for over 30 years (first as a Black & Decker tool and Elu tool). On the other hand, the Bosch 1617EVS is a relatively new tool with some innovative features. Each of the routers has its own personality and its own set of strengths and weaknesses.

THE DEWALT 610

As mentioned above, the DeWalt 610 design is at least 30 years old and essentially unchanged. A rack and pinion gear raises and lowers the motor in the housing. It can be adjusted, like the 690, to zero at any point in its

DeWalt 610	
Weight	7.3 lbs.
Speed	Single, 25,000 rpm
Amp	9
Soft start	no
Horsepower	1.5
Height adjuster/mechanism	Rack & pinion
Collets	¼ in. & ½ in.
Baseplate diameter	6 in. (shown with an accessory offset base)

DeWalt 610

The three motor pack projections add another 1 in. of travel to this DeWalt 610, which is also shown with round collet nut and collar.

travel and its depth ring is indicated in $\frac{1}{64}$ths. A wing nut is standard for tightening the casting around the motor, but a short lever is better (a Reid tool, KHB-14, for example). The casting is not sawn through as on Porter-Cable; rather, a $\frac{3}{4}$-in. strap (band) of the casting is cinched on the motor on the rack side of the base. The grip is not as sure compared with the Porter-Cable, but the motor never slips.

Two positive changes in the DeWalt 610 that warrant praise are its collet nut and motor barrel extensions. The collet nut has been milled to fit inside its accessory collar guides. The closer the collet can get to its template, the less deflection there is with the cutter—a nice touch. The 610 (and its ancestors) have never had much up and down motor travel and used to be quite popular in the router table nevertheless. When the tool carried the Elu and Black & Decker labels, its motor pack was redesigned to accept a longer rack for its depth pinion gear. This clever change added another $\frac{7}{8}$ in. of travel for a total of about $1\frac{3}{4}$ in. However, more travel is at the expense of security. If the $1\frac{3}{4}$-in. depth is exceeded, the base casting's grip on the motor pack isn't secure.

The 610 hard-start, $1\frac{1}{2}$-hp router is more sensitive to cutter imbalance than other routers its size. It's fine with small, squatty profile cutters like ogees, roundovers and bevels, but it vibrates more than I like with long ($1\frac{1}{2}$ in.) cutters of equivalent diameter. This gets more pronounced with bearing-guided router bits. The motor rests well upside down for cutter changes, and requires two different size wrenches to unlock its collet. Through the succeeding years its castings have deteriorated some and self-tapping subbase screws have replaced through-hole machine tapping.

While under the Elu label, the 610's collet was at its best: eight-slotted and self-releasing. Under the DeWalt label the collet was simplified to a single slit, nonreleasing design. Its short length (¾ in.) probably contributes to its vibration sensitivity. Nevertheless, it does grip the cutter well and cutters do not stick in the collet.

The 610 accepts few accessories, but DeWalt does have clear round and offset subbases for this tool in their catalog. With its short, stable geometry, its ability to project the collet into a collar guide, and with its transparent accessory subbase, the tool is particularly well suited for dovetail and box-joint template work. It is just as stable along the edge of stock with decorator cutters. The early Black & Decker tools with essentially the same design were designed to go right back to work after a 6-ft. drop to the floor. The switches last forever but the wire sets seem to have about a two-year life span if used regularly.

THE BOSCH 1617EVS

Bosch is the first to produce an all-new router since the Porter-Cable 690 crossed over from Rockwell. It is, however, a standard-looking router and requires close inspection and a few practice cuts to be appreciated.

The base casting is equipped with a two-stage depth adjuster. It is by no means a micrometer, but small, continuous depth changes can be made by turning the screw adjuster while the motor lock is disengaged. The motor has three small rectangular notches on ½-in. centers milled into it or on opposite sides. The depth adjuster engages a notch for its rough position and the vernier is used for the fine adjust. The total motor travel is about $1\frac{11}{16}$ in. It's not a good idea to exceed that. If the motor isn't engaged with its depth adjuster assembly, the lock system won't work properly. One interesting note: The motor can be inserted in two diametrically opposed positions within the casting, so that you can easily adjust the switch position for ease of operation.

BOSCH 1617EVS

Bosch 1617EVS	
Weight	7.7 lbs.
Speed	Variable, 8,000–25,000 rpm
Amps	12
Soft start	Yes
Horsepower	2
Height adjuster/mechanism	Three ½-in. increments, with secondary continuous micro
Collets	¼ in., ½ in., & ⅜ in.
Baseplate diameter	6 in.

A spring lock engages a notch in the casting for the rough ½-in. changes on the Bosch 1617.

Bosch designed this tool with variable speed, double insulation and soft start. The castings are magnesium, and with its 2-hp motor it's as light as the DeWalt 610. High power and light weight don't usually go together. You might expect the tool to run away from you like its 1604 single speed predecessor. On the contrary, the 1617EVS is a delight to rout with.

The collet seat is milled right into the end of the armature; there are no couplings. This, along with its precision bearings, alignment, armature design, and balance make this the smoothest-running motor of all the routers I know of.

Bosch has solved the motor lock problem that plagues some other routers. The base casting is split through its height on one side and has a very user-friendly over-center lever lock much like a toggle clamp. It is adjustable for wear and stretch, and is designed for a close fit between the motor and the base casting.

The base casting is drilled for its own subbase, and has the same three-hole pattern used for the Porter-Cable 690 specialty accessory subbases and router table. The design of the interior of the base casting and its subbase allows the guide collar to get within 0.004 in. or better of center. The 1617EVS is useful for all fixed-depth cutting with a 2-hp router. It has unique advantages in close quarters, and its forgiving soft start will prevent an unwanted kick into an uncut area. Moreover, its feedback electronics start the tool gradually (soft start) and provide a new measure of safety not found in hard-start tools. The 1617EVS can also absorb kinetic accidents such as an unexpected dig into the uncut material. If I'm into experimental work, I'll choose the 1617EVS for this reason, because routing can be dicey. In ordinary work, the motor behaves like a single-speed tool, but if there is an instantaneous overload this is the router I want to be using. It also has an additional ¼-hp rating over the single-speed 1617 for this purpose.

MILWAUKEE 5680

The Milwaukee is a 2 hp, single-speed hard-start commercial grade router that has remained essentially unchanged for its lifetime of over 20 years.

The motor height is adjusted with a plastic ring engaged in a spiral ground around the outside of the motor. The motor is "hung" in the casting by this ring, so the mechanism doesn't work when the router is upside down. It's not a great choice for the router table. There's also no way to "zero" the vertical position in the router. All depth changes are therefore relative to the last reading of the depth ring. The motor travel is about 1½ in.; after that, the casting begins to lose its grip on the motor.

Milwaukee is credited with the first multisplit self-releasing collet. Its 1⅛-in. overall length and eight-sided nut is a combination not to be found in any other router. The motor has a very flat and large head for easy bit changes upside down.

The Milwaukee 5680 is one of the noisiest and toughest of routers, designed to flop around in the back of a pickup truck, and has long been the standard for carpenters and outside tradesmen. The 5680 is well balanced and ergonomically acceptable, but the initial kick-back on startup has got to be the most powerful of any 2-hp tool. Its squat, heavy motor helps keep the tool flat on edge cuts.

Prevent Accidental Gouging

A powerful router, especially one without a soft-start feature, will lurch when you first flip the switch. To help prevent contact with the workpiece, keep the router a full router-bit diameter away from the work at startup.

Milwaukee 5680	
Weight	8.5 lbs.
Speed	Single, 26,000 rpm
Amps	12
Soft start	no
Horsepower	2
Height adjuster/mechanism	Ring-hung motor, twist ring
Collets	¼ in., ½ in., & ⅜ in.
Baseplate diameter	6 in. (shown with an accessory offset base)

Milwaukee 5680

The Milwaukee 5680 has the only eight-sided collet nut and is one of the first with an eight-slotted self-releasing collet.

The Milwaukee castings are better than most, but still need some deburring. In my view, their split-base casting design holds the motor well but their wing nut assembly for tightening is too small. I've replaced mine with a set screw and nut. The unique screw-on collar guide system, ample motor travel, and high power of this router make it particularly useful for dovetail/box joint template work, all edge cuttings, and pattern cuts.

THE PORTER-CABLE 7518

The Porter-Cable 7518 is the largest fixed-base router. Bosch and Black & Decker used to compete in this niche but the 7518 is now alone in this class. It's not often this happens. I suspect the reason for this is pricing and the economies of scale; nevertheless, this is just a lot of router at a price

Porter-Cable 7518

Porter-Cable 7518	
Weight	14.5 lbs.
Speed:	Variable, 5 speed 10,000–21,000 rpm
Amps	15
Soft start	Yes
Horsepower	3.25
Height adjuster/mechanism	Continuous motor twist
Collets	¼ in., ½ in., ⅜ in., & metrics option
Baseplate diameter	7 in. (shown with accessory offset base)

With its long motor barrel the Porter-Cable 7518 has more up and down travel than any router, fixed or plunge.

that can't be beat. This heavy-duty machine is the most powerful fixed-base U.S. router at 110 volts and 3¼ hp. Everything about this router is big. It weighs in at more than 1½ times (14.5 lbs.) its closest rival. It has at least as much up-and-down motor travel as any router. It has the largest base casting footprint of any router. And it has an overall height of more than a foot. One would expect this machine to be hard to handle, and it can be with big cutters, but it is deceptively tractable in normal use.

The motor fits in twin spirals within the base casting and one motor revolution translates into 1 in. of cutter height change. The tool is double insulated, soft start, and incrementally variable in steps of 3,000 rpm.

The five-speed motor is very well balanced dynamically and with its massive armature and bearings able to absorb kinetic accidents and tolerate out-of-balance cutters better than most routers regardless of size. If it's power I need, I use the 7518. If a new big cutter is suspicious (perhaps resharpened and out of balance), the 7518 at 10,000 rpm is my proving-ground tool. With its locomotive glide and flywheel momentum, it is a graceful and fun router, whether engaged in light work or heavy lifting.

All Porter-Cable routers use the same two stamped wrenches for their self-releasing collets. The base casting of the 7518 has two cast D-handles and the same small wing nut to tighten its split casting on the motor.

Porter-Cable supplies specialty square, round, and offset subbases, edge guides, collars, and dust collection accessories for their fixed-base routers.

The best use of this router is in heavy fixed-depth long duration cuttings of all sorts, especially deep template cuts for pattern work. The 7518 has the power to break small cutters if overfed, but small cutters should be used in smaller routers. It is also my choice for testing, new, oversize, or prototyped tool bits, jigs and fixtures. If these won't work with the 7518, they won't work with a lesser tool. The tool has become the industry standard for the router table.

MAKITA RF-1101

This 2¼-hp fixed-base router is the newest entry in this category. It has state-of-the-art features such as variable speed, a soft start, and low noise output. It's nicely finished with respectable ergonomics and balance. The tool somewhat resembles both the PC-690 and the Bosch-1617. My sample weighed in at just over 8 lbs., which is similar to other comparable routers.

The over-center toggle motor lock is excellent, but it will pinch you if you're not careful. The wide 4-in.-diameter motor top provides a stable platform so you can easily perform bit changes with the router upside down. Collets are nicely machined and hold cutters well; they use two stamped steel wrenches. The base casting is very similar to the Porter-Cable 609 and accepts Porter-Cable subbases, as well as collar and edge guides.

Makita
RF-1101

Makita RF-1101	
Weight	8.06 lbs.
Speed	8,000-24,000 rpm
Amps	11
Soft start	yes
Horsepower	2.25
Collets	¼ in. & ½ in.
Depth adjust mechanism	4 casting pins engage 2 motor pack ground helixes
Baseplate diameter	5¾ in.

The up-and-down motor slop is substantial, and, as such, depth adjustments may take several tries. There is about $1\frac{3}{4}$ in. of motor travel once all four pins in the base casting engage both ground helixes in the motor pack. The depth adjustment ring is all black, difficult to read with the engraved numbers, and hard to turn. The depth ring can, however, be set to zero at any position, making the setting operation easier. The small toggle switch position changes (with respect to the handle axis) as the motor rotates in the base. It is handy for this woodworker but, at a glance, I can't tell if it's on or off. This is not an exclusive Makita oversight.

Department Store Routers

There are perhaps eight to 12, 1-hp to 2-hp "consumer grade" fixed-base routers on the shelf at any one time. Ryobi and Craftsman are the primary players. Often they are the same tool with different labels. Their prices may vary from $50 to $100. These tools are typically loaded with attractive features but accessories that are often troublesome. In my view, the simplest of these tools is usually the most useful. For occasional light duty weekend hobby work the consumer tool will be acceptable. They are often designed only for $\frac{1}{4}$-in. shaft bits and should not be expected to compete with industrial/commercial routers.

Sears offers a comprehensive selection of cutters and accessories for their routers. If you are uncertain of your future in woodworking, you can test the waters with a minimum investment with these tools and I'd recommend it. On the other hand, just because a tool, a car, or whatever is relegated to part-time use, that is no excuse for a compromise if a quality product is affordable.

Best Fixed-Base Applications

Fixed-base routers are more stable than plunge routers along the edge of the work—especially with an offset subbase. They are also valuable on inside cuttings if there is a pathway for the cutter from the edge. The blind inside cut with a fixed base is dangerous and requires a plunge router. A bit that's jabbed into an inside excavation will self-feed the router—and you may lose control.

Fixed-base tools, then, because of their low centers, work better on the outside edges of the work or off a template. Your first choice for dovetail, template tools, open dadoes, full or fractional thickness template cuts, and all ball-bearing profile cutters should be the fixed-base router.

Deep cuts are also less risky with a fixed-base router. The levers and knobs of plunge routers are, by design, higher than those of the fixed-base; they are, after all, fastened to the motor head, not the base casting. Deep

Basic notches are another strong point of the fixed-base router.

This step and repeat decorative cove can be managed well with a fixed-base router, a collar guide and an offset subbase. Make sure to pull the collar firmly against the template. Any deviation will spoil the whole pattern.

Fixed-base tools are the best choice for template-edge cuts. They have a low center of gravity and are less likely to tip than a plunge router.

plunge router cuts with a cutter fully extended may cause a router to tip as you push the tool along, especially with a short-base footprint in the direction of travel. (Plunge routers don't generally have round subbases.) All fixed-base routers have round subbases that better support the tool under these conditions.

The fixed-base router is a necessary router for the lifetime woodworker or hobbyist. Neither a plunge nor fixed-base router will cover all types of routing safely—so plan on owning one of each.

Plunge Routers

T he plunge router, which has been around for about 50 years, differs from a fixed-base tool primarily with the integration of the motor with the rest of the tool and the incorporation of a pair of tubes that provide the mechanism for controlling the up-and-down motion. The whole assembly is designed to function as a single unit and doesn't come apart for bit changes or anything else.

All plunge routers all comprised of a base casting, and the two polished tubes for the motor to "pogo" (move up and down) on. A stop turret is a common feature and used to regulate the depth changes. An up-stop is often used to set the motor head at the same starting point. Also standard on most plunge routers are motor locks, handles, switches, edge-guide accessories, depth gauges, and split self-releasing collets. Some other useful features sometimes found are: a soft start so the machine doesn't jump when you flip the switch; variable speed; two-step safety switches; vacuum funnels for chip collection; spindle locks; protective bellows for the plunge tubes; two-stage microadjusters for precise depth control; and electric braking.

Plunge routers are designed to be used in your hands with the aid of gravity; they aren't really meant for the router table where many of them are found today. (The issue of just what makes a good table router will be discussed in chapter 6.) In my view, the plunge router can be utilized wherever use of the fixed-base seems risky or is clumsy. To be sure, a plunge router can be modified, jigged or fixtured for nearly any cut that a fixed-base machine can do, but this doesn't always make sense. Simple is best.

This squared-off base casting is a typical plunge router configuration. Fixed-base castings are round. The polished tubes and plunge bearings in the DeWalt 621 provide the tool with a smooth plunge action.

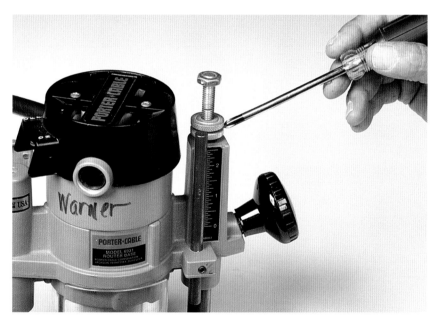

The up-stop on this Porter-Cable 6931 can be used with a fine-adjust knob for continuous adjustment. It also can be set so you know the cutter is clear of the work when the head is up.

The plunge router's essential advantage is its ability to start up with the cutter retracted and stab into the workpiece in a controlled fashion. Thereafter, it can remove the remaining stock in equal passes, changing depth, and cleaning up its mess (in many cases), all while its motor is running. What could be sweeter?

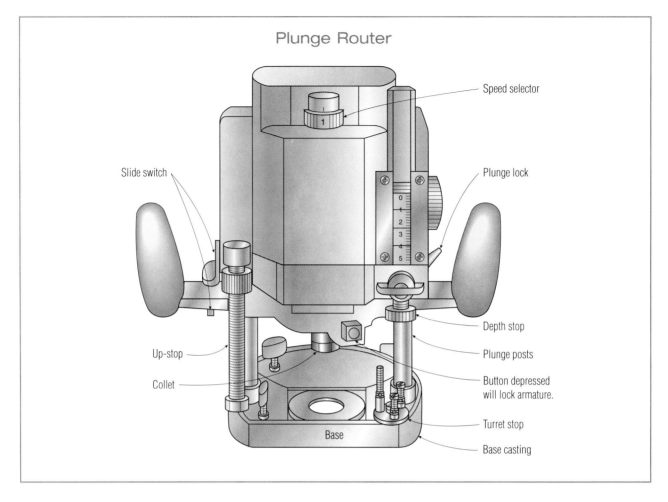

Plunge Router

Speed selector

Slide switch

Plunge lock

Up-stop

Depth stop

Collet

Plunge posts

Button depressed
will lock armature.

Turret stop

Base

Base casting

Basic Anatomy

Plunge routers lack the designer's touch. The machines are designed for function, not looks. And although they have common features, the manufacturers use a variety of ways to the put the components together.

MOTOR HEAD

The motor head is a combination of aluminum and reinforced engineering plastic. The head is the heaviest component of the router and is the reason for its tipsiness. The handles, switches, depth mechanisms, motor lock, speed controls, and motor are all part of the head assembly. The ergonomics of these features and functions differ somewhat from router to router. What is reasonable and comfortable for one worker will not suit the next guy. All of the motor head functions are safe and work well within practical limits. I would not rule out any one tool on the basis of a quirky switch or the feel of its handles. There will be things both pleasant and uncomfortable to all of us.

The RT-1800 plunge router from Fein is the newest of at least eight 3-hp machines. It has soft start, variable speed and a 3-in. plunge stroke.

The DeWalt 621, right, has its motor lock in the left-hand knob. Spin it to lock or unlock. The Porter-Cable motor lock, left, is "on" in its default position. A twist of the lever unlocks it.

PLUNGE TUBES

All motor heads are fastened to, locked on, and pogo on a pair of plunge tubes. They are hardened, usually polished, and sometimes covered with protective bellows. If a wrench slips off the collet nut, it will ding a tube and spoil the smooth travel of the motor head. (Some machines now use one of the tubes for chip collection when attached to a vacuum.) The idiosyncrasies of the tubes are not reason enough to accept or reject a router, but their interplay with the motor head and column bearings is. You should carefully check for a smooth action when considering a purchase.

The springs that pogo the router on the posts should be such that they pick the motor head up to its stop in a measured and nearly buoyant fashion. An oversprung motor head—that is, one with too much spring—will prevent a smooth plunge action.

BASE CASTINGS

The base castings of plunge routers are all different sizes and shapes. The reason for such diversity is control. The designers of these devices assumed that a straight section on a base casting could be used against a guide for more control and accuracy. In practice, the subbase/casting is the least accurate and most troublesome method of guiding a router. In fact, these truncated castings along with the elevated motor head are the reason plunge routers are so unwieldy. A round base casting is the best compromise. The Porter-Cable 7539 has the biggest; the DeWalt 621 has one of the worst, which I will address later. Larger, clear plastic "stability" subbases are available for some plunge routers.

The castings receive the plunge tubes; provide a means for collar guide, subbase, and edge-guide attachment; and support the turret stop. They are sometimes also used as funnels for the vacuum systems. The vacuum systems do work, but the hose can get in the way. During production, the hose is sometimes supported from above the worker.

Checking for Smooth Action

Some plunge routers will jam if you plunge down on only one handle, which you can live with. But if compression on both handles does not result in a smooth up and down glide of the head to its full extremes, that router should be left aside.

Plunge-base castings are all different, but they share some instability when routing along the edges of the work. The plunge router, at lower left, has been fitted with an aftermarket round subbase for greater stability.

The Industry Standard

THE DEWALT 621 has long been the router of choice in midweight plunge routers. This 2-hp, variable-speed, soft-start, 9-lb. machine has an ergonomic design and an excellent plunge action. Its plunge stroke, at 2¼ in., is a bit shorter than some routers, but substantial nonetheless.

The DeWalt has a two-stage depth adjuster on a rack-and-pinion gear. The fine adjuster is a screw "pencil" within the coarse adjuster. Adjustments to a few thousandths of an inch are possible. However, a lock to prevent slipping while routing would be an improvement.

Also standard with the 621 is integrated chip-collection capability. The base casting, vacuum funnel, and its exhaust tube (doubling as a plunge tube) were engineered as a package, not an afterthought. The system works very well on inside cuts, the main arena for the plunge router. Hauling a hose as you rout is not great fun, but it's better than getting MDF in your eye.

The 621 has a spindle lock so only one wrench is needed to change bits, but this has its drawbacks. The router must lie on its side for the cutter change; it will not sit upside down. It is easier to accidentally bash one of the plunge posts with a slipped spindle wrench than if you have two wrenches grasped in one hand opposing one another.

The double-insulated router has an 8-ft. wire set that's short for a 6-ft. person. Also, its short subbase axis is in the direction of travel so that the tool can easily tip if the cutter is deeply engaged in the work. An aftermarket large-diameter subbase is available for the 621 that will help keep it flat on the work.

One common feature that's lacking in this plunge router is a stop to limit the upward travel.

DeWalt 621

Weight	9 lbs.
Speed	Variable, 8,000–24,000 rpm
Amps	10
Soft start	Yes
Horsepower	2.0
Collets	¼ in. & ½ in.
Baseplate diameter	4⁵⁄₁₆-in. x 6¼-in. cutter hole offset
Plunge stroke	2¼ in.

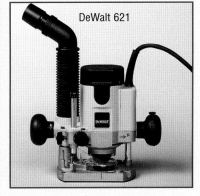
DeWalt 621

Power as an Asset

I think plunge routers do their best work on inside cuts doing multistage work like mortising—jobs they were designed for. A plunge router can approach an inside cut under power, not tip, and waste away stock in stages of an ⅛ in. or so in seconds. Three or four quick passes and you're ½ in. to ¾ in. deep. A cut that deep would break a lot of router bits in a fixed-base tool. A ³⁄₁₆-in.-deep cut with a ½-in.- or ¾-in.-diameter straight bit and a 10-amp tool is a cakewalk with a plunge router. With more power you can do it faster and take deeper cuts but not much more; the cutters can't take it. Consequently, for a lot of plunging, much more than 2 hp is wasted.

Plunge routers range from 1 hp to 3 hp and from 5 lbs. to 17 lbs. The heavier plunge routers are often in the router table, working against gravity, and usually not in the hands of the woodworker for which they were designed. The midweights are the most popular of the plunge routers to be used with jigs, edge guides, and so on, and consequently are the most visible in portable use.

Adding Stability

All routers, whether fixed-base or plunge, are stable when their base castings are surrounded by the work. They will require more skill to handle when less than half the casting is on the work, as is the case with edge cuttings. The plunge router tends to tip more on edges than the fixed-base. As mentioned before, the reasons for that are simple. The motor head rests high on the plunge tubes, the handles are far apart (10 in. to 12 in. or more) and the base castings are light in weight and frequently truncated. Plunging with only half the router on the work is risky.

Wherever the plunge router is stable, whether in fixture or simply on solid ground, it's a safe tool. Releasing the motor lock, plunging, locking, and routing another pass is easy to learn and fun to do. The components to do this vary from tool to tool, and their comfort and efficiency in your hands is a matter of preference. I have tried most plunge routers and can manage them all. For me, the most sensible and comfortable system is embodied in the DeWalt 621. The armored ball knobs each have two functions, which in turn always keep your hands on the knobs. The right hand is for plunge control and switching, and the left is also for plunge control—but a twist of this knob locks the motor head.

Helpful Features

The result of so many different plunge routers is much diversity and novelty. This section discusses the different features and their importance.

ELECTRIC BRAKE

Two plunge routers include an electric brake: the Makita 3612C and Porter-Cable 7529. This is a good option, because accidents do occur on deceleration. I have broken cutters and ruined jigs, fixtures, and the work itself on deceleration. I probably have done more damage with the switch off and the cutter slowing down than most people have done under power. In my view, all routers should have an electric brake.

PROTECTIVE PLUNGE-TUBE BELLOWS

Bellows seem like a good idea; they protect the posts from impact damage and preserve lubricant. The Freud FT2000E and Bosch 1613 use them. Other routers, notably the DeWalt 621 and 625, work endlessly without them.

Increasing Stability

Most plunge routers have relatively small subbases and tend to tip. You can easily increase the stability by making a larger, ¼-in.-thick, round subbase from clear plastic. Transfer the mounting hole locations from the existing subbase to make it any convenient size.

CHIP COLLECTION CAPABILITY

Integrated vacuum collection systems are a good idea. The DeWalt 621 and 625 and the Porter-Cable 7529 (and other Porter-Cable routers) are "vacuum ready." Aftermarket vacuum accessories are becoming common. Chip and dust collection are not only important for our health, but the quality of work can improve, too. A recut chip wears on the cutter and "fouls the footway" in tight quarters, especially with template mortising. Collars and bearings transmit edge and template defects into the work. If a bearing rolls over a chip, it can cause a bump on the work. The vacuum hose is troublesome but better than a chattered profile. Some work, especially with plastics, will require exhaust right at the cutter.

REMOVABLE HANDLES

For hand control, grips are essential. For router table use, they are unnecessary. The DeWalt 625 and Freud FT2000, for example, have removable handles for easier installation. The Hitachi plunge routers all have handles that pivot.

220 VOLTS

The only plunge router with 220 volts is the Bosch 1615 and it is soon to be phased out. The 2-hp Bosch 1617 (fixed-base) has a 220-volt option. Routers with 110 volts are capable of heavy work, but they are not production tools. Sometimes they are used in production work, but the equivalent operation is usually done on the shaper if hours or shifts of the same operation are called for. Short, very heavy-duty cuttings are likely to burn out a standard router; the 220-volt tool will run cooler longer, which is its essential benefit.

Even if shaper power and durability were available in a router, the present-day $\frac{1}{2}$-in. shank tools couldn't stand the stress. The power to take a deeper cut at a higher feed rate is nice, but the limiting factor is the cutters, which are likely to break.

SPINDLE LOCK

Spindle locks are found on most plunge routers. In my view, the two-wrench systems are easier and less likely to cause accidental harm to the router and to the "squeezer." I suspect their presence on plunge routers is more for marketing purposes than practicality. How else can you explain their absence on fixed-base tools?

COLLETS

All routers have collets. A cutter seizing in the collet used to be an ordinary experience. But today essentially all routers use multisplit self-releasing designs. They all let go of their cutters handily on demand and hold the cutter tight. Not much can be said about collets except keep them clean (inside and out) and throw them away every 300 hours to 500 hours or so, or immediately if a cutter slips in one.

Preventing Theft

Some shops use a 220-volt router as a means to prevent theft on the theory that most potential thieves won't have the right electrical outlet to use the tool.

This offset subplate can be used with Porter-Cable collar guides.

These collets are similar. Mark them so you won't accidentally put one in the wrong router. Since the collets are captured on their nut, they pull out of the armature and never stick in the router.

Best Uses for Plunge Routers

Clearly, a plunge router can be used wherever the fixed-base router can, but the fixed-base router poses some risks to the operator in applications where the plunge router does its best work. We have already established that the plunge router is handicapped doing edge work, so what can it do best?

MORTISING

Mortising with a fixed base is rarely practical or safe. A plunge stab with a fixed base and cutter extended may cause the router to self-feed or break the cutter. A plunge router is the best tool for mortises. For speed and accuracy, a jig should be used with an edge guide on both sides of the work and jig. Mortise depths to about 2½ in. are the practical limits, although

Critical Plunge Router Features

Plunge stroke action

A smooth, uninterrupted plunge stroke is essential; why bother with any-thing less? A plunge router is for plunging: Spindle locks, variable speed, microadjustment, fancy switches, brakes, double insulation, or any other special features won't make up for a poor plunge action. So check the action carefully. Even push the router down on one side to see if the stroke still works well. It should be smooth and not difficult to push. The retraction after the cut should be even and not jerky.

Plunge stroke length

Plunge stroke length is important, with typical length being 2 in. to 3 in. A lot of range makes deep cutting easier, but this also has a down side because the high motor position on the posts reduces stability. You can make up for this by using short cutters and shallow cuts to bring the motor closer to the work for more stability.

Buoyancy

If the plunge springs are well matched to the weight of the motor, then it will be easier to plunge. In my view, near-buoyancy is preferred; any more spring force than what it takes to get the head all the way up is wasted, and will make it a little tougher to adjust the depth.

Stability

All plunge routers are difficult to control compared to their fixed-base counterparts. The rounder and larger the base casting on the plunge router, the more stable it will be. But you should expect some degree of instability with plunge routers, because they tend to be so tall and have such small subbases relative to that height.

given two plunge routers with the same setup, 3 in. or more are possible without having to change any cutters.

CIRCLES AND ELLIPSES

Cutting a circle is generally a multistage task, so a plunge router works well because it can be lowered gradually to cut through the stock. A template is often the first stage of the process and the template then is used on the work with trim cutters. A template can be cut out of an MDF or plywood blank. A disk or oval will break out of the blank on the final pass. It should be screwed down onto another substrate to prevent it from vibrating against the cutter. Fastening a plunge router to a circle or ellipse jig is the most accurate and least costly of methods when making these shapes. A bandsaw can be used more efficiently, but not to the precision or finish quality of a router and straight bit.

HALF LAPS, SLOTS, AND TENONS

Slotting, lapping, and tenoning are user-specific operations. There are no textbook standards for these chores. For me, all three are multistage.

You can rout from both sides of the work when making a disk or hole. Obviously, use the same pivot hole. If you leave a thin membrane, you can just snap it out of the blank.

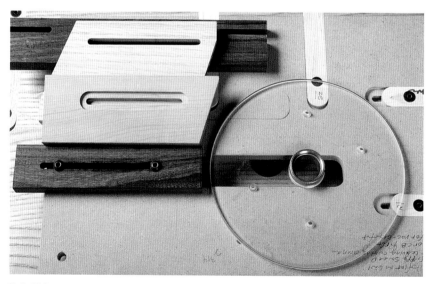

Full-thickness slots are multistage cuts. The work is clamped below the window where the collar guide is sitting. A sample is shown on the jig. There is plenty of platform support for the router.

The tenon-making jig with a window and a broad ski allows you to cut tenons deeper than the ⅝-in. bit. To make a 1½-in. tenon, use the plunge router for progressively deeper cuts. The bearing sets the depth of cut and establishes the shoulder of the tenon.

Cutters are just too short, often too fragile, and the work too demanding or dangerous for a fixed-base tool in one pass. I've made jigs to accommodate and support the plunge router in each case.

CUTTER-BREAKING TROUBLES

The most important time to use a plunge router is when the cut is deep or large enough to risk breaking the cutter. If the depth of cut is such that a single pass of the tool will break the cutter, or burn it out, then a plunge router is called for. Even edge work can fall into this category. Any time the cut will require two passes, it's best to rig the operation to use a plunge router, even if that means building up support on the outboard side of the base to prevent tipping.

Edge work here also refers to the edge of templates (and dovetail jigs are templates). Dovetail bits are single-depth cutters by design; they can't be used at two depths on the same center. The dovetail bit is one of the most fragile and easiest to break. If its pathway is partly cleared by a pre-plow from a straight bit, the dovetail cutter has an easier time and is less likely to chatter. A plunge router can pare away the pathway in two or three steps with a straight bit and do it quickly. I would use the plunge

The use of this ¾-in.-radius roundover bit limits the amount of base casting on the work during startup to less than 40 percent, so I screwed an equal thickness stick to the casting for support.

router in this "utility" function without hesitation, its instability notwithstanding. Moreover, any cutting error from the straight bit will be completely erased by the dovetail bit. For the best dovetail cuttings try to preplow with the next smaller dovetail bit rather than a straight bit.

ROUTER TABLE USE

Plunge routers are probably the most popular choice for router tables, especially for heavy use. This is mainly because there are more choices in the 3-hp range than with fixed-base routers. They're also relatively inexpensive—as 3-hp routers go.

But the choice does present several problems. Since the plunge router motor head is inseparable from the rest of the router, you can't change the bit easily if the tool is bolted right to the tabletop. Consequently, most folks compromise by attaching the plunge router to a big piece of plastic or metal that's inset into the tabletop. The whole assembly is removed for bit changes.

In my view, this compromises the routing process as well as the tabletop integrity and flatness. Inevitably, the top will cup up slightly and so will the plastic insert. Expect interruptions as the work bumps into the transitions where the plastic meets the top. Moreover, expect the plastic to deflect as you press the work down and against the cutter. Close work will be frustrated when a table has the insert construction. It's not so much the plunge router being in the table; it will work, but it is the insert and its installation that are problematic. I prefer a fixed-base router bolted directly to the underside of the router table top.

Porter-Cable 7529	
Weight	11 lbs.
Speed	Variable, 10,000–23,000 rpm
Amps	12
Soft start	Yes
Horsepower	2
Collets	¼ in., ½ in., ⅜ in., & metrics option
Baseplate diameter	6½ in.
Plunge stroke	2½ in.

Porter-Cable 7529

Porter-Cable 7529

The Porter-Cable 7529 plunge router is new in the U.S. market and designed to compete with the best of them.

For openers, the Porter-Cable has a hefty plunge stroke (2⁹⁄₁₆ in. total) and a large, stable base casting with a round subbase. The Porter-Cable has an up-stop that does double duty as a full range microadjuster in both directions of travel. The 7529 also has a spindle lock, but the company's standard pair of wrenches can also be used.

This double-insulated, 2-hp, variable-speed, soft-start tool also has an electronic brake, an important safety feature. It has a relatively quiet and well-balanced motor, with a 10-ft. power cord.

The armored ergonomic grips are close to the controls. One control, the depth stop, can be adjusted with the left hand while holding the grip— all the while maintaining control of the router, a Porter-Cable exclusive.

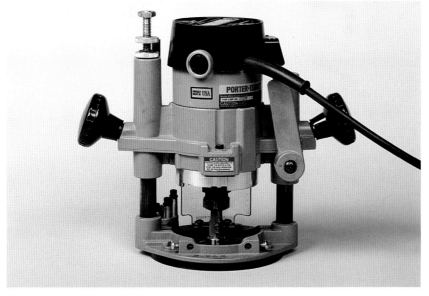

The Porter-Cable 6931 plunge router.

The depth stop on the Porter-Cable 7529 can be worked while your left hand is still on the grip, a smart safety move.

Porter-Cable has also designed the base casting as a vacuum funnel with a connection for a 1-in. vacuum hose. Collectors are also available for edge trimmings, which are harder to pick up.

The variable-speed selector is safely out of the way, but is difficult to rotate. The tool has two switches with thermal overload protection, but I have trouble with the trigger switch coordinating the two steps to lock it on. The plunge glide is acceptable, but the head will jam if downward pressure is only applied to one knob. The tool is heavy at 11 lbs. and much wider than it is thick, making it unstable—but less so than most.

Another plus is that Porter-Cable has designed this tool for router table or hand use with a mechanism that provides for continuous adjustment either upside down or right side up.

Porter-Cable also has two other plunge routers. The 6931 plunge router is essentially the 691 fixed-base router with a plunge base. The 7538 and 7539 are plunge versions of the Speedmatic $3\frac{1}{4}$-hp fixed-base routers.

DeWalt 625

The industry standard in the heavyweight class is DW-625, formerly the Elu 3338. Like all routers, it is not perfect but deserves its position as the best big plunge router. Its controls are well situated and function smartly. The plunge glide, as on the DW-621, is as good as it gets. The maximum plunge depth is $2\frac{7}{16}$ in. Its features are otherwise unremarkable except for its conspicuous up-stop. It limits the up-travel and functions as the fine adjustment knob.

The 625 is a double-insulated, 3-hp, variable-speed, soft-start, 13.3-lbs. tool. It has a spindle lock for one-wrench cutter changes, a two-stage depth adjuster, and a trigger switch with a lock. It's a good tool.

It suffers from the usual plunge router instability problems because the base is so small, but an offset subbase will keep the tool flat on the work. Also, its base casting is truncated and the cutter opening is so wide that it can snag on the corners of the work. Another minor problem is that the action of the up-stop quick release button is stubborn.

DeWalt 625	
Weight	13.3 lbs.
Speed	Variable, 8,000–24,000 rpm
Amps	15
Soft start	Yes
Horsepower	3
Collets	¼ in., ½ in., & ⅜ in.
Baseplate diameter	5⅝ in. x 6¹¹⁄₁₆ in.
Plunge stroke	2⁷⁄₁₆ in.

DeWalt 625

4

Router Tables

A router table can handle most routing procedures, but not all of them safely and efficiently. The router table has a big advantage whenever its broad control surfaces (fence and top) are required. The table's most efficient use employs the wide surfaces to support the workpiece for edge routing. The most difficult operation on a table is routing on the ends of long, narrow sticks like stiles and rails. But even difficult jobs can often be safely accomplished by using jigs and fixtures designed to securely hold the workpiece and keep your hands safely away from the cutter. But it's also important to remember that a hand-held router can be the best solution, especially for large or awkward workpieces.

And, as with all router operations, never forget that the spinning cutter is unforgiving and provides no second chances.

A router table can range from the simple to the ridiculously complex; most are over-engineered. For some people, a production-made plastic-laminate table will do. For others, a handmade, job-specific contraption is better. To be sure, a good table with basic features does take time to make well if you build your own.

Router Table Basics

The router table has lots of applications, but it does have its limitations. You can rout short or odd shapes otherwise unsafe to rout with the hand router, but you can't rout big, wide, long sticks or anything so big it might tip the table over. Edges and faces of narrow workpieces are easily routed,

The author's router table has an MDF top that's supported by a series of ribs underneath. He uses a fixed-base router so he can permanently attach the casting and remove the router motor for bit changes.

but a table isn't appropriate for working on the ends. Fortunately, in those cases where the router table is not suitable, a hand-held router will do the job. Nevertheless, 70 percent to 80 percent of all jobs can be safely and accurately routed on the table.

Table routing is often more efficient than hand routing. Most of the work needn't be clamped or worked with a fixture; a fence with a vacuum system will keep the table clean. Adjustments are easy and setup is quick. The same stick or panel can often be routed on its edges, faces, or ends with no changes in setup. An enclosed router table is also relatively quiet.

Since the work can be fed just as easily on its edge or face, a cutter may have more application on the router table than in the hand router.

Using a fence with a cutter allows you to use more of the cutting surface. The ball-bearing design restricts cutting to a small portion of the edge. By raising this cutter and positioning the fence I can use a section of the cutter that has not yet seen any wood.

I made this fence for chamfering the edges of round subbases. The work rolls on two ½-in. bearings and the depth of cut is determined by raising or lowering the cutter.

A 30-degree bevel cutter, for example, can produce a 60-degree bevel if the work is fed on edge. The fence and cutter height can also be adjusted so any part of the flute can be used to better distribute the wear. The same piloted cutter in the hand router will wear out its flutes near the bearing, leaving sharp carbide near the shank.

A router table can be a platform for routing with piloted bits and collars, or you can use the fence. Most cuttings on the table use the fence, and as such no ball bearings are needed on the cutters. The same cutter without a bearing is often smaller and safer, but not necessarily cheaper. When cutter bearings are absent and the fence receives all of the horizontal force from the work, the router and bit are under less stress and last longer. Moreover, when bearings are not used, edge defects are not telegraphed back into the profile, and in general router fence cuttings are crisper, with less chatter.

THE STAND

A typical router table has a stand, top, and fence. The stand's essential function is to bring the height of the work up to a comfortable level. It should also provide a means for supporting, flattening and attaching the top. Material (usually MDF) and rigidity will inhibit vibration and contain noise. A stand made from ¼-in. plywood and 1-in. by 1-in. legs will support a router. But a stand with 2-in. by 2-in. legs, 1½-in. by 2½-in. rails, and ⅝-in.-thick MDF will be stronger and support the components in the subassemblies.

A router stand should be like the stands for jointers, planers and band-saws: no drawers or storage, maybe an access door, and a place for electrical equipment. It should be strong enough to be pulled around without coming apart. I am not opposed to casters, either permanent or detachable. I have a wire winder in mine, as well as an 18-in. straightedge and a ⅜-in. shoulder bolt to lock a set of spacers on the top to lift the work to various heights in relation to the bit.

A 15-amp rocker switch buried in a mortise prevents accidental startups, but is easy to shut off.

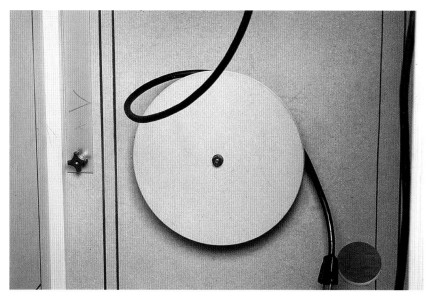

The wire winder can hold about 18 ft. of wire. There is a 6-in. disk beneath the 10-in. one you see. The straightedge at left comes in handy for setups.

The router table box rests on four 1-in. ball casters that are screwed into threaded brass inserts. Two Lexan brakes keep the 80-lb. box from rolling away.

I use a 2-ft.-wide by 2-ft.-deep by 39-in.-high stand. It can just manage a hefty 6-ft. board, which is also my physical limit, so I wouldn't need a bigger stand. The bigger these things get, the heavier they get—and the more likely they are to warp.

Router work is not like chiseling or other common woodworking activity. You should not expect most shop furniture to be at the optimum height for routing. I'm 6 ft. tall and all my routing surfaces are high—about 38 in. to 44 in.

Obviously, the stand is used as the support for the top. As such, you should put some framing into the upper rails to support and connect it. My table has six upper rails that I struggled to get into the same plane. They provide the means to keep the top flat so the top itself can be as thin as is practical.

The material, design and thickness of the top depend somewhat on the router table design and whether a fixed-base or plunge router is used. But before I address that, I would like to present my case for a fixed-base router in the table. Using a fixed base simplifies the top and improves routing accuracy.

FIXED-BASE OR PLUNGE

Although both types of tools are used in router tables, I prefer to use a fixed-based rather than a plunge router. One reason for that is that it's not practical to bolt a plunge router to the underside of the table. Its motor is permanently fastened to the casting, so cutter changes upside down are complicated. Most people screw the plunge router to large metal or plastic subbases, which in turn are nested into rabbeted windows within the top.

With this arrangement, cutter and depth changes can be made, since the router can now be easily extracted. Nevertheless, that one maneuver brings about one compromise after another. For example, the tops themselves get overly complicated with tee-moldings or laminations of fiberboard, plywood, or particleboard. The window has to be a precise match for the large subbase, and the absence of a third of the top (for the window) will spoil its integrity and promote cupping and twisting in what is left.

Moreover, the edges where the insert plate and tabletop meet become dust collectors and need constant cleaning to prevent the work from hanging up. Precision work will be more difficult because the plastic insert can bend with downward pressure, causing small changes in depth of cut. Every time you pull the router and insert out of the table, you need to level and inspect the rabbet seat and insert for a good fit. A fixed-base casting bolted directly onto an MDF top has none of these problems. You simply remove the router motor from the casting to change the bit.

Simplicity, again, is always the best option. This does limit your router choices, however. For serious router table work such as raising panels, you may need a 3-hp machine—and there are many more available as plunge routers than as fixed-base routers. However, the Porter-Cable model 7518 does fill that bill. For lighter-duty router tables, there are a host of machines in the various power categories.

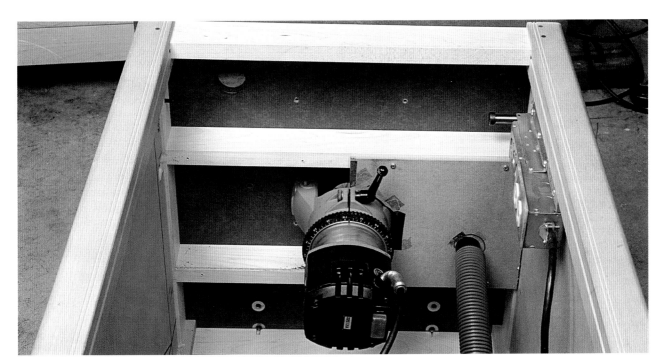

The hefty supports underneath the top ensure that the MDF panel stays flat—a key consideration for router table design.

TABLETOP MATERIAL

Given the fixed-base option, then, the material of choice is MDF—thin (⅝ in.) MDF if your table is stressed with reinforcing rails. Cabinet-grade MDF (such as Medite brand) is finish-sanded to a uniform thickness. This untreated surface will wear and scratch easily. However, two or three coats of Watco will impart a Masonite-like toughness to it and do no harm. It will not be as tough as plastic laminate, but it will resist wear and last a long time. What could be easier?

I would not expect to use cutter-hole inserts for the same reasons I wouldn't use a baseplate insert. A 2-ft. by 2-ft. by ⅝-in. MDF slab is about $2, so it's better to make a spare than degrade either one with an insert. Make one with a hole for your biggest cutter and one with a cutter hole for general use, exchanging them as necessary.

MDF can be bolted down on a table frame without dimensional consequence; no allowance is necessary for changes in humidity or temperature. I would minimize overhang, though, as unsupported surface can cup.

This top has seen hundreds of hours of routing with little wear. Flatness along the cutter path remains within 0.002 in.

A dial indicator on a router table fence may be overkill, but for precise joinery it can save precious time.

The Fence

The fence is the most critical element of a router table. Ideally, it should be straight and square to the tabletop. A stick on a pivot will do, but for speedier adjustments, a split fence with a screw-driven adjustment is better. Also note that making a precise router fence is much easier if you already have a fence. So you may want to find a good straight board to use for a starter fence. Moreover, even the most comprehensive and sophisticated of fences may not be compatible with all cutters. For example, it may not make sense to over-complicate the design of your fence for the occasional use of a 3½-in.-diameter panel bit. Instead, you can make a second, much simpler, fence with a 3½-in. cutout for that operation.

The router fence has two essential functions: One is to guide your stick by the cutter and the other is to regulate the horizontal depth of cut. The guidance function, as implied, is not that difficult to design into the

A router table fence can be as simple as a pivot stick and a couple of clamps.

The author's router table fence is driven with a machine screw. The 1-in. aluminum bars fit into ways cut into the bottom of the fence so that it tracks straight and doesn't twist.

fence; a well-jointed stick will do that. The depth-of-cut function is also easy to manage, but it is more of a challenge and is often overlooked.

Router bits, horsepower and the nature of wood are usually in such conflict that the desired full depth of cut is not possible in a single pass (the easiest way to manage this problem is with an adjustable fence). I know of three methods of moving a fence: the tap and clamp, the pivot, and the screw drive. The first and simplest fence is clamped to the table and tapped with a hammer for adjustment. It's unsophisticated, unrepeatable, and frustrating—but it's the most common method. The second system uses a stick with a pivot so only one clamp is needed. (Stops and screws can be used to advantage here.) The third method and the least common incorporates a lead-screw to drive the fence. My own is assembled on a carrier through which a couple of clamp levers secure the whole thing. The levers are coupled to tee-nuts beneath the top.

Protection from the Cutter

A router bit is an unforgiving cutting tool. One of the safety features of a router table is that most of the time the cutter is buried in the stock or behind the fence, so you are protected from it. If your fence is split, it's good practice to minimize the cutter opening to reduce the cutter exposure. When routing full thickness, allow only $1/16$ in. or so of cutter above the stock, again to hide as much tool as possible. Plastic cutter guards are valuable in some circumstances, and you should use one if you need more protection. For me, if I think a plastic cutter guard is necessary, then I know I'm at risk, and I work out an alternate routing strategy to minimize it. If the work is too narrow, short, or peculiar, or puts my hands too close to the bit, I'll build a holder or a special utility fence.

A router fence has a number of uses besides the usual functions, such as guiding the stock, hiding the cutter and controlling the in-and-out depth of cut. It's also handy for placing a variety of stops and offers a platform for dust-collection equipment. My fence has a vacuum port right behind the cutter, and does an excellent job of picking up the chips. Plastic vacuum accessories for router fences are common.

Using a straightedge and shims, the author adjusts the outfeed half of the fence for a 0.020-in.-deep cut. The cutter lines up with the outfeed fence to make a full thickness pass for a jointed edge.

Whether your fence is split or not, you can use it for jointing operations and making other full-thickness cuts. With a carbide straight bit you can joint plastic, wood, MDF, plywood, and some nonferrous metals. However, MDF and plastic will ruin HSS jointer knives. The outfeed fence should move in and out about 3/64 in., and if you adjust it parallel to the infeed fence and in line with the highest point of the cutter, it will function like a jointer. It will take a thin slice from the full thickness of the workpiece. You can do the same thing with a one-piece fence by attaching some thin (0.010-in. to 0.0025-in.) metal shims on the fence beyond the cutter. A straightedge placed on the outfeed side should just touch the high point on the cutter.

Open mortises and other "stopped" cuts are easy to do on the router table. Often these cuts are only 2 in. or 3 in. in length, so the outfeed fence can be positioned slightly rearward and out of the way. I made a stop with a slot to slide and lock on the outfeed fence—a nice convenience. It's designed to stay above the table so it won't accumulate a pile of chips.

There are more things you can add to a fence. Several small companies are even making a business out of it. Join-Tech, Wood Haven, and Incra, for example, make fences and accessories for dovetails and box joints. Nonetheless, your fence must always be straight and square to the table to be accurate. My fence faces are unfinished, so I can sand, scrape and true them up. I keep them flat to plus or minus 0.001 in.

The 1½-in. plastic tube is a DeWalt 621 router accessory (328592-00) that comes in handy for chip collection on a router table. A brass (chrome-plated) 1½-in. drain tube is also a good choice.

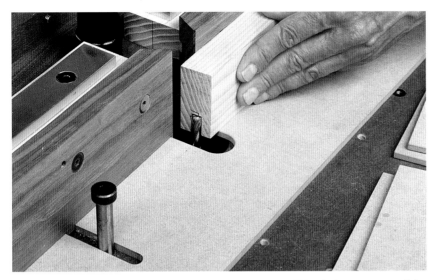

A deep, open mortise like this one, if attempted in one pass, will break the cutter or stall the motor. Routing on ¼-in. lifts solves the problem; remove one for each depth change. The shoulder bolt keeps the lifts from sliding.

I use an 18-in. Starrett ground straightedge to verify the straightness of the fence halves. A 0.0015-in. feeler gauge cannot get under the straightedge.

Depth of Cut Strategies

Material to be cut on the router table must be flat, uniform in thickness, straight and square. That is not a peculiarity; all woodworking machines require it. If your work is cupped, bowed, or otherwise distorted, your cutting results will vary. Given suitable material, a good router table will cut to plus or minus 0.002 in. To cut this close, you need a good fence and a flat tabletop. If any of the three (stock, top, or fence) legs of this triad is less than acceptable, your results will vary.

Router Table or Shaper

THE ROUTER TABLE IS CLEARLY borrowed technology from the shaper. As such, it's a powerful and adaptable tool, but don't expect shaper performance from one.

Both tools are stationary and the operator moves the work, not the tool. Both use fences, collars, or bearings to control the path of the work. But shapers are essentially for edge or end cuttings. They are cabinet-shop and millwork tools and as such are heavy-handed, heavy-duty, and heavyweight. The biggest tool bit in a common router has a ½-in. shank. The smallest spindle on a shaper is ½ in. Moreover, shaper spindles are sophisticated precision-ground components in vibration-dampened, iso-lated assemblies, separate from their drive motors. In a router the spindle is one and the same with the armature and performs double duty, so its bearings are the first things to wear out.

Shapers are designed for all-day door, drawer, or molding operations. Duty cycles are measured in "shifts," not minutes. They are production animals. Their cutters are big (way over 2 in.) and expensive. Shapers spin slower than routers, usually in the 7,000 rpm to 14,000 rpm range, and their power output starts where routers leave off (around 3 hp).

Router tables sacrifice production for versatility. The router table, unlike the shaper, can do inside work as well as edge, face and end cuttings. Dadoes, mortises and other blind inside excavations are not possible with shapers, nor are dovetails—a distinct argument for the router table.

Router bits for all sorts of woodworking are common, and there are probably more router bits than shaper cutters except for door, drawer, handrail, and window applications. The router is an offshoot of the shaper, not a substitute for one. Its price range is well within the reach of most woodworkers; shapers of any quality start at $1,500.

Router tables are easy to set up, and fill an important need for a wide range of cabinet and furniture applications. They are great for short-run solutions, but as mentioned before, don't expect shaper performance from one.

Controlling a Deep Cut

For a cut that is deep and inside (such as open mortises, dadoes, and grooves) the cutter should be placed at the maximum height. The work should then be routed on a stack of spacers, removing one for each depth of cut. Cuttings done this way are safe and precise.

Simplification is another important factor in quality woodworking. The more operations and machine changes, the more chance for error. Obviously, we strive for excellence; good fixtures, good wood, experience and simplification will take us there. To simplify and increase quality control on the router table, any changes in depth of cut have to be well-managed.

VERTICAL DEPTH OF CUT

Often cutters require multiple passes to achieve the desired profile. Sometimes there isn't enough power to get there in one pass; sometimes the cutter can break in a single pass; and sometimes the stock will burn, split, or tear with a heavy cut. If you expect such difficulty, then stage (multiple pass) work is essential. The depth of cut in the router table can be adjusted by the router or the fence. It should be adjusted by one or the other (not both) for a given cutter. Changing both will easily double your chances for a screw-up. Fortunately, the choice of which to manage for a given cutter is easy to make.

HORIZONTAL DEPTH OF CUT

Large-diameter bits are usually short, often intolerant of vertical depth changes, and are used on the edge of stock; to stage-cut with them you move the fence. To do this, set the vertical "depth" to its final position initially and move the fence in equal increments. The diameter of the largest available router bit is around 3½ in.—and ½ in. of that is usually for a bearing. That leaves 1½ in. for the profile, so three or four ⅜-in. fence changes will complete the cut. Using spacer lifts and fence changes at the same time should be avoided. If you find yourself doing both, you should consider moving up to a shaper.

The sample on the left has a pretty good side wall, but the outside edge of the corner is torn. The sample on the right has been climb cut (fed left to right) but only about 1⁄32 in.

I use this sled holder if the work is too narrow or too deep to work safely. I hold the sled by the toggles.

Climb Cutting

The conventional and safe work-feed direction on the router table is from right to left as you face the cutter. In this way, the feed is against the cutter rotation, and as such the work is safely pulled into the fence, covering up the bit. Like planing against the grain, the router bit can cause tearout if the work is fed against the cutter rotation. Sharp cutters and spiral flute design can make this less of a problem, but expect some tearout, especially on difficult woods. Feeding the work from left to right, the climb cut will markedly reduce tearout, but at substantial risk. The climb cut is so named because of the tendency for the router or work to pull (or climb) as you try to feed evenly. The work is constantly being pulled from the hands and away from the fence. This cut is chiefly used for difficult woods in which the grain changes direction. It is less efficient than other cuts, and as such more force is required to control the work. This is risky business. Fortunately, there are counter-measures.

The main use for the climb cut is as a very light "score" made as an initial pass. The light $\frac{1}{32}$-in. depth of cut helps prevent the severe climbing action. Note that you should make a habit of placing the work in a holder that keeps your hands well away from the cutter for climb cuts. Using this technique without such common-sense protection is extremely dangerous. The only time to use a climb cut without a holder is with workpieces that are so large that your hands remain well away from the cutter. In any case, don't take off more than a $\frac{1}{32}$ in. for a single pass.

An MDF work holder is pretty heavy and resistant to power transfers from the cutter in a climb cut. Even if an accident should occur, your hands are on the jig and cannot be pulled into the router bit.

Finally, safe climb cutting can always be done with a power feeder. But you should note that a router table should not be considered a production tool—the very reason for a power feeder. The setup is also technique-sensitive, and your router table has to be a quality one. The feeder will press down hard on the top and against the fence. If either should deflect, your cuttings will vary.

The Miter Gauge

The miter gauge can be useful on the router table, but it's not my favorite choice. I just can't hold the work on one and keep it from slipping. Moreover, most miter-gauge cuts are across the grain and subject to tearout as the cutter exits the work. A back-up waste piece is almost always required—confounding handling even more. A miter slot in the face of the table can weaken it or cause other minor problems. If a miter gauge is needed, a better solution is to use two temporary pieces of $\frac{3}{8}$-in. MDF to trap the blade of the gauge rather than cutting into the top. With this strategy, the fence can remain in play for added work support. A better solution yet is to build a sled fixture with stops and toggle clamps to hold the work. Well-designed fixtures are imperative for good work, reducing accidents and injuries.

Two pieces of $\frac{3}{8}$-in. MDF clamped to the table provide a temporary pathway for the miter-gauge blade. This method doesn't compromise the router table by cutting into it for a groove.

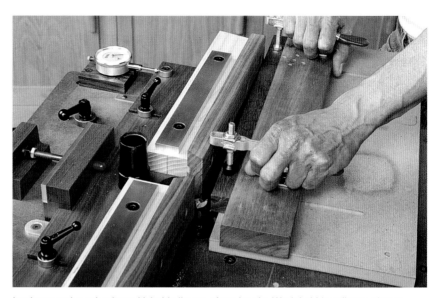

It takes a major calamity to kick this jig out of my hands. Work held in a fixture always machines well.

Router Table Safety

It is clear that high-speed spinning cutters have two possible results: one is to cut the stock; the other is to cut you. There are other threats on the router table, but none as formidable. Safety is an attitude that when followed will improve your efficiency and cutting results. Once in a while, there are genuine surprises but most emergency room visits are due to carelessness. A shoddy setup, difficult wood, inferior machinery, and a fighter-pilot mentality are some of the factors. This book can help you with the unexpected, but not your disposition. And frankly, if you are clumsy, accident prone, and impatient, you should not be a woodworker. The automobile industry has done a yeoman's job of protecting you from yourself and others: air bags, seat restraints, safety glass, and so on. However, the woodworking industry is a work-safety disgrace. Start to believe that, and you will be a conscientious woodworker.

CUTTER SAFETY

Edge routing is the most common table routing practice. You can rout the whole edge or part of it. Either way, there isn't much cutter exposure except at the end of the cut. Routing narrow sticks ($2\frac{1}{2}$ in. or less) can be scary because your hands are placed near the cutter for best results. Whenever possible, press down and against the fence beyond the cutter. Should you have a slip, your hands will dash away from the cutter. While paying attention to that maneuver, prepare for the cutter's sudden appearance at the end of the work.

When edge-routing the full thickness—jointing for instance—project only ¹⁄₁₆ in. of cutter beyond the work. Any more is unnecessary and risky. For best results, match the flute length to the thickness of the work.

Push sticks are always acceptable, but hold-ins, hold-downs, and featherboards can present their own dangers. In my view, they get in the way, upset the uniform travel of the work, and present some risk themselves. To me, they signal that trouble is near; the work is too narrow, too short, too long, or too awkward.

I'm the first to act when it comes to safety. If you see the need for a hold-down or featherboard, then start looking for a jig, fixture, holder, or an alternative method. It could easily be that what you're trying to do is not a table-router operation at all. Some dangerous router table cuts are uncomplicated when done with a fixture and a hand router. And just because you've seen an operation in a book or a magazine, don't assume it's safe. If your results are inconsistent, you don't like doing it, or you are otherwise uncomfortable, you are probably at risk and should consider another method.

Always push down and against the fence *beyond the cutter* when operating a router table.

TRAPPING THE CUTTER AND THE WORK

Because routers generate so much torque, it's crucial to keep the cutters from getting trapped. The work can be trapped between the cutter and the fence or under the cutter. The bit can also be trapped in the work or stuck in the side of the stock. Three of the four situations should be avoided altogether. The fourth is essential to routing and quite common, but done at a risk you should know about.

Trapping the work between the fence and the cutter is about as bad as driving on the wrong side of the road. The question isn't whether an accident will occur, but when. Never set the fence so that the workpiece is sandwiched between it and the cutter. Any slight deviation in stock thickness will jam the workpiece and (very likely) pull your fingers into the bit.

You can also trap the work under the cutter. This is far less common, but the hazards are nearly the same. There is less risk of the work self-feeding, but it will likely ruin the cutter and the work. Be aware: if this happens, it is the result of unsafe practice.

An inside cut like a slot or dado again traps the work between the cutter and the fence. A bad feed or an ill-prepared (poorly jointed edge) workpiece will ruin the cut, may break the cutter, or kick back the work. This is common practice on table-saw dovetail and box-joint jigs and the reason for caution when using a fixture for such a cut. The cutter simply has no place to go in the event of an accident except into an area of the work you didn't want to rout.

The same size dovetail is possible on different thicknesses of stock if both cuts are referenced from the same side of the work. But this strategy should be avoided; it is very risky.

A tongue produced this way—both cuts referenced from the same face of the stock—is high-risk woodworking. If your thickness planer is well-tuned, there is never a need for this.

If there is a "safe" method of widening slots it is on the router table. But beware of the surprise climb cut. With the work trapped between the fence and the cutter a bad feed may break the cutter and jettison the work. The safe feed direction to widen the slot is always against the cutter rotation (left to right in this case).

An accidental climb cut can also occur while widening the pathway on inside cuts if you ignore the cutter rotation. Widening the slot as shown in the photo above with a right to left hand feed is a climb cut and will, in all likelihood, rip the work out of your hands. A feed from left to right is not a climb cut but any deviation in workpiece travel can spoil the cut nevertheless.

This door cutter is stuck in the work. If the work is lifted, the cut will be spoiled; if it is bowed or twisted, the panel and rail fit will be compromised and the stick may kick back.

A blind through slot (like on this sample) is a risky act on the router table. The slot was cut with the jig, a collar and a plunge router. The work is clamped under the window.

Some cutters—such as those for slotting and forming glue joints—are buried in the work for normal operation. That is to say, if you lift the work while routing it, you will spoil the cut. Again, you can break a cutter this way and the work can kick back. You need to make sure you never lift the work while using these cutters. Moreover, if the work is bowed, twisted or cupped, its trip down the router table will be tippy and it could jam and fly back at you. Intermittently pressing and relaxing the force down on a bowed workpiece will increase its chances for a kickback. A hold-down may unexpectedly tip the ends up on small work. The best defense against such a calamity is good stock preparation with flat surfaces and square edges.

BLIND-END TABLE CUTS

As mentioned, there are plenty of unsafe but relatively common woodworking practices. The router has its share—maybe more so than the jointer and table saw. Blind-ended cuts are those cuts that begin and end inside the stock and do not exit or enter through the edge. It is possible to do this on the router table, but clearly the cutter is trapped in the work. The heroics go like this: the daredevil first clamps stops down on the router table top, turns on the router, butts the work against the stop, tilts it up, and drops it down on the turning cutter. Next, the operator slides the work to the other stop and lifts it off the table. If successful, said craftsman keeps his afternoon bungee jump appointment.

The above procedure will burn the wood at both ends of the pathway and the slightest waver will ruin the cut on both sides. But the proper alternative is obvious. It is the express purpose of a plunge router to facilitate blind-end cuts. They should be done with the work in a jig or fixture and routed with the portable plunger and edge guide, never on the router table.

Router Bits

I t is interesting to note that the purchase of 10 to 15 router bits can easily exceed the dollar value of the most expensive router. These highly engineered carbide router bits can stand four to six regrinds, even though most hobbyist woodworkers rarely sharpen them.

But despite this durable material, a new cutter can and will tear out, break out, or chip out a perfectly good straight-grained piece of wood. The cutter sharpness or geometry doesn't matter nearly as much as a solid understanding of which bit to use—and how to use the bit once you're there.

A few premium cutters can often exceed the price of the router they're used in. These retail for about $227—enough to purchase nearly any 2-hp router.

The cutter is a critical factor. The setup and the type of router are the other two parts of the big picture. All three factors play together in the cutting process. The wrong router, an ill-conceived setup, or a poorly chosen router bit can ruin the work. Working with these variables does take experience, but a closer look at cutters can certainly help the operator make some informed choices.

Evaluating Performance

Manufacturers have a lot to say about router bits. Some of the more common buzzwords are super micro-grain, fatigue-proof steel, spun balanced, anti-kickback, precision ground, optimum hook angles, and Teflon coated. But the bottom line is performance, which can't be predicted from simple inspection or even knowledge of routing. A single manufacturer's cutters can vary in quality, and distributors don't always carry a manufacturer's entire inventory, so selection can be perplexing.

As in other products, a manufacturer's reputation and longevity in the business are reasonable considerations. Very cheap bits should be suspect, since you will "get what you pay for." A good rule of thumb is to select one or two cutters and evaluate their performance. The following will show you how.

FINISH

The finish that a new cutter leaves on wood should be nearly flawless. Rough grinding will telegraph itself onto the work. When used properly you should expect little or no tearout, no burning, and an otherwise smooth and glassy finish. Use the router table to evaluate this; it is the least sensitive to technique.

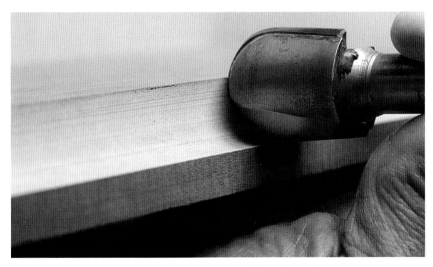

Any grinding defect on a carbide bit will show up plainly on the work.

To check for vibration in a large bit, start it at the slowest of speeds and increase the speed a notch at a time. This PRC trimmer is the longest of all commonly available router bits.

VIBRATION

Vibration is your worst enemy. Clamps loosen, screws unwind, fences squiggle, cutters slide up the collet, and the work can resonate against the cutter. In the worst case, the cutter breaks or comes out of the collet.

Minor vibration of the router bit, once uncommon, seems more and more frequent. But any vibration, in my view, is unacceptable. To test for cutter vibration, use a variable-speed router and start the tool at its slowest speed. Hold the router in the air and advance the speed selector a step at a time. If you feel vibration, stop the router before going to the next speed. (With a hard-start tool you don't have this luxury.)

Cutters whose diameters and flute lengths are less than 1⅝ in. should spin to 25,000 rpm without vibration. Bigger cutters are far more likely to vibrate even though they are supposed to be in balance beyond 30,000 rpm. Be suspicious of all new big cutters and all newly reground cutters. A bad collet will make most medium-sized cutters vibrate, balanced or not. Bearings, good or bad, may make a bit vibrate, too, so to rule out the cutter as the sole vibrator remove all bearings and screws from the bit.

ACCURACY OF GRIND

Just how close does the manufacturer grind to the stated specification such as radius and diameter? Most makers hold the shank diameter to an extreme tolerance of plus or minus 0.00025 in., but the rest of the tool may vary. For decorative bits, ovolos, beads, and roundovers, for example, it doesn't matter much if a radius is off by a few degrees, but joinery cutters should be more precise. The fit from tongue-and-groove tools, glue-joint cutters, cope-and-stick bits, and dovetails is very sensitive to grinding errors.

Cutter Risk

THE RISKS INVOLVED WITH CUTTERS are very real, but manageable. Although cutters can break, it doesn't often happen when they are used within normal limits. Cutters can also come out of the collet, but not if proper care is taken when inserting and tightening the bit (5⁄8 in. minimum for 1⁄4-in. bits, 3⁄4 in. minimum for 1⁄2-in. bits). Cutters do, of course, present a risk by virtue of their

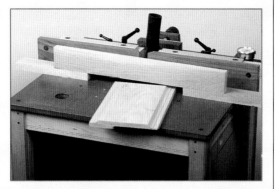

Large bits, such as raised-panel cutters, require extra attention to safety. My "letter slot" fence prevents me from getting my hands close to the cutter no matter what happens.

very sharpness, but careful handling will go a long way toward preventing a cut. And certainly a cut from handling a cutter that's not spinning won't likely send you to the emergency room.

It is true that broken cutters can turn into projectiles, but they rarely do so. They typically break against the stock, so most of their kinetic energy is spent on impact with the work. On occasion, a carbide weld will fail, but that is rare. Safety goggles are a reasonable line of defense. Many dovetail and narrow straight bits often break in a tunnel cut and can't get out, so with these there is little risk. The router sub-base also acts as a shield to cover up the missile.

Adjustment for Bit Wobble

Make some trial cuts in the intended material and adjust your jig to account for the cutter's actual profile. If your spacing between dovetails actually measures, say, 0.76 in. because of cutter deflection—and you want exactly 3⁄4 in.—adjust the spacing on the template to reflect the practical error (in effect, 0.01 in. closer).

The shank of a router bit is held to a very tight tolerance. Rarely is this ever a problem, because the shank has to be the exact diameter to be secured for its own production.

The overall measurements of the router bit are somewhat difficult to establish precisely without elaborate equipment. Top dead center can be difficult to find; the cutter needs to be placed in a special holder or jig, and special measuring gauges are required. A more practical strategy is to measure the work cut by the tool. If your setup is good and your milling is precise, it will be easy to measure your cutting results. For example, a dial

Making a test cut and measuring the results with a set of calipers is a sure-fire way to check the accuracy of a router bit.

Straight cutters come in three primary styles: spiral bits, first and second from left; on shear; and standard straight cutter. The spiral and on-shear bits cut more cleanly than the straight bit.

caliper can measure the depth of a rabbet more easily than it can measure the major and minor diameters of the cutter that made it.

EFFICIENCY

The design and sharpness of the cutting flutes essentially determine the power demand for a bit. Router bits come in a variety of cutting configurations. These include spiral ground, with an up or down pattern to the spiral, and on-shear, where the cutting edge hits the work at a slightly skewed angle. Bits are generally available with two, three, or four flutes. You can assume spiral-ground and on-shear tooling is more efficient. The importance of efficiency is in control. Whether the work is hand fed on the router table or worked with the hand-held router, you'll get better results when the work or the router is easier to control.

Sharpness and flute design are the essential elements that provide for efficiency and good control. Spirals are the most efficient, followed by on-shear and then straight. The number of flutes also plays a role, but two-fluted cutters dominate. Single-flute tools have balance problems, and three- or four-fluted bits (the least popular) sacrifice deflection resistance for cuts per inch. Spiral-ground bits have an advantage in both efficiency and wear. On-shear tools, with the edge at a slight angle, usually require a ¾-in. minimum diameter, so the majority of straight and other small-diameter bits are usually found without shear flutes. Decorative profile cutters are often shear-fluted, and they are plentiful.

Given the choice, I'd buy an on-shear tool over a straight perpendicular flute. The efficiencies are particularly noticeable in production, as the power demand will decrease with the on-shear tool. For the hobbyist who may only rout a few weekends a month, the difference may not be noticed. Heavy users, however, may get by with less horsepower because of the efficiency—and the cutter will run cooler and last longer.

Cutter Life

Some carbide bits last longer than others, but the difference is relatively small. There are too many variables to make a science out of testing the bits. The results from one type of test may not be significant for another type. For example, pathway cutting (cutting a tunnel) is at least twice as abusive on the same cutter as an edge cut.

Carbide bits are fairly equal, except that solid carbide lasts somewhat longer than carbide bits with welded or brazed cutting edges. (The carbide for solid carbide tools has been selected for hardness and durability, not braising, which compromises durability.)

Think about cutter life in terms of how it affects the work. If precision and cleanliness on a long run are essential, whether for joinery or decoration, I opt for two-stage cuts. I'll do 70 percent to 80 percent of the cut

Shaper cutters, which have holes for the arbor, cut the same profiles as router bits—such as the straight cutter at right—but will outlast them by a factor or 10 or more.

Close inspection reveals the cutter wear line on the work. The slight step will frustrate or prevent a close-fitting joint.

with one cutter and finish-cut the remaining 20 percent to 30 percent with a new tool at full depth in one pass. Uniform, light cuts may extend cutter life three to five times.

Your cutter is ready for a regrind when it starts burning stock, needs more hand-feed pressure and shows wear lines on the work. Joinery cutters (glue joint, rabbet, straight, or dovetail) used for extended periods at one depth will show wear lines at another depth. If you run 50 ft. of a ¼-in. by ¼-in. rabbet on MDF and then make a ⁵⁄₁₆-in.-square rabbet, the ¼-in. wear line will likely show up. For a decorative profile cut, the wear line may not matter; but for a dovetail and socket, the parts may not fit properly. Both cutters will still cut, but they are effectively dead soldiers.

Materials

Router bits vary in material. HSS used to be the cheapest and most commonly available. But most router bits for the small shop are now either carbide welded onto steel or solid carbide. Polycrystalline diamond is another option, but is used in production work only.

HIGH-SPEED STEEL

HSS is good material, and capable of very sharp edges that can be sharpened by the end user—but it doesn't hold up under prolonged use. With HSS, expect only 10 percent to 20 percent of the running time of carbide. Its value today is for the very short-run, custom profiles or perhaps for an experiment. If you're wondering about how the actual profile of a $35 carbide ogee might look, an $8 bit will give you the answer. And it might even serve for the short run in a given project.

Another advantage to HSS is that woodworkers skilled in tool grinding can make their own custom profiles. HSS router-bit blanks are available for this purpose. I especially like HSS bits for mortising, since they are often ground to plunge better than a carbide-faced steel bit, and a mortise run for a piece of furniture is usually a short run.

CARBIDE

Carbide on steel (the most common material and design) will outlast HSS 5 times to 10 times. Its actual life will vary, but it is clearly the best compromise for router-bit flutes, both economically and practically. The material can be reground (but never as well as the factory setup) sharp enough to run nearly as long. In my view, hand diamond honing is largely symbolic, and professionals should grind carbide for results and safety.

Carbide is the gold standard in tool-bit material today, although it does vary in hardness, durability, and density. Some carbide bits are selected for their durability in specific materials; one grade does not fit all occasions.

POLYCRYSTALLINE DIAMOND

Polycrystalline diamond (PCD) is very hard material, running 50 times to 100 times longer than carbide. This is strictly production material, mostly custom-made and designed to run for hours or days in materials like MDF, fiberglass, and aerospace composites. But cutters are very expensive, starting at about $200.

This Wisconsin Knife Works cutter has an over-center grind in the end of the flute for better plunging.

Shank Diameter

Shank diameters in the United States are $\frac{1}{4}$ in., $\frac{5}{16}$ in., $\frac{3}{8}$ in., and $\frac{1}{2}$ in.; metric sizes are common in Europe. Large shanks provide more surface area for the collet to surround, and also greater stiffness. Consequently, $\frac{1}{2}$-in. shanks are the most popular. For a given tool geometry, there's often less machining required for a $\frac{1}{2}$-in. tool than the $\frac{1}{4}$-in. equivalent. Consequently, they are about the same price. The advantage to smaller-shank tools is their small radii for closer inside cuts, or where it just makes no sense to use the larger shank. Trim routers use only $\frac{1}{4}$-in. shanks.

Cutter Types

There are many ways to classify router bits. They include piloted (with bearing) or unpiloted, bottom and side cutting, decorative profile, and joinery bits, as well as various combinations. Here's a sampling with special features you should know about.

BEARING BITS

The bearing used to guide a cutter can be placed on either end of the router bit or between a set of cutters, depending on the intended use. In all cases, they limit the cutting depth. Cutters with bearings on the end of the tool typically roll along the work and are often attached to decorative pro-file bits. Bevels, ogees, roundovers, coves, and beads are the typical cutters. They can be used in the hand router or on the router table. Essentially, they cut various profiles. These cutters are plentiful, cheap, competitive and probably the most popular of all router bits. They remove a lot of wood—and some (raised-panel bits) are enormous. Often, they are of anti-kickback design.

Solid carbide bits last longer than the same-sized bit with brazed-on carbide tips, left. Unfortunately, few cutters are solid carbide.

The Amana Nova Cutter System has replaceable carbide cutters that lock into the arbor assembly. Their carbide, not having to be brazed, has been selected for its keen edge.

Bearings come in a variety of sizes and can fit above, below, or between cutters.

The anti-kickback tool has a lot more steel in it than a conventional bit, and runs smoother because of its greater mass and even balance. The cutter design is such that it can only chop at the rate of 1 in. to $\frac{3}{64}$ in. per revolution. The gullets of these bits are shallow, and stock doesn't get caught in them; they don't kick back the work. I must add that the cut quality at 20,000 rpm is indistinguishable from that of a standard cutter at that speed—and that both will certainly cut you.

The sandwich of template-work-template shows two bearing and cutter options for the same result. The top-bearing pattern bit is easier to set up and there are more cutter options.

BEARING IN THE MIDDLE

A few bits have bearings sandwiched between two cutters top and bottom. The bearing maintains the space between the cutters and provides a means to limit the sideways depth of cut. It is strange that the most popular of these, the rail and stile sets, use a bearing at all. This is a router table tool only, and most door work is straight-line and should be worked off the fence. Nonetheless, these sets are supplied with bearings. Tongue-and-groove cutters and a few other miscellaneous bits are supplied with cutters or bearings sandwiched between each other.

BEARING ON THE TOP

Straight bits with a bearing mounted on the top are most often used with templates. They roll along the edge of a template for an exact transfer of the design to the workpiece. The practical and safe limit for full-thickness template cuts is about 1½ in. Longer cutters are common but should be avoided. You can, however, use incremental steps to reach deeper. If a 2-in.-thick piece of work, for example, is routed with a 1½-in. trimmer, you can use the machined surface of the stock to complete the cut. Essentially, all top-bearing tools are used with the template on top of the work. Using a template below the work requires a trimmer with a bearing on the end.

DECORATIVE PROFILE CUTTERS

Most cutters that decorate do so along the edges and ends of the work. They are important and occupy one-third to one-half or more of most cutter catalog inventories. These cutters usually have ball bearings to limit the depth of cut to about one radius. Moreover, the bearing-guided tools were designed primarily for the hand-held router. Ogees, bevels, beads, coves, and so on are generally supplied with R-3 bearings (O.D. = $\frac{1}{2}$ in., I.D.= $\frac{3}{16}$ in.). If the work is manageable and the cutter won't come apart, these profiles should be routed on the table without bearings. These cutters produce a lot of waste that can be easily collected, and the work is more efficient when guided off the table fence. There is also less operator risk than with the hand router.

For example, a 6-in.-diameter router (the typical base casting diameter) always has less than 50 percent of its footprint on the work while edge routing. If a $1\frac{1}{2}$-in.-diameter ogee bit is in the router, then on startup there is only 38 percent of the router on the work—a hazard indeed. When the bearing (say an R-3) does finally engage the edge of the work, that number increases to 46 percent. But as the router turns the corner to rout the ends, less than 25 percent of the base is fully supported. This momentary instability is a big reason that burning and kickback are so likely at the ends of a workpiece. This doesn't happen on the router table.

BEARING ON THE BOTTOM

Flush-trim bits are designed to trim a workpiece to the size of the template or underlying substrate. These cutters are typically used with the hand router, but can just as easily be used on the router table. With a router table, more time and skill are required to make the template and safely fasten the template to the work. It is relatively easy to just clamp the template to the work on the bench and use the hand router.

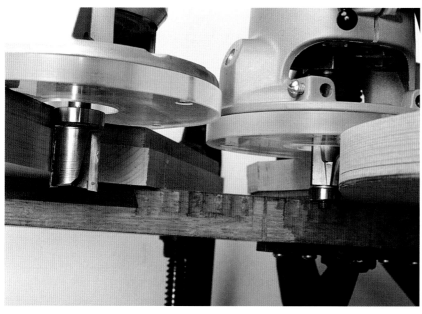

A pattern bit, left, has to have its entire flute extended for the bearing to engage the template. The end-bearing flush-trim bit can be extended the minimum amount to engage its template.

Flush-trim bits are safer than top-bearing-guided tools because they do not "bottom cut," and you can always extend just enough bit to do the cutting. But with the shank-bearing tools, the whole flute has to be extended for the bearing to engage the template. Moreover, these tools (top-bearing cutters) are bottom cutters, and as such present another cutting surface where none is needed. The end bearing on the flush trimmer covers up the sharp edge at the end of the tool for additional safety.

Flush trimmers are very popular but due to the poor selection of standard bearings most are only ½ in. diameter with narrow webs of ⁷⁄₃₂ in. or less. What that means is increased deflection. No matter how sharp or who supplies them, these tools will deflect significantly when their flutes are an inch or longer. There just isn't sufficient metal left in the core of the tool to keep it from bending. The few ¾-in. cutting diameter (½-in. shank) flush trimmers are very strong, however.

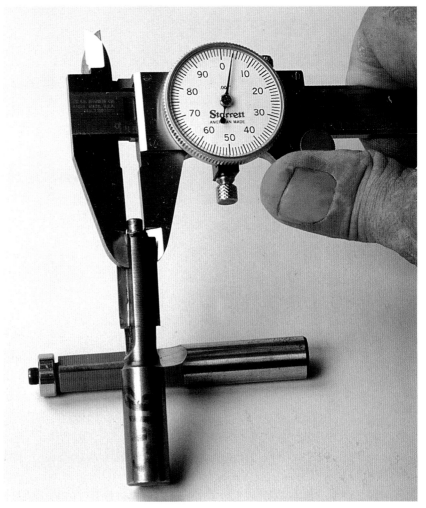

In spite of its ½-in. diameter, this trimmer is pretty narrow in the web, less than ¼ in. at the end of the tool.

Bits for interlocking joinery must meet high grinding standards to do their job. Your setup must also be exact to minimize errors.

Testing Joinery Bits

Joints made with dovetail and straight bits are usually quite forgiving, but it is good practice to take a light swipe on the edge of some maple or birch deeper than you intend to use on the joint. If any wear lines or "chip telegraphy" are evident on the sample, expect to have problems with the fit. These defects are never canceled on opposite sides of the joint and are destined to frustrate close joinery.

Though the faces of this glue joint don't line up, the profiles do nest in one another.

JOINERY BITS

Routers are good at joinery. Common joints include half lap, tongue and groove, mortise and tenon, cope and stick, scarf, finger, glue, and dovetail. Many cutters are precision-ground precisely for the job; others are not. Some dovetail bits are job-specific; so are the glue joint and cope-and-stick cutters. Half-lap, tongue-and-groove, and mortise-and-tenon bits are non-specific but require precision nonetheless. For the most part, good joinery is quite dependent on good milling and good jigs and fixtures—and less on

Interchangeable cutters used on a separate arbor provide an alternative to individual bits with arbors.

the cutter itself. Nevertheless, it can be very frustrating to discover that a poor fit is caused by the cutter.

As a matter of routine, I make a practical check on the fit of a sample joint before I commit the cutters to joinery on real project sticks. Direct cutter measurement may not reveal the potential for error, and certain cutters require sophisticated measuring tools and a good understanding of trigonometry and geometry to predict their behavior. It is easier and more important to actually test a cutter on scrap. If you don't, you'll risk spoiling expensive stock.

MULTIPIECE BITS

Most manufacturers of router bits make a few cutters that are assembled onto an arbor. Sometimes it's done out of necessity for the speed of production. It might just be cheaper to make the cutter than grind the whole thing out of one chunk of metal. Sometimes it's done to give the user a choice, say an 1/8-in. vs. a 1/4-in. slot cutter. Sometimes it's done for the sake of economy.

Expect a little more vibration with multipiece cutters and pay attention to the assembly directions. A cutter accidentally placed upside down can burn out in a minute, or break.

Examples of scary, potentially dangerous bits, from left: The 10-oz. lock miter's diameter is 5½ times larger than its shank. The rabbet bit is five times greater. The big dovetail bit has less than a ³⁄₁₆ in. of steel in the web. The HSS spiral bit is so flexible it "zings" when it cuts. And the carbide O-flute is 12 times longer than its diameter.

Sharpening

All cutting tools get dull. As they lose their cutting edge, their power demand to cut increases, the tools are worked harder and dulling increases at a faster and faster rate. A router bit's life is short, so I have developed strategies to increase it. One way to increase cutter life is to sequence its use. A cutter that burns in end grain, for example, may be acceptable on long grain; a cutter that won't cut edge grain will burn the end grain, but you can probably rout MDF with it. If it won't cut MDF, it may cut plastic but not for long. A cutter that won't cut plastic may abrade MDF but won't really slice it. To be sure, for the best of cuts on any material, use a new cutter.

Carbide grinding requires sophisticated diamond tooling; the stuff is hard. You can diamond hone it a little and you can sharpen high-speed steel. But to get the maximum time between sharpenings, expect to have your tools professionally ground. It is very cost-effective. Four to six regrinds are possible if the cutter has incurred no serious fractures. It is important to note that if 80 percent of the cutter life (if reground four times) is from the grinding service, not the manufacturer, finding a good grinder may be more important than finding a good manufacturer.

Router Accessories

As mentioned, routers can't do much without a guide of some sort. A cutter without a bearing on it will require a router table or an accessory to control its pathway. Even cutters with bearings often require a jig or template to guide the tool around. It so happens there are quite a few accessories for routers—some that are manufactured and some that you can easily make yourself. Here's a sampling.

Guides and Bases

The collar guide is available from the manufacturer for most routers, whether fixed-base, plunge, or trim. These devices fasten to the subbase or the base casting, surround the cutter, and with the cutter act like a pattern bit, but with an offset between bit and guide. They are used with templates, especially with dovetail and joinery jigs. The router is pulled against the template to establish contact with the collar. The collar slides along the template and cuts a swath parallel or concentric to the pattern. A 1-in.-diameter tool bit is about the largest cutter that can be used with a collar.

INLAY KITS
Inlay kits include a collar, sleeve, and $\frac{1}{8}$-in.-diameter cutter. The sleeve will offset the cutter pathway to compensate for diameter differences of the cutter and collar. If the cutter was like a laser and could cut with no waste, the plug and the recess it fits into could be created without the sleeve on the collar.

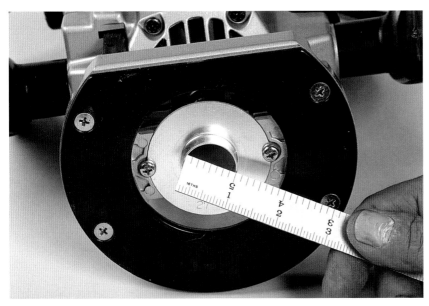

Collar guides that fit the opening in the router's baseplate allow the router to follow templates and other cutting jigs. The largest practical cutter diameter that can pass through most collars is 1 in.

Inlay kits use a pair of matched collar guides so you can follow the same pattern for both the excavation and the insert. The sizes are designed to compensate for the diameter of the bit.

Don't expect to do anything more than shallow decorative inlay work with these systems. The cutter is only a ⅛ in. in diameter—which is very short and not capable of deep or wide work. Note that you'll need to make pattern templates for most work with these kits.

With an aftermarket offset subbase and a shop-made edge guide, it's nearly impossible to spoil this decorative cut.

EDGE GUIDES

Edge guides fasten to the router-base casting with a pair of rods. Nearly all routers are designed to accept them, though not all manufacturers make them for their routers. The guides provide a means to cut parallel to the edge of the work. They are continuously adjustable and generally used with pilotless cutters. Add-on or replacement fences can be made concentric to inside or outside radii so the whole package (edge guide, router, and bit) can travel along curved edges.

ROUTER SUBBASES

Round, offset, square, and other shapes of subbases are available for transparency, control, and specialty application. Sears, DeWalt, Porter-Cable, Woodhaven, Vermont American, and others compete in this aftermarket niche (see Sources on p. 379).

CIRCLE CUTTING AND ELLIPSE MAKERS

Plastic pivot subbases are in most catalogs and the all steel and aluminum Micro Fence jig can cut precision circles (shown at right). The jig is also designed to work with an ellipse base, shown at far right, which provides an easy way to adjust the minor and major axes.

Wrenchless Collets

OLDER ORIGINAL EQUIPMENT ROUTER COLLETS often would let their cutters slip, or "glue," themselves to the cutter. Two wrenches, frequently different, were and still are a necessity for cutter exchanges. Newer collets are fastened to their collet nuts, rarely slip, and always free themselves from the bit. Still, there are those who think that is not enough.

Two aftermarket companies have been trying to create a market for wrenchless collets. The Jacobs Power Collet is toolless and the Eliminator chuck uses only a T-handled hex-key. They are somewhat router-specific, but given sufficient distribution, they should be available for all routers soon. They are bigger than the original collets and hold their cutters well, but they can vibrate more.

The Jacobs Power Collet replaces wrenches with a snap-in system that releases and tightens with a click.

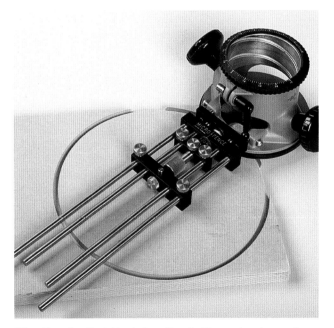

Micro Fence's adjustable circle cutting jig fits most routers and can be tuned to within a few thousandths of an inch.

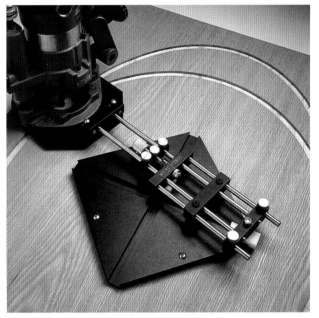

Used with an aftermarket jig, the Micro Fence can be used to rout precise ellipses. The mounting plate and a set of pivoting blocks provide a way to quickly set the minor and major axes of the ellipse.

The DeWalt 621 plunge router has an accessory adjustment knob for fine adjustments—useful whether the router is upside down or right side up.

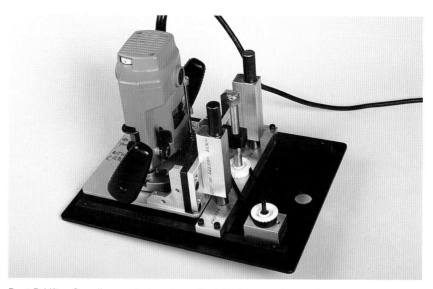

Rout-R-Lift, a Canadian product, replaces the table insert and cutter height adjustment with one product. A removable crank raises and lowers the router with a screw drive from the top of the table.

Rout-R-Lift top view.

Lee Valley's Router Bit Jack is attached to the depth stop of a plunge router. The tool allows depth changes with a lever. (Photo courtesy Lee Valley.)

Router Table Accessories

Routers are essentially designed for hand use and as such do not necessarily adjust up and down very well against gravity when underneath a router table. Extracting the springs from plunge routers and retrofitting the router with an aftermarket fine-depth adjuster are common strategies that can help.

A couple of different devices from Lee Valley and Jessem Tool Companies accomplish the same thing. The Jessem Rout-R-Lift is a substitute router table insert that carries the router in a crank-driven mechanism. The Lee Valley Router Bit Jack uses a ratchet mechanism fastened to a threaded rod of an upside-down plunger.

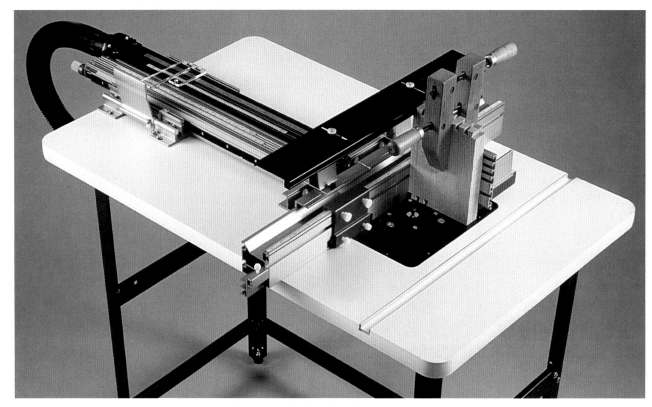

The router table fence from Incra Jig can be used as a standard fence and, with an attachment, for cutting dovetails. (Photo courtesy Incra Jig.)

ROUTER TABLE FENCES

Incra and JoinTech are the key players in aftermarket router table fences. The Incra Jig fence system moves a notch at a time on a saw-tooth rack, with a knob for fine adjustments between stops. The JoinTech uses a screw for continuous adjustment throughout its range.

PIN ROUTING

Pin routing is an interesting template method of routing whereby an overhead pin, in line with the cutter, engages the edge of the template fastened to the work. The cutter then trims the work even with or parallel to the template. Inside work is also possible with the system.

DOVETAIL/BOX-JOINT MAKERS

There are at least five dovetail jigs for hand routers; three of the five are capable of box, finger, and other case-corner joints. The Omni Jig is a Porter-Cable tool with many templates for box, through, half-blind, and sliding dovetails.

The JoinTech fence adjusts continuously and can be used on other stationary tools. (Photo courtesy JoinTech.)

The Porter-Cable Omni Jig is an industrial dovetail jig that has many accessories for various kinds of dovetails, as well as other joinery. (Photo courtesy Porter-Cable.)

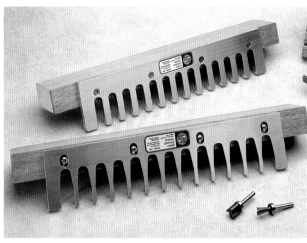

The Keller Dovetail System uses matched templates to cut precisely through dovetails on fixed centers. The idea is to do only through dovetails, but do them well and with a minimum of setup. (Photo courtesy Keller & Co.)

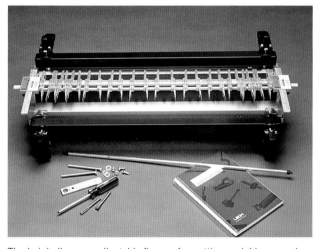

The Leigh Jig uses adjustable fingers for cutting variable-spaced dovetails, and it has become the industry standard for this operation. Leigh offers a wide variety of accessories for other joinery applications as well. (Photo courtesy Leigh Jig.)

Half-blind dovetail jigs—Porter-Cable 4112 is shown—are commonly used for drawer construction. The setup is rather fussy, though, and can require several test cuts. (Photo courtesy Porter-Cable.)

The Keller jig is a set of templates that clamp to the work, one for tails and the other for sockets or pins. The openings in the aluminum templates are fixed so the dovetails are cut on fixed centers.

Leigh Jig is the most versatile of the joint makers, capable of variable-spaced dovetails, box joints, and decorative interlocking joints shaped like flowers. The work is clamped to the bench-supported jig.

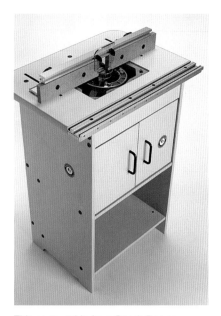

This router table from Bench Dog comes with an adjustable split fence system and built-in tracks for accessories. (Photo courtesy Bench Dog.)

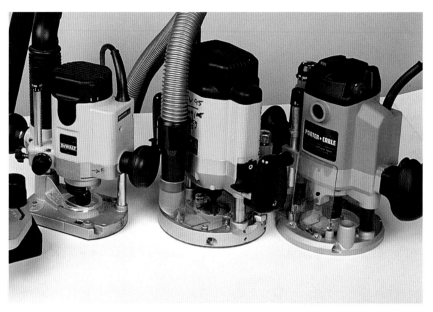

Many routers are now being fitted with chip-collection tubes. From left: DeWalt 621, DeWalt 625, and Porter-Cable 7529.

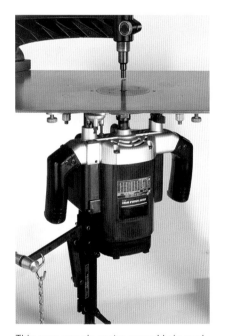

This over-arm pin router assembly is used with a template attached to the top of the workpiece. It's very efficient for making multiples of pieces with a complex shape. It's also capable of inside template routing. (Photo courtesy Lee Valley.)

The Katie Jig and the Stotts Template Making Jig also compete in the fixed-space, through-dovetail jigs for hand routers.

Finally, there are a number of half-blind dovetail makers by Porter-Cable, Sears, and many others. These are for making drawers in varying widths.

Chip Collection

Routers make a lot of waste. At 300 cuts to 400 cuts per second, they can only produce wafer-thin chips. These should be collected as soon as possible for your health and the quality of the cut. The DeWalt 625 has an aftermarket vacuum funnel accessory, as does the Porter-Cable router system. Router tables, the biggest chip producers, should all have a vacuum system.

A router table is a necessity rather than an accessory for many woodworkers. There are at least 16 choices, varying in size, material, design, and price. Prices with both accessories and router can run up to $500 or more.

Simple Shopmade Jigs

S hopmade router jigs and fixtures use the router to its limits. These jigs and fixtures can be very simple or extremely complex. Some of the fixtures I've seen are so sophisticated that you'd need to be a machinist to build them.

Router jigs and fixtures essentially serve to hold and index the work, as well as provide a guide for a controlled cut. At times, the jig or fixture holds the work so the cutting can be done on the router table. At other times, they hold the work so a handheld router can be used easily and safely. Either way, jigs and fixtures can be thought of as safety devices for precise, manageable and controlled routing.

Right-Angle Templates

Right-angle templates are similar to bench hooks used as holders and cutting guides with hand tools. Used with clamps, they hold the work and establish a pathway for the router to cut perpendicular to the edge of the work. Use them with collar guides or pattern bits.

I make mine from ½-in. MDF. The template should be at least as long as the work is wide and 6 in. to 8 in. wide. Two or three different lengths are better than one size for all. Screw and glue a 1x2-in. cleat to the bottom of the template. To get the most out of one of these, square both working edges to the front edge of the cleat.

Right-angle bench hooks register off the front edge of the work. They can be used with a collar guide, as shown. Backup scrap is clamped to the rear of the template to prevent tearout and breakout.

The adjustable stop on my fence is useful for cuts like open mortises.

Slot Makers

Adjustable stops with slotted ways are quite common in woodworking, but without a jig they're not easy to make. I solve this problem by creating a window slot template. I clamp the work under the template and use a collar guide and plunge router to make the slot. The width of the slot is usually one cutter diameter, and its length is regulated with the stop.

Make the platform from ½-in. MDF and big enough to clamp to the work—about 11 in. by 17 in. Make the narrow opening just wide enough

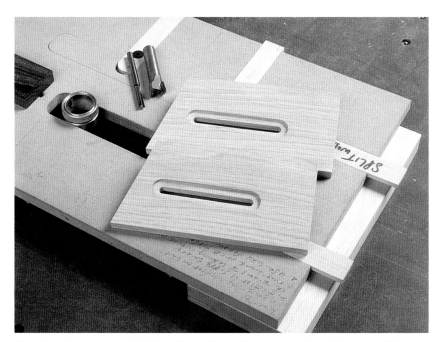

Slotted mortises require a jig. Here, the workpiece fits underneath, and the pattern bit runs in the slot.

for your collar to slip in—1 in. is a common collar diameter. Make the slot longer than the longest slot you plan to use—6 in. in my case.

You'll need some fences underneath to register the work, and on which to mount a clamp. Slot the MDF fences for a pair of screws and washers so they are easy to adjust.

Shopmade Mortiser

A good mortise is essential to quality joinery. There are many ways to make them, each with its advantages and limitations. Given well-milled material, a good plunge router, two edge guides, and my shop-built mortiser (see the top photo on p. 134), I can index and excavate a mortise up to $2\frac{3}{8}$ in. deep in just a minute or so.

A block of straight-grained hardwood is the foundation of the jig. Make it about $1\frac{1}{4}$ in. by $4\frac{1}{2}$ in. by 24 in. and screw on some $1\frac{1}{2}$-in. by $1\frac{1}{2}$-in. stock of the same species for more router surface. Add a cleat to the bottom of each side—one for jackscrews to support the work, and the other as a hold-down.

A set of three toggle clamps screwed to one of the cleats will secure and index the work. To be sure, a pair of adjustable stops on the top of the jig will simplify the mortising process. Position and slot them for the lengths of mortises you expect to make. A big, flat washer and machine screw will hold them in place.

This mortising jig uses a pair of sliding rods so it can easily adjust to make many mortise widths.

This simple tenoning jig uses a rabbeting bit with a ball bearing and an oversized router base to cut square tenons. The plunge mechanism allows you to cut a deeper tenon than the width of the rabbeting bit.

Tenon Maker

Square shouldered, clean-faced straight tenons are a snap with my shop-made tenoner (above). The windowed platform, combined with a plunge router on a wide wood base, are the key components to routing precise tenons. The work is indexed, clamped, and squared up from below, and the long-shank rabbet bit makes the tenon cheeks from above. Shoulder widths vary as the diameter of the bit and bearing differ.

For the body of the jig, use ¾-in. MDF or maple. Screws, dadoes, and angle brackets are used for the assembly. Cut a window in the top for work and cutter access. Also cut one in the vertical member so the cutter can access the entire section of the work.

You can clamp the jig to the bench when routing short stock, or clamp the work in a vise with the jig clamped to the work for big and long sticks.

An adjustable fence that pivots will permit angled tenons. A small toggle clamp on the fence will facilitate setup, but at least one other C-clamp will be needed to hold the work safely.

Tenon Maker

With this tenon maker and a ball-bearing guided rabbeting bit, you can easily form tenons on the end of the workpiece. The window cutout allows access to the end, while the workpiece is secured to the base of the jig by a clamp.

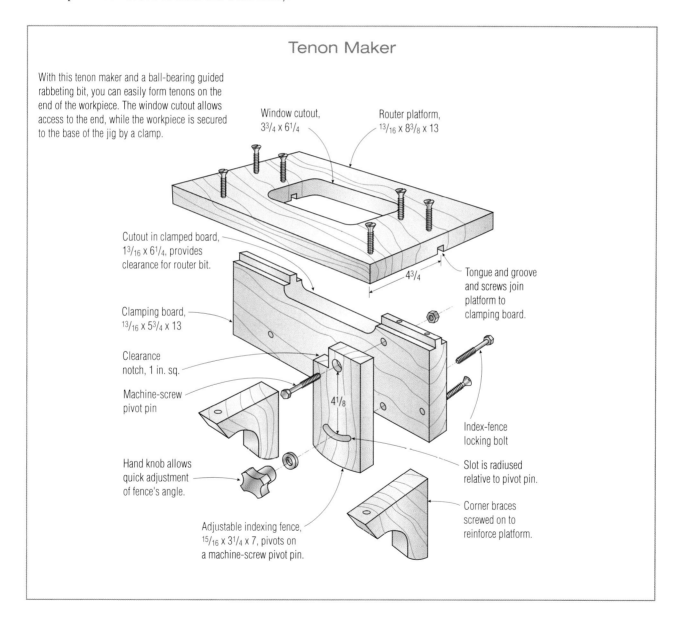

Window cutout, $3^3/_4$ x $6^1/_4$

Router platform, $^{13}/_{16}$ x $8^3/_8$ x 13

Cutout in clamped board, $1^3/_{16}$ x $6^1/_4$, provides clearance for router bit.

$4^3/_4$

Tongue and groove and screws join platform to clamping board.

Clamping board, $1^3/_{16}$ x $5^3/_4$ x 13

Clearance notch, 1 in. sq.

Machine-screw pivot pin

$4^1/_8$

Index-fence locking bolt

Hand knob allows quick adjustment of fence's angle.

Slot is radiused relative to pivot pin.

Corner braces screwed on to reinforce platform.

Adjustable indexing fence, $^{15}/_{16}$ x $3^1/_4$ x 7, pivots on a machine-screw pivot pin.

Shown is the underside of a half-lap jig. The workpiece is clamped in place and the router excavates the lap through the window.

End-Lap Template

End laps are simple enough visually, but hard to cut precisely. The shoulder must be square and the face must be equal to the mate it overlays. The lap is usually cut to half its thickness. A pattern bit and template are about all you need. The work is clamped under the template and exposed to the cutter through the window. A right-angle fence squares the work to the critical edge of the template. I use a large subbase on the router to keep it from tipping into the window.

Since lap cuts are so shallow, this jig can be made from ⅝-in.- or ¾-in.-thick MDF. This template and its construction are similar to the tenon jig—only this time, the work edge of the window must be at a right angle to the fence.

Make the jig big enough to clamp to the bench. Hold the work with toggle clamps fastened to the fence. A cleat fastened just beyond the window with a screw through it can serve as an adjustable stop. The end of the workpiece is butted against the screw, but below the work's thickness centerline to prevent an encounter with the router bit. If you work on both faces of the stock, you can make two-faced tenons.

Adjustable Tenon Maker

Dovetail and straight tenons are made with a fixed or plunge router using bearings or collars. The work has to be reversed and cut equally from both sides to yield centered tenons. The straight template is coupled to a screw and rotating lever for continuous adjustment. The work is clamped to the fixture, which is clamped to the bench/beam.

Make this one out of wood, aluminum, and MDF for the adjustable template. Make a right-angle assembly as long as the widest stock you plan to work, plus 8 in. or so for a fence, a clamp pedestal, and a hold-fast. You must be able to fix the jig to a rigid structure.

The template should be 5 in. or wider for plenty of router support. It travels on a set of 1-in. parallel bars mortised into the platform and the

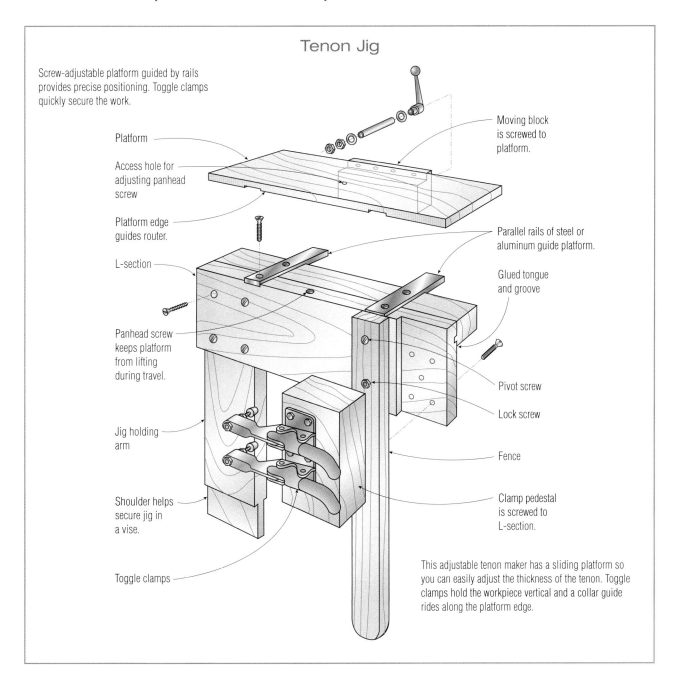

Tenon Jig

Screw-adjustable platform guided by rails provides precise positioning. Toggle clamps quickly secure the work.

Platform

Access hole for adjusting panhead screw

Platform edge guides router.

L-section

Panhead screw keeps platform from lifting during travel.

Jig holding arm

Shoulder helps secure jig in a vise.

Toggle clamps

Moving block is screwed to platform.

Parallel rails of steel or aluminum guide platform.

Glued tongue and groove

Pivot screw

Lock screw

Fence

Clamp pedestal is screwed to L-section.

This adjustable tenon maker has a sliding platform so you can easily adjust the thickness of the tenon. Toggle clamps hold the workpiece vertical and a collar guide rides along the platform edge.

This adjustable tenon jig is used with collar guides to cut precise tenons. One turn of the lever is 0.055 in. of template travel.

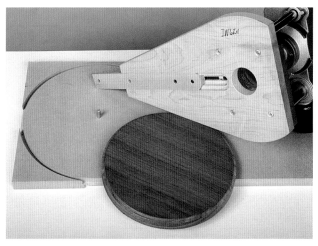

A homemade circle jig can be easily made up from hardwood scrap. An adjustable slide rides in a groove and pivots on a pin.

A router horse elevates the work and is more convenient than a router table for many operations.

template itself. It is driven by a screw that is ⁵/₁₆ in. in diameter by 18 threads per inch.

Two clamps on the pedestal secure the work. A fence (pivoting a few degrees) squares the work to the template. The hold-fast is 4 in. wide and screwed and rabbeted to the jig.

Circle Maker

This subbase (above) has a sliding pivot stick to make circles or disks. Use it with a plunge router and a solid carbide straight bit for best results.

The shape of the tool is not critical, but should be as small as practical. The bigger it gets, the more likely it is to bang into clamps as it revolves. You could also use a paddle with holes in it, but a jig with a fully adjustable arm is a lot handier.

Make the jig from ⁵/₈-in. maple with a long slot in it for an adjustable slide. If you want, make several slides of different lengths for convenience. Put a few holes in the slide for a pivot pin. A flat-head machine screw enters the bottom of the slide, and extends through the slot and into a nut on top to secure the arm.

Router Horse

Most hand-routed work is either done on an assembly or a loose stick. Assemblies are usually stable enough to rout clamped to the bench without much ado. Sticks, on the other hand, could use a lift. This short beam, shown at left, was made with lots of overhang to get the work up high enough to rout comfortably. Normal 34-in.- to 36-in.-high assembly benches are too low to rout on.

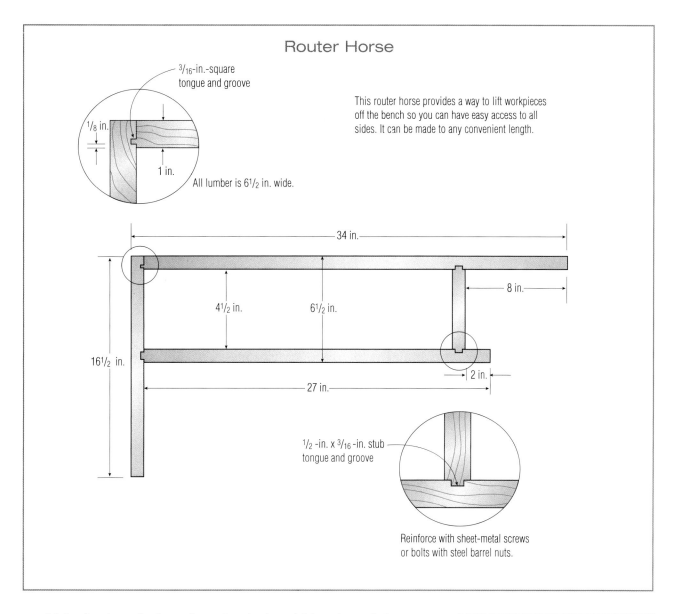

Router Horse

3/16-in.-square tongue and groove

1/8 in.

1 in.

All lumber is 6 1/2 in. wide.

This router horse provides a way to lift workpieces off the bench so you can have easy access to all sides. It can be made to any convenient length.

34 in.

8 in.

4 1/2 in.

6 1/2 in.

16 1/2 in.

27 in.

2 in.

1/2 -in. x 3/16 -in. stub tongue and groove

Reinforce with sheet-metal screws or bolts with steel barrel nuts.

Make this 1-in.-thick jig about 6 in. high and 36 in. long. A 6-in. to 8-in. width will support a 10-in.- to 12-in.-wide workpiece. The tool is joined in four places. The overhang on the horizontal surface is somewhat arbitrary: allow about 4 in. to 8 in. The vertical end piece is overhung by 10 in. to allow better support for workpieces held on end.

There is no need to complicate this; just hold the jig together with shallow dadoes and a little hardware. The bottom stick is used to hold the jig down and is pinned by a clamp. After assembly, add a fence to the vertical panel and again, some handy toggle clamps to hold the work on end. The right-angle jig can be used to advantage here, for making tenons or dadoes.

Permanent C-Clamps

A clamp with a welded-on plate can permanently attach a deep C-clamp to a jig. With a clamp screwed down through the steel plate, a jig becomes a sturdy platform that can support beefy workpieces, so all sorts of routing can be done from many directions.

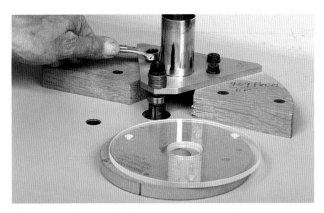

The shop made pin router jig will allow you to easily make multiples of complex shapes. The template goes on top and rolls against the pin.

This jig is used to cut bevels on the edges of round stock. The work rolls on the two bearings and the cutter is exposed through the cutter window.

Pin-Routing Jig

Pin routing is essentially a router table operation. A bearing or pin is suspended above or hung below and in line with the cutter. A template and work sandwich is rolled along the bearing, which follows the template contour and transfers that to the workpiece. The system is nearly the same as routing with end bearings, but in this case the isolated pin (or idler bearing) gets all the sideways stress, and thus the cuts are cleaner. As a rule, the pin router is a production tool.

You needn't make the jig quite this fancy (above left), but these are production tools. Mine is cut from a 1-in.-thick by 12-in. oak semicircle. Use thicker material if you plan on routing more than $\frac{3}{4}$-in.-thick stock. Add an equal share to the thickness of the jig for additional work thickness. Cut a notch in the front for a chip pocket. A vacuum tube on top of the jig collects the chips.

I used aluminum plate for mounting the pilot bearing. A $\frac{1}{4}$-in. shoulder bolt secures the bearing to the plate. The plate's screw holes are $\frac{9}{32}$ in., and the screws that go through these holes are $\frac{1}{4}$ in.

45-Degree Bevel

On occasion, I'll make a run of round replacement subbases. The two bearings ensure the disk has two points to roll on. I raise or lower the cutter to adjust the depth of cut.

I made this tool (above right) from $\frac{3}{4}$-in. MDF. The bearings can be situated in three places for different-sized disks. The small wooden platform, also screwed to the jig, is for a vacuum tool holder. The sub assembly also makes it harder to get my fingers near the cutter. The jig gets bolted down to the router table; its position is not critical. The base is 9 in. by 15 in., but size isn't important. Be sure to make it big enough if you're clamping it to the table.

Alignment Aid

To center and align a pin-router bearing, use a $\frac{1}{4}$-in. pilot pin installed in the router collet. The pin is available from most woodworking supply houses and is simply a machined piece of steel used for alignment chores. Simply project the pilot pin through the hole for the shoulder bolt in the aluminum plate—then tighten the screws down on the plate. Remove the pilot pin and install the $\frac{1}{4}$-in. bolt and bearing.

Router Safety

Compared to other technologies, woodworking and machinery processes change slowly. The hazards and risks associated with power and hand tools are essentially the same as they were decades ago. It's a dangerous business and accidents are common—a fact that's reflected by insurance rates for woodworkers.

Working with wood requires sharp cutting tools often used very close to the operator's body. It should come as no surprise that butchers use bandsaws on animal carcasses, and orthopedic surgeons use hammers, chisels, circular saws, drills, knives, and sanders on humans.

The rules of router safety are similar from manual to manual, but it's still a good idea to read them.

Hearing protection and a dust mask are sensible precautions.

Woodworking machinery is in the dark ages compared to the automobile, as far as safety goes. The automobile industry has done a thorough job in protecting drivers while in the cars they are driving and from the ones they may crash into. Seat restraints, air bags, hazard lights, ABS brakes, door panel guards, telescoping steering columns, safety glass, and padded dashboards all protect the driver. However, defensive driving skills are still as important as ever. In woodworking as well, it's just as important to play an active role in your own safety, to learn how to prevent accidents and to practice that skill constantly.

I make it a point to read all router safety rules in texts, articles, and router owners' manuals. These manuals are very poor; but you should read them nevertheless, because in this book, I am going to omit information on routing in an electrical storm, wearing OSHA-approved safety glasses, and the regulations on jewelry, long hair, long sleeves, and long extension cords. I am also not going to repeat the material on overreach, children in proximity, operator fatigue, the influence of alcohol or drugs, forcing the tool, good housekeeping, or saving instructions for future use. I will tell you about the things that have scared me, nearly injured me, and taken me by surprise. These experiences have led me to develop some precautions that you won't find in the operator's manual.

I should point out that all of my accidents and near-accidents were entirely my fault. I've never had an accident due to equipment failure. I've wrecked an acre of wood, but I've never drawn blood from a broken tool or a machine failure. And as we all know, there are general health issues besides the direct physical dangers of routing.

Hand-Router Safety

Fixed-base and plunge routers were first designed for upright use in the hands of the woodworker—not to be inverted under a router table. If they are used within their design limits, they are pretty safe. They are intimidating and scary, but they are safe.

CUTTING RESISTANCE

The amount of cutter engaged in the work determines its "grip" in the stock. Cutter traction increases roughly by the square. In other words, the area swept out in a ⅜-in. by ⅜-in. cut is nine times greater than a ⅛-in. by ⅛-in. rabbet, not three times. As such, the cutting dynamics are somewhat

The cutting procedure for the ⅛-in. by ⅛-in. rabbet, left, is the same for the ⅜-in. by ⅜-in. rabbet, right, but the volume swept out in the latter is nine times greater than the smaller cut. Expect substantial changes in handling as you scale up.

Neglect the motor lock in the router table and expect the depth of cut to change like it did while routing this slot.

unpredictable. Don't expect the same control when doubling the cut. If you're in doubt, make depth changes in small increments. The differences are especially noticeable in end grain where the fibers are at right angles to the cutting direction. Expect more exertion on end-grain or cross-grain cuts like dadoes.

SPONTANEOUS DEPTH CHANGES

On occasion, a motor may spontaneously shift in the casting, or a cutter may loosen in the collet. A plunge motor may also move on its posts if it's not tightened down enough. The consequences can range from a minor mishap to ruined work.

It is your responsibility to make sure the motor in a fixed-base tool does not move under power. They rarely do, but I believe wing-nut lock levers should be replaced with longer levers for more tightening purchase. Plunge levers should also be positioned so they don't run out of twist-travel before locking up the motor. All plunge lock levers have an adjustment for this.

INSTABILITY

Routers can unexpectedly tip when under power. They can be awkward to use and difficult to hold securely as you work. Fixed-base tools are sometimes used on narrow edges, or with less than half their baseplates on the work. In either case, a bobble can cause the cutter to dig into the work, even breaking or bending the cutter and resulting in kickback. Often, the router table is a better choice for narrow stock because it allows much better control. You can also use offset router bases, as shown below, that allow for more control by making it easier to press down directly over the workpiece. In this case, even an oversized subbase can make a big difference.

The locking lever of this Porter-Cable 690 router has been replaced with a longer version. The extra length provides more torque for easier locking.

Adding an oversized subbase to a plunge router, shown at lower left, can add a lot of stability to the tool.

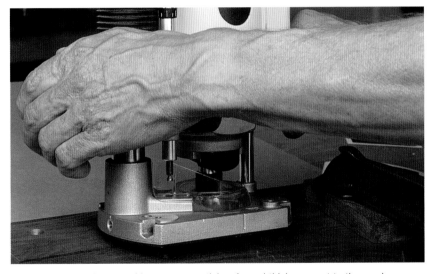

The cutter is loosely trapped between two sticks of equal thickness, set to the maximum intended depth for the cut. Test with a 5-lb. or 10-lb. push to see if the tool is unstable.

A plunge router under similar conditions can also tip. The handles are widely spaced and often high up on the posts. If a long cutter is engaged in a deep cut, your hand-feed forces may tip the tool over.

VARIABLE SPEED AND SOFT START

Variable speed is a relatively new feature in routers and a good one—especially for slowing down large-diameter cutters. Also, all variable speed tools have soft (ramp) start, a nice safety feature. Nevertheless, slow-speed routing can be risky. At slower speeds, cutting efficiency is reduced and it

Dry Run to Test Setup

Even though you won't be cutting stock, it's a good idea to get the feel of a plunge cut before you start the motor. Simulate the cut with the motor off and the cutter at its maximum depth. Move the router along to get the feel of it and to make sure the operation will go easily and smoothly. For difficult cuts, it's always a good idea to do a test cut in scrap stock.

takes more hand-feed force to move the work or router. As a result, the risk for up-ending the router increases and adequate clamping is essential. Before routing at slow speed, push and pull on the work, fences, stops, and edge guides to check their security: you'll be using more force than usual.

If you do start a cutter spinning and engage it in the work before it reaches maximum cutting speed, you may break or bend it. A soft-start tool has little rotational kinetic kickback on startup, so the likelihood of the cutter slamming into something before it is at maximum rpm is less of a problem. Consider a soft-start variable-speed tool to be the equivalent of a shock absorber in your car, thus making accidents such as bit grabbing in end grain less terrifying. Without this feature, the kinetics (reaction forces) during cutter jams and bobble are spontaneous and much more frightening.

Aftermarket Speed Controls

CLAIMS ARE MADE THAT AFTERMARKET SPEED CONTROLS are as good as the variable-speed feedback microprocessors in new routers. In my view, that is not true, and some toolmakers will not guarantee their tools with aftermarket devices in use.

Variable-speed controls on routers are not particularly accessible—and for good reason. Speed-control devices are used to slow down large-diameter tools; at high speeds they present more risk. If the speed control is very accessible, it could accelerate with an accidental bump, thus causing an accident.

In any case, if you use one of these, protect it from an accidental dial change. Early advertisements showed the contraption on the operator's belt—a very unsafe practice.

Big cutters require larger clearance holes than is necessary for most operations. A spare MDF fence can solve the problem.

With this template on a slight incline, you can rout a grip into the side of this box.

Incorporating a switch in the outside of a router table base provides safety insurance by allowing for quick shut-off in the case of an emergency. The switch is mortised so it can't be accidently struck.

KEEPING THE ROUTER HORIZONTAL

There will be occasions when routing with the router sideways (spindle horizontal) may look like a tempting solution to your woodworking problem. I would resist that temptation. Not only will you get chips in your face and hair, but the dynamics of the operation are so peculiar that it is invariably dangerous. Routing on an angle, however, is safe as long as the angle is not steep enough to make the router easily tip.

Router Table Safety

As a router table woodworker, you should keep a few things uppermost in your mind. Most basic of all is keeping the router secure in its casting while mounted upside down in the table. Failure to tighten the clamps can also have obvious drastic consequences. And clearly, your router table must be secured while you work. Also key is wiring a switch into your router table so that you can quickly turn it off.

With these basic precautions, the router table is pretty safe most of the time, but there are some risks. In general, you should use a split fence for safety's sake. You can more easily true up fence halves and slide the halves left and right to crowd the cutter, thus exposing the minimum steel. Vacuum collection and a solid means of securing the fence are essential. Without a secure fence, a slip could make the router grab the work, or you could lose your balance.

This pair of 2½-in.-long levers, at 6 in. from either end of the fence, securely lock the fence in place. The levers lock into T-nuts under the table.

Don't do this. Sliding the work down the fence onto this spinning cutter is done at considerable risk. If the fence moves, you can lose your grip on the work; or if the work is bowed you can break the cutter.

SMALL WORK

Work that is too small for the hand router can be table routed, but a great table and fence are not reason enough to get your hands close to the cutter. Avoid unnecessary reliance on hold-ins and hold-downs whenever possible. They obscure the cutter and hinder control of the workpiece. If the work seems hazardous enough to use hold-downs, it should be the signal that another kind of jig or fixture is required. You'll need a fixture big enough to keep your hands away from the cutter and sturdy enough to serve as a platform for stops and clamps. The jig may not be easy or quick to make, but your results will be better—and much cheaper than an emergency room visit.

DOUBLE-BLIND ENDED TABLE CUTS

Dropping the work on a spinning cutter is dangerous. It is a common but risky practice. Selecting the end points of the cut is guesswork, changing depth for mortises (and other cuts) is difficult, and handling the work is precarious. Any relaxation or momentary loss of control is "curtains." Expect chattered walls and burns at the ends of the piece as you reverse direction. You'll kill the cutter prematurely, and this is an unsafe practice. The hand plunge router was invented to accommodate these blind cuts, so you should use it.

THE HIDDEN CUTTER

It's common when working on a router table to have the cutter buried much of the time during a cut, only to have it appear unexpectedly at the end. It's important to stay alert; you must play an active part in your own safety. The sudden appearance of the cutter is just as threatening as a cutter that is always in your face.

ROUTING CURVY WORK

For routing on a curve, the usual strategy is to use bearing-guided cutters with a starting pin off to the side so you can ease the workpiece into the spinning cutter. Without one, the work is likely to kick away from the cutter. Even with a pin, it's possible that the cutter will catch the starting corner and whisk the work out of your control. Whenever possible, add a little sacrificial material to the end of the work for an easier start. In any case, you should feed the material against the cutter rotation.

Making the groove is so effortless, one may forget there is a cutter soon to emerge as the work passes over it.

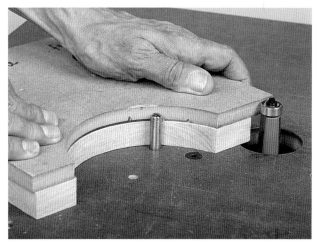

A starting pin allows you to start the work in a controlled way—a safety essential with curved work.

Cuts that run around the entire workpiece can begin anywhere, but it is safer to start on the long grain. Pin routers are sometimes used here instead of bearing-guided tools, especially for full-thickness cuts.

BIG CUTTERS

In my view, any cutter with a diameter over 2 in. is too big for a router. And even with so many kitchens being homemade today, big cutters occupy only a small percentage of most router-bit manufacturers' inventories. They are hazardous, not only because of their sheer size, but also because of the required slower speeds. Slower speed means greater hand-feed forces, and greater forces in turn require the setup to be more secure. If you do a lot of raised panels, consider using a shaper, which has the power and durability for this type of work.

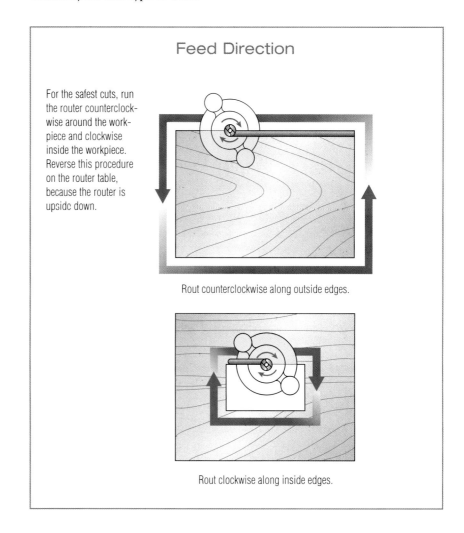

Feed Direction

For the safest cuts, run the router counterclockwise around the workpiece and clockwise inside the workpiece. Reverse this procedure on the router table, because the router is upside down.

Rout counterclockwise along outside edges.

Rout clockwise along inside edges.

Climb Cutting

The safe hand-routing feed direction should be left to right (against the cutter rotation) on the outside of the work. On an inside excavation, the feed direction should be clockwise, also against the cutter rotation. This is a good rule, but feeding against the cutter rotation usually causes some tearout. The effect is similar to chopping against the grain with a chisel while moving the chisel in the direction of the chop. It is very efficient, but the cutter can grab and tear out some stock. If the router is fed right to left, only the most recalcitrant of materials will tear out—the only real incentive to climb cut.

There is some risk in feeding with the cutter rotation; the router can self-feed. The cutter transfers its rotational force into a forward pull and tends to pull away from the work as it self-feeds. This doesn't happen with the standard cut because the operator is pushing against that force. But when you're pushing the router in the same direction as its self-feeding tendency, it's much harder to control. However, light cuts with small bits transfer very little force back into the router. Climb cutting with them is relatively safe. The bigger the cutter, the greater the power transfer. The problem also gets more serious on end-grain, where the cutters have the most traction.

On the router table, the climb cut can transfer a lot of energy into a relatively light workpiece. It's very easy to lose the work when feeding left to right. And once the workpiece starts to self-feed, your fingers can be pulled into the cutter, a disaster indeed. If you have the work in a holder that has some additional mass, the likelihood of a self-feed is reduced, and you can keep your hands safely away from the cutter. A workpiece not

Climb Cutting

Reversing the router's feed direction results in the risky climb cut—so-named because the router bit tends to pull—or climb—its way along the workpiece.

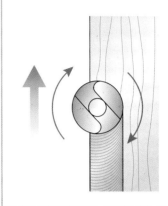

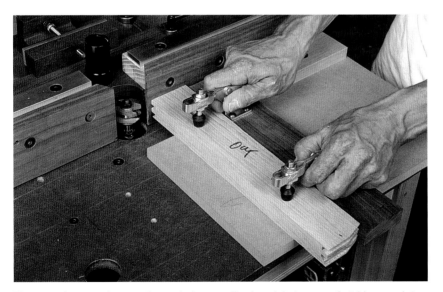

These toggles not only press the work down on fiberboard, but are comfortable enough to use as handles.

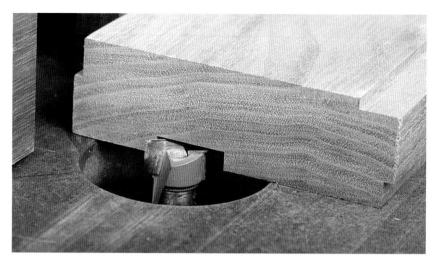

Feed the stock from left to right if widening slots on the fence side (nearest the fence). Feed from right to left if the slot is being widened on the operator's side. The initial groove should be made feeding right to left.

fixed into a holder of some sort is very hard to control when climb cutting. Climb cutting is always risky. Take very light cuts with small bits to learn about the phenomenon, and know your enemies. The self-feed of the climb cut is one of them.

THE ACCIDENTAL CLIMB CUT

Widening inside cuts (as in dadoes and slots) can be hazardous. Taking the cut on the wrong side of the pathway may result in a climb cut. Pay attention to cutter rotation (counter-clockwise on the router table) and cut against the rotation when widening tunnels. Dovetail sockets, ways, and box joints are commonly widened with specialty joinery fences.

Stock Preparation

Work that has been poorly milled will yield variable results and may self-feed or kick back unexpectedly, especially if the cutter is trapped in the work, like a slot cutter (on edges) or straight bit in a dado. There is also potential for the work to self-feed or kick back on edge cuts if the work is bowed. As the work is pressed down and relaxed on the table, it may cut more on the top or the bottom of the profile. If the bow is quite pronounced, a sudden reduction of down force may kick back the work. Crooked or poorly edged material may be the cause of unexpected self-feeding or kickback on inside cuts.

Removing a lot of material on the table may also distort a stick that started out flat and straight. This phenomenon is often seen while ripping on the table saw. The two halves of a rip often go their separate ways. Inspect your work often while table routing. If you are removing enough material to relieve stress and the work changes shape, then kickback, self-feeding, or torn cuttings can be expected.

Cutter Surprises and Risks

Router bits cut or destroy most things in their pathway even if they're dull. They can even get hot and burn you. They can also break, especially if they're small in diameter. Most of the cutting and force on a cutter at work is at the end of the bit. The lever (distance) from the end of the tool to its weakest point can be long enough to break the tool in modest working conditions: dovetail bits are notorious for this. To minimize breakage when no other cutter will do, use solid carbide or take the cut in stages with a plunge router. Also note that a sloppy setup increases the likelihood of breaking the tool. Keeping a cutter confined to its pathway helps stack the odds in your favor.

No countermeasure will prevent all accidents. Cutters break. Fortunately, cutters that break in inside cuts lose their kinetic energy quickly against the wall of the cut—and they are usually trapped there by the cover of the subbase. They are rarely dangerous. A cutter breaking along the edge of stock is a threat, but rare. I've heard horror stories, but I think you're more likely to get hit by lighting than a ballistic tool bit. I've put in thousands of hours behind routers with all sorts of cutters—new, used, experimental, unbalanced, reground, and so on—and I have never broken a cutter while edge routing. I've also chipped a lot of carbide when hitting nails, knots and embedded hardware, but I've never been hit by cutter shrapnel.

This table leg, out of square, will rout differently on the router table depending on which face is against the fence. If it is too far out of square, it could break the cutter.

This slot cutter is engaged in the work. Lift up the work while routing and anything can happen—usually what happens is not good.

THE TRAPPED CUTTER

A trapped cutter is any bit that will destroy the work if you lift the router. These include slot cutters, keyhole bits, and dovetail bits. Any of these will ruin the work if you tip or lift the router. If the cutter is in the router table and you lift the work, you'll also ruin the cut. You may also unwittingly dislodge or pull the cutter from the collet and change its cutting depth, causing both dangerous and unexpected results. There is not much you can do about this but pay attention.

OUT-OF-BALANCE CUTTERS

Bent, self-sharpened, reground, big, long, single-flute, and even ordinary cutters can be out of balance. Dirty or worn collets can send a well-balanced tool into a resonant frenzy, too. With any of the above, test the tool in a variable-speed router for vibration first. Hold the motor with both hands, with your thumb on the off switch. Accelerate a step at a time and shut the tool down the instant any vibration is felt. Operate the bit only at speeds below resonance (marked vibration) or not at all. Frankly, I would return an out-of-balance bit for a refund or replacement. Unfortunately, I have seen new cutters from most suppliers that have some vibration.

Let your collet fill up with a resinous mess from a softwood routing session and the next cutter in the collet may not be secure. Collets should be immaculate; if they're not, you'll see a loss of holding power.

Health Concerns

Routing is a dirty, dangerous, noisy business. Eye protection is essential, and goggles that won't let a chip in anywhere are cheap. Ear protection should not be overlooked. Routers are noisy, and with a vacuum they are doubly noisy. Noise suppressors safe to NRR:25 dB minimum should be worn at all times when routing, as sound-energy insults are cumulative and can lead to noise-induced hearing loss.

Every reasonable effort should be made to collect the dust and chips from a router to prevent nasal and lung damage. The router table is very easy to set up with dust collection equipment, and you should use this whenever possible. Repeated exposure to wood dust is a recognized health hazard, so you need to minimize exposure. (For more on this, see *Woodshop Dust Control* by Sandor Nagyszalanczy, The Taunton Press.)

POSTURE

Most shop furniture is too low for routing, not only for inspection of the work but for your posture. For me, the best height is around 36 in. to 38 in. high for table routing, and about 40 in. for hand routing. Select the best height using the adjustable height of the drill-press table as an experimental surface. There's no sense in stooping and tiring before you're ready to quit.

Hearing protectors, safety goggles, and dust masks help prevent long-term health damage from frequent router use.

Working with Sharp Corners

Routing can produce very sharp-cornered workpieces—sharp enough to cut your hand. Although routing with gloves can have its own hazards, I do use rubber gloves from time to time for protection. Be cautious, though. If a cutter catches a glove it can pull your hand with it, winding up the glove in a second.

Introduction to the Table Saw

The table saw is one of the most important and versatile power tools for anyone who works with wood, from carpenters to furniture makers. It's the tool that allows you to rip, crosscut, and join wood or sheet goods most efficiently. If you are new to the craft of woodworking, a table saw will most likely be your first major power tool.

Although the table saw was originally invented to do rip cutting (that is, cut wide boards into narrower pieces along their lengths), it didn't take long to see the advantages of using this saw to make accurate crosscuts as well. For the most part, the table saw's purpose—to efficiently and accurately cut wood of almost any size—remains the same today as it did years ago.

Different types of table saws are marketed for various levels of use and expertise. There are saws for the home hobbyist, the carpenter or contractor, the small production shop, and large industry. But whatever the saw, the basic working principles are the same. A motor spins a circular sawblade, which protrudes through a table, and the workpiece is moved through the blade.

In this chapter, I'll discuss the functions of the various table-saw parts to give you a basic understanding of how the saw works. I'll also discuss the types of saws in brief, and what they were designed for. In the next chapter, I'll delve into much more detail about the advantages and disadvantages of the particular types of saws and their features to help you in your purchasing decisions.

Basic table-saw design hasn't changed much in the days since this classic old Oliver® saw was made.

Table-Saw Anatomy

All table saws share standard features, although the design, materials, and quality vary from model to model. The basic external features include a base, a table and its extensions, rails and a rip fence, a miter gauge, a throat plate, adjustment wheels, and a power switch. The internal parts include the motor, trunnion brackets, carriage assembly, arbor and arbor assembly, and sector gears.

THE BASE

As its name implies, the base, or body, of the saw supports the table. It is freestanding or is used in conjunction with a stand that is positioned at an average comfortable working height of about 34 in. The base contains the internal mechanisms and incorporates the adjustment wheels and power switch. Some bases house components for efficient dust collection, but many just serve as dust containers.

Exterior of a Table Saw (Contractor's Saw Shown)

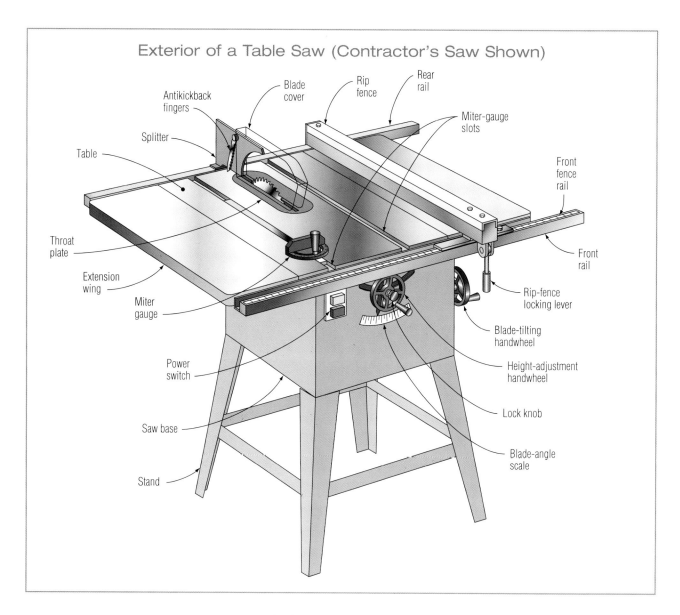

The base protects the working parts of the machine from damage and prevents the operator from getting caught by the revolving parts of the machine. The body is generally made of steel—with thicker-gauge steel used in higher-quality saws. The bodies on some portables are made of high-impact plastic designed to withstand rough treatment and extreme weather conditions.

THE TABLE AND EXTENSIONS

Ideally, the table on a saw provides a stable, durable, flat working surface for the workpiece to ride on as it is presented to the sawblade. For the saw to cut correctly, the table surface must be as flat as possible. Therefore, heavy cast iron is the material of choice for most table-saw surfaces

Interior Mechanisms (Contractor's Saw Shown)

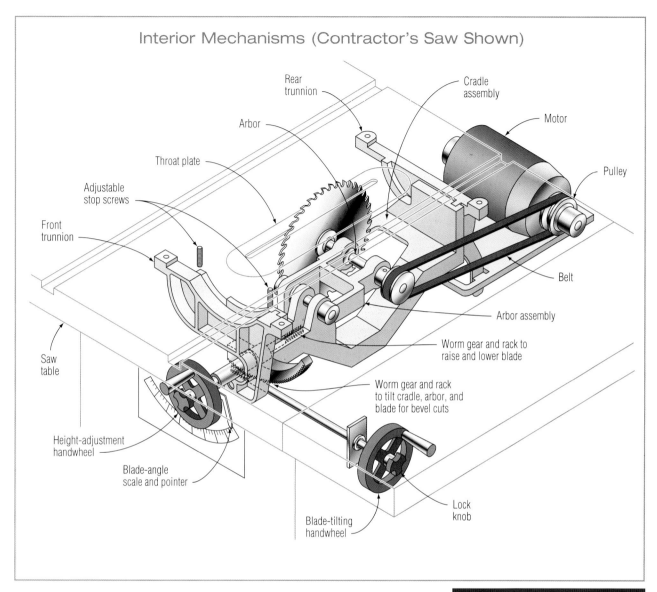

Rear trunnion

Cradle assembly

Arbor

Motor

Throat plate

Pulley

Adjustable stop screws

Front trunnion

Belt

Arbor assembly

Saw table

Worm gear and rack to raise and lower blade

Worm gear and rack to tilt cradle, arbor, and blade for bevel cuts

Height-adjustment handwheel

Blade-angle scale and pointer

Lock knob

Blade-tilting handwheel

because it provides an extremely flat and durable surface. Its weight also adds stability to the saw and helps absorb vibration. The less vibration, the longer any machine tool will maintain its accuracy. Minimal vibration also helps reduce operator fatigue.

Because a flat table surface is of paramount importance to accurate sawing, today's manufacturers of iron table-saw tops use precise technology in the production processes. The end result of careful iron manufacturing processes is a table saw that is accurate and durable enough to give generations of service.

Table extensions increase the size of a top, making large workpieces more manageable. The extensions, often called "wings," add 16 in. to 20 in. to the width of a top and increase stability by adding weight to the

Table Extensions

Shopmade table extensions can increase the effective table size of any saw, allowing you to more easily cut large stock and sheet goods.

A GOOD CAST-IRON TOP can give generations of service. Today's manufacturers of cast iron can maintain precise control in the chemistry of iron composition. Better electric furnaces, modern patterns, and machining processes can provide the end user with a top that is within 0.005 in. flat over its entire surface. The level of control is such that there is no longer any reason to "cure" the iron after casting to relieve stresses. Formerly a standard practice, the curing process could add as much as a year to the manufacturing time.

When the consideration is table-saw portability, the table surface is made from cast-aluminum alloys, which are much lighter than cast iron. Anodizing the aluminum increases durability, and a coating such as Teflon® can be added to the surface to aid in hardening and to reduce workpiece friction. Even precision-machined aluminum won't make as flat or durable a tabletop as cast iron, but it provides an economical, sufficiently accurate, lightweight alternative.

Tabletops on European saws tend to be long and narrow. Instead of incorporating a fixed center top with a left hand, a long sliding table on the left of the saw carries the workpiece across the blade.

Webbed cast-iron extension wings provide a compromise between stamped-steel wings and solid cast-iron wings. They're flatter and more solid than stamped steel, but less expensive than solid cast iron.

saw. On saws other than portable saws, the table-saw surface consists of a main center section measuring about 21 in. by 27 in. The wings are bolted onto either side. On larger stationary saws, the wings are made of cast iron. On smaller home-shop saws, cast iron may be an option, but less expensive stamped-steel extensions are more common. Another option may be cast-iron wings in a "webbed" style (see the photo above). The webbed style is a compromise that provides stiffness, weight, and a flatter surface than stamped steel.

European table-saw tops differ from North American saws in that the center section tends to be smaller from side to side but deeper from front to back. The extra depth, which adds support for the workpiece, is a European safety requirement. The table extension is added to the right side of the saw. To increase the width to the left, European manufacturers typically add a sliding table that doubles as an efficient crosscutting solution (see the photo at left on the facing page).

THE THROAT PLATE

The throat opening in a tabletop is large enough to allow access for blade changing, arbor maintenance, and, on some saws, adjustment of the guard assembly. The throat plate is a separate, removable insert that sits in the throat opening, surrounding the blade. The throat plate is made of a soft, nonferrous material that won't spark or damage the blade if it comes into contact with it. A stock throat plate has a slot opening that is long enough and wide enough for the blade and a splitter or riving knife to pass through it at any angle or height.

Leveling screws in the throat plate sit on cast pods in the opening to allow height adjustment of the plate relative to the tabletop (see the photo below). The throat plate may also have one or more screws or a clip to secure it, as required on Canadian saws. Optional throat plates with wider openings are available for use with dado heads or molding heads. And custom throat plates are easy to make from plywood, plastic, or other materials.

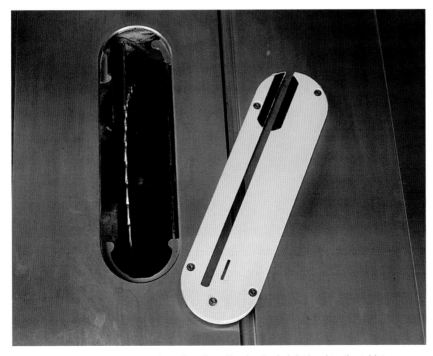

The leveling screws in a throat plate allow for adjusting its height level to the tabletop.

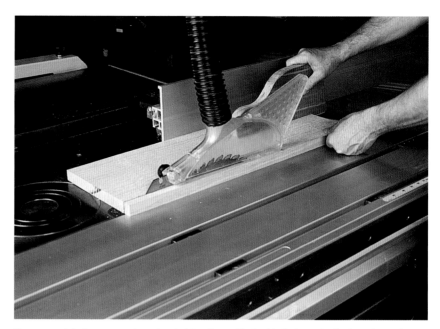

European-style fences can be retracted to align with the blade for safe ripping of reactive boards that splay apart once past the blade.

The fence rails on this Inca table saw can be adjusted to the right or left to accommodate cutting on either side of the fence.

THE RIP FENCE AND RAILS

The rip fence guides wood parallel to the blade as the wood is being cut along its length, a process known as ripping. The fence head is made of metal and rides on the rails. The fence body has a facing of plastic, aluminum, or laminated wood. Some facings are adjustable to the table surface and may be replaceable. On European saws, the fence body can be pulled back to align with the beginning of the sawblade for safe ripping of warp-prone boards (see the top photo on the facing page).

The fence moves along one or two fence rails that are attached across the front and the back of the table-saw top. The length of the rails determines the ripping capacity of the saw, with 24 in. to 52 in. being the standard. A measurement scale attached to the front rail is used in tandem with a cursor on the fence head to set the fence a specific distance from the blade. Some table saws have sliding rails that can be adjusted to the left or the right to give maximum cutting capacity to either side of the sawblade (see the bottom photo on the facing page).

A clamping lever or knob on the head of the fence locks the fence to the rails. The lever or knob works by means of a cam that pushes against the front rail when the lever or knob is tightened. On some fence systems, locking the front also pulls on a rod that tightens a J-clamp on the rear rail to help secure the fence. Some fences have a microadjust knob that allows dialing in fine adjustments rather than tapping the fence into position.

THE MITER GAUGE AND MITER SLOTS

The miter gauge is used to guide the workpiece during most crosscutting operations, usually at 90 degrees. The miter gauge on most saws consists of a soft, cast-metal protractor head attached to a length of ¾-in.-wide bar stock. The head pivots on the bar to the left and right for cutting angles from 30 degrees to 90 degrees in either direction. The gauge can be locked anywhere in between these angles using the calibrated protractor scale. Most models have adjustable stops at the most frequently used angles of 45 degrees and 90 degrees.

The miter gauge slides in slots that are milled in the tabletop parallel to each other to the left and right of the blade. On most U.S. saws, the slots are fairly standard at ¾ in. wide and ⅜ in. deep. Most miter-gauge guide slots are in the shape of an inverted T to accommodate a washer that's screwed to the bottom of the miter-gauge bar at its far end. This arrangement traps the end of the bar in the slot, preventing the gauge head from dropping when pulled out in front of the saw.

Most European-style miter gauges come equipped with a long, adjustable extruded-aluminum fence facing. The facing provides added support for the workpiece as it approaches and meets the blade. European-style miter gauges are typically equipped with adjustable drop stops that ride in a T-channel in the top of the body. These miter gauges are supplied with European saws that don't have sliding tables. Saws with sliding tables incorporate an adjustable fence that travels with the sliding table for crosscutting operations.

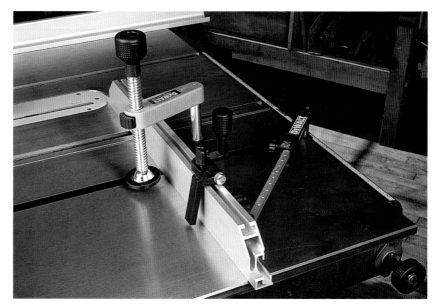

European-style miter gauges include a longer fence for better bearing and integral flip-down stops for repetitive cutting.

Trunnion Styles

The connection between the front and rear trunnion contributes to accurate cutting. A one-piece cast-trunnion assembly is preferable to trunnions connected by rails, which can flex, affecting the cut.

INTERNAL MECHANISMS

Underneath the saw table lie the parts and mechanisms that permit the machine to cut wood at varying heights and angles and allow the motor to transmit power to spin the sawblade. A good understanding of how these parts work together is essential for maintaining a safe and well-tuned table saw.

Arbor assembly The arbor assembly is at the heart of the internal mechanisms. The assembly includes the arbor and the sector gear for raising and lowering the blade. The arbor is a metal shaft that holds the blade as well as its driver pulley(s). Depending on the drive system, one or more pulleys are located either at the end of the arbor opposite the blade or at the center of the arbor. The blade end of the arbor is threaded to accept a nut that sandwiches the blade between a removable outside flange and a fixed inside flange. The pulley or pulleys attached to the arbor drive the blade by means of a motor and belt(s). Portable saws, by contrast, are direct drive, meaning that the arbor is directly attached to the motor shaft.

On most portable saws and all home-shop and 10-in. cabinet saws, the arbor is ⅝ in. in diameter. On some saws, the arbor diameter is larger through the bearings and then turned down to a smaller diameter at the blade end, allowing for a more stout arbor and bigger bearings. Table saws with 12-in.-dia. blades use a 1-in. arbor at the blade end. The most common European arbor diameter is 1³⁄₁₆ in. (30mm). The length of the blade end of the arbor can vary—an important consideration when thinking about mounting a wide dado or molding head.

Carriage assembly The carriage assembly, also referred to as the cradle, consists of the front and rear trunnions and the yolk (or rails) that connects them. The carriage assembly also serves as the mounting for the arbor assembly and motor, keeping them aligned as the carriage assembly is tilted. The carriage assembly rides in channels, or ways, milled into the trunnion brackets. The front trunnion includes a sector gear for tilting the assembly.

A one-piece, solid-cast trunnion assembly is preferable to one that uses rails to connect the trunnions because the rails can cause some twist when tilting the unit. A one-piece assembly can also more easily incorporate an efficient dust port in the casting.

Trunnion brackets The trunnion brackets at the front and rear of the saw support the carriage assembly and allow it to be tilted. On home-shop saws, the brackets are bolted to the underside of the table. On stationary saws, they are secured to the cabinet itself. The trunnion brackets are most commonly made of heavy cast iron on stationary saws and lighter-weight cast iron on home-shop saws. Other lightweight metals are used on portable saws.

Sector gears A table saw has two arc-shaped sector gears for adjusting the blade. The arbor-sector gear is part of the arbor assembly and provides for raising and lowering the blade. The bevel-sector gear, part of the carriage assembly, allows tilting of the blade for beveling. Teeth on the sector gears mesh with, and are driven by, worm gears on the ends of the handwheel rods. Better saws include an adjustment on either the sector gear or the worm gear to minimize backlash between the two. Most saws include an adjustable stop at either end of the bevel-sector gear to stop the blade at exactly 45 degrees and 90 degrees.

Adjustment wheels Changes in blade height and angle are accomplished by means of handwheels that extend through the saw body. The height-adjustment handwheel is at the front of the saw body. It is used to raise and lower the blade and can be prevented from turning by using the locking knob at its hub.

The blade-tilting handwheel is located either on the right or left side of the saw base on most home-shop and stationary saws. On portable saws, it is located on the front of the saw where it is combined with the height-adjustment wheel. The blade-tilting handwheel is used to tilt the blade for bevel cuts and to set the blade at 90 degrees to the tabletop for square cuts. The handwheel has a corresponding degree gauge, typically on the front of the saw base, that indicates the approximate cut angle. Like the height-adjustment handwheel, the blade-tilting handwheel has a locking knob at its hub. For some high-end saws, an optional dial indicator is available for clear indication of the exact blade height and angle.

Power switch The power switch is located on the front of the saw. Switches come in various sizes, shapes, and colors, but there are two basic mechanisms: magnetic and manual. The contacts on a magnetic switch are maintained by electric current only, whereas a manual switch maintains an electrical contact by physical pressure.

The important difference lies in the way that the switches react to a power failure. If the power fails (due to a tripped circuit breaker, for example), a magnet switch will automatically disconnect and remain off until the "on" button is pressed again. This ensures that the saw doesn't jump back to life on its own when the power returns—a potentially dangerous risk that you run with a manual switch. A magnetic switch is required on any table saw in a commercial or educational setting. Switches that can be shut off with the press of a knee are required on table saws in Europe.

Basic Safety Equipment

The table saw is a tool with great potential—for both creativity and accidents. Manufacturers recognize the dangers and provide basic safety equipment on every table saw they sell. The stock safety equipment on saws sold in the United States is somewhat similar to that on European saws, but it differs in name and ease of operation. Standard safety equipment includes a blade cover, a splitter or riving knife, antikickback fingers, and belt and pulley guards. (For a more detailed discussion of safety features, see chapter 11.)

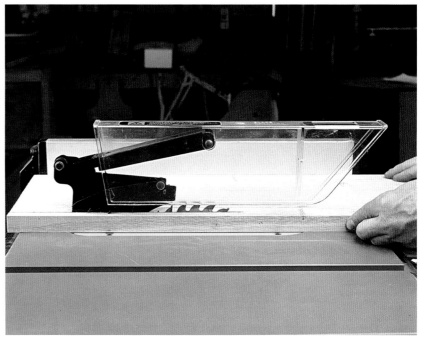

The blade guard on a typical American saw is made of metal or clear plastic and is attached to the flat metal splitter that projects up through the saw's throat plate.

BLADE COVER

The blade cover, sometimes called a blade guard, helps to prevent your hands and other objects from accidentally meeting the blade. The blade cover also deflects away from the operator the wood chips and sawdust thrown by the blade. The cover may be made from clear plastic, metal, or a combination of metal and plastic (see the photo on the facing page). A good blade cover surrounds the blade but does not interfere with normal cutting operations.

SPLITTER OR RIVING KNIFE

A splitter or riving knife is a piece of metal located directly behind and in line with the blade. It is crucial to the safe operation of a table saw. It denies the workpiece access to the rear saw teeth, which can cause it to be picked up and thrown violently toward the operator—a dangerous situation known as kickback. It also helps prevent reactive wood from pinching the blade, causing it to bog down or burn the wood. (Read more on kickback and safety in chapter 11.)

ANTIKICKBACK FINGERS

Antikickback fingers, or pawls, are a safety addition on saws sold in the United States. Antikickback fingers are normally attached to the splitter but are sometimes part of the guard. The sharp fingers allow the workpiece forward motion by pivoting out of the way, but supposedly prevent reverse motion by digging into the workpiece if it is forced backward. European safety standards don't require antikickback fingers.

BELT AND PULLEY GUARD

On a contractor's saw, which has an exposed motor, a belt and pulley guard keeps objects (and fingers) from getting caught up between the belt and the pulley during operation.

Types of Table Saws

With the burgeoning interest in woodworking as an American pastime, the types, features, and even names of table saws are changing at a fast pace. It is exciting to see saws developed and introduced into the market with features that are better able to meet the needs of all the various people who work with wood. In addition to the usual selection of saws available on the U.S. market for years, we're beginning to see the introduction of more European saws, giving us the chance to learn how European woodworkers approach safety and versatility issues.

The descriptions that follow provide an overview of the types of saws currently available to help you understand their purposes and basic features. In the next chapter, I'll discuss their features in much more detail and address changing terminology in the field of table saws.

Blade Guards

Stock blade guards are often poorly designed, as explained in chapter 4. Before buying a particular saw, consider the future costs of upgrading it with good aftermarket safety accessories.

The portable saw is a light- to medium-duty tool, popular with do-it-yourselfers and job-site carpenters.

PORTABLE SAWS

Portable table saws are small, lightweight machines that are designed to be carried by one person (see the photo at left). Portable saws come without legs and are meant to be clamped or bolted to a commercial or shopmade stand or work surface. Even though portable saws are diminutive in size, they are capable of most of the operations of larger saws.

The portable saw is a direct-drive tool. Instead of a separate arbor assembly and arbor that is driven by a motor, the shaft on the motor is the arbor. Unlike the heavy industrial direct-drive machines of old that used a large induction motor, the portable table saw uses a small, lightweight universal motor. Universal motors are used in portable hand tools of modest power, such as routers, circular saws, and drills. The largest of these motors on a table saw can handle a 10-in. blade and can cut softer woods at full height, but they have trouble doing so on hardwoods.

The smallest portable saw is the model maker's saw. As its name implies, it is a craft-specific tool. Sizes for these saws run from 2 in. to 4 in. (With table saws, size refers to blade diameter.) The most powerful model maker's saws will cut 1-in.-thick balsa or basswood and ¼-in.-thick hardwood, depending on the type of blade used. The model maker's saw can be belt driven or direct drive. It is not unusual for the saw to have variable speeds spinning from 3,500 rpm to 7,000 rpm for cutting nonferrous metals, wood, and plastics.

The next largest portable saw is a lightweight saw with minimal extras. Often called a benchtop saw, it has the basic features of any table saw—a fence, a miter gauge, and a tilting arbor—but all have been reduced in size and weight. This saw has an 8-in. or 10-in. blade and a small motor. The benchtop saw is suitable for the do-it-yourself home handyperson with limited space, a tight budget, and perhaps minimal needs for a table saw. As small as this tool is, it can still be a handy tool for light-duty work.

The largest portable saw is designed with the carpenter or contractor in mind. This user needs a saw that is truly portable but that can cut the size and type of materials used in the building trade. Manufacturers have supplied this market with 10-in. portable saws that offer extended capacity fences, larger and flatter work surfaces with expandability, and strong motors. Even with all of this, manufacturers have kept the weight to under 70 lb.

HOME-SHOP SAWS

The type of saw used most often by serious home woodworkers was originally designed for the contractor during the housing boom that took place right after World War II. This table saw was a scaled-down version of the very large industrial table saw. At the time, this "contractor's saw" seemed light in comparison with the industrial version. Even though it weighed in at more than 200 lb., it could be moved as necessary by a couple of stout

The traditional contractor's saw is still popular today with many home-shop woodworkers.

workers. The motor that hangs out the back is removable to make transportation easier.

Today, contractors use portable saws unless the job demands finer finish work. What is commonly known as a contractor's saw is actually a full-sized saw with a medium-weight, cast-iron table (see the photo above). The cabinet is attached to an open stand constructed of sheet steel. This saw uses standard 10-in. blades and will accept a host of accessories. Contractor's saws are adequately powered for cutting dimensional lumber, but the typical 1½-hp motor often labors when cutting heavier hardwoods. The motor is mounted on a pivoting frame at the back of the saw cabinet and delivers power to the saw arbor by a single belt.

Some manufacturers are recognizing the need for a saw specifically designed for the home woodworker and have created a saw for the home shop. This saw tucks the motor back into the cabinet, thereby freeing up shop space and giving the saw better balance and reduced vibration. Home-shop saws come with features such as accurate fence systems, improved dust collection, and sturdier bases.

CABINET SAWS

Cabinet saws are considered stationary saws. The primary difference between these saws and home-shop saws is their weight. Intended for heavy-duty use, a cabinet saw doesn't normally get moved around in the shop. In its standard configuration, the footprint of a cabinet saw is really no bigger than the previous saws mentioned. But in weight these saws can be 200 lb. to 600 lb. heavier.

The cabinet saw is the choice of professional woodworkers due to its accuracy, stability, and power.

The extra weight on a cabinet saw is due to its beefier parts. The thicker cast-iron top and extension wings, heavier cast internal mechanisms, larger motor, thicker enclosed base, larger adjustment wheels, fence, and even the miter gauge all contribute to the extra weight (see the photo above). The components on the cabinet saw are heftier and machined to closer tolerances, resulting in a saw that is more accurate and stable. The larger internal mechanisms are built to handle a more powerful motor and to run longer with less vibration.

Cabinet saws are powered with motors in the 3-hp to 5-hp range. The motor used is a totally enclosed, fan-cooled (TEFC) unit, which makes for a longer life inside a dusty saw cabinet. The motor drives the arbor using two or three short belts to eliminate belt slippage and deliver maximum power. Short belts also create less vibration and noise than the long belts on home-shop saws. As their name implies, cabinet saws have a fully enclosed cabinet, to which the saw table is attached. The cabinet also adds heft and stability to the saw, and because it encloses the motor and internal parts, it muffles some of the noise and contains the sawdust.

EUROPEAN SAWS

European table saws differ from their American counterparts in two distinctive ways. The first is that their safety and dust-collection features are much more effective. The second is that these saws incorporate a sliding table, which makes handling of large workpieces such as sheet goods much easier.

The sliding-table design came about as a direct result of the devastation of Europe in World War II. The scarcity of trees and need for rebuilding after the war demanded more efficient use of wood in the form of plywood and other sheet goods. That, in turn, prompted the development of saws that could more easily handle sheet goods.

A sliding table is basically a platform that easily carries a workpiece past the blade—a much better alternative to pushing a workpiece with a miter gauge. On most European saws, the sliding table is an integral part of the machine. On a few saws, the table is an add-on, often called a rolling table. An integral table is preferable because it comes right up to the blade, providing a more accurate and safer way to cut any workpiece. An add-on sliding table is adequate for many operations but not as precise. Sliding tables are available in various sizes. Larger tables are capable of carrying sheets up to 5 ft. wide and 10 ft. long.

COMBINATION MACHINES

Combination machines incorporate a number of woodworking machines in one package. These machines typically include the five most commonly used stationary tools in woodworking: the table saw, jointer, planer, shaper, and horizontal mortiser. All five tools can be combined in a machine that takes up less space than two table saws placed side-by-side (see the photo below).

These machines are masterpieces of economy. Each individual tool shares space, capacity, mass, and features with other tools on the machine. The best combination machines come from Europe, where space is a luxury in short supply and the demand for quality is high. Sizes and capacities of combination machines vary to meet the needs of the small home shop or large professional shop.

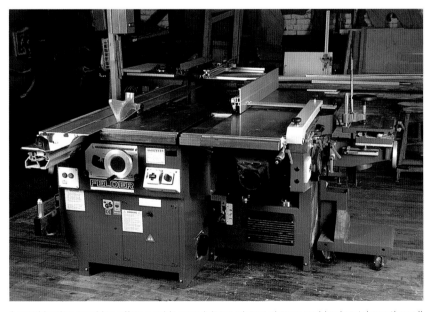

A combination machine offers a table saw, jointer, planer, shaper, and horizontal mortiser all in one relatively compact, high-quality package.

Table-Saw Blades

A table saw's blade is just as important as the machine itself. To get the most from a table saw, it needs to be outfitted with a good-quality blade that's appropriate to the work being performed. But picking the right blade for the job can be confusing because there are so many different types with different tooth configurations to choose from.

In this chapter, I'll tell you how to select the right blade to suit your work and how to identify a good-quality blade. I'll also discuss specialty blades such as dado heads, scoring blades, and molding heads. Protecting your investment in blades is also important, so I'll cover blade care and maintenance as well.

Blade Design and Anatomy

A sawblade consists of three basic elements: the body, the arbor hole, and the teeth (see the illustration on the facing page). Here are some important things to look for when you are trying to decide which blade to buy.

BLADE BODY

The body of a sawblade is a steel plate that must be flat and stay stiff when in use. It is typically made of carbon-steel alloy. The flatter the plate, the smoother the blade will cut and the quieter it will run. Cheap blades are merely polished or quickly ground; better blades will show fine circular grind marks emanating from the arbor hole outward to the rim of the blade. Better blades also typically have slots cut in the body to allow the rim to expand without distorting out of flat as heat builds up at the cutting edge.

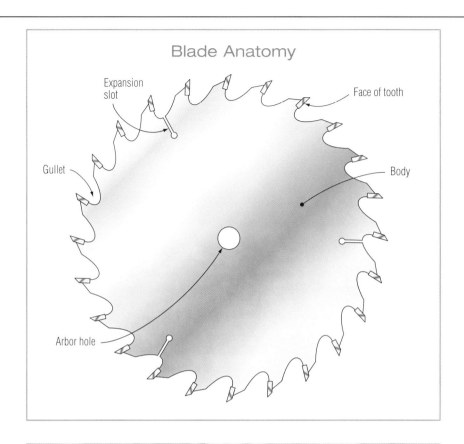

Blade Anatomy

Expansion slot

Face of tooth

Gullet

Body

Arbor hole

A good straightedge will detect serious warp in a blade.

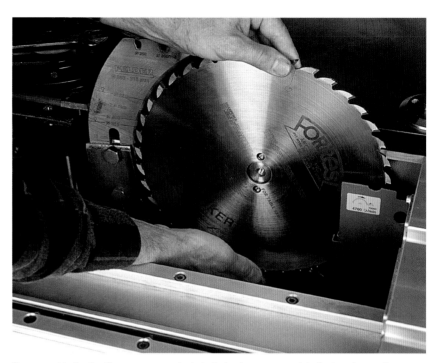

Some sawblades for European saws include holes to accommodate brake pins on the saw arbor.

Blade warp isn't necessarily obvious; however, a bad warp can be detected by checking it with a good straightedge (see the photo on p. 143). To do this, back up the straightedge with a strong light and try to detect light between it and the plate. Test various areas of the plate. That's just a rough check, though; the best way to check a blade's flatness, or runout, is to mount it on the saw and check it with a dial indicator (see "Aligning the Miter-Gauge Slots to the Blade" on p. 198).

Any runout detected with the blade mounted on the saw will represent the combination of arbor-flange runout and the blade runout. But it's that total measurement that you're most interested in anyway, because it determines the quality of the cut you'll get with that particular blade on the saw. Runout of somewhere between 0.005 in. and 0.010 in. is to be expected. If it exceeds that, try to determine if the runout is being affected by something other than blade warp: Make sure the arbor-flange runout doesn't exceed 0.001 or that worn arbor bearings aren't causing the problem. Also check for debris between the arbor flange and the blade. If blade warp appears to be the primary problem after all, it can often be fixed by a saw smith.

ARBOR HOLE

The arbor hole should fit as snugly as possible around the arbor. A snug fit is one indication that the blade was carefully manufactured, because it's

Thin-Kerf Blades

NOT ALL BLADES ARE MADE TO THE SAME THICKNESS. Thin-kerf blades are made with thinner bodies and narrower teeth that typically cut a ³⁄₃₂-in kerf, although the teeth on some blades are even narrower. The advantage of these blades is that they require less power to run because they remove less wood. Therefore, they're well suited to low-powered portable saws and contractor's saws. The disadvantage of a thin-kerf blade is that the thin plate is more prone to vibration, causing it to run less true and cut less cleanly than its thicker counterpart. It can also be noisier and more prone to heating up quickly.

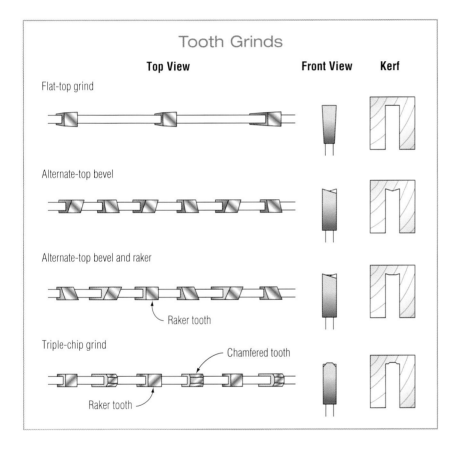

Tooth Grinds

easier and quicker to make an oversized hole than one that's precisely sized. On some inferior blades, you can see a metal lip or burr where the hole was simply punched through. On better blades, the hole is first laser-cut undersized, then reamed out to within 0.001 in. to 0.0015 in. oversize, leaving a smooth, clean-edged hole. Some European sawblades include holes that slip over short posts on the arbor flange called brake pins (see the photo on the facing page).

Carbide vs. Steel

NOT VERY LONG AGO, STEEL BLADES were the only choice for the table-saw owner. However, with the development of tungsten carbide, steel blades have been almost totally replaced in the modern woodshop by blades with carbide teeth. Tungsten carbide is an extremely hard alloy formed by bonding tungsten, carbon, and cobalt.

Although carbide blades are more expensive than steel blades, the higher initial cost is more than offset by the carbide's longevity, low maintenance, and cutting performance. A carbide blade can cut smoothly up to 50 times longer between sharpenings when cutting hardwoods, and up to 400 times longer when cutting man-made materials such as particleboard. Today, when choosing a blade for your table saw, it's not really a choice between steel or carbide; it's a matter of what to look for in a carbide blade.

TEETH

Sawblades employ variations on four teeth configurations, called grinds (see the illustration on p. 145). The four configurations are called flat-top grind (FTG), alternate-top bevel (ATB), alternate-top bevel and raker (ATB&R), and triple-chip grind (TC). The teeth on a typical carbide-tipped sawblade are $\frac{1}{8}$ in. wide, producing a $\frac{1}{8}$-in.-wide cut, or kerf. Each type of tooth configuration has its own particular strengths and applications. I'll focus on carbide-tipped blades here because steel blades are of little real use to woodworkers these days (see the sidebar above).

Flat-top grind (FTG) Flat-top grind teeth have a flat face and a flat top. FTG teeth are primarily rip teeth and work like a chisel, cutting well with the grain but poorly across the grain. A blade designed for ripping generally has 24 to 30 FTG teeth, with deep gullets between the teeth to eject the large chips produced and to cool the blade body. Because of the grind of the teeth, an FTG blade doesn't produce a very smooth cut, but it's the best blade to use for fast, heavy-duty ripping.

Alternate-top bevel (ATB) The teeth on an alternate-top bevel blade are ground at alternating angles. ATB teeth slice through the wood with a shearing action, producing a cut with little or no tearout across the grain. On some blades, the angle of the bevel may be as little as 5 degrees, but on others, it may be as much as 40 degrees. Teeth with steeper bevels produce less tearout, but they dull more quickly.

General-purpose combination blades—which work well for both ripping and crosscutting—employ the ATB grind. Although these blades do not rip as quickly as an FTG blade with fewer teeth, they will rip a smoother cut without too much more feed force. They also won't cut as smoothly as a crosscut blade with a greater number of ATB teeth, but they do cut with a minimum of tearout in both solid wood and sheet goods.

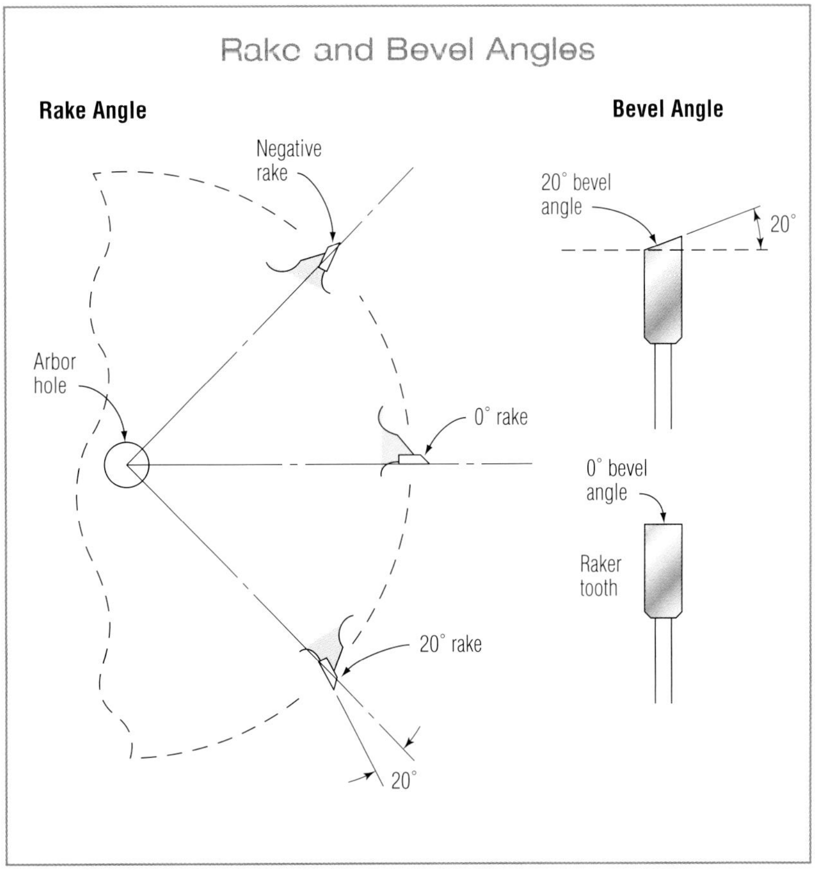

THERE ARE TWO ANGLES TO A TOOTH THAT DETERMINE ITS FUNCTION. The first, called rake, is the angle at which the body of the tooth attacks the workpiece. The second, called the bevel angle, is the angle across the top edge of the tooth.

The rake, or hook, angle is determined by drawing a line from the center of the blade to the tip of a tooth (see the illustration at right). A tooth whose face is parallel to that line has a 0-degree rake. If the face of the tooth leans forward of the line, it has a positive rake. If it leans backward, it's considered a negative rake.

The greater the rake angle, the more aggressive the cut, but also the more tearout you'll get on the exit side when crosscutting. A blade with a lower rake angle will give you less tearout when crosscutting, but will require more feed pressure when ripping. For ripping, a 15-degree to 20-degree angle is about right. For crosscutting on the table saw, 10 degrees to 15 degrees is fine. Blades with a 0-degree or negative-degree rake are designed for radial-arm saws and sliding compound miter saws to prevent the blade from driving the saw carriage forward too aggressively.

The bevel angle is the angle ground across the top of the tooth. A tooth with a 0-degree angle is straight across and is represented by the teeth on an FTG blade. This is the most efficient design for ripping, as the entire edge of the tooth splits the wood along the grain as it enters the workpiece. But this also produces a rough cut and tearout when crosscutting. The bevel angle of teeth on an ATB blade typically ranges from 10 degrees to 20 degrees. The steeper the angle, the cleaner the cut because the point of the tooth scores the wood fibers just before the bevel shears the wood. The tradeoff is that a steeply angled tooth dulls more quickly.

Rake and Bevel Angles

Teeth: More or Less

BECAUSE 10-IN. BLADES ARE THE MOST COMMON, all of this talk about the number of teeth on a blade refers to 10-in. blades. To do the same job, an 8-in. FTG blade might have the same number of teeth, but a 12-in. FTG blade might have six more. For ATB blades, figure about 10 fewer teeth for an 8-in. blade and about 10 more for a 12-in. blade. These figures are all relative, of course. There seem to be very few standards when it comes to sawblades.

A 40-tooth ATB blade is the one that you'll want on your saw most of the time.

Alternate-top bevel and raker (ATB&R) As its name implies, an alternate-top bevel and raker blade incorporates both alternate-top bevel teeth and raker teeth. A typical 10-in. blade consists of 10 groups of five teeth separated by deep gullets. Each group is made up of four ATB teeth preceded by a raker tooth. ATB&R blades are the original "combination" blades, created for both ripping and crosscutting. However, the design is basically a carryover from old steel-blade technology and is fast being superseded by the 40-tooth ATB blade.

Triple-chip (TC) On a triple-chip-grind blade, the corners of every other tooth are chamfered at 45 degrees. The teeth in between are either flat-top rakers or ATB teeth. Each chamfered tooth plows a rough center cut, which is then cleaned up by the rakers. Trip-chip blades are designed for cutting dense man-made materials such as particleboard, plastics, and aluminum because the raker-style teeth won't dull as quickly as beveled ATB teeth. TC-grind blades will do an acceptable job on solid wood but typically won't cut as cleanly as an ATB blade.

Selecting the Right Blade for the Job

The proper blade for the job depends on the type of material to be cut. When working with solid wood, it also depends on the kind of cut you want to make (see the chart below). Here are some guidelines.

SOLID WOOD
For ripping operations, I typically use two types of blades. At the beginning of a project, when sawing a lot of boards to rough sizes, I use a 24-tooth FTG blade (see the photo on p. 150). This blade requires less feed force than a blade with more teeth and is sturdy enough to saw through thick hardwoods. It also saves my smoother cutting blade. The

MATCH THE BLADE TO THE JOB

Type of Cut	Appropriate Blades
Solid-wood ripping	FTG (24 to 30 teeth) ATB (40 teeth)
Solid-wood crosscutting	ATB (40 to 80 teeth)
Plywood	ATB (40 to 80 teeth)
Particleboard, MDF, plastic laminate	TC (80 teeth)
Melamine	TC (80 teeth) ATB (40 to 80 teeth)
Plastics, nonferrous metals	TC (80 teeth)

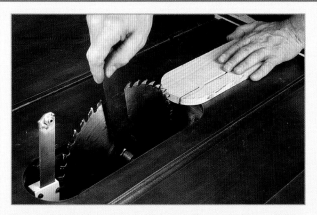

Use a piece of scrap wood or a wooden throat plate to stabilize the blade as you remove the arbor nut.

Commercially made plastic covers are available to protect your blade and hands when changing the blade.

TO CHANGE THE BLADE ON A TABLE SAW, disconnect the power to the saw, then remove the throat plate. Use a wrench to loosen the arbor nut. (I replace the stock, stamped-steel blade wrench with a better-fitting wrench with a longer handle.) If the arbor has left-hand threads, as most right-tilt saws do, the nut is removed by turning it clockwise. A left-tilt saw arbor has right-hand threads, so the nut is removed by turning it counterclockwise. Regardless of the tilt of the blade, you'll always pull the wrench toward the front of the saw to loosen the nut.

I wedge a piece of scrap wood or my wooden table-saw insert against the teeth of the blade to hold it while I turn the nut (see the photo at left above). Alternatively, you could use a rag or a commercially made plastic cover (see the photo at right above). To prevent the nut from falling into the sawdust at the bottom of the saw, place your finger on the end of the arbor and unscrew the nut onto your finger.

Next, remove the washer and the blade, being careful not to cut yourself. Be sure to set the blade

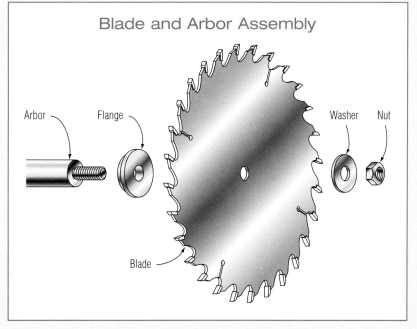

Blade and Arbor Assembly

Arbor Flange Blade Washer Nut

down on a piece of wood to prevent the teeth from chipping on the metal saw table. Install the new blade on the arbor, making sure that the blade's teeth face toward the front of the saw. Replace the washer and the nut, then tighten the nut snugly but not too tightly. Again use a piece of scrap wood to hold the blade stationary. Finally, replace the throat plate.

To really test a blade for tearout, try cutting a piece of oak plywood across the grain. If the exit side of the cut is clean, you've got a good cross-cut blade.

A 24-tooth FTG blade (foreground) serves for fast ripping. A 40-tooth ATB blade (center) does a good job of both ripping and crosscutting. The 80-tooth ATB blade (rear) crosscuts with little or no tearout.

24-tooth blade does leave some saw marks, but that's not an issue at this point because the boards have to be ripped to final size later anyway, at which point I'll use a 40-tooth ATB blade.

For most crosscutting, I use a premium-quality 40-tooth ATB blade, which is the blade that lives on my saw most of the time. When I need an especially clean cut with no tearout, I switch to an 80-tooth ATB blade.

PLYWOOD

Many kinds of hardwood plywood—particularly close-pored woods like birch and maple—can often be cleanly sawn using a sharp 40-tooth ATB blade. However, for cutting oak plywood and other panels with tearout-prone face veneers, use an 80-tooth ATB blade for a clean cut.

OTHER SHEET GOODS

Particleboard, medium-density fiberboard (MDF), melamine, and plastic laminates are all dense materials that can quickly dull sawblades. Although you can cut these panels with a 40-tooth ATB blade, it's best to use an 80-tooth triple-chip blade, which stands up better to the wear.

PLASTICS AND NONFERROUS METALS

Woodworkers occasionally find themselves needing to cut acrylic, other plastics, and nonferrous metals such as brass and aluminum. Although the table saw isn't necessarily the best tool for cutting plastic and metal, it will do the job. Use an 80-tooth triple-chip blade because of the tough, dense nature of these materials.

Gauging Blade Quality

The quality of sawblades varies greatly. In general, you get what you pay for. For the sake of comparison, I'll separate blades into three broad categories: premium blades, mid-grade blades, and economy blades.

PREMIUM BLADES

Premium blades are made to close tolerances and high standards so that they can endure the fast, continuous pace of a heavy production shop. The manufacturing time and labor are reflected in the prices, which typically range from $75 to $200. One indication of a well-made blade is the quality of the brazing that connects the tooth to the plate. The brazing will be smooth without pits or gaps, and the tooth will be smooth and finely ground (see the photo below). The arbor hole will fit the saw arbor snugly without slop and the blade body will often include expansion slots to dissipate heat. The teeth will be sharp and polished, and the blade will be very flat.

One indication of a premium blade is smooth, nonpitted brazing where the tooth attaches to the plate of the blade.

A Basic Blade Set

SO HOW MANY BLADES DO YOU REALLY NEED? That depends, of course, on the type of work you do. If you do general woodworking, cutting primarily solid wood but also some plywood and particleboard, a good-quality 40-tooth ATB blade would be your best first choice. A good second blade to have would be a high-bevel 80-tooth ATB blade for making fine crosscuts and sawing plywood. After that, you could fill out your set with a 24-tooth FTG blade for fast, easy ripping, particularly of hardwoods.

If you work with a lot of dense, man-made boards like particleboard, MDF, plastic laminates, and solid-surface material, your choices would be different. Your blade set might consist of a 40-tooth ATB blade for general wood cutting, followed by a 60- to 80-tooth TC blade for the man-made boards. You might then add a high-bevel 80-tooth ATB blade for sawing tearout-prone panels like melamine and oak plywood.

By the way, don't throw out the typically inferior blade that came with your saw. It can be very handy for cutting through the occasional dirty, nail-ridden board.

MID-GRADE BLADES

Although not quite as durable as premium blades, mid-grade blades are a good value if you aren't involved in heavy production woodworking. These blades are probably the best choice for the serious home woodworker or small-shop professional. You can often get a good deal on mid-grade blades from mail-order suppliers, with prices in the $40 to $75 range; some higher-end blades sell for $80 to $100.

ECONOMY-GRADE BLADES

Economy blades are manufactured to minimum standards for those who want to buy as cheaply as possible, regardless of quality. The blades may have pitted teeth and a rougher finish than mid-grade blades, and they aren't machined as carefully. To me, economy blades are just a waste of money. They cost $40 or less, and after a couple of sharpenings should be thrown away.

Specialty Blades

In addition to the standard blades described above, there are a number of specialty blades designed for specific operations. These include stacking and adjustable dado blades for cutting dadoes and grooves, and molding cutters for shaping the edges of boards into decorative profiles.

DADO BLADES

Dado blades—also called dado heads—consist of a blade or blades that can be adjusted to cut a dado, groove, or rabbet in a single pass. Dado heads are available with steel or carbide-tipped teeth. Because grooving doesn't

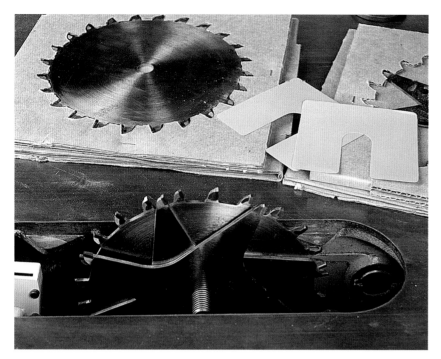

A stack dado head consists of two outside cutters, between which are sandwiched a number of chippers. Thin plastic, paper, or metal shims placed between the blades provide fine adjustment for the width of cut.

normally require very deep cutting, a 6-in.-dia. or 8-in.-dia. dado head is usually sufficient for any shop. In general, use a dado head that is 2 in. less in diameter than the size of a saw's stock blade (e.g., an 8-in. dado head for a 10-in. saw). The arbor on some portable saws isn't long enough to accept a full $^{15}/_{16}$-in.-wide dado-head setup.

There are two basic types of dado heads: stack dadoes and wobble dadoes. A stack dado consists of two outer cutters, between which are sandwiched a number of chippers (see the photo above). The beveled teeth on the right-hand cutter "lean" to the right. The teeth on the left-hand cutter "lean" the other way, resulting in smoothly cut dado walls with minimal tearout. A cutter can have from 18 to 60 teeth. The chippers, which typically sport two, three, or four FTG teeth per blade, are designed to remove material quickly and leave a flat-bottom dado or groove.

A stack dado includes two $^1/_8$-in.-wide cutters, a $^1/_4$-in.-wide chipper, a $^1/_{16}$-in.-wide chipper, and a few $^1/_8$-in.-wide chippers. By using different combinations of chippers (or no chippers at all), you can adjust the overall width of the dado head to cut a dado or groove ranging from $^1/_4$ in. wide to $^{15}/_{16}$ in. wide in $^1/_{16}$-in. increments. You can fine-tune the width of the dado head using paper, plastic, or metal shims.

Another type of dado cutting tool is the adjustable dado head, known as the "wobble" or "drunken" dado head (see the top photo on p. 154).

Wobble dadoes that adjust on a hub provide an inexpensive alternative to stack dadoes. The V-dado on the right employs two blades.

An expensive, high-quality stack dado produces little or no tearout (left), even in oak plywood. The ragged cut shown at right was made with an inexpensive wobble dado head.

With these tools, either one blade (wobble dado) or two blades (V-dado) are mounted on an adjustable hub at an angle, and the pitch of the blades can be adjusted for different-width grooves. (This is the ultimate example of blade runout.)

A premium-quality, top-of-the-line stack dado can cost close to $300. However, if your dadoes and grooves are mostly limited to jig making

A STACK DADO HEAD CONSISTS OF TWO OUTSIDE CUTTERS, between which are sandwiched a number of chippers. After installing the right-hand cutter (typically marked as such), place a chipper against it with the chipper's teeth positioned within the cutter's gullets. Otherwise, you risk distorting the blades and damaging the teeth. Then install additional chippers and shims as necessary to build the dado out to the proper width. Space the teeth on each new chipper equally between the teeth on the previous chipper to prevent the dado head from running out of balance and stressing the arbor bearings (see the photo on p. 153). Last, install the second blade, again positioning the chipper teeth within the blade gullets.

Although you can buy a commercial dado-throat insert for your saw, it's best to make a custom "zero-clearance" throat plate that exactly accommodates the width of the dado head. That way, tearout will be minimized, even with a less-expensive dado set. Remember to clamp down the throat plate when raising the spinning head to cut your initial opening (see "Custom Throat Plates" on p. 197).

where rough cuts don't matter, you can get a wobble or V-dado for $100 or less. In my furniture making, I usually rout dadoes and grooves instead of sawing them. If I sawed a lot of dadoes, especially in plywood, I would buy a quality carbide stack dado for its ability to cut clean-walled, flat-bottom dadoes with minimal tearout (see the bottom photo on the facing page). Forrest makes a great stack dado for about $300 (see Sources on p. 379).

MOLDING HEADS

Molding cutters, which are used to shape stock, can be installed in a special head that mounts on the saw arbor (see the photo on p. 156). Like dado heads, molding heads are dangerous because they remove a lot of stock in one pass. In addition, the workpiece is often fed on edge, so guards have to be specially made to suit the job. Because of these reasons, I generally advise against using the table saw for this kind of shaping unless you use extraordinary safety precautions. Instead I recommend using a router table or shaper for most shaping work.

For the longest time, only two molding heads have been available—one made by Delta and one by Sears®. Neither have any features for safely limiting the depth of cut, which adds to the danger of kickback. Recently, though, a table-saw molding head has come on the market that is made in accordance with strict European safety regulations. Called the Magic Molder, the head has a chip-limiting design to reduce the chance of kickback, and the carbide cutters lock securely into a well-balanced aluminum head (see the photo on p. 156). If you want to use your table saw for shaping, the tool might be worth checking out (see Sources on p. 379).

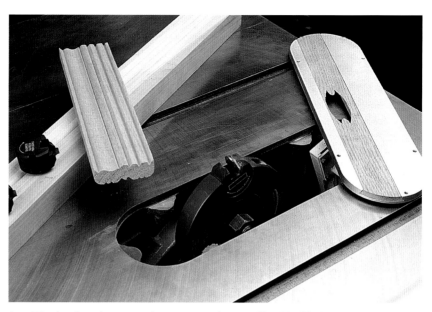

A molding head can be mounted on a saw to shape profiles. The Magic Molder shown here limits the depth of cut to reduce the chance of kickback.

SCORING BLADES

A scoring blade is a small blade (about 4 in. in diameter) that makes a shallow cut ahead of the main sawblade. The scoring blade rotates in the opposite direction, making only a shallow, scoring cut to eliminate possible chipping or tearout from the main blade (see the photos on the facing page). Scoring blades are standard or optional equipment on most panel saws—saws with a built-in sliding table that are capable of handling a lot of sheet goods. At least one company—Modulus—has made an after-market scoring saw attachment that will fit most cabinet saws. The unit costs about $400 (see Sources on p. 379).

Blade Stiffeners

Flanged collars called blade stiffeners are precision-machined washers that help stabilize a running blade. Installed on the arbor next to the blade, they provide extra support to the blade, helping reduce vibration that can cause rough cutting and blade fatigue, particularly when using cheap or thin-kerf blades. Larger-diameter collars provide more support at the outer edges of the blade (see the photo on p. 158).

Typically, a single collar is installed on the outside of the blade, but you can also use two collars—one on the inside and one on the outside. However, placing a collar on the inside—next to the saw arbor's fixed collar—will reposition the blade on the arbor. This means you may have to make a throat plate to suit the new saw slot. You'll also have to readjust

Aftermarket scoring-blade assemblies can be retrofitted to most cabinet saws to eliminate tearout and chipping in plywood and other sheet goods.

The small scoring blade cuts a shallow kerf ahead of the main sawblade, eliminating tearout in fragile facing materials like oak plywood and melamine.

A blade stiffener mounted against the sawblade stabilizes it, reducing vibration and helping produce a cleaner cut.

the cursor on your fence-rail scale if you want to use it to set your rip fence (see "Custon Throat Plates" on p. 197).

Because using a blade stiffener also reduces the depth of cut, it's a good idea to note the blade's cutting capacity with the stiffener installed. You want to remember not to raise a spinning blade in the middle of a heavy cut, jamming the stiffener against a wooden throat plate and smoking up the shop as I have done.

Blade Care

A set of good sawblades can easily cost as much as some table saws, so it's a good idea to take care of your blades. Like other cutting tools, blades must be kept sharp and clean to perform at their best.

Keeping your blades sharp is important for reasons other than just getting clean cuts. Dull blades heat up while fighting their way through the wood. The heat causes gum and pitch buildup, which in turn increases the heat, often resulting in a warped blade. Working dull, hot blades can also lead to cracks in the plate, usually starting at the gullet. Regularly inspect your blades for cracks in the plate or chips in the teeth. Chipped teeth can be repaired by a saw smith, but a cracked blade should be discarded.

After softening and loosening pitch and resin on a blade using a cleaning solvent, scrub off the residue using a plastic- or brass-bristled brush. Oil the blade after cleaning.

Clean your blades regularly, especially when you're cutting resinous woods such as pine or cherry. Either paint remover (not paint thinner) or ammonia in warm water will often remove pitch and resins. Stay away from oven-cleaning products because they tend to break down the cobalt binder that holds the carbide particles together. A number of proprietary blade-cleaning products on the market these days do an excellent job of cleaning blades. I prefer a water-soluble, environmentally friendly cleaner because it's not as nasty to work with as many cleaners (see the photo above). After cleaning, blades should be dried thoroughly, then treated with a light coat of thin oil to prevent rust, particularly around the teeth.

You might think that because carbide is so hard it would be difficult to damage, but it's also very brittle and can crack and chip. Don't use a carbide blade to cut wood that may contain nails or other metal. And take care when handling and storing carbide-tipped blades. Never stack them directly against each other or lay them on the saw table; store them in an appropriate container.

Table-Saw Safety

According to an estimate by the U.S. Consumer Product Safety Commission, there was an average of more than 30,000 emergency-room admittances for table-saw-related hand injuries every year for the last 10 years. I believe it. Nearly every serious woodworker that I know has experienced at least one close call on the table saw. I myself remember being doubled over in front of my saw after getting slammed in

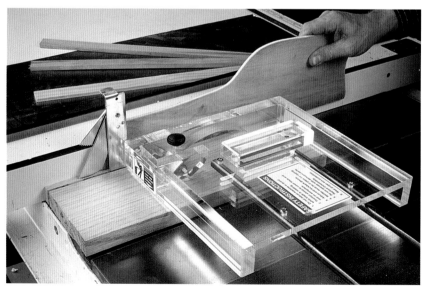

A blade guard and splitter or riving knife are essential table-saw accessories. Using a pusher to feed the wood keeps your hands out of harm's way.

Safety at the Table Saw

MANY ACCIDENTS AT THE TABLE SAW can be avoided by proper preparation and use of common sense. Your best safety precaution is a sharp mind. Concentrate on the task at hand and don't be distracted by conversation. Be aware that many accidents happen right after a large lunch, when you're often less alert.

Try to find the simplest way to make a cut; a fussy setup can invite problems. Use your common sense; if a setup seems dangerous, it probably is. Try a different approach or use a more appropriate tool. And take your time. Rushing is an all-too-common cause of accidents.

Dress Appropriately

Be aware that anything hanging or protruding near the blade can present a danger. Roll up loose sleeves, tuck in your shirt, tie back long hair, and doff any jewelry. Avoid gloves, even if it's cold, because they can catch on things and reduce your sensitivity. Wear shoes with non-skid soles, and avoid sandals. Keep your top pockets free of objects that could drop out onto the table.

Set Up for Safety

Make sure your saw is properly plugged into a grounded outlet because all that metal conducts electricity easily. Operate the saw only in a dry area. Always unplug the saw when changing blades or performing tune-ups, and make all adjustments with the blade at a dead stop. Set the blade no more than ¼ in. above the workpiece, and always double-check the rip fence to make sure it's locked in place before making a cut.

Keep Clean and Sharp

Keep the saw table free of tools, offcuts, and extra workpieces that could creep toward the blade. Use a dust brush instead of your hands to brush sawdust off the table. Use sharp, clean blades; they're less likely to kick back and will cut the work much easier. Resin-covered blades tend to build up heat and resist cutting. It's also wise to wash up after using the saw to minimize skin irritation from certain woods.

Use Proper Cutting Procedure

Use the rip fence for ripping and the miter gauge (or other appropriate jig) for crosscutting. Never cut freehand for any reason! And don't use the fence as a stop block for crosscutting; an offcut trapped between the fence and the blade can kick back violently.

Let the blade build up to full speed before cutting, then push the workpiece fully through the blade; stopping mid-cut invites kickback. Most important, stand to the side of the workpiece being cut. Always wait until the blade comes to a dead stop before picking up cut stock or clearing away offcuts.

the gut by a flying workpiece. I've also had cutoffs whiz by my head on their way to the other end of the shop. Fortunately, I escaped serious injury before learning proper safety techniques, but I know others who haven't been so lucky.

The good news is that table-saw accidents are almost entirely preventable—no exaggeration. In this chapter, I'll explain the causes of accidents and show you how to avoid them. I'll also discuss ways to protect your eyes, ears, and lungs as well as your limbs.

The Risks

Proper planning, dress, and saw setup can reduce many risks at the table saw (see the sidebar on p. 161). However, the three greatest potentials for table-saw harm involve the blade. The most prevalent accidents involve kickback, followed by ejection and laceration. All of these dangers can be eliminated by using the proper safety equipment and technique, as I'll discuss in the following sections.

KICKBACK

By far, the most common cause of table-saw accidents is kickback. Kickback is just the nature of the beast called the table saw. It's not necessarily the "fault" of the woodworker, the machine setup, or the workpiece; it's simply an inherent part of the cutting operation. Unless you're using a splitter or riving knife, kickback can occur even when the rip fence is set properly, the workpiece is flawless, and you're pushing correctly.

Kickback is caused by the tendency of the rising teeth at the rear of the blade to pick up the workpiece, catapulting it toward the operator at speeds approaching 100 miles per hour (see the sidebar on the facing page). As if the risk of getting smacked by the workpiece isn't bad enough, your hand can also be pulled toward the spinning blade in the process. And this all usually happens way too fast for you to pull yourself out of harm's way.

You can minimize the chance of kickback by adjusting your rip fence properly and holding the workpiece firmly against the fence for the entirety of the cut. But that's not the real solution. The only sure-fire way to prevent kickback is by using a properly adjusted splitter or riving knife, which denies the workpiece access to the blade's rear teeth. I'll discuss splitters and riving knives in more depth shortly.

EJECTION

Although a splitter or riving knife prevents kickback, a workpiece can still be ejected straight toward the front of the saw. This force is simply caused by the friction on the side of the rotating blade and is overcome by whatever feed force is being applied to the workpiece. The best protections against ejection are to push all pieces past the rear of the blade, not to cut pieces shorter than the distance between the front and back of the blade, and not to use the fence to crosscut.

You should also use a properly shaped push stick and feed the workpiece with a force and momentum appropriate for the size of and density of

Kickback Speed

A board that's kicked back by the sawblade can hurl a workpiece toward you at speeds approaching 100 miles per hour.

FOR AS OFTEN AS IT HAPPENS, KICKBACK IS NOT WELL UNDERSTOOD. For one thing, it occurs too quickly to observe. Here's what's actually taking place.

As a workpiece approaches the rear of the spinning blade, the rising rear teeth try to lift it upward. This is made worse by the fact that the sawn edge is always trying to press against the rear teeth due to the resistance at the front of the blade and the resistance from the pusher at the opposing diagonal corner. To understand the principle, lay a book on the table and plant a finger (representing the blade) on the table behind the far left-hand corner of the book. Then push the book forward from its right front corner (the pusher). Notice that the book pivots to the left, just as a workpiece pivots into the blade.

When ripping wood, one side of the workpiece is restrained against the fence, pinching the workpiece diagonally between the fence and blade. The workpiece then rides up on top of the spinning blade and is hurled backward and to the left toward the operator at speeds up to 100 miles per hour. The workpiece is typically left with a scar in the shape of an arc as evidence of its rough ride over the top of the blade.

The only way to entirely eliminate kickback is to use a properly aligned splitter or riving knife (see "Aligning the Splitter to the Blade" on p. 203). If you insist on working without a splitter or riving knife (I won't!), you can at least minimize the chances of kickback by taking the following measures, although they aren't foolproof: Keep

the workpiece firmly against the fence for the entirety of the cut. A shoe-type pusher with a long sole will help you provide some side pressure (see "Pushers" on p. 177).

Be particularly careful when trimming square pieces, which are prone to creeping away from the fence. If the workpiece edge that's bearing against the fence is shorter than the adjacent edges, use a miter gauge or crosscut sled instead of the fence to guide the workpiece.

As a workpiece strays from the fence, it can become diagonally pinched between the blade and the rip fence, inviting kickback.

As the workpiece is lifted by the rising rear teeth of the blade, it climbs over the top of the blade, traveling backward.

The workpiece is hurtled diagonally backward toward the operator.

The arched scar on the underside of the workpiece is a result of its travel over the top of the blade.

the wood. Don't let the heel of a push stick ride up over the end of the workpiece. Some splitters include notched pawls or "fingers" intended to prevent ejection, but I've found them to be very unreliable.

LACERATION

Any part of an exposed blade presents a danger to flesh and bone. The best protection is a blade cover, often called a blade guard. A cover prevents your hands from accidentally coming in contact with the blade. It also prevents sawdust and splinters from being thrown at the operator. Many lacerations occur while removing cutoffs from the table before the blade (even a covered blade) has stopped. It's a good habit to lower an uncovered blade below the table when you're finished cutting. Even a stopped blade can hurt you.

Although many woodworkers remove the troublesome stock blade cover that came with their saws, a number of well-designed aftermarket blade covers are available as replacements. There are also other creative ways to cover the blade for specific cutting operations.

Safety Accessories

The essential safety equipment for any table-saw operation includes a good splitter or riving knife and a blade cover. Other accessories such as pushers, auxiliary workpiece supports, featherboards, safety wheels, and power feeders also have their particular uses.

STOCK BLADE GUARDS

The stock table-saw guard systems on most saws sold in the United States are awful. There, somebody has said it. Nearly every woodworker knows this, even though woodworking experts insist in books, magazines, and television shows that we use our table-saw guards. They tell us that *they* have removed the guards on *their* table saws only so we can better see the operation they're performing. Nonsense. The reason why they and so many other woodworkers discard stock guards is that the guards are poorly designed for their purpose.

A stock blade guard is actually a three-in-one system that is bolted to the saw's carriage assembly. The system combines a splitter, a blade cover, and antikickback fingers in one assembly. Unfortunately, this design approach severely limits the usefulness of the system. First, because the splitter is fixed in place and stands higher than the blade, only through saw cuts can be made. To cut dadoes, grooves, rabbets, and many other joints, the entire guard assembly must be unbolted from the saw—not a quick and easy operation.

The splitter also prevents use of crosscut sleds and other jigs. To make matters worse, the blade cover on many assemblies won't stay up and out of the way for blade changing or measuring sawblade height. Ultimately, because removing and reattaching the guard assembly is such a pain, it is often cast aside in a dark corner of the shop to collect dust.

That said, these guard systems are better than nothing at all. They do work; they're just terribly inconvenient. Even so, I would use one rather than nothing at all. However, read on for better alternatives to stock guards.

SPLITTERS AND RIVING KNIVES

A splitter or riving knife is the most important piece of safety equipment for a table saw because it virtually eliminates the potential for kickback—the most common table-saw accident. As I've explained, a splitter or riving knife denies access to the upward rising teeth at the rear of a sawblade, preventing a workpiece from being thrown.

A riving knife, which is attached to the blade-arbor assembly, is a much better solution than a typical splitter, which doesn't rise and fall with the blade. Sadly, riving knives are only available on European saws. Curved in shape, a riving knife sits about ¼ in. behind the blade and a little below the blade height (see the photo below). Therefore, it does not get in the way of any cut or jig that a woodworker normally uses. The only reason to change it would be to install a smaller- or larger-diameter blade.

The fact that the riving knife sits so closely behind the blade ensures that the workpiece is held away from the rear teeth almost immediately after the workpiece passes the blade. Unfortunately, these proprietary splitters cannot be retrofit to a different saw.

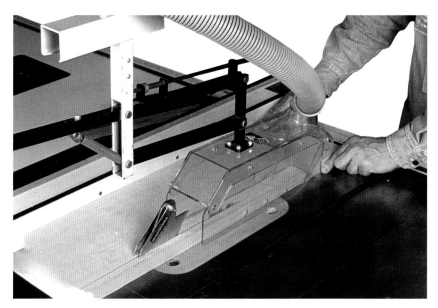

The riving knife on a typical European saw is attached to the arbor carriage and rises, falls, and tilts with the blade.

Riving Knives

Although the terms splitter and riving knife are sometimes used interchangeably, a splitter typically refers to a plate attached to the rear of the saw or to the throat plate. With the exception of the Delta Disappearing Splitter, a splitter cannot be adjusted in height. A riving knife, typically on European saws, is fixed to the blade-arbor assembly, so it always moves relative to the blade and stays in proper position, regardless of blade height or tilt.

The Delta Disappearing Splitter can be pushed down under the throat plate for non-through-cutting operations such as grooving and rabbeting.

A Shopmade Splitter

AS DISCUSSED IN THE SIDEBAR on p. 197, a zero-clearance throat plate has many advantages over the stock throat plate that comes with your saw. In addition, it's easy to create a shopmade splitter by simply gluing a piece of hardwood or other thin material into the blade slot of a zero-clearance throat plate (see photo below).

A splitter is most effective when placed close to the rear of the blade. Because the blade progresses toward the rear of the throat plate as it's raised for thicker cuts, make at least two throat plates—one for cutting stock up to about 1 in. thick and another for thicker stock. To make a throat plate for thick stock, you'll need to elongate the slot by flipping the throat plate end for end, then raising the blade. This allows you to place the splitter farther back.

It's important to align the right side of the splitter with the right-hand side of the blade teeth. To fine-tune the position of the splitter, install a short screw in the end or side of the throat plate to take up any play in its fit. The insert can also be sanded if necessary to reduce its thickness.

A piece of hardwood glued into the slot in a zero-clearance throat plate serves as a shopmade splitter.

The best alternative—short of buying a European saw—is to get an aftermarket splitter designed to fit saws manufactured for the U.S. market. There are currently four models available: two made by Delta, one by Biesemeyer, and one by Excalibur. The other alternative is to make your own splitter (see the sidebar above).

Unlike the splitter on the stock three-in-one system, aftermarket splitters can all be removed and reinstalled easily. Because they all install on the rear of the carriage assembly, some space remains between the blade and the splitter, especially when the blade is set low. Although this allows some potential for kickback, it's very small.

The Delta Disappearing Splitter The Delta Disappearing Splitter is the oldest splitter and the one with which I have had the most experience. It was designed to fit the right-tilting Delta UniSaw® as part of Delta's original UniGuard® system. Although the original UniGuard has been discontinued in favor of the Deluxe UniGuard, the Disappearing Splitter is still available.

This splitter is not removable from its holder. Instead, it can be pushed down below the table into its holder when not needed (see the photo on the facing page). To raise the splitter, you need only remove the throat plate and pull the splitter up, at which point it automatically locks in place. Being nonremovable, it is always at hand and easy to bring into play. Because the Disappearing Splitter is thin and narrow, it will work with thin-kerf blades as well as standard blades. However, the thin metal is also easily bent, calling for caution when handling large or heavy workpieces.

The Delta Disappearing Splitter costs about $100 and will mount only on the right-tilting Unisaw and right-tilting Jet cabinet saw.

The Delta Deluxe UniGuard Splitter This newer model splitter from Delta is clamped to its holder with a knurled, threaded knob, which is unscrewed to remove the splitter (see the photo at right). As with the Delta Disappearing Splitter, the UniGuard Splitter may also be used with thin-kerf blades. Because the UniGuard Splitter is wider than the Disappearing Splitter, it is not as prone to bending, although it's not as sturdy as the Biesemeyer splitter.

The Delta Deluxe UniGuard Splitter costs about $30 and will fit all of Delta's table saws including the left-tilting UniSaw, except the portable saws. It should also fit Jet cabinet saws.

The Biesemeyer Splitter The Biesemeyer splitter is a solid ⅛-in.-thick piece of steel that sits in a heavy-duty holder (see the photo below). The splitter can be snapped into its holder without removing the saw's throat

The Delta Deluxe UniGuard Splitter is clamped in place with a threaded knob, which also allows you to remove it for non-through-cutting operations.

The Biesemeyer splitter snaps easily into its mounting bracket and can be removed by retracting the round knob on the bracket.

The rear of the Excalibur splitter hooks over a rear-mount assembly, while the front end clicks into a mount inside the saw on the blade carriage.

plate. Removal, however, does require getting under the throat plate to retract a spring-loaded rod on the holder. To avoid having to remove the throat plate to access the knob, I drilled a 1-in.-dia. hole in my saw's throat plate that allows insertion of a stick for pulling the knob. This splitter is very sturdy and cannot be easily bent. While contributing to solidity and durability, the ⅛-in. thickness prevents use of the splitter when working with thin-kerf blades.

Biesemeyer splitters cost about $120 and are currently available for all models of Delta saws except portables. They will also fit Powermatic® saws, General® saws, and Jet saws.

The Excalibur Merlin Splitter The Merlin splitter is a bit different from other aftermarket splitters in that it attaches to the rear of a table saw rather than to the rear of the carriage assembly (see the photo above). It's easy to remove and replace and should fit many of the most common tables saws including Craftsman®. I haven't tried it yet, as it was still in development as of this writing.

BETTER BLADE COVERS

As an alternative to stock blade-guard systems, there are currently five overhead blade-cover systems available, sold either as part of a saw package or as an aftermarket accessory. An overhead cover is independent of a saw's splitter or riving knife, allowing non-through-cutting operations to be covered when the splitter or riving knife has been removed. Four of the five aftermarket cover systems also include dust-collection ports, creating a somewhat healthier work environment.

Delta Deluxe Blade Guard.

An overhead cover can be adjusted horizontally to accommodate a tilted blade or to minimize the space between the cover and the fence for easier ripping of narrow pieces. When crosscutting, the side of the cover can be adjusted close to the blade to prevent trapping short cutoffs between the blade and side of the cover. For cutting tall pieces, the cover can be moved entirely away from the blade. All of the systems are removable for those rare occasions when oversized work requires an unusual amount of free space around the blade.

Delta Deluxe Blade Guard The supporting frame of the Delta is a C-shaped piece of hollow tubing, the bottom arm of which is bracketed to the rear of the saw and to the rear edge of the side extension table. The upper arm is a telescoping boom that supports a two-piece basket-style blade cover (see the photo above). A plastic tray mounted on the upper arm will hold a note pad, tape measure, push stick, and a slot to store a removable splitter.

The Delta's split blade cover is an innovative design, providing extra safety in some cutting situations. For example, after crosscutting thick stock, half of the cover drops down for protection even though the cutoff holds half of the cover up above the spinning blade. The cover is sloped at the front to ride up easily onto an approaching workpiece. Stop collars on the arm allow the halves of the cover to flip up out of the way for changing blades and setting up cuts. There is no dust-collection port on the cover.

Although the top arm of the C-frame is only 10 in. above the table, there is still enough access for pushers and crosscut sleds without feeling cramped. The telescoping arm allows for very little movement to the right of the blade, but the arm can easily be removed if it obstructs cutting tall, wide workpieces. Rotating the extended section moves the blade cover forward and backward in relation to the blade. For cutting very long and wide boards, the whole frame can be swung below the work surface by loosening one bolt on each of the frame brackets. However, a rear outfeed table that is wider than 36 in. from the left side of the saw will prevent the arm from swinging down.

This guard is designed for Delta table saws and fence systems. It will not work with fence systems that require use of a rear rail for fence operation. On Biesemeyer-style fence systems, the rear rail is used only to support a side table, and the rail can be replaced with Delta's flat metal bar. Although a flat bar doesn't provide a ledge for supporting a rear outfeed table, a freestanding table could be used.

If budget is a consideration and you have a Delta table saw, the Delta Deluxe Blade Guard is the best buy of all these systems. Considering that it includes a splitter, this package might fit your equipment budget. The lack of a dust-collection port is a disadvantage, but it may be outweighed by the cost savings compared with other models.

Biesemeyer T-Square Blade Guard System Like the Delta, the Biesemeyer support frame is C-shaped. The lower arm of the rectangular tubing mounts with a couple of bolts and screws to the L-shaped rear rail of a Biesemeyer-style fence system. The telescoping upper arm supports a basket-style cover that can accept an optional dust-collection port (see the photo below). A perpendicular channel at the end of the arm allows easy fore-and-aft adjustment of the cover, as well as its removal.

A counterbalanced mechanism allows the cover to self-adjust to suit any thickness of workpiece while staying parallel to the saw table. When

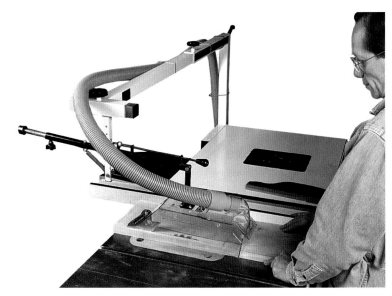

Biesemeyer T-Square Blade Guard System.

lifted all the way up, the cover locks into place about 7 in. above the table. The cover can be moved well to the right of the blade for using tall jigs or cutting vertically supported workpieces. The telescoping movement is controlled by an internal threaded rod connected to an adjusting crank on the far end of the upper arm.

A release lever allows for quick, gross adjustments of the arm, but I still found this somewhat cumbersome. To overcome the problem, I removed the threaded rod altogether, allowing for quick, easy adjustments made from my normal working position.

Because the post mounts to the rear of the extension table, you can crosscut any length workpiece up to 12 in. wide before it is stopped by the post. For easy removal of the entire system, I attached it to the rear fence rail with 3-in.-wide plastic wing nuts. Alternative mountings include a bolt-down floor stand or a ceiling mount.

The Biesemeyer is one of my favorite systems because of its overall ease of use and relative unobtrusiveness. It's only real disadvantage is its inability to be used on saws that require a rear rail for fence operation.

Excalibur Overarm Blade Cover The Excalibur consists of a square post that supports a round, hollow, telescoping arm to which the blade cover is connected (see the photo below). The two-piece post is bolted to the end of the extension table rather than to its rear edge. This means the Excalibur can be used with any fence system since it won't interfere with rear fence rails. The lower section of the post extends to the floor and is held upright by two metal braces that connect to the extension table. The upper section of the post slides into the lower section, locking in place with a lever, which allows you to easily remove the entire upper section of the system if necessary.

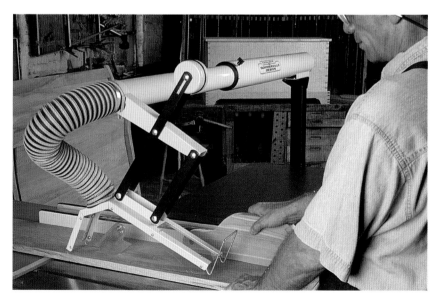

Excalibur Overarm Blade Cover.

Exaktor Industrial Overarm Blade Cover.

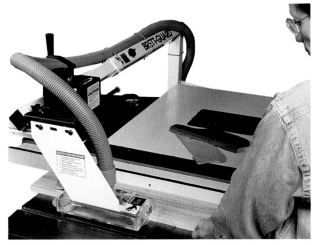

Brett-Guard Cantilever Mount.

The basket-style blade cover can be locked in place at any height up to 8 in. above the table. A lever allows you to lock the cover down onto a workpiece for safer cutting of thin stock and dadoes. A wire handle at the front of the blade cover offers a safe, convenient grasp of the cover and allows the cover to ramp up onto approaching stock. The rear plastic panel can be removed to accommodate a stock or aftermarket splitter. The cover can be moved fairly easily 24 in. to the right of the blade.

For dust collection, a length of hose connects the blade cover to one end of the upper arm. A 4-in.-dia. dust-collector hose connects to the opposite end of the arm. The whole arm is sealed for optimum vacuum efficiency.

The Excalibur offers sturdy quality and superior dust collection. However, the unit is heavy and places a lot of weight at the end of the extension table, which can cause the table to twist, so this system may not be the best choice for a saw mounted on a mobile base.

Exaktor Industrial Overarm Blade Cover The Exaktor consists of a two-piece round post that supports a round, hollow, telescoping arm that carries a basket-style blade cover. Like the Excalibur, the post attaches to the end of the extension table so it won't interfere with any fence system (see the photo at left above). The lower section of the post can be bolted to the floor for a sturdy installation. The post is further stabilized by means of a turnbuckle extending from the bottom section of the post to the underside of the extension table. The upper section of the post (along with the telescoping arm) can be lifted completely out of the lower section after releasing a locking handle on the post. The arm can also simply pivot out of the way in its post.

The cover assembly lifts easily out of the way for setting up cuts and can be locked at any height. A dust port on the cover connects via a hose to the hollow telescoping arm. A rubber collar at the opposite end of the arm adapts to fit a standard 4-in.-dia. dust-collector hose. The dust-collection system works great. Unfortunately, the blunt front end of the cover does not allow an approaching workpiece to slide under it. You must either lift the blade cover onto the work or lock it to hover above the workpiece.

The cover will slide well to the right of the blade by pushing the telescoping arm to the right. However, it takes two hands to lift and push the arm because the fit is a bit rough. Also, the lack of a registry channel between the two pieces of the arm allows the inner arm to rotate when unlocked. This can cause the blade cover to move out of parallel to the table surface or workpiece. In its favor, the arm sits about 19 in. above the table surface, allowing plenty of unrestricted space to work.

The rear of the cover includes two slots to accommodate a splitter. The unused slot is covered when not in use. Unfortunately, with a splitter installed you are not able to adjust the cover horizontally for finer adjustments—for example, when ripping narrow pieces.

The Exaktor is less expensive than most of the other models and is sufficient as a blade cover, but it lacks the sturdiness of the Excalibur and the lightweight efficiency of the Biesemeyer. Because the Exaktor mounts on the floor, it also lacks mobility. It is, however, a very efficient collector of dust at the blade, and you can purchase the blade-cover assembly separately for ceiling mounting or other custom installations.

Brett-Guard® Cantilever Mount The C-shaped frame on the Brett-Guard Cantilever Mount guard screws to a rear support angle, which is not needed if the table saw already has a Biesemeyer-style rear fence rail. Fence systems that require a rear rail for fence operation can still be used with this system. The blade cover is connected by a bracket to a control housing that is hinged to a platform on the end of the upper arm (see the photo at right on the facing page).

The Brett differs from the other blade covers in that it does not use a basket-style cover. Instead, a clear, thick, plastic box that provides great visibility connects to a control housing that the user adjusts manually. The underside of one edge of the cover is scalloped, so the blade can be set right at the edge of the cover for ripping narrow stock (see the photo on p. 160).

The cover height is adjusted using a crank on top of the housing. Unlike typical gravity-controlled covers, all adjustments are positive; the cover does not lift or drop on its own. Adjusting the cover to hold down a workpiece helps reduce kickback. (The cover includes an antikickback device, but I couldn't get it to work properly no matter what.) Of course, when the cover is fixed at the height of a thick workpiece, the blade is somewhat exposed after the cut. Although the cover comes with a dust port, you must provide your own hose and fittings.

The SawStop™

TABLE-SAW SAFETY IS IN FOR A REAL SHAKE-UP. A recent invention called the SawStop promises to revolutionize saw safety by stopping the blade upon contact with skin. The device consists of a heavy-duty, spring-loaded, replaceable brake pawl that slams into the blade, stopping it within one-quarter of a turn and causing it to drop immediately below the table. This action takes place in a few milliseconds, turning what could have been an amputation into just a minor cut.

The SawStop works by sensing the electrical conductivity of your body. When your skin touches the blade, it affects a fuse in the device that releases the brake. Cutting wet wood doesn't trigger the brake, although metal will. Before cutting aluminum, brass, or other soft metals that can be cut on a table saw, you'll need to turn off the SawStop.

Unfortunately, the SawStop cannot be retrofit to existing saws and, in fact, calls for an internal redesign of existing saws. Although it's not in production at the time of this writing, there's little doubt that the SawStop will become an integral part of table saws produced within the next few years.

As great an invention as it is, the SawStop is really a second line of defense on the table saw and protects only against laceration. It won't protect against kickback, which is the most common accident at the saw. To prevent against kickback, you need to use a properly aligned splitter or riving knife, as discussed on pp. 165–168. That said, saws of the future that include a European-style riving knife as well as a blade brake like the SawStop will be a welcome addition indeed to any woodshop.

The cover can easily be flipped up out of the way for setting up a cut. It can also be moved 20 in. to the right of the blade when necessary, although the heavy control housing requires using a bit of force to slide the upper arm. When the arm is slid over fully and the housing and blade cover are flipped up out of the way, there is plenty of access for a crosscut box or tall workpieces.

Unfortunately, the Brett allows little accommodation for an aftermarket splitter. A splitter has to sit outside of and behind this cover. After adjusting the cover forward, I was still only able to use the narrow Delta UniSaw Disappearing Splitter. The Brett comes with its own splitter, but it bolts in place just like a stock table-saw splitter and is just as inconvenient. This cover really calls for a shopmade splitter in the throat plate.

Brett-Guard Original Mount   Like the cover on the Brett-Guard Cantiliver Mount, the cover on the Original Mount is a heavy-duty, square plastic box that provides great visibility of the blade. However, this model is suspended on two metal rods that attach to a platform that mounts on your saw's left or right extension wing (see the photo on the facing page).

The guard is easily removed and reattached and can be slid out of the way for blade setups. An adjustment crank on the platform raises and low-

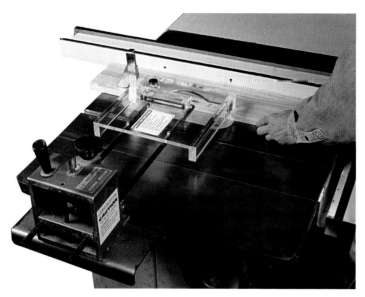

Brett-Guard Original Mount.

ers the cover, which is meant to ride lightly on top of the workpiece. You can adjust it to hover above the blade right next to the rip fence, making it ideal for ripping narrow pieces (see the photo on p. 160). Because the unit attaches to the saw table, your cutting capacity is limited to the distance between the cover and its platform.

Like the Brett-Guard Cantilever Mount, this table-mounted version allows little accommodation for an aftermarket splitter, although the Delta Disappearing Splitter is small enough to use. Alternatively, you could use a shopmade splitter.

FEATHERBOARDS AND SAFETY WHEELS

Featherboards and safety wheels are shopmade or commercial hold-down devices that prevent kickback by holding workpieces firmly against the table or fence, allowing you to keep you hands away from the blade. As helpful as they are, these devices are not intended to be a line of first defense against kickback. To prevent kickback, you really need a splitter or riving knife. However, featherboards and safety wheels can help during operations when using a splitter or riving knife is difficult or impossible.

Featherboards, or fingerboards, are wood, metal, or plastic accessories that clamp in the miter-gauge slot or to the table to prevent the workpiece from moving backward from the blade toward the operator (see the top photo on p. 176).

Although featherboards are available commercially, it's easy to make your own (see the sidebar on the facing page).

Safety wheels consist of a pair of wheels that mount directly on the rip fence or on an auxiliary fence. The wheels adjust for various thicknesses of materials and, when set properly, hold the workpiece against the fence and

A featherboard applies springlike pressure to hold a workpiece against the fence or table, preventing backward travel at the same time.

Pushers can be bought or made in various shapes to suit particular ripping tasks.

table. One-way bearings prevent backward rotation. Many woodworkers who use safety wheels find them most beneficial when cutting sheet goods or other large panels and when cutting grooves and rabbets.

Although safety wheels seem to be a popular substitute for a missing guard assembly, I find them somewhat obstructive. In many cases, you have to either use a low push stick to push the workpiece under the wheels or else pull the stock out from the rear of the saw. Of course, with a splitter or riving knife, guard, and antikickback fingers in place, the wheels aren't necessary for most operations.

Shopmade Featherboards

A FEATHERBOARD CAN BE MADE FROM ANY CLEAR, fairly straight-grained scrap wood. Depending on the application, you can use either 4/4 or 8/4 stock. About the only time I use featherboards at the table saw is for edge grooving or rabbeting, which are both cases where a thicker featherboard works better. For edge grooving, the thicker featherboard helps steady the vertical workpiece while holding it flat against the fence. When rabbeting, a wide, thick featherboard acts as a blade cover while holding the work down on the table.

To make a featherboard, select a scrap 3 in. to 6 in. wide and long enough to overhang the left edge of the saw table for clamping purposes. Mark a line across the board about 6 in. from the end and cut that end off at about 30 degrees. Using a bandsaw or a jigsaw, make a series of parallel cuts ⅛ in. to ¼ in. apart from the angled end of the board. This will make the flexible feathers that allow the work to be fed in only one direction.

Pushstick Design

The ideal pusher is one that keeps your hand well above the fence and that provides pressure over a good length of the workpiece. A comfortable wooden pusher will have no sharp edges.

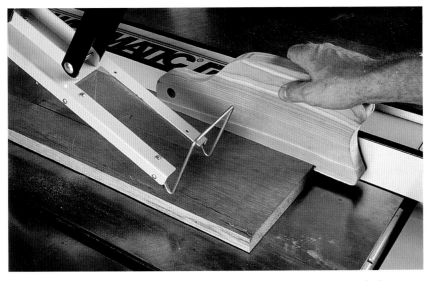

The long sole on a shoe-type pusher provides great bearing and control when ripping.

Pushers Pushers are used as extensions of your hands to push the work through the sawblade. Made of wood or plastic, they are an important piece of safety equipment to help protect your fingers. A well-designed pusher will also provide good control of the workpiece. Like many accessories, pushers are available commercially, but you can also easily make them yourself in many shapes, sizes, and styles (see the bottom photo on the facing page).

The pushers I use the most are shaped like a shoe, with a long sole, a toe, and a heel. The long sole and heel work in combination to hold the work to the table and against the fence (see the photo above). The length and height of the toe can be varied to negotiate tight places. For example, a long, narrow toe will fit under antikickback fingers when ripping very narrow workpieces. I bandsaw my own pushers from scrap wood, making them tall enough to keep my hand above the fence. My pushers range from ⅛ in. to 2 in. thick—I use a ¾-in.-thick pusher the most.

Power feeders For production sawing, a power feeder attached to the saw can be a good option. The motor-driven wheels on these units feed the work automatically into the sawblade. This pretty much eliminates any danger when ripping, since your hands are nowhere near the blade. Power feeders are expensive though, ranging from about $350 to more than $1,500.

Outfeed supports Auxiliary outfeed supports for the table saw are more than a convenience; they're an important safety addition. Without outfeed support, even the shortest pieces of wood will fall off the table at the end of a cut. To prevent them from falling, you would have to reach over the spinning blade to retrieve them—a very dangerous move, even with a guard. Although an outfeed roller can help, it doesn't provide a flat surface to carry the workpiece. An extension table is a much better solution, even if it extends only 18 in. behind the saw (see "Auxiliary Supports" on p. 217).

HEARING PROTECTION

The table saw is a loud machine, and prolonged exposure to the noise can subtly but permanently damage your hearing. Noise is measured in terms of decibels. Hearing loss begins with prolonged exposure to noise above 85 decibels, and a table saw typically operates at about 100 decibels. Do the math: Use ear protection. It's also a good idea to have your hearing examined periodically to keep tabs on your hearing health.

Hearing protectors are the main line of defense against noise-induced hearing loss. When investigating hearing protectors, compare noise-reduction ratings (NRR). The NRR is the amount of noise, measured in decibels, that a protector blocks out. Acceptable hearing protectors for the table saw should have an NRR of at least 25.

Safety gear is worthless if inconvenience deters you from using it, so get hearing protectors that are comfortable and convenient. There are three types of hearing protectors: hearing bands, earmuffs, and ear inserts (see the photo on the facing page). The first two are the types I use most frequently.

Hearing bands Hearing bands are my favorite type of ear protection. They are lightweight, plastic bands that fit under the chin or behind the head and don't interfere with wearing glasses. Because hearing bands are very lightweight, you can comfortably carry them around your neck so they're right at hand when needed. Plastic or foam pads at the ends of the band fit into or over the ear canal. I prefer soft foam pads to plastic cones. The cones are made to fit into any size ear canal, but after a while, I feel as though they're painfully widening my canals. Hearing bands cost less than $10 and are available through woodworking or safety-supply catalogs.

Hire an Electrician

If you're at all uncertain about electrical matters, hire a competent licensed electrician to do any wiring you need in your shop.

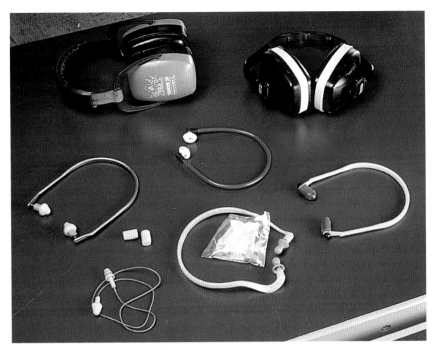

Earmuffs, hearing bands, and ear inserts are available in a wide range of styles, materials, and colors.

Earmuffs I also use full-sized earmuffs to protect my ears from machine noise. The first set of earmuffs I bought were heavy and uncomfortable, and I didn't like wearing them. The ones I use now are lightweight and more comfortable, so I'll wear them for longer periods of time. The main reason I don't use earmuffs as much as hearing bands is that muffs feel like they're choking me when I carry them around my neck. And if I set them down, they never seem to be at hand when I need them. (If you prefer ear-muffs, belt loops are available for them.) When wearing muffs, be careful that glasses or spectacles don't break the seal around the ear. Any air that gets to the ear will carry sound, reducing the effectiveness of the muffs.

Ear inserts Ear inserts are small cylinders, typically made of foam, that expand inside the ear canal to block out noise. They are inexpensive and comfortable to wear, but my invariably dusty hands soil them quickly, so I tend not to use them.

EYE SAFETY

In my early days as a woodworker, I didn't give a lot of thought to eye pro-tection. I wore regular prescription glasses, used a blade cover, and had dust collection hooked up to my saw. I figured I was pretty well protected. Eventually, though, I learned that regular prescription glasses aren't designed to withstand a heavy impact. Even with a blade guard and dust collector, you're still susceptible to eye injuries ranging from sawdust in the eye to serious puncture wounds requiring immediate medical attention.

Safety spectacles provide cheap and effective eye protection for most sawing tasks. Goggles (right) wrap fully around the eyes for maximum protection during particularly dusty tasks.

Set Your Speed Dial

If your shop phone has speed-dial capability, it's wise to dedicate a button or two for emergency dialing of your local fire or ambulance service.

These days, there's a great variety of safety eyewear available (see the photo above). You can get everything from basic frames to wraparound designer frames with tinted lenses and adjustable temples. Accessories like ear pads, elastic holders, and safety cords make safety glasses more comfortable and convenient than ever. And they're relatively cheap—starting at about $2. Choices of safety eyewear include safety spectacles, safety prescription glasses, and goggles.

Safety spectacles Safety spectacles approved by the American National Standards Institute (ANSI) are antifog, antiscratch, and antistatic. They are moderately impact-resistant but not unbreakable. Whenever there is a danger of severe impact, it's a good idea to wear a face shield in addition to safety spectacles.

Safety prescription glasses I have been using scratch-resistant safety lenses in my prescription glasses for quite a while. (Contact lenses aren't suitable for a dusty shop environment.) Safety prescription lenses are available for regular, bifocal, or multifocal lenses. When you order safety prescription lenses, be sure to specify polycarbonate for high-impact resistance. Prescription safety lenses aren't as protective as regular safety glasses because they typically lack top and side shields, but these are sometimes available as options.

Goggles Goggles—which wrap totally around the eyes—provide the kind of protection that is needed when performing dust-intensive tasks such as cutting coves or finger joints. I used to avoid wearing goggles at any cost because they were so uncomfortable and scratched so easily. Today, much better quality goggles are available, and I have a good comfortable pair that is fog- and scratch-resistant.

IT'S IMPORTANT TO KNOW HOW TO DEAL WITH EYE INJURIES in the woodshop. Eye injuries can range from irritating to painful to sight threatening. The most common injuries involve small particles of dust. If these are not removed by normal tear flow, they can usually be flushed out with clean water running over an open eye. An eye cup, available at pharmacies, can also be used to flood the eye.

Often, a small particle that is stuck under the upper eyelid can be removed by pulling the upper lid down over the lower lid. In the process, the eyelashes of the lower lid wipe the inner surface of the upper lid to dislodge the particle.

To remove particles from the lower lid, you can pull the lid down to expose the inner surface, then lift the particle with a sterile piece of gauze. Never try to lift a particle with a sharp object such as the tip of a knife. Try to resist the urge to rub your eyes; you can scratch your eye or drive a particle deeper into it. Once a particle is removed, it may still feel like something is in there. If pain persists, seek medical attention. Sometimes particles may be virtually invisible but can be detected by using a dye administered by a medical professional.

If you're not wearing safety eyewear, small chips or splinters thrown by the blade can stick in the eye or, worse yet, puncture it. Never try to remove these yourself. Instead, cover the eye with a bandage compress and have someone take you to a doctor. If you're alone, call an ambulance.

If you get smacked in the eye with a piece of wood, a cold compress will alleviate the pain and swelling. If you feel pain inside the eye or experience blurred or double vision, get medical help as soon as possible. Blood under the cornea is usually a sign of a cut eye. Seek medical attention immediately. Don't rub the eye—putting pressure on a cut eye can force out the inner fluid or even the retina, resulting in partial or total blindness. Protect a cut eye by covering it with a sterile bandage. A piece of cardboard or other stiff material placed over the bandage will protect the eye from pressure.

Don't treat eye injuries lightly. It's better to get professional medical attention immediately than to risk possible loss of sight.

Dust Protection

Although the table saw doesn't produce the volume of dust that a sander does, it's enough to cause a health hazard. Exposure to dust from wood and composition materials has been associated with skin and eye irritation, allergic reactions, asthma, nasal cancer, colon cancer, and salivary gland cancer, among other illnesses. The dusts of certain woods may be especially irritating to some woodworkers. And wood dust doesn't have to be noticeably irritating to be doing damage to your system.

Wood dust spewn from a saw can be hazardous in other ways too. It's slippery, and a sawdust-covered floor in front of the table saw can be a danger when ripping, which requires sure-footedness. (A nonskid mat in front of the saw can help with this.)

DUST MANAGEMENT AT THE SAW

There are a number of ways to reduce the amount of dust produced by your saw. For one, keep your blades sharp; sharp blades make shavings, whereas dull blades make dust. A second way is to use a blade cover, which will deflect dust and shavings downward onto the table instead of at you. Of course, this also helps protect your eyes, skin, and lungs. Third, you can install a dust-collection system, as discussed on p. 212.

DUST MASKS

Over the years, I've been dissatisfied with most of the dust masks I've tried. Most of them are uncomfortable, fit poorly, and cause my glasses to fog up. I eventually found two types of masks that I can tolerate: a soft silicone half-mask, and a double-strap paper face mask (see the photo below). The silicone half-mask fits tightly over the face and has a one-way valve for exhalation to reduce moisture collection in the mask. You inhale through replaceable dust filters. This mask can also be fitted with organic vapor filters for protection against chemicals in finishes and strippers. I use these masks for prolonged sanding and other heavy dust protection.

Double-strap dust masks are approved for lower dust concentrations. They are disposable and cost less than $1 each. I use these masks for short bouts with sawdust and to outfit occasional helpers. Don't confuse the double-strap masks with the more common single-strap masks, which are thinner, ill fitting, and not safety approved.

Half-masks with replaceable filters serve well for extended sawing and sanding operations. Double-strap paper masks provide adequate protection for brief bouts with dust.

First-Aid Procedures

Woodworkers should become familiar with basic first-aid procedures for removing splinters, dealing with eye injuries (see the sidebar on p. 181), and controlling bleeding. The best way to educate yourself about these procedures is to add a first-aid guide to your shop library. Standard references include *The AMA Handbook of First Aid and Emergency Care* (Random House®, 1990) and *First Aid Guide* (National Safety Council, 1991).

It's also critical to know what to do in the event of severe hand lacerations or amputated fingers, which unfortunately are not uncommon occurrences at the table saw. I asked a local hand surgeon for a list of recommended procedures for dealing with serious hand injuries, and I strongly advise you to do the same.

Every workshop should have a well-equipped first-aid kit in a convenient location (see the photo below). A fire extinguisher is another essential piece of safety equipment. Keep the phone numbers of your doctor, hospital, and ambulance service in plain view at the phone, and make sure you know the fastest route to the hospital. If you have a programmable phone, one-button emergency dialing can save your life.

First-Aid Kit

A basic first-aid kit for the shop should include the following:

- sharp tweezers
- scissors
- adhesive tape
- 2-in. by 2-in. and 3-in. by 3-in. sterile pads
- 1-in. by 3-in. sterile bandages
- antiseptic wipes
- antiseptic ointment
- instant cold compress
- mild pain reliever
- plastic gloves

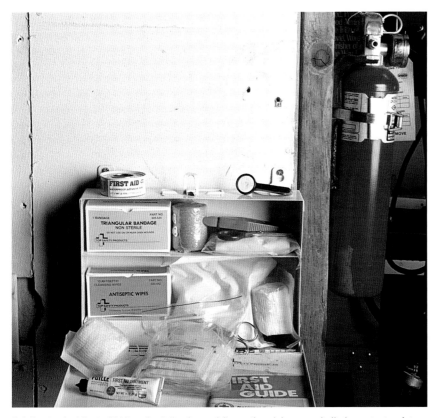

A fully stocked first-aid kit and a fully charged fire extinguisher are vitally important safety accessories for any woodshop.

Table-Saw Tune-Up and Maintenance

A table saw does not come finely tuned and ready to do its best cutting straight from the box. Even if it was assembled by the dealer, it's likely to need fine adjustment and diagnosis. In this chapter, I'll explain how to set up your saw for accurate, safe, dependable use and how to keep it that way. The adjustments that I'll describe generally apply to all table-saw models; any differences between types of saws will be pointed out. You'll find drawings of your particular saw in your owner's manual.

Initial and Periodic Tune-Ups

Many table-saw adjustments may need to be performed only once or twice during the lifetime of the saw. Others should be viewed as part of a regular periodic checkup. Some adjustments need to be performed more frequently, depending on the quality of your saw, how it's used, and whether it's moved around a lot. A more expensive, well-made saw will generally hold its adjustments longer than a lightweight, inexpensive saw.

A proper tune-up requires a particular sequence of adjustments, as listed in the sidebar on the facing page. It's important to perform them in the proper order because one step often affects the next. The procedures I discuss here include a thorough inspection of a saw, whether brand new or used. On a new saw, you're not likely to encounter serious problems such as loose bearings, but don't skip their inspection in any case.

Arbor and Bearings

The first things to check on a saw are the arbor and bearings. Wear or looseness in either can be a serious problem, resulting in excessive runout, where the spinning sawblade wobbles and cuts a kerf wider than the blade teeth. It's unlikely that a new saw will have problems in these areas, but if it does you'll want to find out right away, as you may want to return the saw. If you come across an old saw for sale with a bad arbor or bearings, I suggest you think twice about buying it. Even if you can find the parts, replacing them may cost you more time and money than the saw is worth.

To check the arbor and bearings, first unplug the saw and remove the blade. Inspect the arbor and flange for dirt and for burrs and nicks that have raised the metal. Some imperfections can be removed carefully with a fine-cut file. However, deep grooves that cause a sloppy blade fit probably call for replacement of the arbor.

To check the bearings, remove the drive belt(s) and turn the arbor by hand while feeling for any stiffness or coarseness in the movement. Grasp the arbor and gently pull up and down to check for any slack in the bearings. Roughness, resistance, or slack generally indicates faulty bearings in a new saw or worn bearings in an old saw.

Every table saw suffers runout to some small degree, even if the arbor and bearings are in great shape. Unfortunately, there is no such thing as an arbor flange that is precisely 90 degrees to the arbor. Most modern manufacturers press the flange onto the arbor and then turn it, resulting in a flange with less than 0.001-in. runout, which is acceptable. Saws with an added or loose arbor flange often don't fare as well. Minimizing arbor

To measure flange runout, place a dial indicator against the flange and slowly rotate the arbor. A magnetic base holds the dial indicator solidly in place.

runout is important because any runout at the flange multiplies toward the perimeter of a sawblade, affecting the quality of cut.

To measure runout of the flange, hold a dial indicator against the flange and slowly rotate the arbor (see the photo above). Runout should be less than 0.001 in. More than that will cause enough vibration in even a good sawblade to cause rough cutting and splintering. The best way to correct the problem is to remove the arbor assembly and take it to a machine shop for truing.

You should also check your blades for runout. In this context, runout refers to any deviation from true flatness, and there's no such thing as a perfectly flat blade. It's important to understand that operable runout, which is what affects your cutting, is the result of both blade runout and arbor runout combined. For example, take a 10-in.-dia. blade that is out of flat by 0.006 in. If you mount it on an arbor flange that has 0.001-in. runout, that 0.001 in. is multiplied by the 5-in. blade radius to create 0.005-in. runout at the perimeter of the blade. Add that 0.005-in. runout to the 0.006-in. runout in the blade itself, and you end up with a blade wobbling 0.011 in. at its perimeter—not good. I consider runout more than 0.006 in. to be excessive.

To check the operable runout of a blade, place a dial indicator at the perimeter of the blade body as you slowly rotate the blade. If runout varies all around, the cause is probably a warped blade. If the extremes are 180 degrees apart, the cause is more likely to be runout in the arbor flange.

Cleaning and Lubricating the Internal Parts

Regular cleaning and lubrication of a saw's internal parts are essential for smooth, accurate operation. I've never gotten organized enough to set a schedule for this; I just tend to it a few times a year, depending on how often I use the saw and whether I notice stiffness and resistance in the adjusting mechanisms. If you've never tended to the guts of your saw, now is a good time to do it.

CLEANING

Begin by vacuuming the interior and brushing off the gears. Pay particular attention to sawdust packed around the motor and the blade-height and blade-angle adjusting mechanisms. Take the opportunity to check the assemblies for excessive wear or damage, especially the teeth on the sector gears. (If these are worn excessively or if teeth are missing, the gears can be replaced.) Scrub the trunnion grooves and gear teeth using a rag or toothbrush and nonflammable solvent to clean off any pitch, grease, or crud from the parts. On new saws, the gears typically come with a thick packing of grease, which needs to be removed. Otherwise, the grease will accumulate sawdust, becoming a sticky mess gunking up the works.

LUBRICATING

Lubricate the gears and trunnion grooves. The best lubricants to use for these moving parts are ones that do not pick up a lot of sawdust, such as furniture wax or a dry lubricant. There are a number of dry lubricants on the market; ask at a bike shop. If you use wax, you can apply it with a brush (see the photo at right). There's no need to buff it off. To lubricate the entire length of the trunnion grooves, begin with the motor set at 90 degrees, clean the exposed sections, then crank the motor over to 45 degrees to access the remainder of the grooves.

The only other interior parts that may need lubrication are the sections of the two adjusting rods where they enter the cabinet and where their stop collars ride against the rack assemblies. In both places, you can loosen the stop collars and slide them back on the rods, then clean, wax, and return them to their original positions. Use lithium spray to lubricate assembly pivot points and other hard-to-access areas.

Most newer saws and motors are built with permanently sealed bearings, but if yours has lubrication fittings on the motor or arbor assemblies, squirt them with some light machine oil at least twice a year. Don't overdo it, and don't oil anything that doesn't sport an oil fitting. Exposed oil will only collect sawdust and congeal into a gummy substance. Rubber drive belts will also deteriorate if exposed to oil.

Apply wax to the sector gear teeth using a toothbrush. There's no need to buff it off.

Eliminating Gear Backlash

If you can turn the blade-tilting or height-adjustment wheel more than one-eighth of a turn without moving the blade, it means there is excessive play between the internal worm gear and its sector gear. This is called backlash, which can result in the blade shifting or dropping a bit during a cut. (Tightening the locking knob in the center of the tilt wheel only locks the position of the tilt; it does nothing to take out the play.) Backlash must be removed before you can accurately align the trunnion/carriage assembly to the miter slots.

With the saw unplugged, check for backlash by trying to move the arbor and carriage assembly by hand. First, tilt the carriage off the 90-degree stop, then grab the motor and try to shift it back and forth. There should not be any play in either direction. If there is, most saws can be adjusted, as explained next. (If you have problems with your particular saw, you can consult your owner's manual or call the manufacturer for technical support. But often, the adjustment will become apparent after scrutinizing the mechanisms.)

On a contractor's saw, remove the motor, turn the saw upside down, and loosen the screws that hold the wheel-bearing retainer to the outside of the saw body. You will then be able to shift the wheel downward. This forces the worm gear against the bevel-sector gear, producing a tighter fit. Retighten the screws and check that the wheel turns smoothly without binding, which can cause excessive wear on the meshing teeth.

On most cabinet saws, an adjustment bolt inside the cabinet at the front of the saw moves the worm gear against the sector gear for a tighter fit. Refer to your saw manual for specific instructions on the adjustment.

Unfortunately, not all saws provide an adjustment for stabilizing the carriage assembly. On certain saws, some backlash may exist even after making adjustments. On these saws, temporarily clamping the rear trunnion to its bracket will eliminate any play. Some older saws have a built-in trunnion lock to temporarily secure the carriage at any setting.

Pulley Alignment and Belt Inspection

To minimize vibration and noise on your saw, it's important that the pulleys on the arbor and motor shafts are aligned to each other and that the belt(s) are in good shape.

PULLEYS
To check the pulley alignment on a home-shop saw, lay a straightedge across the faces of the pulleys. The straightedge should contact both edges of each pulley (see the illustration on the facing page). If it doesn't, loosen the setscrew in the motor-shaft pulley, adjust the pulley as necessary, then tighten the setscrew.

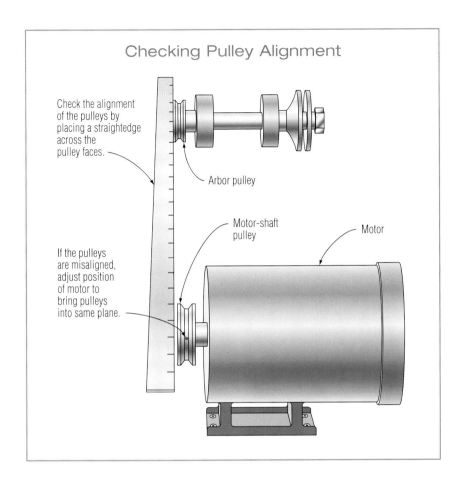

Checking Pulley Alignment

Check the alignment of the pulleys by placing a straightedge across the pulley faces.

Arbor pulley

Motor-shaft pulley

Motor

If the pulleys are misaligned, adjust position of motor to bring pulleys into same plane.

When you make this adjustment, it's best that the pulley is as close as possible to the motor bearing to prevent unnecessary strain on the shaft and bearings. If necessary, loosen the motor mount and slide the motor over into a better position. While you're at it, inspect the motor mount for damage or evidence of sliding. Lock washers on the motor-mount bolts should prevent the latter.

The stock pulleys on a contractor's saw are typically made of light-weight, die-cast aluminum. These can be out-of-round, contributing to saw vibration. Turned machine pulleys—available for most saws—are a much better option. You may need a small bearing puller to remove the pulley from the arbor, especially on an older saw. But it's easy to exchange the motor pulley, and this alone can help reduce vibration.

BELTS

The condition of a saw's belt or belts can also affect power and vibration. Most modern table saws employ V-belts, which ride against the inside walls of the pulleys. To maximize torque transmission, the sides of the belt need to make maximum contact with the pulley's inside walls. The shape of the belt should perfectly match the slope of the pulley walls and fill the pulley groove entirely.

The grooved belt on this Ridgid® saw is more pliable than a typical V-belt and transmits power better.

Segmented belts provide better pulley traction than standard V-belts because the links prevent the belt from taking on a set shape and slapping on the pulleys. The turned steel pulleys also shown here are more concentric than typical cast pulleys and reduce saw vibration.

A belt that is too wide will ride above the pulley rim, causing some loss of power. On the other hand, a belt that is narrow or worn will bottom out in the pulley's landing, reducing contact with the sides and causing slippage. The ensuing friction and heat can cause excessive wear to both the pulley and the belt. Worn or frayed belts will cause vibration and should be replaced. Vibration transmitted to the blade accounts for rough cutting even with the best of blades.

V-belts have a rubber body with interior cording that is strong enough to carry the load and resist stretching. Always replace worn belts with new ones that match the original. Never try to fit a new belt to a badly worn pulley; instead, replace the pulley. If your saw uses multiple belts, replace them all as a set, even if only one is worn. Otherwise, the load will be unevenly distributed, causing vibration and premature wear.

A V-belt is not really the best choice for a drive belt, especially on a contractor's saw, which typically uses a long belt. Often, this type of belt retains some memory of its packaged, oval shape and tends to "slap" in use, causing vibration. Some new-model saws employ a wide, flat, grooved belt that is more pliable and an excellent power transmitter (see the top photo on the facing page). A good replacement option for a contractor's saw is a segmented belt, which is made up of individual links (see the bottom photo on the facing page). This type of belt can't assume a set shape, thereby reducing vibration.

| **Used Belts** |
| Save used belts to use as spares for temporary emergency use. |

Setting the Blade-Angle Stops

Now that things are cleaned up inside your saw, check the accuracy of the blade-tilt stops. One stop should register the blade at 90 degrees to the tabletop, and the other stop should register it at 45 degrees. Begin with the 90-degree setting.

THE 90-DEGREE STOP

Raise the blade to nearly its full height, making sure that the tilt wheel is cranked fully over against the 90-degree stop without applying excessive pressure on the stop. Also make sure there is no sawdust or crud on the stop or on its area of contact on the bevel-sector gear. Place a large, accurate square on the table and against the body of the blade between the teeth. If the angle appears to need adjustment, crank the sector gear away from the stop and loosen the lock nut on the stop bolt. Turn the stop bolt in the direction necessary to correct the tilt (see the photo on p. 192). Crank the blade back over against the stop and recheck the setting with your square. Repeat the process until the blade stops at 90 degrees.

A more practical test, which will compensate for any errors in your square or eyesight is to check the accuracy of the cut itself. First, make sure that the locking knobs on the height and angle wheels are tightened. Then mill a piece of wood about 2 in. wide by about 18 in. long. Its thickness isn't important, but the piece must be planed flat and square, with its opposite edges parallel to each other. Mark a large X on the face of the board, as shown in the top illustration on p. 193. Set your miter gauge at 90 degrees, stand the board on edge, and crosscut through the center of

An Allen screw at the end of the sector gear provides an adjustable stop for setting the sawblade at 90 degrees.

the X. Flip one of the halves in relation to the other, then place both pieces against a good straightedge.

Any deviation from square will be doubled, making it easy to see. If necessary, adjust the tilt stop as described above and make another test cut. When the two pieces meet squarely end to end, you're set. Tighten the lock nut on the stop bolt while maintaining the stop bolt's position, then check the cut accuracy one last time. When you're satisfied, set the pointer on the tilt wheel to its 90-degree mark.

THE 45-DEGREE STOP

If your saw has a 45-degree stop, tilt the blade over until it stops. To check the angle, crosscut another accurately milled piece of scrap at 45 degrees, then place the two pieces against a try square as shown in the bottom illustration on the facing page. If the 45-degree setting is accurate, the pieces will form a 90-degree angle. If they don't, adjust the stop in the same manner as before.

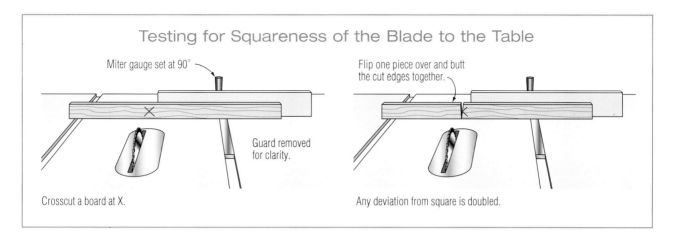

Testing for Squareness of the Blade to the Table

Miter gauge set at 90°

Crosscut a board at X.

Guard removed for clarity.

Flip one piece over and butt the cut edges together.

Any deviation from square is doubled.

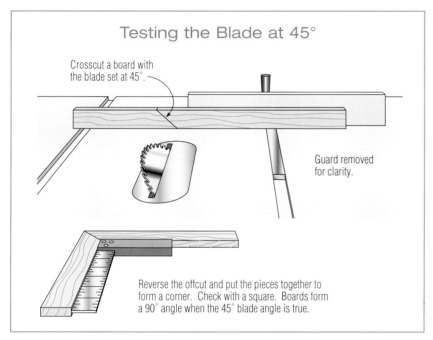

Testing the Blade at 45°

Crosscut a board with the blade set at 45°.

Guard removed for clarity.

Reverse the offcut and put the pieces together to form a corner. Check with a square. Boards form a 90° angle when the 45° blade angle is true.

Be aware that the stops will only get you close to the angle that you want. A little pressure more or less against the stop can make a difference. Turning the crank a little too much will almost always twist the carriage assembly. Whenever I need an accurate angle, I adjust the blade using a square or bevel gauge, then make test cuts to verify.

Stabilizing the Base

A table-saw base needs to sit solidly on the floor without rocking. Instability can be a safety hazard when cutting and can contribute to vibration. It's also best if the tabletop is level. To stabilize a saw that sits on a bolted-together stand, place a level on the tabletop, then loosen the bolts and shift the parts of the stand until the saw sits solidly on all of its legs with the top level. Retighten the bolts. For a saw with an enclosed base, strategically place shims under the base to level and steady it. Some saws include adjustable levelers for this purpose.

If your saw is lightweight or top-heavy, adding sandbags or bolting it to the floor will improve stability and reduce vibration. If you bolt your saw to a wood floor, check that the floor area underneath doesn't vibrate. You can also run the bolts through rubber pads under the saw feet to further reduce vibration. Outfeed tables attached to a saw can help improve stability as well.

Aligning the Tables

Because the table surface is the reference used to present the workpiece to the blade, it needs to be as flat as possible to ensure accurate cuts. As discussed in chapter 2, an out-of-flat tabletop can affect cutting, particularly a dip or hump near the blade. However, not every deviation in a top's flatness will affect the accuracy of your cuts. The only way to really tell is to make cuts with variously sized pieces of wood, then check them for square.

A tabletop can also be twisted, where two diagonally opposed corners are higher than the others. Fortunately, a twisted top—unlike a humped or dipped top—can often be corrected, as explained on the facing page. It's important that any attached extensions be aligned to the main table as well. Table alignment should be taken care of before making the remaining adjustments discussed in this chapter.

Mark the Location

If you have to move your saw often, first mark its original stable position on the floor so that you can return it there later. Attaching a thin pad of wood or plastic to each foot helps prevent scratching your floor when moving the saw.

An accurate straightedge placed diagonally across the main table will reveal twist. The low spot between the table's two high corners can be measured with a feeler gauge.

THE MAIN TABLE

Begin by checking the flatness of the main table. I have been surprised to find that many tables are twisted; cast-iron tops are more flexible than you might think—especially many of today's lighter-weight tops. Aluminum tops are even more flexible.

To check the main table for twist, place an accurate straightedge across the table diagonally in both directions. A twisted top will expose a low spot between one pair of corners and a high spot between the opposite pair (see the photo on the facing page). Sometimes a top may be twisted simply because the top of the body or cabinet isn't flat. In that case, you can shim under the bolts until the top is flat.

Sometimes a twist is caused by the weight of a long extension table and rails and maybe an overarm blade guard cantilevered off the side of the saw. Even if an extension table has legs, the legs may be standing on an uneven floor, effectively pulling down the side of the saw table. In either case, proper shimming may bring the tabletop back into flat.

EXTENSION WINGS

The extension wings need to be adjusted flush with and in the same plane as the main table. I check the joint first with a short straightedge, then I check the span of the main table and extension table with a long straightedge (see the photo below).

In order for the table and extension to meet in the same plane, the edges of both must be 90 degrees to the top. I've found that this is rare and that it's often necessary to shim the joint to make the two surfaces level.

Use a long straightedge and shims to set the extension wings level and flush to the main table.

It's also best to first check both mating surfaces for any foreign matter or imperfections. Clean the edges and smooth out any protrusions using a fine, flat file.

To shim the joint, you must first loosen the bolts enough to insert shims either at the top or the bottom of the joint to drive the wing up or down as necessary. Gauging the number and thickness of the shims is a trial-and-error affair. For shims, you can use anything that you can find around the shop, including paper, cellophane, or aluminum from a soda can. Use a clamp at each end of the joint to hold it flush as you tighten up the bolts. Sometimes it takes a bit of tapping with a dead-blow hammer to align.

Pressed-steel wings are often twisted but can be made relatively flat by loosening their connections to the fence rails, adjusting the position of each connection, then retightening the bolts.

EXTENSION TABLES

Extension tables to the side and rear of the saw are great for supporting workpieces during and after cutting. Side tables are typically bolted to the main table and set flush and level to it. It's best if a bolted-on table is supported on its own legs to prevent its weight from introducing wind into the main tabletop. A rear outfeed table can be freestanding or attached, and it doesn't hurt to have it set just a bit lower than the main table (but never higher). You can use a long, jointed board for checking the alignment of an extension table with the main table.

THE THROAT PLATE

The throat plate is an important part of the table surface and needs to be stable and flush to the table. Stock aluminum throat plates typically have leveling screws and a wide opening that allows the blade to be tilted for bevel cutting. However, narrow pieces of wood can wedge in the opening, causing them to be thrown back at the operator.

I suggest that you replace the stock throat plate with a zero-clearance throat plate that leaves no open space to either side of the raised blade. You won't be able to use it for bevel cutting, but it will serve you much better for the majority of your cutting, which is at 90 degrees anyway. A zero-clearance throat plate provides solid bearing right up to the blade, resulting in safer cuts that will also be cleaner because fully supported wood fibers are less likely to fray or tear out. Throat plates are easy to make (see the sidebar on the facing page). Commercial throat-plate blanks are also available for most table saws (see the photo on p. 198).

For throat plates with leveling screws, use a short straightedge as a guide to level the throat plate to the tabletop. Adjust the leveling screws or shim the underside of the plate with tape to bring it flush to the table-top. Make sure that the plate doesn't rock in any direction. Some wood-workers set the plate a hair low in front to prevent a workpiece from

Custom Throat Plates

THE STOCK THROAT PLATES THAT COME WITH A TABLE SAW have too wide of an opening for safe, clean cutting. I prefer to make my own zero-clearance throat plates that support the workpiece right to the sides of the blades.

You can make the throat plates out of almost any dry, stable hardwood at hand, avoiding figured or defective stock, which might compromise stability. When making test cuts, first thickness-plane the stock to be exactly flush with the tabletop. Once you get the exact thickness setting, plane enough stock to make several plates because it's handy to have a number of throat plates with different-sized openings.

If you don't have a planer, or if you want to make your plates adjustable, you can use ½-in.-thick hardwood plywood or ultra-high molecular weight (UHMW) plastic, which is very slick and stable. To make these plates adjustable, install setscrews that will rest on the tabs in the throat-plate opening.

When sizing the plate, take measurements from the throat opening rather than from the stock plate, which tends to be undersized. I use the stock plate only to lay out the profile for the rounded ends. Cut close to the layout line, then use a disk sander for final fitting. Sand a bit at a time until the fit is snug. You may need to chamfer the bottom edge of the throat plate slightly to get it to seat properly in its opening. If you are replacing a particularly thin plate, you may need to rabbet the underside of a ½-in.-thick plate to fit it into its opening. Alternatively, you could glue a heavier piece to the underside of thin stock. Drill a finger hole at the front of any throat plate for easy removal, and ease the edges of the hole for comfort.

To cut the saw kerf in the throat plate, clamp the blank down using a narrow board spanning the table-

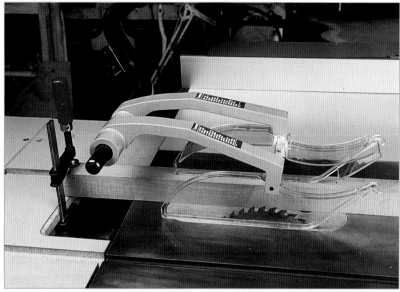

To cut the blade slot in a zero-clearance throat plate, clamp the blank to the table using a long, narrow board that spans the tabletop. Raise the spinning blade slowly into the throat plate.

saw top (see the photo above). Then turn on the saw and raise the blade slowly into the plate. On many saws, the standard blade will not retract enough to allow you to completely insert the throat-plate blank. In this case, use a smaller-diameter blade to start the kerf, then switch to the desired blade to finish the cut. If you don't have a smaller blade, you can chisel a narrow starter channel to accommodate the top edge of the blade.

After cutting the kerf, mark out the splitter slot, aligning it with the kerf. Then cut the slot using a bandsaw or a small handsaw. Waxing the plate afterward will minimize wood movement and reduce feed friction. To prevent any possibility of the plate lifting in use, you can attach a small wood catch or metal washer to the underside at the rear. You can also fit the throat plate with a shopmade splitter (see the sidebar on p. 166).

catching on it. This is a safe practice, but I prefer to keep the plate as level as possible because the accuracy of some joinery operations depends on a perfectly level plate.

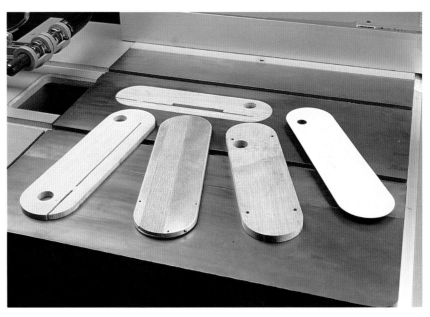

Shopmade or commercial throat inserts provide zero clearance around the blade, making for safer, cleaner cutting.

Aligning the Miter-Gauge Slots to the Blade

For accurate ripping and crosscutting, the sawblade should be perfectly parallel to the miter-gauge slots. Unfortunately, a machine seldom comes exactly aligned from the factory. For ripping, you can compensate for this misalignment by adjusting the rip fence parallel to the sawblade. However, that won't correct the problem for crosscutting because a miter gauge, crosscut sled, or similar jig must travel in the miter slots. And if the slots aren't parallel to the blade, the blade will cut into the work with both the front and then the back of the blade. Changing the angle of approach won't correct the problem.

To determine if the blade is misaligned to the miter slots, you'll need to measure from the blade to a miter slot. There are a number of great commercial products made specifically for this purpose (as well as other machine tuning), but I find that an inexpensive dial indicator clamped to a miter gauge does well for this job (see the sidebar on the facing page). A dial indicator provides measurements in thousandths of an inch for great accuracy and is easy to read while you're adjusting the alignment.

If you don't want to buy a dial indicator, I'll also discuss a low-tech method for aligning your blade to its miter slots. Both methods that I'll explain require the use of a miter gauge that fits snugly in its slots. Yours may not, so I'll cover that first.

To effectively widen a miter-gauge bar that fits sloppily in its grooves, pound a series of chisel grooves across the edge of the bar.

TUNING THE MITER-GAUGE FIT

The bar on a stock miter gauge often fits sloppily in its slots. One way to eliminate this side-to-side play is by slotting the edges of the bar with a cold chisel (see the photo above). The raised metal around the chiseled depressions essentially widen the soft metal bar, taking out the slop. Space the depressions evenly all along one or both edges of the bar—not just in a section or two. You want the bar to stay snug even when it's extended partially off the table. If you've made it too snug, run a fine-cut file lightly over the chiseled edge of the bar.

Although this fix will last quite a while, it's only temporary; eventually the soft metal will wear down, producing slop again. If you use a miter gauge a lot (I don't, as explained later), consider buying a better-fitting

Some miter-gauge bars include Allen screws or other fittings for adjusting the width of the bar to better fit its slot.

A dial indicator provides an immediate readout for adjusting the blade parallel to the miter groove. A bar clamp locked onto the rear trunnions provides a lever for easy adjustment of the trunnion position.

aftermarket bar. Some have built-in adjustments (see the top photo). Some are longer than stock bars, which helps create a better fit because any deviations are spread over a greater distance.

Aligning the Blade to the Miter-Gauge Slots

Contractor's saw

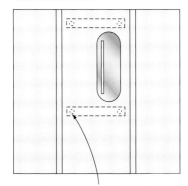

Loosen the bolts that hold the trunnions to the tabletop. Shift the trunnions relative to the table to align the blade and miter slots.

Cabinet saw

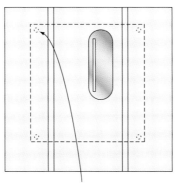

Loosen the bolts that secure the tabletop to the saw base. Shift the top to align the blade and miter slots.

MAKING THE ADJUSTMENTS USING A DIAL INDICATOR

Now that your miter-gauge bar fits well, you're ready to make the blade-to-miter-slot adjustment. With the power disconnected, elevate the blade just short of its maximum height. Never crank the blade hard against its stops, which will twist the internal mechanisms.

Screw the dial indicator to a piece of wood that extends out toward the blade. It doesn't matter if the miter gauge isn't at a perfect 90-degree angle to the blade. Clamp the wood so that the plunger is lightly depressed against the perimeter of the blade plate, not against a tooth (see the bottom photo on the facing page).

Rotate the scale on the dial indicator until its reference pointer is at zero. Using a felt-tipped pen, make a reference mark on the blade near the plunger. Slide the miter gauge to the opposite end of the blade, then rotate the blade until your reference mark is under the plunger. The dial indicator will show the amount of difference between the two positions, indicating the amount of misalignment between the plane of the blade and the miter slot.

The reason for rotating the blade is that no blade is perfectly flat. Therefore, you can't just measure the distance at the front and rear of a blade without introducing error. For the same reason, you shouldn't measure to a straightedge placed against the blade.

To bring the blade and miter slots in line with each other, you'll need to adjust either the carriage or the tabletop, depending on the type of saw (see the illustration above). On portable saws and home-shop saws, adjust the carriage. Slightly loosen the bolts that hold the trunnions to the top. Don't loosen them too much; it's best to have just a bit of resistance when you're trying to move the carriage only a few thousandths of an inch. You can tap the trunnion with a mallet to move it, but I find it much easier to clamp the trunnion and carriage assembly together with an F-style bar clamp, then use the bar as a lever to move the rear of the carriage (see the bottom photo on p. 200).

After you make an adjustment, you may need to reset the reference pointer on the dial indicator before rechecking the alignment. When the dial indicator registers the same distance at the front and rear of the blade, tighten the trunnion bolts, then recheck the alignment. It may take several efforts to get the alignment dead on, but it's worth it, and you may only have to do this once or twice for the life of the saw.

On a stationary cabinet saw, the trunnion mechanisms are fixed to the cabinet, so it's the tabletop that you need to move instead. Loosen the tabletop bolts a bit, then tap the edge of the tabletop to bring it into proper relation to the blade.

THE LOW-TECH APPROACH

If you don't have a dial indicator, you can use a long piece of wood and a feeler gauge instead. Spring-clamp the piece of wood to the miter gauge as before, but this time bring the wood right up to the side of the teeth. Using the piece of wood as a reference, first determine whether the front or rear of the blade is closest to the miter slot. Mark a tooth at that spot with chalk or a felt marker.

Next, rotate the marked tooth to the opposite end of the throat-plate slot and take a feeler-gauge measurement of the gap there (see the photo

Enlarging Bolt Holes

S ometimes trunnion bolt holes are too small to allow sufficient movement for proper adjustment. In that case, simply drill or file the holes to elongate them in the proper direction.

If you don't have a dial indicator, you can use a feeler gauge to measure the distance between the blade and a piece of wood clamped to a miter gauge.

on the facing page). As mentioned in the previous section, don't trust measurements unless they're taken from the same spot on a rotated blade. If the difference between the front and rear of the blade is more than 0.003 in., adjust the alignment as explained above.

Aligning the Splitter to the Blade

For optimum performance and safety, the splitter or riving knife must be properly aligned with the sawblade. If misaligned, it can steer a workpiece into or away from the rip fence, leading to inaccurate cuts or difficult feeding. Stock splitters are typically thinner than the blade, whereas aftermarket splitters vary from about $\frac{3}{32}$ in. thick to $\frac{1}{8}$ in. thick. A stock splitter typically aligns with the center of the blade, but I prefer to shim it out so it's even with the right side of the teeth (the side closest to the fence). This way, it will firmly hold the workpiece against the fence, resulting in a clean—as well as safe—cut.

To adjust a splitter, loosen the bolts that attach it to the carriage assembly. With the blade set at 90 degrees, use a square to set the splitter perpendicular to the table. Using a straightedge, line it up with the right side of the blade. The flimsy stock splitters that come with most saws bend out of shape easily, but they can just as easily be bent back into shape.

Adjusting the Rip Fence

For proper cutting, a rip fence must be adjusted parallel to the blade. The faces must also be straight and flat, as well as square to the table. A rip fence that is out of alignment with the blade will cause a number of problems. A fence that angles away from the rear of the blade will cause the workpiece to skew away from the fence, burning the waste side of the cut and creating a hollow workpiece edge in the process.

The more dangerous situation is when the fence angles toward the rear of the blade. In that case, the workpiece will bind between the fence and the teeth at the rear of the blade, burning the workpiece and inviting kickback if no splitter or riving knife is installed. Don't bother to adjust the rip fence until the blade has been adjusted parallel to the miter-gauge slots, as discussed previously.

To check your fence alignment, lock the fence in position and measure from it to the opposite ends of the miter-gauge slots, again using the dial indicator attached to the miter gauge. Alternatively, you can place blocks of ¾-in.-thick stock into the miter-gauge slot at each end, then gently lock the rip fence against the blocks to see if they contact the fence at the same time. If not, the alignment needs adjustment.

Many old-style stock fences made of stamped steel are adjusted by loosening the two bolts on the top of the fence, moving the body until it is parallel to the miter-gauge slot, then retightening the screws. An adjustment screw at the front of the fence regulates the grip of the hook on the back rail that locks the rear of the fence in place.

Biesemeyer-style fences are adjusted by turning Allen screws on the crossbar that rides on the fence rail. The fence needs to be removed to adjust the screws, then replaced to test the alignment (see the photo at left below). This trial-and-error adjustment isn't difficult, though, and doesn't take long.

I like to set my rip fence so that it is no more than 0.001 in. farther from the rear of the blade than it is at the front of the blade. This way, the rear teeth just barely touch the workpiece, providing a smooth, unburned cut without steering the workpiece away from the fence. I use a feeler gauge or dial indicator to measure the distance between the fence and the teeth.

The faces of a fence should also be square to the table all along their lengths. Check them with a good square. A tilted fence can result in inaccurate cuts when ripping stock of different thicknesses, edge-grooving, or tenoning when using the fence as a reference surface. A few fences provide for making this adjustment (see the photo at right below). If yours doesn't, you can add an auxiliary fence and shim it out as necessary.

Make Sure the Fence is Straight

Old-style stamped-steel fences are notorious for not having straight faces. Whatever fence you have, check its straightness using an accurate straightedge. If the fence is bowed or twisted, add an auxiliary wood fence, shimming it to correct any imperfections.

To adjust a Biesemeyer-style fence parallel to the blade, remove the fence from its rail and adjust the Allen screws on the crossbar that presses against the rail.

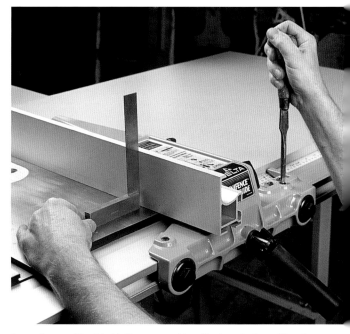

Some fences, like this Unifence, provide adjustments for setting the face of the fence perpendicular to the saw table.

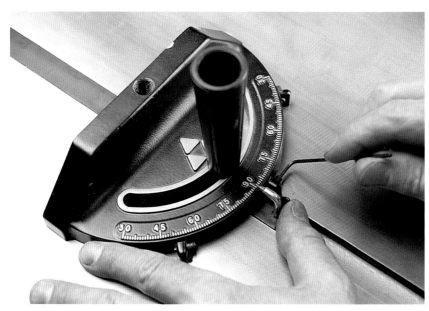

Once you've set the miter gauge at 90 degrees to the blade, adjust the setscrew that presses against the stop.

Adjusting the Miter Gauge

An accurate stock miter gauge is a contradiction in terms. Most of them are sloppily made, and I almost never use mine. But a lot of woodworkers do use them, so I'll address here how to adjust miter-gauge stops.

Begin by placing a large square against the gauge and the blade body, avoiding the teeth. When the relationship appears square, lock the miter-gauge head on its body. Next, crosscut a 3-in. piece off of a ¾-in. by 1½-in. by 18-in. board. Flip one of the cut pieces and place the sawn edges together against a straightedge.

Just as when you made a test cut earlier to check the blade perpendicularity to the table, any deviation from 90 degrees will be doubled when you put the sawn edges together (see the top illustration on p. 193). Readjust the miter-gauge angle and make more test cuts as necessary until the two sawn edges meet perfectly. Then set the stop and indicator so you'll be able to quickly set the gauge to 90 degrees repeatedly (see the photo above).

To set the miter-gauge stop at 45 degrees, adjust the gauge to approximately 45 degrees using a drafting triangle or sliding bevel gauge. Then crosscut a piece of scrap wood as explained above. Flip one of the pieces, then put the pieces together to form a corner as when making test cuts for checking the bevel angle of a blade (see the bottom illustration on p. 193). Check the corner using a square. Once again, any deviation from 90 degrees will be doubled. Readjust the miter-gauge angle as necessary until an exact 45-degree angle is achieved. Finally, set the 45-degree miter-gauge stop.

Cleaning and Maintaining Work Surfaces

A clean, smooth, waxed saw table is essential for safe, accurate, easy feeding of workpieces, as well as for the longevity of your saw. Wax reduces feed friction and helps prevent rust. I clean and wax my saw table and accessories whenever I start encountering feed resistance, which usually works out to three or four times a year.

Begin by cleaning the table. On a new saw, you may first need to wipe off the heavy antirust protectant using lots of mineral spirits and rags. On an old saw, you can remove heavier rust and stains using 400-grit wet/dry sandpaper lubricated with mineral spirits. Metal polish and coarse automobile rubbing compound also do a good job of rust and stain removal. Most tables can simply be scrubbed with mineral spirits and coarse steel wool to remove any light rust, pitch, gum deposits, and old wax.

Next, apply a thin coat of wax, rubbing it into the entire surface, including the miter-gauge slots. I use furniture paste wax, but most car and floor waxes will work equally well. Avoid floor waxes that contain antislip additives, and don't use products that contain silicone, which can cause finishing problems if it contaminates a work surface.

Allow the wax to dry to a haze, then buff it off. As long as all of the excess is removed, there's no danger of contaminating a work surface. Even if a small amount is transferred to the workpiece, normal sanding will remove it. I also clean and wax my saw's fence rails, extension tables, and rip fences and wipe down any plastic parts with a damp cloth.

Wax and other surface coatings help to protect the saw from rust but won't stop it. Rust is always ready to attack, so it's important to keep the table free of moisture. Common sense will tell you not to set drinks, green wood, or damp rags on the table. However, a more pernicious form of moisture is condensation—caused by a cold metal surface coming in contact with warm humid air from the outside or perhaps from a nearby clothes dryer. In these cases, a cardboard or specially designed cover can help protect the metal.

Preventing Rust

Rust is most common on tools that sit unused for long periods. If you're not going to be using your equipment for some months, it might be wise to lightly coat the top with oil or thin grease.

The Table-Saw Workstation

Properly set up and configured, the table saw is much more than just the primary tool in your woodworking arsenal. Along with its attendant fixtures, accessories, and extension tables, it's actually a workstation where you perform some of the most critical processes in woodworking. As such, it's important to carefully consider the saw's ideal placement in the shop as well as its lighting, wiring, dust collection, and relationship to other tools in your shop.

Saw Placement

The table saw is the heart of the shop in a number of ways. Not only is it central to many woodworking operations, but it's also often physically located in the middle of the shop and is the tool around which other processes often revolve. Unlike most other stationary woodshop tools, the table saw requires space on all four sides for ripping and crosscutting large workpieces.

For a table saw, a working space 17 ft. long and 12 ft. wide will accommodate most of the boards needed for many woodworking projects. The 8 ft. in front of the blade and the 8 ft. behind it allow enough infeed and outfeed room for ripping 8-ft.-long boards or panels. And if you situate the saw with 6½ ft. to the right of the blade and 5½ ft. to the left, you'll have plenty of room for crosscutting boards almost 8 ft. long.

If your shop doesn't allow you to dedicate such a large, permanent space to a table saw, think mobile. A good mobile base allows you to easily move a saw about in the shop to gain cutting room when needed (see the

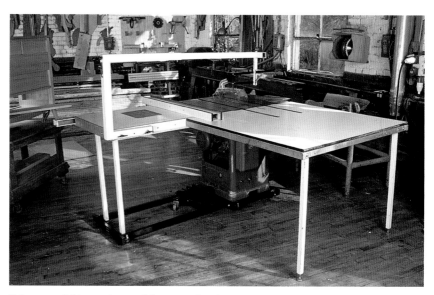

Set up your table saw in a well-lit, convenient location, with saw accessories close at hand and as much space around the saw as you can afford.

A mobile base allows you to move your table saw around in a small shop to create infeed and outfeed areas as needed.

photo above). For that matter, you can leave your saw stationary and put surrounding machinery on mobile bases for clearing room around the saw when handling large workpieces.

You can also take advantage of open doors and windows by aiming long workpieces through them when ripping. For very small shops or garages, a portable saw can easily be moved about to make the most of the space that you do have. You can even take it outside if you're really cramped.

Arranging Machinery for Workflow

Table-saw placement

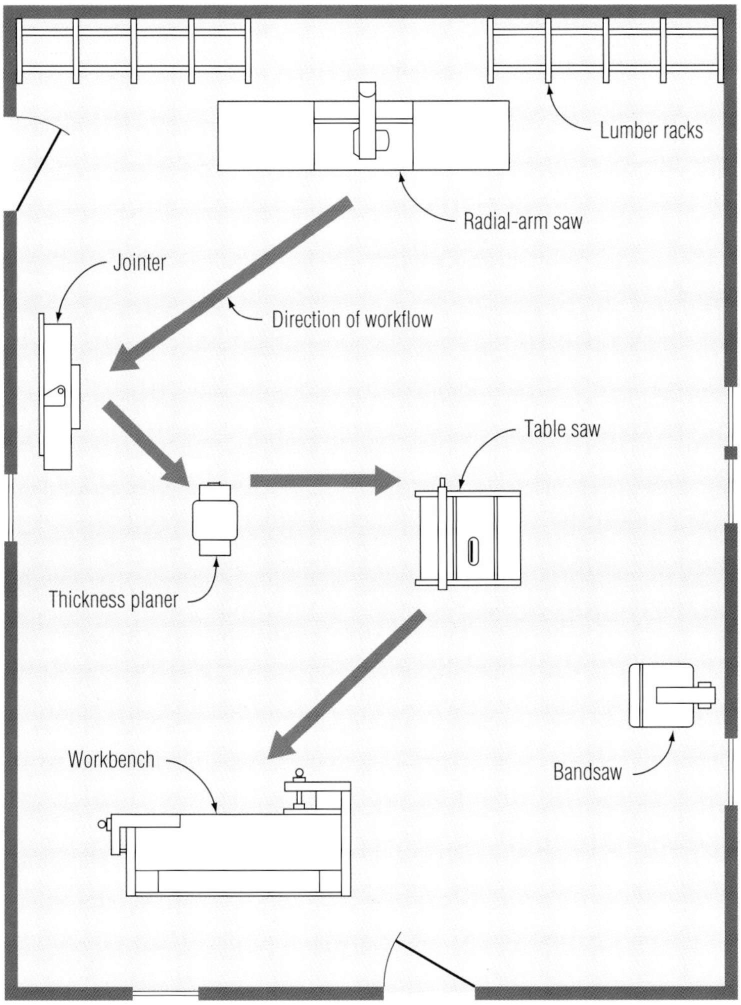

Arrange machines to suit your order of operations and economize movement. In the example shown here, work begins near the lumber racks, where boards are cut to rough length on the radial-arm saw. Workpieces are then milled at the jointer and planer before moving to the table saw for cutting to final size. Finally, joint-fitting and assembly takes place at the workbench.

Avoid Surprises

When possible, place your table saw so you're facing your shop entrance when working. This can prevent you from being startled from behind by visitors when concentrating on a cut.

Your table saw's placement in relation to other tools and operations is important because it affects workflow. Try to arrange your machines to follow your particular order of operations and to economize movement as much as possible. For example, my work generally begins at the cutoff saw near my lumber rack, where I crosscut boards to rough length. From there, I move to the nearby jointer and planer to do my initial stock dressing. After that, work moves to the table saw for cutting to final size (see the illustration on p. 209). For more information on machine placement and general shop setup, check out *The Workshop Book* by Scott Landis (The Taunton Press, 1991).

Wiring

Whatever type of saw you have, it should be connected to an appropriate electrical circuit—for reasons of both safety and efficiency. Most saws that are marketed for home use, including portable and contractor-style saws, come with motors rated at about 1½ hp. The horsepower, voltage, and amperage ratings for a motor can be found on its information plate.

The motors on these saws come wired for 115 volts, the common U.S. household current, making them ready to plug in and use without any need for special wiring. Because these motors draw around 15 amps, a saw should be plugged into a dedicated circuit that won't serve any other tools at the same time the saw is running. Since motors can draw more than their specified amperage upon startup, the circuit breaker should be rated at 20 amps. For Underwriters Laboratories (UL) approval, a 115-volt motor that draws more than 15 amps should use a special plug and matching receptacle.

230-VOLT CIRCUITS

A 230-volt circuit provides a more efficient use of electricity, resulting in fewer circuit overloads and longer motor life. The 1½-hp induction motors on most home-shop saws are dual-voltage motors, meaning they can be wired for either 115 or 230 volts. If you have a 230-volt circuit in your shop, it's definitely to your advantage to wire the saw motor for 230-volt use. If you don't have a 230-volt circuit, it's usually not difficult for an electrician to install one. Whenever adding or changing wiring, be sure local electrical codes are adhered to.

To rewire the motor for 230-volt use, remove the lid on the wiring box that's attached to the motor. Under the lid is a wiring diagram for changing the voltage. Once you've switched the wiring connections in the box, you'll need to replace the standard 115-volt plug on the end of the cord with a 230-volt plug (available at hardware stores).

ELECTRICAL OUTLETS AND CORDS

Ideally, the electrical outlet for the saw should be as close at hand as possible. For one thing, you don't want to have to use an extension cord (see the sidebar on the facing page). For another, it's important to be able to easily disconnect the power for saw maintenance and blade changing.

Since the table saw is often placed in the center of the shop, the power cord typically has to run across the floor to a wall outlet. If so, keep from tripping over an electrical cord by using a shopmade or commercial cord cover that's grooved on the underside to accommodate the cord (see

---

Needs of 3-hp to 5-hp Saws

If you're planning to buy a stationary saw with a motor ranging from 3 hp to 5 hp, you'll need a 230-volt circuit because these saws require it.

the photo at right). Cord housings are often available at office-supply stores.

Sometimes an outlet can be installed under the saw or extension table. Outlets set face up into the floor of a woodshop are definitely not a good idea because they'll just clog with dust. However, an outlet that sits above the floor on a short post works well and makes for easy power disconnects. Although overhead outlets work for some machines, they're often in the way at the table saw, especially when cutting sheet goods or large panels.

SWITCH PLACEMENT AND MODIFICATION

If your saw switch is mounted on the right side of the saw, consider moving it to the left if possible. Because most table-saw operations take place from the left side of the blade, it makes sense to place the switch there. When you are standing to the left of the blade and reaching over for a switch on the right side of the saw, you put your body in line with the blade, increasing the potential for injury. On most saws, moving the switch to the left side isn't difficult. It's usually just a matter of drilling a new mounting hole and rerouting the wire. Just make sure you have enough wire on the switch to reach the new location.

A shopmade knee switch is another feature that provides convenience as well as safety. My knee switch is simply a length of wood hinged to the fence rail with a cutout for finger access to the on switch (see the photo on p. 212). A block of wood glued to the back presses against the off button, effectively turning the entire piece of wood into a giant "panic switch" that can easily be hit in an instant. For example, I have been in a predicament where a workpiece kerf closed on the blade and I was afraid to let go of it to turn off the saw. In such situations, a large knee switch is an extra edge on safety. Even during ordinary operations, it's helpful not having to feel around for small buttons.

A cord cover prevents tripping over cords snaking across the floor to the table saw.

Lighting

Safe, accurate work at the table saw requires good overhead lighting that casts no shadows and creates no glare. Ideally, lots of natural light is the best choice, but that's often not an option. Instead, a fluorescent light fixture positioned above your saw with incandescent lighting to either side

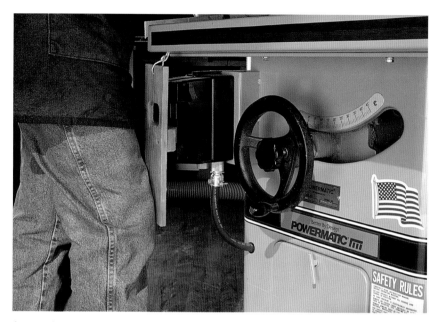

An oversized knee switch allows you to turn the saw off quickly without taking your hands off the workpiece. Turning the saw on, however, requires deliberately reaching through the cutout to push the on button.

can give you plenty of light with no perceptible fluorescent flicker. You can test a lighting scheme by standing a 12-in. dowel on the table-saw surface and adjusting the lighting so the dowel casts no heavy shadows. General shop light can be improved by painting the walls and ceiling white to help reflect available light.

Dust Collection at the Table Saw

Making piles of sawdust is one of the table saw's many talents. Dust from every cut is discharged in several directions. The majority is packed into the blade gullets between the teeth, then ejected beneath the saw table. Above the table, a steady stream of dust is thrown toward the operator. Last, the smallest and most unhealthy dust particles remain in the air for us to breathe, finally settling as a film on all shop surfaces. Some sort of dust collection at the table saw is essential to health and general shop safety.

The problem is that most table saws sold in the United States aren't well suited to dust collection, either below or above the table. Contractor's saws are particularly problematic because of the wide open base. Some manufacturers offer an optional base plate with a dust port for connection to a dust collector (see the top photo on the facing page). However, a lot of dust still escapes from the open back of the saw.

Cabinet saws are better at capturing dust because of their enclosed bases, but they're still not very efficient because the cabinet is not sealed

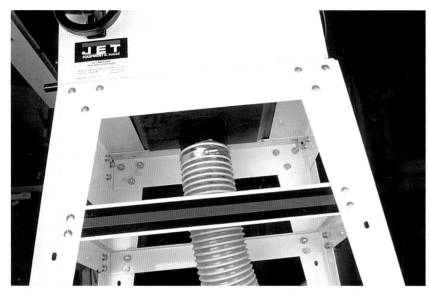

Outfitting a contractor's saw for dust collection requires installing a panel with a dust port under the saw cabinet. For better dust collection, the back of the saw should also be covered with a panel.

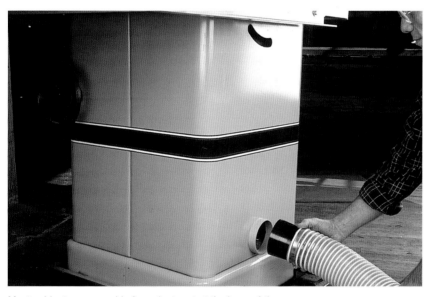

Most cabinet saws provide for a dust port at the base of the saw.

by any means. For dust-collection purposes, many cabinet saws offer only a port at the base of the cabinet that can be connected to a dust-collector hose (see the bottom photo above). Instead of a port, there may be a panel that can be replaced with an optional port attachment from the manufacturer. Newer-model cabinet saws feature an internal ramp to help direct the sawdust to the collector port.

To their credit, a few manufacturers are improving dust collection by taking cues from European table-saw design. Some newer-model portable

Doing the Best with Dust

Although sealing up a saw can help improve dust collection, don't expect miracles. The truth is that without a dust chute surrounding the blade, you're fighting poor dust-collection design.

IN AN ENCLOSED SHOP, FINE DUST PARTICLES can float high in the air long after a cut is made. These fine particles are a real health hazard and should be evacuated or filtered. If you don't have good air circulation to the outside, an ambient air cleaner will quietly filter the finest dust particles from the air in your shop. A number of models and sizes are available to suit any size shop (see Sources on p. 379).

An ambient air cleaner filters from the shop air the very fine dust that is most harmful to the lungs.

and home-shop table saws include a dust chute that partially surrounds the blade. The chute, which is connected to a dust collector, efficiently gathers the dust right at the source. This system has been standard on European saws for some time.

For capturing dust above the table, a blade cover with a dust port does the trick. This type of cover is standard on European saws. For saws sold in the United States, there are several aftermarket blade covers available (see "Better Blade Covers" on p. 168).

SEALING YOUR SAW

For saws without a dust chute, the best approach to improving dust collection is to seal up as much of the saw as possible. On cabinet saws, you can apply silicone to any small openings on the saw's body. For larger openings, such as the area between the tabletop and the cabinet, you can use duct tape. Taping the interior walls to the floor also helps. As for the large handwheel slot on the front of the saw, you can attach a slotted piece of inner tube to help seal the opening. Adding a shopmade inclined ramp of

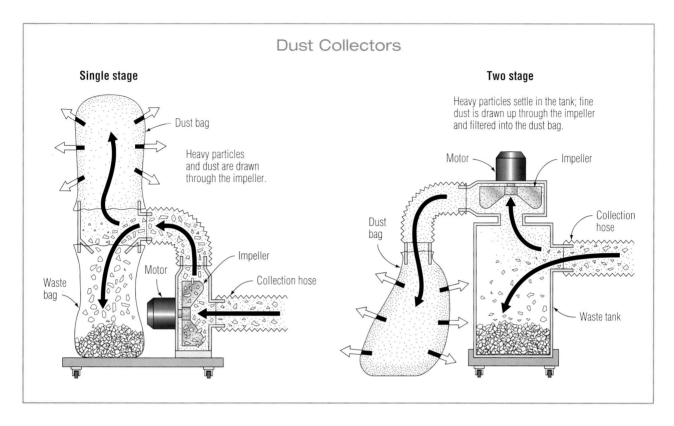

Dust Collectors

Single stage

Dust bag

Heavy particles and dust are drawn through the impeller.

Impeller

Motor

Collection hose

Waste bag

Two stage

Heavy particles settle in the tank; fine dust is drawn up through the impeller and filtered into the dust bag.

Motor

Impeller

Collection hose

Dust bag

Waste tank

sheet metal or plastic laminate to older saws can help direct dust toward a low-placed dust port.

Sealing up a contractor's saw is another challenge altogether. Because the motor hangs out the open back of the saw, it's difficult to seal up this saw, but that's what you have to do to capture the dust. Because most sawing is done with the blade set at 90 degrees, you can make a simple removable back to fit the saw set up for this angle. When a different angle is needed, you can remove the back easily.

DUST COLLECTORS

The first dust collector I tried using on my table saw was a shop vacuum, simply because I had one. Unfortunately, even industrial-quality shop vacs don't move enough air to be effective on most table saws. A table saw, like most shop machinery, requires a minimum of about 300 cubic feet per minute (cfm) of airflow at the point of connection for effective dust collection. An industrial shop vacuum typically produces only about 140 cfm. Most other shop vacuums produce only 100 cfm to 120 cfm and have a limited hose-diameter capacity.

The one exception is that a shop vac will work on a saw that incorporates a dust chute. As previously discussed, the dust chute partially surrounds the blade underneath the table and includes a port that can be connected to a shop vacuum or dust collector. The chute effectively retains the dust in an area small enough for a shop vac to evacuate.

For most table saws, though, I recommend a dust collector that is rated higher than 350 cfm. Any commercially available dust collector with at least a 1-hp motor should have enough drawing power for the table saw.

Dust collectors are available as either single-stage or two-stage units (see the illustration on p. 215). Single-stage systems draw all of the sawdust directly into the blower impellers. Heavy particles then drop below into a bag or other container, and fine dust is filtered by the upper bag. Two-stage systems draw particles into a tank or cyclone first, where the heavy particles drop, leaving only the fine dust to pass through the impeller blades and into the filter.

Both types of units have their pros and cons. Single-stage systems are generally less expensive and can be easier to empty out because the chips and sawdust end up in an easily detachable bag. However, single-stage systems are very noisy, and metal pieces that accidentally enter the system can damage the blades or cause sparks that can potentially ignite a dust fire. Two-stage systems are more expensive but tend to last longer because there is less wear on the impeller, housing, and motor.

Single-stage dust collectors There are two types of single-stage dust collectors: one is a small, single-bag unit, and the other is a double-bag unit that is often mounted on a mobile stand. A single-bag unit is powerful enough to use with a portable saw and lightweight enough to move around easily on a job site. Just be prepared to empty the small dust bag often.

A double-bag unit—typically 1 hp to 2 hp—is powerful and capacious enough to handle planer and jointer shavings as well as table-saw waste.

A conversion lid placed on a waste can between the saw and a single-stage dust collector creates a two-stage system because the heavy dust falls into the can before reaching the dust-collector impeller.

Fitted with a quick disconnect, it can easily be moved from machine to machine. These units are tall, though, and can be top-heavy. In some cases, this can make them awkward to use in a cramped shop. Note that you can convert a single-stage collector into a two-stage collector by employing a conversion lid that directs heavy waste into a trash can while allowing the finer dust to continue on to the dust collector (see the photo on the facing page).

Two-stage dust collectors There are also two types of double-stage collectors: a barrel-type unit and a cyclone unit. A barrel-type unit is fairly low profile. Because it's shorter than a table saw, it won't interfere with handling or feeding large workpieces. Cyclones are more efficient but are very tall and hardly portable.

Central dust collection Depending on the size of the woodshop, many woodworkers find it convenient to connect all of their machines to a central dust-collection system. For the table saw, the connecting ductwork can be run from the collector across the ceiling, then down a shop wall close to the machine. Where the duct meets the floor, you can connect a length of flexible hose to the duct work with a quick disconnect fitting. It is then easy enough to move the hose out of the way when the need arises.

For more information on setting up dust-collection systems, see *Fine Woodworking* #67 and *Woodshop Dust Control* by Sandor Nagyszalanczy (The Taunton Press, 1996).

Shop Accessories

Several accessories will make your table saw easier to use. Some, such as auxiliary supports, are virtually essential; others, such as carts and storage racks, are enormously helpful. Below are some of the setups I've developed in my many years as a woodworker.

AUXILIARY SUPPORTS

Auxiliary supports increase the working surface of the table saw, carrying long or wide workpieces at the tabletop height. Outfeed supports are a necessary safety feature because most table saws provide less than 6 in. of support behind the blade. You definitely don't want to be reaching over the blade to prevent a piece from falling after the cut. An auxiliary side table supports the edges of panels when making wide cuts.

Auxiliary supports can take many forms, ranging from a simple set of sawhorses spanned by a piece of sheet material to plastic-laminated extension tables projecting from the rear and right side of the saw. Workbenches are about the same height as the saw table, so I have used mine many times as an outfeed-support surface.

Fold-down tables and steel-roller systems that attach to the rear of the saw are convenient for a small shop because they drop out of the way when not in use. (see Sources on p. 379). You can also buy roller stands as separate units, but I have found that if these are not aligned at exactly 90 degrees to the blade, they tend to steer the workpiece to one side or the other.

If you have the room, a large extension-table system is much better when it comes to handling large workpieces. Biesemeyer offers two laminated outfeed-support tables—one "professional" size and one for the home shop—that are designed to attach to the back rail of a Biesemeyer fence system. The tables are adjustable in height and come with milled slots to accommodate an extended miter-gauge bar or jig runners (see the top photo on p. 208). The extra table area is also useful for drawing and assembly work. I keep it waxed to resist glue.

Of course, you can make your own extension tables instead of buying them. Attach a two-legged extension table to the saw table with clamps or with brackets through the guide rails. Alternatively, build a freestanding four-legged table. An outfeed support should be at the same height, or slightly below, the saw table (see the photo at left). A side extension table should be at exactly the same height as the saw tabletop.

CARTS

Wheeled carts or tables can be used for moving lumber from machine to machine or for holding project parts as you are processing them (see the photo at left on the facing page). When working at the table saw, I find it more convenient and safer to work from a stack of parts on a cart rather than piling things on the saw table. Parts stacked neatly on a cart are easy to count and missed joints are clearly evident.

Carts are easy to obtain. You can get them at furniture-factory auctions or you can recycle food carts from hospital junk piles. You can also build your own or make one by attaching casters to an old table. It is useful to have some carts that are low to the floor and some at bench height.

RACKS, DRUMS, BOXES, AND BUCKETS

In a well-organized workspace, frequently used table-saw tools and accessories are kept within reach of the saw. These include your push sticks, arbor wrenches, miter gauge, fences, throat plates, guards, maintenance supplies, and featherboards. You might also want to store your sawblades, jigs, clipboard, and patterns nearby.

Some saws come equipped with brackets for holding the accessories that you use the most—the rip fence and miter gauge, as well as the arbor wrench. If your saw didn't come with brackets, they are easy enough to make.

Since a set of good sawblades can easily cost more than your table saw, it makes sense to take good care of them. I made a simple wall-hung saw-

Setting Up Extension Rollers

If extension rollers aren't set perfectly perpendicular to the sawblade, they can steer a workpiece out of line while feeding it.

An extension should be at the saw height or slightly below the saw table. Some tables can fold down out of the way when necessary.

Wheeled carts can conveniently ferry workpieces and work in process from machine to machine. A cart can also serve as an extension table when needed.

A simple wall-hung box keeps blades organized and separated to protect them from damaging each other.

blade box to protect my blades while keeping them at the ready (see the photo at right above). I keep my collection of pushers on top of this box.

Large 55-gallon drums are handy for holding wood scraps or sawdust. With a panel placed across the top, they can be used as temporary parts tables. A drum is also a handy place to set the rip fence if you have to remove it from the saw temporarily—better than the floor, where it's likely to get damaged or tripped over. A scrap box or bucket next to the saw (not that I always hit it) helps control the mess from cutoffs. Pieces in the bucket either go into the 55-gallon drums or serve as fuel for the wood-stove. Larger pieces go to my scrap shelves if I think they can be used later.

Tools at the Table Saw

There are two types of important tools I keep by the table saw: layout tools for measuring, marking, and checking the workpiece, and tools for setting up the table-saw blade, miter gauge, and rip fence for various cuts. You will be repaid many times over by investing in good tools and keeping them in good condition. Good tools enhance accuracy, and the more accurate your work at the table saw, the better your projects will turn out.

Squares and rulers are the tools that you'll probably use the most at the table saw. You'll need a 6-in. try square to check fence and miter-gauge setups and the ends of your crosscuts. A machinist's combination square is handy for checking 45-degree miters and for gauging lines, as when used as a marking gauge. A framing square is useful for layout and square reference on larger panels and as a straightedge for confirming flatness.

Handy Square
I like to carry a 2-in. engineer's square in my shop apron for checking edges.

Use a sliding bevel for checking and marking angles other than 90 degrees on the workpiece, the blade, and the miter gauge. A gauge with the locking nut at the end of the handle is more versatile than one with a wing nut on the side at the head.

DRESSING FOR SUCCESS

I LEARNED TO WEAR A SHOP APRON FROM MY WIFE, who looks unkindly at saw-dust and wood chips hanging precariously off my clothes when I come into the house. Of course, a shop apron serves other purposes besides protecting my clothes and marriage. The apron's breast and waist pockets hold the tools that I use the most at the table saw: a pencil, a 6-in. ruler, a 2-in. engineer's square, and 4-in. sliding calipers.

Shop aprons are reasonably priced at hardware and discount stores, and you can probably order a dozen aprons at a time even more cheaply. Even though I wash my aprons, the glue that ultimately cakes on them forces me to throw them out, so I'm glad for the ones kept in reserve.

Check each square periodically for accuracy by placing it against the straight edge of a board and marking a line with a sharp pencil. Flip the square on the same edge and check the blade's alignment with the mark. Any deviation from 90 degrees will be doubled.

I usually carry a 6-in. metal precision ruler with metric measurements on one side and English measurements (inches) on the other. The metric measurements come in handy for calculations because they allow for finer gradations and don't involve fractions. The pocket rule will take care of much of the close work done at the saw.

For longer measurements, I find that both a folding rule and a short tape measure have their own advantages. The tape measure hooks onto the end of a board, making it easy to take long measurements. A rigid folding rule is easier to handle and is better for the more exacting work of marking joinery. Because rulers often vary from each other, it's best to use only one ruler on a job. You can check your ruler for accuracy with a machinist's rule.

A 4-in. sliding caliper with metric and English measurements is handy for checking stock thickness and narrow widths. The caliper can be used for inside and outside measurements and is more precise than measuring with a ruler.

Pencils are essential marking tools. I keep a #2 pencil behind my ear or in the top pocket of my apron. A carpenter's pencil or beginner's #308 school pencil with a thick lead is best for marking wood in the milling stage. Save your thin-lead pencils for writing, sketching, and marking joints.

Masking tape is indispensable in the woodshop. A few of its myriad uses include marking on the table-saw surface for rough cutoffs, leveling the throat plate, keeping small parts together, shimming jigs, fences, and stops that are a smidgen out of square, and taping back chips until you can glue them back in.

Ripping

R ipping and crosscutting are the most basic and common operations performed on the table saw. Ripping is sawing with the
grain—in other words, along the length of a board. Crosscutting is
sawing across the grain of the wood. The two operations are fundamen-
tally distinct and require different cutting approaches.

In this chapter, I'll discuss techniques for safe and accurate ripping of
solid wood and sheet stock. I'll address crosscutting in the next chapter.

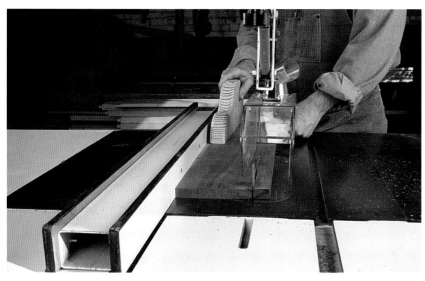

For a typical rip cut, a board's jointed face and edge are pressed against the saw table and
fence. The operator stands to the side of the board and finishes the cut using a pusher.

Preparing Wood

For safe work, a piece of wood ideally should be prepared with one straight edge and one flat face. The straight edge, which rides against the fence, prevents the board from binding between the fence and the blade. The flat face, which rides on the saw table, keeps the workpiece from rocking while being fed through the blade.

A workpiece that doesn't ride firmly against the fence and table is an invitation for dangerous kickback (see the sidebar on p. 163). Kickback can be eliminated by using a properly aligned splitter or riving knife, but I'm forced to acknowledge that many woodworkers don't currently use one. I want to reiterate here that I don't recommend using a table saw without a splitter or riving knife!

The easiest way to straighten an edge and flatten a face is to run the workpiece over a jointer. If you don't have a jointer, you can handplane the stock or buy surfaced lumber from most suppliers. If an edge is extremely irregular, like that on a rough-cut slab, it's much faster to saw the edge than to joint it. One approach is to strike a straight line, cut to it using a bandsaw, then finish straightening the edge on a jointer or with a handplane.

Alternatively, you can attach a straight-edged guide to one edge of the slab, then run the guide against the fence (see the illustration below). You'll now have a straight edge on your workpiece that you can run against the fence. Another way to rip irregular stock is to use a sled that secures the work at the front against a wooden stop (see the top photo on the facing page). If you have a European saw, you can also rip a board using the sliding table (see the bottom photo on the facing page).

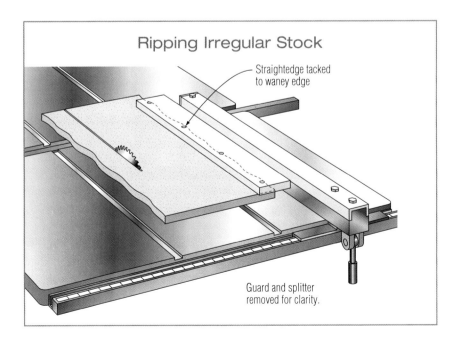

Ripping Irregular Stock

Straightedge tacked to waney edge

Guard and splitter removed for clarity.

To rip irregular stock, you can place the stock on a panel jig guided by a runner in a miter-gauge slot. The front end of the stock is pressed against a stop that's screwed to the leading end of the jig. Snipped-off brads projecting from the stop prevent the board from slipping. The trailing end is held down firmly against the sled.

The sliding table on a European saw can be used to rip irregular stock. The leading end of the stock gets jammed under an angled plate at the end of the sliding table.

RIPPING AN UNSURFACED BOARD

It's not always possible or desirable to joint and thickness-plane stock before ripping. For example, jointing a wide board to remove a large cup or twist often leaves the board too thin for your purposes. In that case, it's best to rip the pieces to rough width before jointing. That way, there's much less cup to remove on the jointer.

WOOD OFTEN CONTAINS STRESSES THAT ARE RELIEVED when a board is cut. So-called reactive wood can spread apart or pinch together as it's being ripped. This can cause the board to bind between the blade and the fence, causing dangerous kickback if you don't have a splitter or riving knife.

One way to prevent reactive wood from binding is to allow room behind the blade for the workpiece to spread out. To accomplish this on a European saw, you can slide the fence toward you and lock it in place so that it ends at the front of the blade. If your fence doesn't have this sliding fore-and-aft adjustment, you can outfit your fence with a half-fence to serve the same purpose.

A half-fence is easy to make (see the illustration at right below). Use a stable material such as maple or good-quality hardwood plywood. Applying a plastic laminate face will reduce feed friction. The fence should be taller than the thickest stock your blade will handle. Like all auxiliary fences, the half-fence should include a ⅛-in. by ⅛-in. rabbet along the bottom edge to prevent sawdust and small chips from lodging between the workpiece and fence.

You can make a simple stationary fence that clamps or bolts to your rip fence with the end of the half-fence extending about 1 in. beyond the forward gullets. But a sliding half-fence, like that shown in the photos at right, works better because you can fine-tune its position. Ideally, the end of a half-fence should extend 1 in. past the gullets at the front of the blade. Because the position of the gullets varies with the height of the blade, a sliding fence allows for the necessary fore-and-aft adjustment. The cove at the leading end of the fence accommodates varying thicknesses of stock to some degree, minimizing necessary fore-and-aft adjustments.

Using a half-fence can feel a bit awkward at first because the workpiece is unsupported once it passes the blade, but you get used to the process pretty quickly.

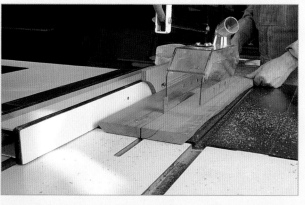

A half-fence, which extends just beyond the cutting edge of the sawblade, allows the workpiece to spread apart after being cut, reducing the risk of kickback.

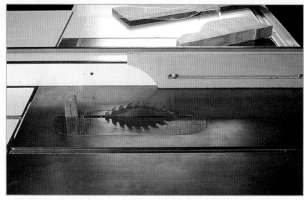

A Shopmade Half-Fence

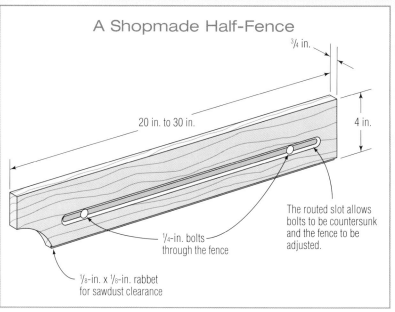

20 in. to 30 in.

¾ in.

4 in.

¼-in. bolts through the fence

The routed slot allows bolts to be countersunk and the fence to be adjusted.

⅛-in. x ⅛-in. rabbet for sawdust clearance

The safest way to rip unsurfaced stock is to use a bandsaw, but it can be done on a table saw. Unfortunately, ripping a warped board on a table saw can be dangerous, especially without using a splitter or riving knife, even when the stock has a straight edge for riding against the fence. A cupped board fed through the blade with the concave side down is fairly stable until it reaches the end of the cut, when it can collapse, pinching between the blade and the fence.

On the other hand, if a board is fed with the concave side up, it won't collapse at the end of the cut but it can rock from side to side while being cut. Of the two approaches, I favor the former. Even though the workpiece can collapse at the end of the cut, a splitter or riving knife can prevent it from being thrown backward. A half-fence is useful here too (see the sidebar on the facing page), as is ripping with a sliding table.

Basic Ripping Techniques

The standard procedure for ripping a board involves selecting the blade, setting its height, setting the fence, then making the cut with a blade cover and splitter or riving knife in place. Your stance at the saw is also critical to safety and accuracy.

SETTING THE BLADE HEIGHT

The blade-height setting has an effect upon feed resistance, heat generation, and exit tearout. On the one hand, the higher the blade, the less feed resistance and the cooler the blade runs. On the other hand, a high blade presents more danger and produces more tearout on the bottom of the cut. It can also produce more forceful kickback if you're not using a splitter or riving knife. (Again, I don't recommend sawing without one!)

However, if you don't have a splitter or riving knife on your saw, set the blade about ⅛ in. above the top of the workpiece. With a sharp blade and a properly tuned saw, the benefits of setting the blade high are minimal. Ask me how high to set the blade and I'm likely to ask you how deeply you want to cut into your fingers.

If you're using a blade cover and a splitter or riving knife, you can safely set the blade as high as you like. For the most efficient chip removal, set your blade so that the primary blade gullets clear the top of the workpiece.

SETTING THE FENCE

Move the rip fence in position for the desired width of cut. For accuracy and safety, it's critical that the fence be parallel to the blade or cocked just a hair away at the rear of the blade. If you have a premium rip fence that's adjusted properly, it should stay properly aligned to the blade regardless of the fence's position on its rail. However, if you have an old-style fence, you'll probably need to check parallelism to the blade for

When initially ripping a number of boards to rough width at the beginning of a project, I recommend using a 24-tooth FTG blade. This blade is designed to cut easily through stock, even thick hardwoods. The rough edge left by a 24-tooth blade is not an issue because you can rip workpieces to final size later using a good-quality 40-tooth ATB blade, which leaves a much smoother edge.

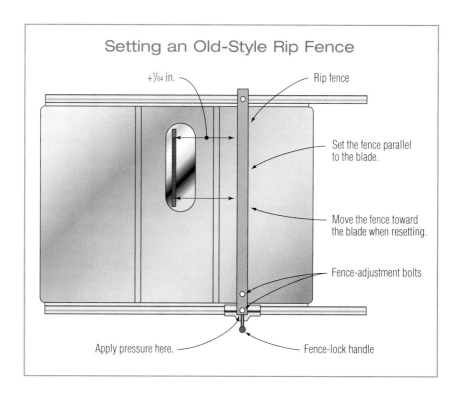

Setting an Old-Style Rip Fence

+1/64 in.

Rip fence

Set the fence parallel to the blade.

Move the fence toward the blade when resetting.

Fence-adjustment bolts

Apply pressure here.

Fence-lock handle

every cut, since these fences are notorious for locking to the rail at a slight angle to the blade.

To set an old-style fence for a cut, begin by moving it toward the blade rather than away from it. This helps prevent the drag on the rear fence rail from cocking the rear of the fence toward the blade. While moving the fence, push the front sleeve against the rail to help keep the fence square to the rail, then lock the fence in place (see the illustration above). After locking the fence, double-check your setup by measuring from your fence to both the front and rear of the blade.

When setting the fence for your width of cut, you can use the cursor and scale on a premium fence, or you can measure the distance between the fence and blade using an accurate ruler. Sometimes, you may want to use a previously cut workpiece to set the fence.

MAKING THE CUT

Put on your safety gear, ensure that the blade cover is working properly, and see that the saw table is free of debris. Make sure your splitter or riving knife is aligned properly to prevent kickback (see the sidebar on the facing page). Whenever possible, orient the workpiece with its finished, or outside, face up so that any tearout takes place on the underside.

Turn on the saw and allow the blade to reach full speed. Place the workpiece on the table with its straight edge against the fence, and move the stock into the blade. Feed the work through the blade at a steady rate, pushing it about as fast as the saw will cut. The proper feed rate is deter-

Licking Kickback

THE DANGER OF KICKBACK IS CONSTANTLY LURKING AT THE TABLE SAW. No matter how perfectly your fence is aligned and how carefully you feed a workpiece, the rising rear teeth of the blade may pick up the workpiece, hurling it at you at fierce speeds. The only sure way to prevent kickback is to use a properly aligned splitter or riving knife. I don't cut without one. If you don't like the inconvenient stock splitter that came with your table saw, there are several aftermarket models available (see "Splitters and Riving Knives" on p. 165).

To maximize stability when ripping, stand at the front of the saw to the left of the blade with your left foot in contact with the base and your hip against the front rail.

mined by the type of blade, the power of the saw, and the density of the wood. Feeding too slowly can overheat the blade and burn the workpiece, whereas feeding too fast can strain the motor on an underpowered saw. Listen to the saw as you cut. If the motor slows down as you cut, feed a bit more slowly.

Be sure to pay attention to your stance when ripping. It's dangerous to stand back from the table saw because the farther away you are, the more you have to overreach to make the cut. This is awkward and can throw you off-balance. The correct approach is to stand at the front of the saw to the left of the blade with your left foot in contact with the base and your hip against the front rail (see the photo on p. 227). In this position, the saw helps to stabilize your body, leaving your arms free to manipulate the work. Keep your right arm in line with the workpiece being pushed along the fence to the right of the blade. At the end of the cut, you'll be in a comfortable, balanced position.

It's wise to use a pusher when ripping stock that's less than 8 in. wide between the blade and the fence. A pusher acts as an extension of your hand, giving you added control as well as an extra measure of safety. (For more on pushers, see p. 177).

When ripping, pay close attention to where the workpiece meets the fence, not the blade. Keep the workpiece against the fence for the entirety of the cut. You can use your left hand to apply light pressure to push the workpiece against the fence in front of the blade. (Keep your left hand stationary on the saw table well in front of the blade. As soon as the work-

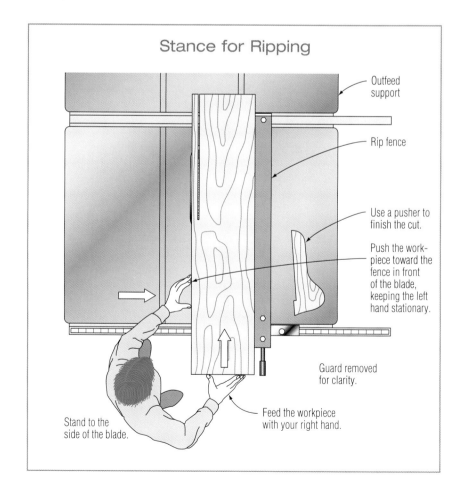

Stance for Ripping

Outfeed support

Rip fence

Use a pusher to finish the cut.

Push the work-piece toward the fence in front of the blade, keeping the left hand stationary.

Guard removed for clarity.

Feed the workpiece with your right hand.

Stand to the side of the blade.

piece passes, remove your hand from the saw table.) As the cut comes to an end, use a pusher in your right hand to hold the work down and against the fence (see the illustration on the facing page).

Ripping Long Stock

As you rip, you need some form of outfeed support, even if it's just a short outfeed table. When ripping long boards, additional support is necessary. I always use a long extension table, but if you don't have one, you can use an auxiliary support stand or a human helper.

Auxiliary supports can be freestanding or fixed to the saw. Commercial units of various sorts are available, but you can just as easily make auxiliary supports yourself. A sawhorse set at the proper height will serve, but an extension table is much more useful (for more on auxiliary supports, see p. 217).

A helper, or tail-off person, who understands how a table saw operates can make cutting long boards safer and more efficient. The helper is a human support stand who can also return the work to you. A helper should never pull on a board, but simply support it with both hands from underneath. It's up to the operator, not the helper, to guide the board (see the photo below). After each board is cut, the helper can stack the work-pieces and either dispense with the offcut or push it back to the operator for further cutting. Working together, the saw operator and a helper can develop a rhythm for efficient, safe cutting.

Long-Board Strategy

When you are cutting just a few long boards, a support stand or outfeed table will do, but if you have a lot of long boards to cut, get a helper if possible.

When you are ripping a lot of long stock, using a helper to accept the boards can be very efficient. The helper should never pull or guide a board, but simply support it with palms upraised.

Before ripping a long board, always prepare one straight edge and one flat face. Keep your pusher on the saw table near the fence so it's at the ready when you need it. Line up an outfeed support to receive the cut pieces.

Begin by propping the board against the saw, then turning on the machine. Holding the trailing end of the board in your right hand, lift it slightly to ensure that the leading end of the board contacts the tabletop. Place your left hand as far forward on the edge as you comfortably can to apply diagonal pressure to keep the board against the fence. Walk the board forward until its end reaches the saw table, then grab a pusher to complete the cut (see the photos below).

When ripping long boards, hold the end of the board in your right hand, with your left hand extended as far forward as comfortably possible. Lift the rear end of the board slightly and walk forward, keeping the board against the fence. Move right up against the saw to finish the cut.

Ripping Sheet Stock

I don't use plywood or other man-made boards very much in my work, but there are times when I need to rip sheet stock—for example, when building jigs or doing utility work around the shop. Ripping sheet stock refers to cutting pieces to width using the rip fence. The two biggest challenges when cutting sheet stock concern maneuverability and tearout. I'll talk about maneuverability first.

Feeding full-sized 4-ft. by 8-ft. sheets across a table saw can be unwieldy. It demands use of auxiliary supports or a helper because the material is often either heavy or thin and floppy. You should place sturdy auxiliary supports at almost the level of the saw's tabletop. When dealing with wide offcuts, you'll need side support as well as infeed and outfeed supports.

An extended fence can also help when cutting sheet goods by providing more bearing surface against the fence (see the illustration below). You may need to clamp down the rear end of the fence to resist the increased sideways pressure.

The thin face veneers on many sheet goods are particularly prone to tearout. You can minimize this by using the proper blade (see chapter 3). Also, a zero-clearance throat plate will provide maximum backup on the exit side of the cut (see "The Throat Plate" on p. 196). Of course, it's wise to place the "show" side of the workpiece up because the cut on the top side will be cleaner.

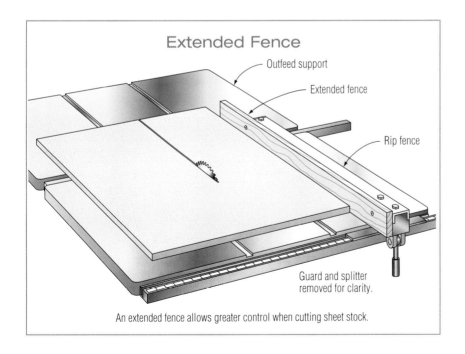

Extended Fence

Outfeed support

Extended fence

Rip fence

Guard and splitter removed for clarity.

An extended fence allows greater control when cutting sheet stock.

Ripping Sheet Goods

RIPPING FULL-SIZE SHEET GOODS can be challenging. To make it easier on yourself, use outfeed supports and approach the process as shown here.

1 Begin the process of ripping a sheet by bracing it against the front of the saw table.

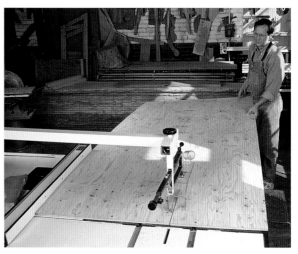

2 Standing at the rear left corner of the sheet, walk the piece forward while applying pressure diagonally against the fence in front of the blade.

3 Maintaining pressure against the fence, walk the sheet forward until the saw is bearing the entire weight of the sheet.

4 Move around to the rear of the sheet, with your right hand centered between the blade and the fence. Push straight forward to complete the cut.

The Importance of a Good Rip Fence

THE IMPORTANCE OF A GOOD RIP FENCE CANNOT BE OVERSTATED. A fence that is straight and that firmly locks parallel to the blade makes all the difference when it comes to safe, accurate, efficient ripping. Many new fence systems are available to replace old-style sheet-metal fences that tend to have bowed faces and that often don't lock parallel to the blade.

One fix for a bowed fence is to outfit it with an auxiliary fence. The auxiliary fence—made from a straight piece of plywood or straight-grained hardwood—can be bolted or clamped to the rip fence (see the illustration below). If necessary, shim behind the auxiliary fence to straighten it or square it to your saw table. A ⅛-in. by ⅛-in. rabbet along the bottom edge serves as an escape chute for chips and sawdust that might otherwise get trapped between the fence and workpiece.

Just as important as the type of fence is its proper alignment to the blade. An improperly adjusted fence invites kickback and burning of the stock. Make sure that your fence is properly adjusted before you rip any wood (see "Adjusting the Rip Fence" on p. 203).

Practice Feeding Sheet Goods

When learning to cut sheet goods, you may find that it helps to lower the blade below the table and practice feeding a sheet before making the actual cut.

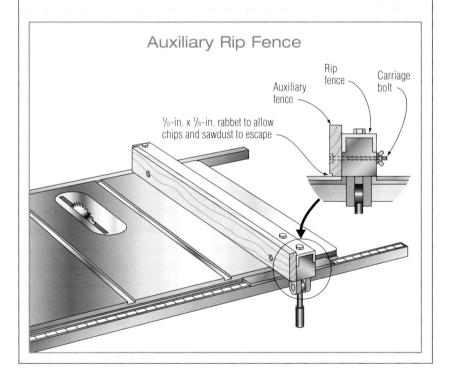

Auxiliary Rip Fence

Rip fence

Carriage bolt

Auxiliary fence

⅛-in. x ⅛-in. rabbet to allow chips and sawdust to escape

If the work is fragile (a fine laminate, for example) and you're experiencing tearout at the bottom of the cut, try making a preliminary pass with the blade set for a very shallow scoring cut. This will slice the fibers clean, and there should be no tearout when the piece is cut through. If you work a lot with sheet goods, consider using a scoring blade, as discussed on p. 156.

When cutting sheet stock, you generally stand much farther to the left of the blade than when ripping solid wood. The best place to stand to rip a panel is at its far left rear corner. From there, you can guide the piece in a straight line along the fence, pushing forward at the same time. With your left hand, grasp the left outside edge about 1 ft. from the corner. Place your right hand on the rear edge, with your arm extended (see the photos on p. 232).

Begin the cut by walking the sheet forward, maintaining pressure against the fence in front of the blade. Do not apply sideways pressure once the blade has entered the workpiece. As you approach the saw, shift your body closer to the line of cut. Position your right hand on the rear edge of the sheet between the blade and the fence. Move your left hand closer to the corner, where it will help keep the sheet against the fence in front of the blade. As the cut comes to an end, slightly reduce the forward pressure of your left hand to prevent cocking the offcut into the blade.

Cutting a 4-ft. by 8-ft. sheet can be challenging, but as long as you have auxiliary supports properly set up and you feed the work as described, you'll do fine.

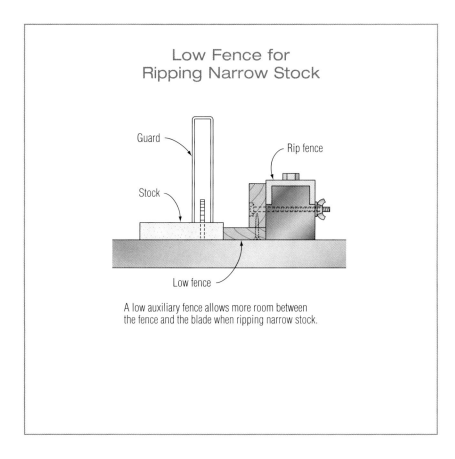

Low Fence for Ripping Narrow Stock

Guard

Rip fence

Stock

Low fence

A low auxiliary fence allows more room between the fence and the blade when ripping narrow stock.

Ripping Narrow Stock

The difficulty in ripping narrow stock is the fence's proximity to the blade and blade cover. When ripping very narrow stock, there is very little space between the fence and the blade cover in which to manipulate a pusher, and many blade covers impede the process.

As a result, many woodworkers remove the blade cover and splitter to rip narrow pieces. However, it's a dangerous mistake to work without the protection of these devices. There are safe ways to rip narrow stock with the cover and splitter in place.

First, if the piece you need is at least 2 in. wide, you can attach an L-shaped auxiliary fence to your rip fence (see the illustration on the facing page). The additional space that the fence provides allows more room for your hand and pusher.

You can also make a simple jig for ripping workpieces that are less than 2 in. wide. The jig is nothing more than a straight piece of wood with a handle on top and a stop on the side (see the illustration below). This jig works well for pieces that aren't very long, because the jig needs to be almost as long as the stock being cut. To use the jig, place the stock against the edge of the jig and the stop at its end. Hold the jig's handle in your right hand while using a pusher in your left hand to steady the

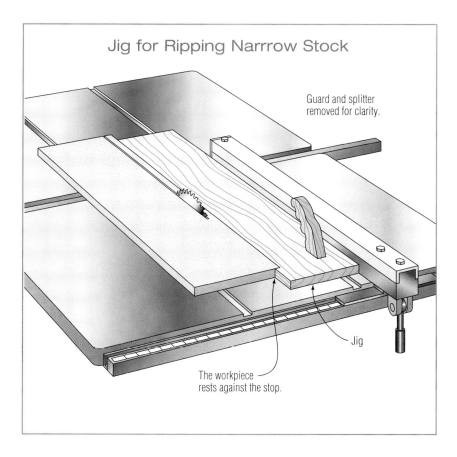

Jig for Ripping Narrrow Stock

Guard and splitter removed for clarity.

Jig

The workpiece rests against the stop.

workpiece against the jig. When ripping very narrow pieces, use a zero-clearance throat insert to prevent the rippings from falling into the blade opening (see the sidebar on p. 197).

A third alternative is to use a box-style blade cover such as the Brett-Guard (see the photo on p. 160). Unlike basket-style covers, the underside of one edge of the Brett-Guard is scalloped, so the blade can be set right at the edge of the cover for ripping narrow stock. By using a pusher that is thinner than the space between the blade and the fence, you can rip stock as thin as ⅛ in.

One final way to safely rip narrow stock is to saw it from the outer edge of the stock, rather than from the edge that rides against the fence. This technique doesn't work well for multiples of the same size though, since it requires resetting the fence for every cut.

Ripping Short Pieces

Trying to rip a short piece of wood is asking for trouble because the wood may not reach the splitter or riving knife before the end of the cut, so it can be easily thrown. Ideally, short pieces should be cut to length from longer rippings, but that's not always practical. The best way that I've found to safely rip short pieces is with a cutoff box, using a hold-down (see the photo below).

If it's not practical to rip short pieces from longer rippings, secure the short pieces in a crosscut sled using a hold-down.

Ripping Thin Stock

Ripping stock that is ⅛ in. thick or less requires a pusher with a shallow heel and a sole that is long enough to keep the piece from lifting up onto the blade as it is being cut. Some people use featherboards or safety wheels to hold down the workpieces, but I find that they just get in the way. An appropriate pusher will hold the work flat for the entirety of the cut.

If your rip fence doesn't closely meet the saw table, the workpiece can creep under it. To prevent that, attach an auxiliary fence that sits tightly against the table. Outfeed support also helps when handling thin, floppy material.

Ripping Thick Stock

The thicker the workpiece, the harder the saw has to work to cut through it. When ripping thick stock, use a 24-tooth FTG blade, as discussed in chapter 3. As you cut, listen to the saw motor and adjust your feed rate accordingly. As with other ripping operations, feed the stock as quickly as possible without bogging down the motor. If you encounter stiff resistance even when using a sharp FTG blade, try using a thin-kerf blade, which cuts easier because it's removing less wood.

If the workpiece is thicker than the cutting capacity of the blade, make one cut from one side, then flip the board over to complete the cut (see the photos on p. 238). Pay careful attention to feed speed when making the first cut. Because the blade is totally buried in the wood, chip ejection is less efficient and the blade can run hotter. Make the cut as quickly as possible without taxing the motor.

Standing at Ease

MY FIRST SHOP HAD A CONCRETE FLOOR, and it didn't take too many hours of standing to appreciate the relief that a rubber mat afforded. Although I'm fortunate to have wood shop floors now, I still stand on a rubber mat at the table saw, as well as at other machines. These mats greatly reduce leg fatigue and provide a nonslip surface among the sawdust and shavings on the floor. (For suppliers of rubber mats, see Sources on p. 379.)

A good pair of shoes also goes a long way toward keeping your legs and feet from developing problems. When standing in one place for long periods, worn-out or cheaply made shoes can be a real pain.

In addition to standing on a mat and wearing good shoes, it sometimes helps to adjust your vertical position at the saw for more comfort. For example, when cutting a lot of finger joints, I've found that standing on a low plywood platform helps reduce leg fatigue by raising me up to a more comfortable position for this tedious operation.

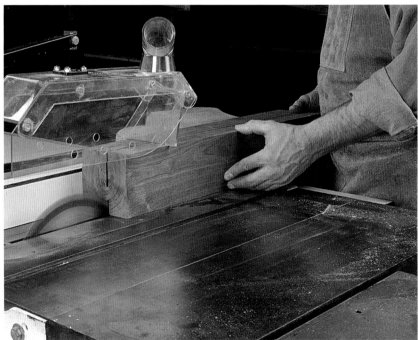

If the thickness of a workpiece exceeds the capacity of your blade, rip the piece in two opposing passes. To prevent kickback, I use a Delta Disappearing Splitter with the fingers removed. Instead, you could use a shopmade splitter. To make the second cut, flip the board end-for-end, raising the blade only as much as necessary.

Resawing

Resawing means sawing a piece of work on edge to yield two or more thinner pieces. Sometimes woodworkers will resaw by making opposing cuts into the edges of a workpiece, as described on p. 237. This is very dangerous because the buried blade can overheat or bind, a blade cover can't be used, and balancing the workpiece can be awkward. Because of the dangers involved, I strongly discourage resawing on a table saw. Use a bandsaw instead.

Ripping Angles

There are times when you need to rip a board at an angle—that is, not parallel to the edge of a workpiece. Cutting tapered legs is a common example of this. There are also times when you may want the grain on a board angled in a particular way for appearance or strength. Sometimes, you may need to make an angled cut to avoid a bow or defect in a plank, or you may be able to get more yield from a board by ripping it at an angle.

To rip a board at an angle, secure it with hold-downs to a sled that either rides in the saw's miter-gauge slots (see the photo below) or against the rip fence. The hold-downs are adjustable across the sled's width, allowing you to hold work safely at almost any angle.

Rip in One Pass if Possible

When you are ripping thick stock, it may be tempting to make a series of shallow, multiple passes. However, this is not a good idea because the workpiece can distort in the process, yielding a bad cut.

Tapers can be cut safely using a sled with adjustable hold-downs.

Always rip bevels with the blade tilted away from the fence and the finished workpiece (not the offcut) riding against the fence. For right-tilt saws, the fence will usually have to be positioned to the left of the blade.

Ripping Bevels

Sawing a bevel along the grain is similar to standard ripping except that the blade is tilted at an angle other than 90 degrees. To avoid kickback and burning and to get the cleanest cut possible, be sure to angle the blade away from the fence and use a splitter or riving knife. The cut piece you want to save should always ride along the fence, with the beveled edge above the tilted blade (see the photo above). If you trap it under the blade and against the fence, it can burn and kick back. Most table saws tilt to the right, meaning you'll need to work with the fence on the left side of the blade.

Crosscutting

Crosscutting means sawing wood to length across the grain. Wood is generally crosscut after it has been ripped to width. The workpiece is fed crosswise into the blade, guided by a miter gauge, crosscut sled, or sliding table.

For the most part, crosscutting is a less dangerous operation than ripping. Since the workpiece isn't confined between the blade and the fence, there is little danger of it kicking back. With miter-gauge cutting, the danger lies with the offcut that's left near the blade, where it's prone to be thrown. As with ripping, the splitter and blade guard are important safeguards.

Guiding the Workpiece

Just as the rip fence is necessary to guide a workpiece when ripping, you'll need a safe and accurate method of guiding a workpiece when crosscutting. The two most common accessories for crosscutting are the miter gauge and the crosscut sled. In this section, I'll discuss how to best modify a stock miter gauge for effective crosscutting and how to make a crosscut sled. I'll also address crosscutting with a sliding or rolling table.

MITER GAUGES

The miter gauge is guided by a metal bar that slides in slots machined in the table-saw top parallel to the sawblade. The body of the gauge, which

One of the best ways to crosscut a board to length is to use a crosscut sled that slides in your saw's miter-gauge slots. The sled is much more stable and accurate than a stock miter gauge.

can be set to any angle from 30 degrees to 90 degrees, guides the workpiece as it's pushed through the blade.

For most crosscutting operations, I find the stock miter gauge inaccurate and awkward because of its small body and single guide bar. The truth is, I hardly ever use a miter gauge. However, if you do, the best improvement you can make to your stock miter gauge is to add an auxiliary fence, which will provide an increased bearing surface for the workpiece, stabilizing it during the cut (see the top sidebar on the facing page).

One safety problem when using a miter gauge is that small offcuts tend to gather around the sawblade as you make repeated cuts. These pieces can be easily thrown if they contact the spinning blade. If the offcuts are very thin, they can also wedge into the throat-plate opening, catching the workpiece and possibly lifting the throat plate in the process. The best solution here is to use a splitter or riving knife and a zero-clearance throat plate. Additionally, you can make an auxiliary fence that extends past the sawblade to support the pieces and carry them past the danger zone (see

Making an Auxiliary Miter-Gauge Fence

MAKE YOUR AUXILIARY FENCE FROM ¾-IN.-THICK, stable, straight-grained stock with two parallel faces. The fence can be any length, but 24 in. seems to work fine for most operations. As with any auxiliary fence, cut a ⅛-in. by ⅛-in. rabbet along its bottom edge as a clearance chute for sawdust and chips.

A piece of sandpaper attached to the fence face with contact cement will help prevent the workpiece from slipping. This is particularly useful when making miter cuts, which tend to push the workpiece away from the blade.

Screw the auxiliary fence to the miter gauge through two predrilled holes in the miter-gauge body. Position the fence on the gauge so that the first cut will trim off the end of the fence. That way, you can use the end of the fence as a reference for cutlines.

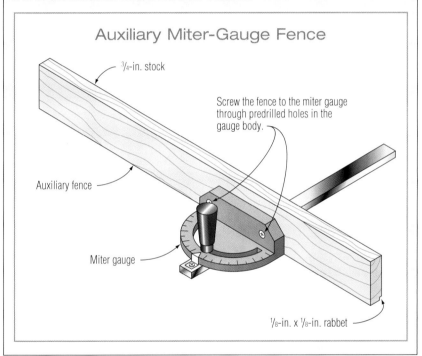

Auxiliary Miter-Gauge Fence

¾-in. stock

Screw the fence to the miter gauge through predrilled holes in the gauge body.

Auxiliary fence

Miter gauge

⅛-in. x ⅛-in. rabbet

Replacement Miter Gauges

THE INADEQUACIES OF STANDARD MITER GAUGES have led to the development of a number of aftermarket replacement miter gauges. Most of these gauges, which range in price from about $50 to $150, have a long body to provide greater support for the workpiece. The fence is typically an aluminum extrusion, which is adjustable to provide support right up to the blade at any angle. Some systems have adjustable drop-stops that make setting up for repetitive crosscutting easier and more efficient. Many of these features are standard on miter gauges that come with some European table saws.

An auxiliary fence that extends past the blade will push cutoffs past the blade so they can't be thrown at the operator. Sandpaper attached to the fence prevents workpiece slippage.

the photo above). To prevent cutting off the end of the fence, you'll need to make the fence taller than the workpiece being cut.

CROSSCUT SLEDS

Years ago, after I struggled with large workpieces supported only by an auxiliary fence on my miter gauge, it dawned on me that there had to be a better way to make accurate crosscuts. And so was born the first of my crosscut sleds.

A crosscut sled is basically a panel with runners that slide in the table saw's miter-gauge slots. A fence on the operator's side of the panel guides the workpiece. A rail at the rear simply serves to hold the two halves of the sled together there. For safety, a clear Lexan blade cover fits between the fence and rear rail, and a rear exit guard covers the blade where it exits the fence. You'll be thrilled at how easily and accurately you can cut workpieces using a crosscut sled.

It's not difficult to make a crosscut sled (see the sidebar on pp. 246–247). My first sled was made primarily to handle wide workpieces such as tabletops and chest sides. However, much crosscutting and joinery done at the table saw involves fairly narrow pieces, so you can make scaled-down sleds, which are easier to handle.

A sliding table—like the one on this DeWalt® 746 saw—allows easy, accurate crosscutting of long, wide, or heavy workpieces.

A number of crosscut sleds are available commercially if you choose not to make one. These sleds include a variety of features including drop-stops and adjustable fences that can be angled for miter cuts (see Sources on p. 379).

SLIDING TABLES

These days, I do all of my crosscutting—particularly of larger pieces—using the sliding table on my European table saw. A sliding table allows accurate, safe, effortless crosscutting because it is solid, precisely machined, and it nestles right up to the sawblade (see the photo above). A sliding table, which is integral to the saw itself, should not be confused with aftermarket rolling tables, which I'll discuss in the next section.

A sliding table is particularly useful when it comes to crosscutting sheet goods and other wide panels, but it's also great for crosscutting long, thick stock. The fence on a sliding table can easily be adjusted to any angle for sawing miters or compound bevels on the ends of workpieces. Many fences include drop-stops for convenient repetitive cutting.

ROLLING TABLES

For woodworkers who are looking to expand the crosscutting capacity of their existing saws, rolling tables are available as aftermarket add-ons (see

A CROSSCUT SLED MUST BE MADE OF STABLE MATERIALS. I made mine from high-quality, nine-ply, ½-in.-thick Baltic birch plywood. Although the mid-sized box shown in the illustration on the facing page was made for my Delta Unisaw, the design can easily be adapted to any table size and any size workpiece. The sled's accuracy depends on alignment. Your saw's miter-gauge slots must be parallel to the saw-blade, and the sled's fence must be perpendicular to the blade's line of cut.

Cutting the Parts

Cut out the sled's components to the sizes indicated in the illustration or to fit your own saw. The base should be 1 in. wider than the saw table; the fence and rear rail should match the length of the base.

Laminate the 1-in.-thick fence and rear rail from two pieces of plywood. Joint their bottom edges square, and saw a ⅛-in. by ⅛-in. rabbet along the inside bottom face of the fence for sawdust and chip clearance. On the inner face of the fence and rear rail, cut ¼-in. by ¼-in. dadoes to receive the ends of the blade cover. Next, bandsaw the fence and rear rail to the dimensions given in the illustration, proportioning yours to suit your saw table. The fence is higher in the center for holding workpieces vertically when necessary. The ends of the fence are lower for clamping pieces to the sled.

Make the runners from a hard, stable material such as plastic or metal. Rip the runners to fit snugly side-to-side in the miter-gauge slots, but make them a bit thinner than the depth of the slots so the base sits flat on the table.

Attaching the Base to the Runners

Insert the runners into their slots and place the base on top of them with its front end aligned with the front edge of the saw table and its left edge extending 1 in. beyond the saw table. Mark the base over the centerline of each runner, then drill pilot holes and countersink for #8 x ¾-in. flathead screws about every 4 in.

If the base doesn't glide freely, remove it from the table and take down any high spots on the runners using a scraper or a rabbet plane. When the sled glides well, wax the runners and the underside of the base to reduce friction.

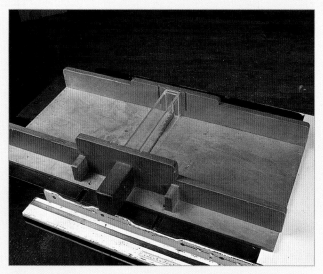

A crosscut sled is a great improvement over a miter gauge in terms of both safety and performance. This sled includes a clear polycarbonate blade cover that can be lifted onto the workpiece before making a cut.

Attaching the Rear Rail and Fence

Fasten the rear rail to the base using #10 x 2-in. flat-head screws spaced about 3 in. apart. Avoid the blade-cover dadoes and the blade path. The rear rail doesn't need to be exactly square to the blade because it's not used as a fence. Next, slide the assembly into its slots and cut a kerf through the base, stopping a few inches short of the front.

For your sled to be accurate, the fence must be absolutely straight, flat, and square to the blade. Use a square to check that the face of the fence is square to the base. If it isn't, joint the bottom edge of the fence and recut the rabbet if necessary.

Squaring the fence to the saw kerf isn't difficult, but it can take some patience. First, mark the position of the fence, setting it about 2½ in. in from the front edge of the base. Next, with the fence removed, turn the base upside down and drill and countersink a screw-clearance hole at the right- and left-hand ends of the fence location. Slightly elongate the left-hand countersink and hole, which will allow you to pivot the fence a bit to adjust its angle later.

Place the sled runners in their grooves so that the front edge of the sled overhangs the table saw. Align the fence to its positioning marks, and lightly clamp it to the base. Using an accurate square, adjust the fence perpendicular to the kerf in the base, then

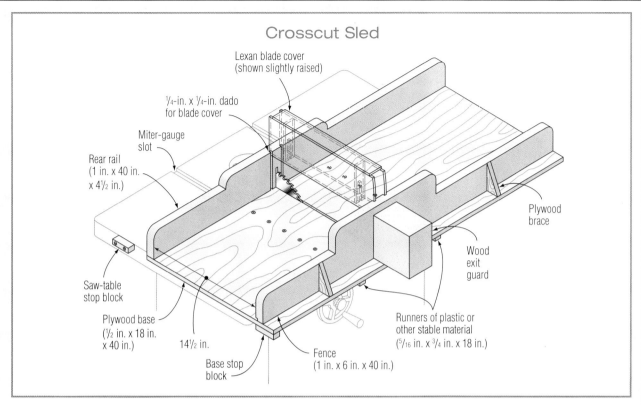

Crosscut Sled

Lexan blade cover
(shown slightly raised)

$\frac{1}{4}$-in. x $\frac{1}{4}$-in. dado
for blade cover

Miter-gauge
slot

Rear rail
(1 in. x 40 in.
x 4$\frac{1}{2}$ in.)

Plywood
brace

Wood
exit
guard

Saw-table
stop block

Plywood base
($\frac{1}{2}$ in. x 18 in.
x 40 in.)

14$\frac{1}{2}$ in.

Base stop
block

Fence
(1 in. x 6 in. x 40 in.)

Runners of plastic or
other stable material
($\frac{5}{16}$ in. x $\frac{3}{4}$ in. x 18 in.)

tighten the clamps and drive screws through the base into the fence. Now crosscut a wide piece of scrap using the sled.

Afterward, flip one piece over, then butt the ends of the two pieces together with their edges against the fence to check the cut for square as when testing the squareness of the blade to the table (see the top illustration on p. 193). If the fence needs adjustment, loosen the screw in the elongated hole, adjust the fence angle, and recut and check the test piece again. When the cut is square, fix the fence in place with screws spaced about 3 in. apart.

Triangular plywood braces help keep the fence rigid and square to the base. Glue and clamp them about 8 in. in from the ends of the sled to allow clamping space for attaching an extension fence for repetitive crosscutting.

Making the Blade Cover and Stop Blocks

The blade cover for the crosscut sled is a necessity. It protects your fingers and shields you from offcuts and sawdust thrown by the blade. I made my cover from $\frac{1}{4}$-in.-thick Lexan, an impact-resistant polycarbonate,

but you could also use a clear acrylic plastic like Plexiglas®. Cut the parts to size on the table saw and assemble them using a suitable adhesive. Check your local phone directory for plastics suppliers, who can supply you with material and the necessary solvent.

After assembly, sand a slight crown on the ends of the cover to allow it to move up and down easily in the sled's fence and rear rail dadoes.

Because the blade passes through the fence for all crosscuts, make a solid-wood exit guard to protect your fingers. The guard should be at least 2 in. thick and at least $\frac{1}{4}$ in. taller than the blade at maximum height. It should also extend at least 1 in. past the fully raised blade when top dead center of the blade intersects the face of the fence. Glue and clamp the guard to the sled with the long-grain surface against the fence.

Fasten the stop blocks to the base and the saw table as shown to prevent sawing through the exit guard. The saw-table stop block should stop the sled when top dead center of the blade meets the face of the fence.

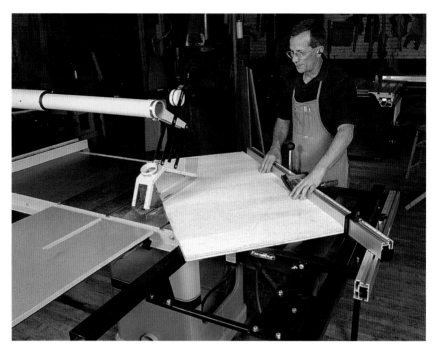

An aftermarket sliding, or rolling, table attaches to the side of a saw, providing increased crosscutting capacity. Although these rolling tables make handling large stock much easier, they are not as accurate as an integral sliding table that comes right up to the sawblade.

the photo above). Often referred to as sliding tables, these attachments might be more properly called rolling tables because their mechanisms are significantly different from those used on integral sliding tables.

As opposed to an integral sliding table, a rolling table typically attaches to the left side of a saw table, leaving some distance between the blade and the table, somewhat affecting accuracy and workpiece drag. Although a rolling table is not as accurate or solid as an integral sliding table, it is a big improvement over a miter gauge, especially for long or wide workpieces.

Like the fence on an integral sliding table, the fence on a rolling table can easily be adjusted to any angle for sawing miters or compound bevels on the ends of workpieces. All rolling-table fences include drop-stops for convenient repetitive cutting.

Basic Crosscutting Techniques

Although I do most of my crosscutting on a sliding table these days, I'll describe techniques for using a miter gauge as well as a crosscut sled. A crosscut sled is an immense improvement over a miter gauge, and I strongly recommend that you make or purchase one.

SETTING UP FOR THE CUT

Mount the appropriate blade on your saw. For most crosscutting, except sawing plywood, use a high-quality 40- to 60-tooth ATB blade. Set the blade height as described on p. 225. Move your rip fence to the outer end of the table or remove it from the table entirely so it won't interfere with the cut or cause offcuts to gather near the blade. Never use the rip fence itself as a stop block—the offcut may wedge between the blade and the fence, causing kickback. Remember to wear safety glasses and ear protection.

When cutting with a miter gauge, hold the workpiece against its fence, aligning the cutline on the workpiece with the edges of the teeth on the appropriate side of the blade. If you're using a miter gauge with an auxiliary fence that extends right up to the blade, you can align the cutline with the end of the fence. Or you could mark the table in line with the blade, then align your cutline to that. However, after a little practice, you should have no trouble simply sighting across the cutline to the blade.

When using a crosscut sled, a stock blade guard would get in the way, so I outfitted my crosscut sled with a custom guard (see the sidebar on pp. 246–247). I lift the guard up, align my cutline with the kerf in my sled base, then rest the guard on the workpiece.

MAKING THE CUT

When you're ready to cut, stand to the same side of the blade as the miter gauge. If you're using a crosscut sled, stand to the side of the blade opposite the offcut. This position is safer and makes for easier pushing. Turn on the saw and allow the blade to reach full speed.

If you are using a miter gauge, use one hand to hold the workpiece against the fence while the other hand pushes the gauge forward into the blade. Don't be tempted to hold the offcut half of the workpiece—a dangerous move. When using a crosscut sled, hold the workpiece against the fence with one hand while making sure to keep your other hand out of the path of the blade.

Feed the workpiece into the blade at a steady, continuous speed. Crosscutting offers less resistance than ripping, so the tendency is to feed the work quickly. However, the proper feed speed depends on the thickness and density of the material being cut. When crosscutting, you should generally feed a workpiece a bit slower than you would when ripping the same piece of wood. When the cut is complete, return the workpiece and fence to their starting point. Slide the wood slightly away from the blade on the return stroke to avoid touching the blade.

Even if your miter gauge is set square to the blade, it's wise to check the sawn end with a square. Sometimes inconsistent feed pressure can cause the workpiece to veer just a bit from a straight line.

Make Sure End Is Square

When crosscutting stock to length, first square one end of the workpiece. The temptation here is to trim off only 1/16 in. or so, or just enough to square up the end. The problem is that if the blade is cutting only on one side, it can deflect, cutting the end out of square. It's best to cut in far enough from the end to leave a fully sawn offcut.

Repetitive Crosscutting

Making repetitive cuts to the same length is a common practice in wood-working. There are several ways to approach this on a table saw. Most setups involve employing a stop block set at the desired distance from the blade, eliminating the need for marking cutlines on individual pieces and ensuring pieces of exactly the same length.

Remember that the first step in cutting a workpiece to finished length is to saw one end square. This will be the end that abuts the stop block for the finished cut. One approach to cutting repetitive pieces is to first cut one end square on every piece. Next, fix a stop block to your miter-gauge auxiliary fence or sled fence and saw the pieces to final length while butted against the stop. The problem with this approach is that it involves handling every piece twice. There are better methods.

USING POSITIONING STOP BLOCKS

One method is to use a long, L-shaped stop block that sits well forward of the blade and simply positions the workpiece on the miter-gauge fence for the final cut. The first step is to cut one end of a workpiece square, disregarding the stop block, which is clamped in place but out of the way. Next, turn the workpiece end-for-end, butt the squared end against the stop block, then push the workpiece forward into the blade (see the photo below).

One way to make repetitive cuts for longer pieces is to position the workpiece on the miter-gauge fence using a long L-shaped stop block. First, crosscut one end of a workpiece square without using the stop, then butt the squared end against the stop before pushing the workpiece into the blade for the second cut.

Repetitive cuts can be made by clamping a thick positioning block to the rip fence well in front of the blade.

A drop-stop allows easy, accurate repetitive crosscutting. First, one end of a workpiece is squared with the stop flipped up out of thc way. Then the stop is dropped down in place for cutting pieces to final length, as shown here.

An alternative approach is to clamp a positioning stop to the rip fence well in front of the blade (see the top photo). Make sure the stop is thick enough to allow plenty of room between the end of the workpiece and the fence to prevent trapping the cut piece in a small space between the fence and the blade.

The disadvantage to using positioning blocks is that the workpiece can slip as you feed it forward. Unless you hold it very firmly during its travel, you can end up with miscuts. When cutting multiples, I've never hit 100 percent accuracy with this method. A better approach is to use drop-stops.

USING DROP-STOPS

A drop-stop provides the advantage of being able to flip a stop up out of the way when necessary without moving the stop's position on the fence. This way, you can flip the stop up to make the initial squaring cut on a piece of stock, then drop it down to make the final cut. When down, the stop holds the workpiece in position against the fence, making for very accurate cuts (see the bottom photo on p. 251).

Drop-stops are available commercially for attachment to an auxiliary miter-gauge fence or crosscut sled (see Sources on p. 379). Many after-market miter gauges come equipped with drop-stops, as do the fences on most sliding and rolling tables.

USING A CROSSCUT SLED

When using a crosscut sled for repetitive cuts, you don't necessarily need a drop-stop. Instead, you can clamp a fixed stop block to the fence at the proper distance from the blade, then make your initial squaring cut with the workpiece riding on the opposite end of the sled (see the photo below left). Afterward, slide the workpiece against the stop to make the final cut (see the photo below right). The stop block should be notched at the bottom to provide clearance for chips and dust.

For repetitive crosscutting using a crosscut sled, first square one end of the workpiece from the right side of the sled.

Next, slide the workpiece over against the stop block to crosscut it squarely to final length.

For repetitive cutting of pieces that are longer than the sled fence, clamp an extension board to the fence, then clamp a stop block to the extension board.

To cut pieces that are longer than the sled fence, you can mount a stop block to an extension fence that's clamped to the sled fence (see the photo above). Make your fence extension from a light, stable wood such as poplar or mahogany. The extension should be thick enough to prevent flex and tall enough to clamp to the fence above the workpiece.

Crosscutting Wide Panels

Accurate crosscutting of wide panels requires some form of solid support to carry the workpiece through the blade. A miter gauge is out of the question in a lot of cases because the operation is too awkward. A sliding table is the best option, but if you don't have one, a crosscut sled will really shine here too.

The procedure is basically the same as for standard crosscutting but with a larger sled. With the guard in place, square off one end of the panel, mark it for length, then align your cutline to the kerf in your sled to make the final cut. On very wide work, I sometimes start the cut by raising the spinning blade up into the workpiece. This can be safer than suspending a large sled in front of the saw in order to begin the cut in front of a raised blade.

If your workpiece is both wide and long (such as a large tabletop or case side), you may need an auxiliary stand or table to the side of the saw

Crosscut very short workpieces using a crosscut sled and a wooden hold-down.

You can crosscut wide panels using a large sled. A wood block clamped to the fence holds long boards down against the base of the sled.

to support the overhanging panel. When the overhang isn't too great, my preferred method is to clamp a thick block of wood to the sled fence to keep the workpiece from lifting (see the top photo).

You'll also need some form of outfeed support to carry the sled as it leaves the rear of the table. Although you can use an auxiliary stand or boards clamped to sawhorses, the best solution is an outfeed table. Mine has grooves that line up with the miter-gauge slots in the saw table (see the photo on p. 218).

Crosscutting Short Pieces

Crosscutting short pieces on the table saw can be dangerous because it can place your fingers too close to the blade. The safest way to crosscut short pieces is with a crosscut sled. Use a wooden hold-down to secure the workpiece down and against the fence, and make the cut with the blade cover in place (see the botom photo on the facing page).

You could also cut short pieces using a hold-down against your miter-gauge auxiliary fence, but the guard can't be used for this operation, and a small piece is more difficult to handle like this. One other option, of course, is to cut short pieces to length using a handsaw at your workbench.

Crosscutting Bevels

Bevel crosscuts, sometimes called end miters, are produced by crosscutting a board with the sawblade tilted at an angle other than 90 degrees. This is a joinery cut that I typically use only for joining molding, although it can also be used for deep picture frames and cases with mitered corners. Because the face of the bevel is basically end grain, the joint needs reinforcement with a spline or biscuits for strength.

To make a bevel crosscut, tilt the blade to the desired angle (usually 45 degrees) and check the setting with a bevel gauge or drafting triangle. For the cleanest cut, set up the workpiece so that the offcut ends up below the blade (see the illustration below).

You can use a miter gauge to crosscut bevels, but for the sake of accuracy, I use a small crosscut sled with a wide blade slot for cutting dadoes and bevels. (I don't use this sled for cutting 90-degree angles because offcuts can drop into the opening unless it's covered with a sheet of thin plywood.)

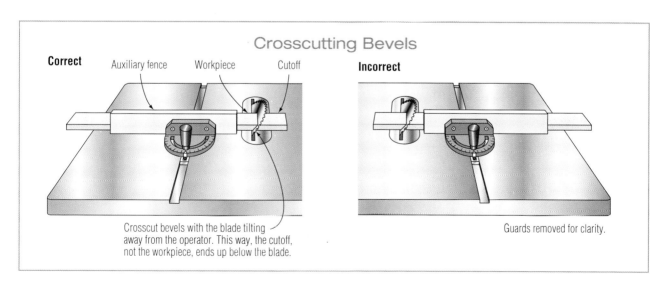

Crosscutting Bevels

Correct — Auxiliary fence — Workpiece — Cutoff

Incorrect

Crosscut bevels with the blade tilting away from the operator. This way, the cutoff, not the workpiece, ends up below the blade.

Guards removed for clarity.

Crosscutting Miters

Miters are produced by feeding the workpiece into the blade at an angle other than 90 degrees. When the sawblade is set at 90 degrees to the table, the cut is called a face miter or flat miter. When the sawblade is set at an angle other than 90 degrees, the cut becomes a compound miter. Miter cuts are made primarily for joinery work.

When cutting miters with a miter gauge, use an auxiliary fence and a stop block.

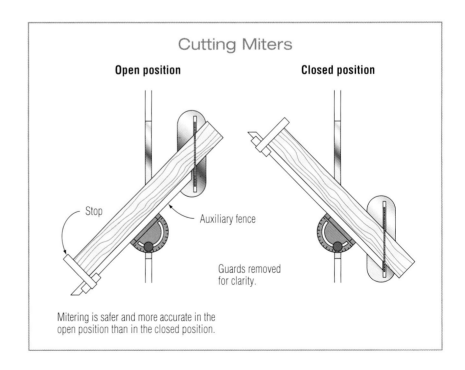

Cutting Miters

Open position   **Closed position**

Stop

Auxiliary fence

Guards removed for clarity.

Mitering is safer and more accurate in the open position than in the closed position.

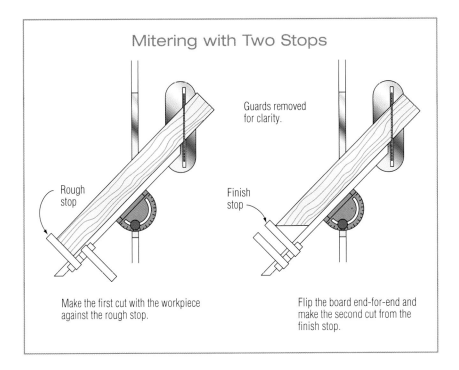

Mitering with Two Stops

Guards removed for clarity.

Rough stop

Finish stop

Make the first cut with the workpiece against the rough stop.

Flip the board end-for-end and make the second cut from the finish stop.

USING A MITER GAUGE

There are a number of ways to set the angle of the miter gauge for making miter cuts. One is to use a bevel gauge or drafting triangle to set the required angle between the miter-gauge body and bar. Another way is to scribe the angle on the workpiece, then turn the gauge upside down onto the workpiece and set the angle to the scribe mark. A third method is to use the stops or angle markings on the miter gauge. Whatever method you use, test your setup using a piece of scrap first.

The miter gauge can be set in either the open or closed position (see the illustration on the facing page). I was taught to use the closed position because it allows you to stand more to the side of the blade and the cut is smoother because of the grain orientation. However, the workpiece is more likely to creep in this position and your hands get closer to the blade as the angle increases. I find that using the open position with an auxiliary fence and stop block yields better results (see the photo on the facing page). Glue sandpaper to the fence to help keep the workpiece from slipping.

Most miter cutting involves making frames, with multiple pairs of workpieces cut to the same length. Unless your workpieces have already been cut to finished length, or at least squared on one end, you will need two stops for the following procedure. (Alternatively, you could miter one end of each workpiece first without using a stop, then miter the opposite end using a stop.)

To cut a workpiece, first miter one end square with the piece butted against a rough stop. Next, flip the piece end-for-end and make the second

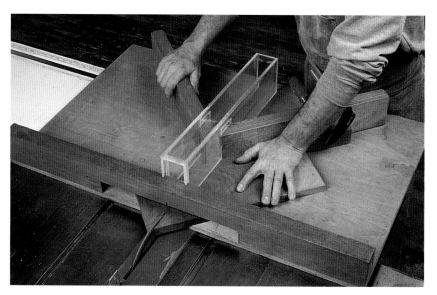

The best way to cut 45-degree miters is to use a crosscut sled with two fences that are perpendicular to each other and angled at 45 degrees to the blade. A cutout in the sled's rear rail allows you to miter wide workpieces.

cut with the piece against a finish stop (see the illustration on p. 257). Make sure the stop is wider than the workpiece so the tip of the miter will contact it. Since most frames are rectangular, you'll need two setups: one for the long sides and one for the short sides.

USING A CROSSCUT SLED

I find that the miter gauge is inaccurate for cutting miters—joints that leave little room for error. Instead, I use a simple shopmade crosscut sled for that purpose. For those rare occasions when I need to cut an angle other than 45 degrees, I either fiddle with the miter gauge until I get the cuts right or I add a spacer or hold-down to my crosscut sled to hold the workpiece at the correct angle.

My 45-degree crosscut sled works basically the same as my 90-degree crosscut sled except that two fences—set at 45 degrees to the blade and perpendicular to each other—support the workpiece (see the photo above). Opposing miters are cut using the opposing fences. That way, as long as the fences are at 90 degrees to each other, the joint will be at 90 degrees even if both mating miters are slightly off of 45 degrees. For long pieces, you can extend the fences to accommodate stop blocks. For wide stock, simply make a cutout in the rear rail. Of course, you can fit a sled with fences to cut any angle.

A miter sled is a good approach to cutting angles, but if you cut a lot of varying angles in your regular work, I strongly recommend getting a sliding compound miter saw. These saws, which are specifically designed for cutting miters, are available in a wide variety of sizes and prices.

Bandsaw Features and Options

Before you buy or use a bandsaw, it's helpful to understand how the machine is put together. Knowing what makes a bandsaw work will make it easier for you to undertake small repairs and give your saw the occasional tweaking it needs to keep it running smoothly. And if you haven't yet bought a saw, knowing what features and options are available will prepare you to make a wise purchase.

Frames

The most important part of any bandsaw is the frame. It supports all the major components of the machine, including the wheels, table, guides, and sometimes the motor. The frame must be rigid enough to resist flexing or bending when the blade is fully tensioned. If the frame is not rigid, it will be impossible to get the blade tight enough to do some operations such as resawing. If you plan to do a lot of resawing, you'll especially appreciate a rigid frame. Although bandsaw designs vary widely, there are essentially only three types of frames: two-piece cast iron, one-piece cast iron (or sometimes aluminum), and the welded steel box.

Cast-iron frames

For more than a hundred years, manufacturers have used cast iron for bandsaw frames and for good reason. Cast iron is strong enough to handle the stress from a fully tensioned blade, and it's great at absorbing vibration. If you've ever stepped up to an old 36-in. Tannewitz bandsaw while it's running, then you already know what I'm talking about (see

Weighing well over a ton, this 36-in. Tannewitz industrial bandsaw has a cast-iron frame that's rigid enough to tension wide blades and heavy enough to dampen vibration.

the photo above). The machine's massive, curved gooseneck frame rises gracefully from the base to provide rigid support for even the widest blades. This iron giant weighs a ton and a half, enough to dampen any vibration from the drivetrain or blade. In contrast, a lightweight bandsaw may vibrate so badly that you'll have difficulty following your layout line.

But you don't have to buy an industrial saw to get a cast-iron frame. Many of today's consumer-grade saws also have

iron frames. The frame is typically cast in two pieces—a base supporting the table, lower wheel, and lower guides, and a column supporting the upper wheel and upper guides. The two castings fasten together at the base of the column. This two-piece frame design allows you to easily increase the saw's cutting height by adding an accessory extension block, which is bolted in the column between the two pieces. The extension block raises the guidepost height by about 6 in. When you buy the block, you also get longer guards and an extended guidepost to support the upper guide. Keep in mind that you'll have to buy longer blades and you may need to buy a motor with more horsepower.

There is another kind of cast-iron frame used primarily on inexpensive bandsaws. Some manufacturers use this design for saws in the 14-in. to 16-in. range, but most saws of this type are smaller and sometimes cast in aluminum. The frame and wheel covers are cast to form a one-piece structure. To achieve rigidity, the casting is heavily ribbed (see the photo at right on the facing page). This design isn't used on large floor-model bandsaws because it just isn't rigid enough for heavy resawing. Because most bandsaws of this type lack the power and capacity for all but the smallest work, many woodworkers who buy a small benchtop saw of this design soon outgrow its limited capabilities.

Even though having a cast-iron frame has definite advantages, it isn't an ironclad guarantee of a smooth-running saw. Nor

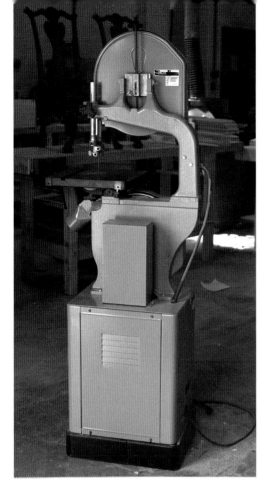

The joint between the two parts of the cast-iron frame of this 14-in. bandsaw is just below the level of the table. A riser block can be bolted between the two pieces to double the resaw height.

Many smaller bandsaws use a one-piece cast frame. This aluminum frame has ribs cast into it to increase strength and stiffness.

is cast iron really necessary. A strong, rigid bandsaw can be made using sheet steel folded and welded to make a box-type frame.

Steel box frames

In the long history of the bandsaw, the idea of using a steel frame is a relatively new one. But the idea has caught on, as steel-frame bandsaws are steadily gaining popularity among woodworkers. To make a steel frame, manufacturers fold and weld sheets of heavy-gauge steel to make a rigid box. A steel-frame bandsaw is considerably less expensive to build than a cast-iron bandsaw of the same size. As a result, many woodworkers are discovering that they can afford the large bandsaw they've always wanted.

Cast iron is excellent at absorbing vibration, while steel transmits energy rather than absorbing it. So how do manufacturers make steel-frame saws that run smoothly? The key is balance. To run

A bandsaw with a welded steel frame, like this European-made model, is stiff and strong as well as being lightweight and moderately priced. Note the plywood platform to bring the table height to a comfortable level.

Wheel diameter and blades

Many manufacturers recommend that their blades not be used on wheels with diameters of less than 12 in. The greater the wheel diameter, the less likely the blade is to get brittle and work-hardened by the severe flexing it undergoes as it spins around a small-diameter wheel.

vibration-free, all of the rotating parts (the wheels and pulleys) are extremely well balanced. There are other items that factor into the balancing equation, such as motors, tires, and V-belts. But the bottom line is that manufacturing has dramatically improved since the days when all bandsaw frames were huge and cast from iron. Today, expensive cast iron is not necessary as long as vibration is kept to a minimum.

Wheels and Covers

The blade on a bandsaw wraps around two (or sometimes three) wheels that are mounted to the frame and hidden behind hinged covers. The wheels keep the blade in tension and transmit the turning power from the motor to the blade. The upper wheel adjusts vertically to tension the blade or to release tension when changing blades. There is also an adjustment to tilt the upper wheel slightly to get the blade tracking on the center of the wheel.

Wheels

As a rule, blades last longer on saws that have large wheel diameters. This is because a blade and its weld are flexed around the wheels several hundred times each minute when the saw is running. This continuous flexing places a great deal of stress on a sawblade. Naturally, blades break more often when they are flexed tightly around small-diameter wheels. Manufacturers of small bandsaws overcome this problem by outfitting their saws with thin blades. However, thin blades flex

Bandsaw wheels cast from aluminum perform well when properly balanced.

Cast-iron wheels have a slight advantage over aluminum wheels. The weight of a cast-iron wheel creates a flywheel effect, and the added inertia helps to propel the blade through the wood.

and twist excessively during contour cutting, which makes it difficult or impossible to accurately follow a layout line.

Another concern with bandsaw wheels is balance. Dynamic balancing of the wheels is a major factor in smooth performance. This involves balancing the wheels as they are spinning by using a machine similar to those used to balance automobile tires. Some manufacturers of

lower-cost bandsaws use static balancing, which is not as precise. Still others don't bother balancing the wheels at all. It's no wonder that some bandsaws vibrate so wildly.

Tires

All bandsaw wheels have rubber or plastic tires to cushion the blade and give it traction. Tires mount to the wheels in one of

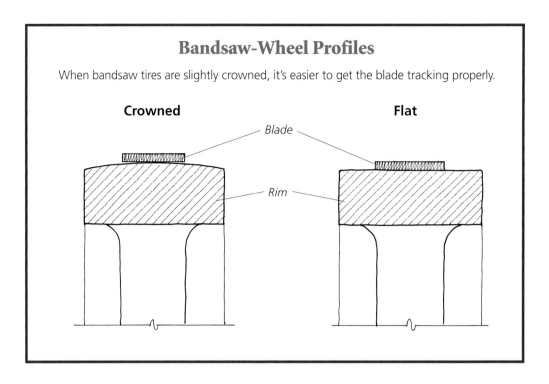

Bandsaw-Wheel Profiles

When bandsaw tires are slightly crowned, it's easier to get the blade tracking properly.

Crowned **Flat**

Blade

Rim

---

three ways: They are stretched onto the wheel, glued onto the wheel, or they snap and lock into a groove in the wheel's perimeter. The snap-on type is the easiest to replace.

To make it easier to keep the blade tracking properly, most bandsaw tires are slightly crowned. This means the middle of the tire's surface is slightly higher than the edges (see the drawing above). On a crowned tire, the blade naturally tends to ride toward the tire's center.

Although most bandsaw tires are crowned, some are flat, particularly those on saws 18 in. and larger. The theory is that flat tires give more support to blades that are more than ¾ in. wide. In practice, I believe it's easier to keep blades tracking on a crowned tire. The crown only needs to be very slight, so wide blades can still have the support that they need.

Just like the tires on your car, bandsaw tires become worn with age and use. And like your car's tires, worn bandsaw tires can create a lot of problems. Narrow blades cut grooves in the tires, and this can make it difficult or impossible to keep the blade tracking. As tires age they crack, and the cracks can cause the blade to vibrate. Cracks can become so bad that chunks of the tire come loose and fly off as the wheel turns. As you might imagine, this can cause the blade to bounce and vibrate wildly.

Sawdust can build up on your bandsaw's tires and cause problems similar to those created by wear. Surprisingly, even a small amount of sawdust buildup can cause problems. Some manufacturers solve this dilemma by mounting a brush that rubs against the lower wheel (see the photo at right). If your saw doesn't have a brush, you can easily install one yourself. A portion of a stiff-bristle scrub brush works well, and it can be attached to a bracket so it contacts the lower tire.

A brush works wonders to keep sawdust from building up on the tires. This one was part of the original equipment, but you can make your own from a stiff scrub brush mounted on a piece of angle iron.

Wheel covers

It's hard to imagine, but the earliest bandsaws had no covers over the wheels and blade. With so many feet of exposed blade, a wrong move could be disastrous—not to mention what could happen if a blade broke or came off of the wheels. Covers on a bandsaw are vital for your safety, and thankfully all contemporary bandsaws have covers to shield you from the turning wheels and moving blade.

Changing a blade requires removing the covers, so to make the process fast and hassle-free, the covers should be hinged and equipped with a quick-release catch. Twenty years ago, many consumer-grade

Keep tires clean
Even if your saw has a brush to scrub away the sawdust, the tires will still benefit from an occasional cleaning.

bandsaws had unhinged covers. Both top and bottom covers had to be removed to change the blade, and each one was secured by two screws. Since I owned a saw like that, I can say that having unhinged covers made blade changing slow and annoying. Unfortunately, some manufacturers still design covers this way.

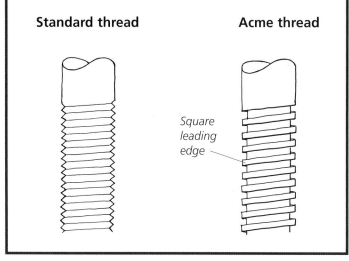
Tension Screws and Gauges

The tension screw on a bandsaw is used to move the upper wheel up or down to tension the blade. Although the tension screw is a simple device, I've seen plenty of problems with inadequate screws. The most common is stripped threads, which are not rare when tension screws are made with standard machine-screw-type threads.

It's better to use Acme-style threads for the tension screw because they can handle more load (see the drawing at left). This is the same style of thread that's found on pipe clamps. Acme threads have a square leading edge rather than a sharp leading edge as do ordinary machine-screw threads. Acme threads are more expensive to manufacture so they are typically found only on premium bandsaws.

The tension screw is turned by a hand-wheel that is located either above or just below the upper wheel. I prefer to have the handwheel located below the wheel because it's easier to reach. I also prefer a

A large, easy-to-grip tensioning wheel makes it easy to crank up the tension on a wide blade.

Tires and tension

To prolong the life of your bandsaw's tires, release the blade tension at the end of the day. Leaving the saw tensioned for days or weeks can leave permanent ridges in the tires. Prolonged tension can even distort wheels and cause bearings to fail prematurely.

large handwheel with spokes so I can get a firm grip while adjusting the blade tension. I've used some bandsaws with small, smooth handwheels that are difficult to grip.

Almost every new bandsaw has a tension gauge that is supposed to tell how much tension is on the blade. The problem is that most are inaccurate at best and many are way off. Use them only as a rough guide to blade tension.

Guides

Bandsaw guides support the blade and limit side-to-side and backward movement. All bandsaws have guides mounted both above and below the table (see the photos below). Each guide has three support members: one on each side of the blade to prevent lateral flexing and one behind the blade to prevent the feed pressure from pushing the blade off the

Guide position

For maximum blade support, the lower guides should be as close to the underside of the table as possible.

The upper guides are mounted on a sliding post that adjusts up and down to accommodate different thicknesses of lumber.

The lower guides are fixed in place beneath the table to provide support as the blade exits the stock. These lower guides are mounted several inches below the table; on some saws the lower guides are much closer to the underside of the table.

Steel blocks are standard on most midsize bandsaws.

wheels. The side supports can be either bearings, which spin when they come in contact with the blade, or stationary steel blocks, sometimes called jaw blocks (see the photo above).

The rear support is called a thrust wheel, which spins as it makes contact with the moving blade. Some thrust wheels are simply a bearing positioned so that the blade contacts the outer edge of the bearing's face. Although this method provides excellent blade support, the face of the bearing eventually becomes worn and the bearing must be replaced. The best thrust-bearing design is one in which a hardened steel disk or wheel is pressed over the face of the bearing where it contacts the blade.

Still another style of thrust wheel is one in which the bearing is positioned so that the blade contacts the edge of the bearing rather than the face. The blade sits in a

groove machined into the edge of the bearing. This is an effective design that is typically found on the guides of heavy industrial saws.

Block guides

Stationary blocks are the most common type of guide. They're used on both industrial and consumer bandsaws. Blocks are popular with bandsaw manufacturers because they are simple and inexpensive. But that doesn't mean that they're inferior or ineffective. In fact, guide blocks provide excellent blade support, especially when cutting curves. This is because they have a broader contact area than bearing guides. Additionally, because of their square shape, guide blocks provide their support closer to the stock, where the cut is actually made. I've tried both block- and bearing-type guides on my bandsaw, and while bearings do have their advantages, I prefer the blocks for contour cutting because of the superior blade support that they provide.

However, there are some disadvantages to blocks. For one, they need periodic maintenance. Friction between the blade and the block wears grooves or steps in the block faces, which limit their effectiveness. This can easily be corrected by occasionally removing the blocks from the guide and truing the block face with a file. Eventually, the blocks end up too short for the setscrew to hold so you'll have to replace them. Another disadvantage is that if steel blocks are adjusted incorrectly and the teeth come in contact with the blade, the blade will be irreparably damaged.

The Truth about Steel Guide Blocks

There has been a lot of misinformation lately about the damage that steel guide blocks inflict on bandsaw blades. Here's the theory: The heat generated by the friction between the steel blocks and the blade shortens the life of the blade by either causing the teeth to lose their temper (which makes them dull rapidly) or by weakening the blade until it breaks. The theory also holds that you must replace steel blocks with plastic or composite blocks.

The theory sounds good, but in reality there isn't enough heat generated by friction with the guide blocks to have any effect on the blade. Blades get hot during cutting, but the heat is generated at the tooth tip, not from the guide blocks. Besides, the heat is only a problem when resawing with a carbon-steel blade. Bimetal and carbide-tipped blades can withstand much more heat at the tooth tip, which is one reason why they are better suited for resawing.

Likewise, the small amount of friction with the guides has no effect whatsoever on the breaking of blades. Blades break when they become work-hardened from flexing around the saw's wheels hundreds of times each minute the saw is running. The guides have nothing to do with it.

Do plastic or composite guide blocks have any advantages over steel guide blocks? Yes. They won't dull the teeth if the blade accidentally comes in contact with them. And when using tiny 1/16-in. scrolling blades, it's best to surround the blade with the blocks for maximum support. But blocks of scrap hardwood work as well as those made of plastic or composite—and best of all, they're free.

Plastic or composite guide blocks wear very quickly and need frequent adjustment and replacement. If you want longer blade life, I recommend you spend your money on better blades.

Cool Blocks You can replace the steel blocks with "Cool Blocks," a brand name for a guide block made from a fibrous material that has been impregnated with a dry lubricant. Cool Blocks make it possible to run tiny 1/16-in. blades on your saw. Since the soft material will not damage blade teeth, you can locate the blocks so that the blade is completely sandwiched between the blocks. Using a 1/16-in. blade and having the guides adjusted in that way, you can cut incredibly tight turns with your bandsaw—the kind of cuts normally made on a scrollsaw.

Aftermarket blocks are easier to adjust and offer more surface area than steel blocks.

Shopmade hardwood guide blocks support very narrow blades without damaging a blade's teeth.

Hardwood guide blocks You can also replace the steel blocks with hardwood blocks (see the top photo at left). I use a dense, tight-grain wood such as maple. To make the guide blocks, I cut narrow strips of hardwood to fit the guides on my saw, then cut the strip into short pieces. I always make several sets of blocks because they wear out so quickly. When they get worn, I simply toss them out and install a new pair.

Bearing guides

Bearing guides, sometimes called roller guides, look similar to block guides except that they use bearings to support the sides of the blade. There are two distinct styles of bearing guides: American and European.

Bearing guides rotate as the blade turns, which reduces friction. American-style bearing guides contact the blade with the perimeter of the guide.

American-style bearings If you've purchased a recent American-made industrial bandsaw, it probably has bearing guides (see the bottom photo at left). You can also purchase aftermarket bearing guides and install them yourself on most popular saws (see Sources on p. 379). Bearing guides use three bearings to support the sawblade. Just as with block guides, a thrust bearing is mounted behind the blade to prevent feed pressure from pushing the blade off the wheels, but this style has two more bearings mounted on either side of the blade for lateral support. Each bearing spins as the blade makes contact, so there is very little friction between the blade and the guide.

European-style bearings In recent years, steel-frame bandsaws imported from Italy have steadily gained in popularity among professional woodworkers and serious hobbyists. These sturdy, smooth-running bandsaws are economical, especially in sizes larger than 14 in. If you've seen these bandsaws in advertisements or in woodworking shows, you've probably noticed their unusual-looking guides (see the photo at right). They have bearings on three sides to support the blade as American-style bearing guides do, but the side bearings are mounted so that the blade contacts the face of the bearing rather than the edge.

As another advantage, European guides have thumbwheels and knurled locking rings for easy adjustments. You don't have to search for tools to adjust these guides. The side bearings have a micrometer-type adjustment with a locking ring to hold the bearing in position. Unfortunately, the thrust bearing doesn't have a micrometer adjustment, but it does have a locking wing nut so you won't have to search for an Allen wrench.

As a disadvantage, European guides are large and take up a lot of space. This isn't a problem on the top guide, which is mounted to the guidepost, but the lower guide is too large to fit under the table. It ends up mounted in the lower cabinet, several inches below the table. Although this arrangement works, I sometimes miss the additional support provided by having the guide directly beneath the table, especially when I'm turning the workpiece through an intricate series of tight turns.

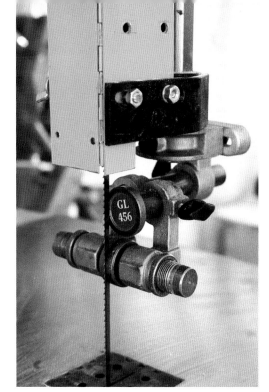

European-style bearing guides contact the blade on their faces and provide a larger bearing surface. They can be adjusted without a wrench and can be lowered closer to the cut than American-style bearing guides.

Installing guides

Before I install hardwood block guides to support narrow blades, I cut a small notch into one of the blocks and position the blade into the notch. This extra support prevents the tiny blade from twisting in the cut.

Guideposts

Mounted to the frame of a bandsaw, a guidepost adjusts the vertical height of the upper guides to compensate for different thicknesses of stock. A sheet-metal guard is attached to the guidepost to shroud the moving blade and prevent accidental contact.

The single most important aspect of a guidepost is its rigidity. If the guidepost deflects, the quality of the cut will be affected. If the deflection problem can be

Typically found on large, premium-quality bandsaws, this sturdy guidepost has a rack-and-pinion system for easy adjustments.

traced to a loose bracket or fastener, then the problem is easily corrected. But when the guidepost is securely locked in the bandsaw's frame and it continues to deflect, it's a sign that the guidepost material lacks sufficient stiffness for the job.

Also important to guidepost design is the squareness of the post to the table. If both the front and side of the post are not 90° to the saw table, you'll have to readjust the guides each time you change the height of the guidepost. This is a real nuisance, and I wouldn't buy any saw with this problem.

The best guidepost designs—those with the greatest rigidity—use a square, round, or octagonal post machined from a bar of steel. If the saw frame is made of cast iron, a hole is machined into the casting to accept the post. If the bandsaw frame is fabricated from steel, bushings are typically welded into the frame as a fitting for the guidepost.

Some smaller bandsaws use heavy-gauge sheet metal for the guidepost. The metal is folded to form an L-shape to give it rigidity. Although not as expensive as a solid-steel post, this design seems to be adequate for the smaller bandsaws on which it's used.

The combined weight of the guidepost, guide, and guard can be substantial, especially on large saws. When you loosen the screw that locks the guidepost, you'll have to support the guidepost assembly to keep it from suddenly crashing down onto the table. On better-quality bandsaws, this problem may be solved in one of several ways.

First, some machines have a counterweight to balance the weight of the guidepost assembly. A steel cable in the saw's column suspends the counterweight. The cable is wrapped around pulleys to keep it moving smoothly through the saw's frame as the guidepost is raised or lowered. The system is reminiscent of an old-style window sash that uses weights suspended inside the window frame. I've used a bandsaw with this design for a number of years, and it's a good system. It makes raising and lowering a heavy guidepost smooth and effortless.

Another system for supporting and adjusting the guidepost is the rack and pinion. Machined into the guidepost are gear teeth, which engage a small gear inside the saw cabinet (see the photo above). The small gear is fastened to a knob or handwheel on the outside of the cabinet. This is an excellent design that makes guidepost adjustments easy as well as precise.

Small saws with stamped-steel guide-posts typically have a friction device to prevent the guideposts from dropping suddenly during adjustments (see the photo at right). Although this design serves its purpose, guidepost adjustments seem stiff and awkward compared to the counterweight or rack-and-pinion designs.

Tables

The purpose of a bandsaw table is obvious: It supports the stock as it is being cut. But some bandsaw tables do this simple job better than others. A good-quality table is one that's made from cast iron that has been machined flat. If you plan to saw thick, heavy stock, the table should be able to support the work without flexing. To maximize strength and stiffness, many tables are heavily ribbed.

To allow for blade changes, a table has a slot that runs from the throat to the table edge, either at the front or right side. Placing the slot to the side allows the trunnions to be spaced farther apart, which makes the table stiffer. To keep the table halves aligned at the blade slot, a tapered pin is inserted into a hole in the table edge. If the blade slot is in the front edge of the table, a fence rail may be used instead of a pin.

If a table is warped, the two halves will suddenly twist out of alignment when the pin or rail is removed. A small amount of misalignment shouldn't be a concern, but a saw with a severely warped table is not usable.

This simple friction device, found on a 14-in. bandsaw, uses a spring-loaded bearing to prevent the guidepost from falling.

The larger a saw's table, the more useful it will be. It's difficult to saw long, curved workpieces such as a cabriole leg when one end keeps dropping off the table. Most tables are square, the length of each side roughly equivalent to the wheel diameter of the saw. Therefore, a 14-in. saw has a table that measures about 14 in. by 14 in. A 36-in. bandsaw has a large table that rivals those found on table saws.

The table is centered on the blade, so it doesn't completely fill the space between the blade and the saw's column (called the throat). On some saws, an iron or sheet-metal auxiliary table is bolted onto the main table to fill this void. This is a nice feature, and the added support is appreciated when sawing large workpieces.

Don't overlook the height of the saw table from the floor. In the United States, the standard height seems to be around 40 in. to 42 in. However, European band-saws can be quite low in height, some having tables only 35 in. high. Bending over a table that low for long periods of time may give you back pain and stiffness. To increase the short stature of my saw, I built a simple plywood box as a stand and filled it with sand to make the saw more stable.

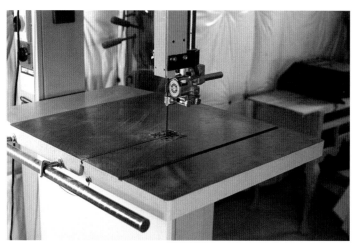

The large table on this bandsaw provides ample support for the workpiece. Note the auxiliary table that fills up the area between the table and the frame.

Trunnions bolted to the underside of the saw table allow it to tilt for cutting angles. (Photo by Scott Phillips.)

Trunnions

The table is fastened to curved supports called trunnions that allow the table to tilt for cutting angles (see the bottom photo at left). For strength, the trunnions should be made of cast iron, although some are die-cast or stamped steel. To stiffen the table, the trunnions should be spaced as far apart as possible.

Although I don't recall ever seeing a bandsaw with a nontilting table, some tables tilt farther than others. There's plenty of room for tilting to the right (as you stand facing the teeth), so tables can typically tilt 45° in that direction. However, the frame of the saw limits the angle of the tilt to the left. Although most bandsaw tables can tilt 5° to the left, some can tilt as much as 15°. In most cases, an adjustable stop is provided that enables you to quickly return the table to 90°.

Inserts

Where the blade passes through the center of the table, there is a large hole to prevent the blade and the table from damaging each other no matter what the table angle. An insert of aluminum or plastic is set into the table to fill the space around the blade. For maximum support of the workpiece at the cut, the insert should be flush to the table.

Miter slots

Most bandsaw tables have a slot for a miter gauge. The slot can be a nuisance because it sometimes catches the workpiece, so you may want to fill the slot with a strip of wood. A hard, dense wood like maple works best. Make the strip to fit snugly, then simply press it into place. You can easily remove it if you want to use the slot for a jig.

The standard miter-slot size in the United States is ⅜ in. by ¾ in. This means that you can use a miter gauge from one of your other machines. European saws typically have a smaller slot, which means you'll have to order an accessory miter gauge from the dealer.

Fences

A fence is invaluable for ripping, resawing, and cutting precision joinery. A good fence should lock firmly in any position to a track or rail on the edges of a table, and it should have sufficient stiffness to resist deflecting under sideward pressure. The best fences are cast iron or extruded aluminum. I'd avoid folded sheet-metal fences. Some fences have an adjustment to compensate for drift.

Motors and Drivetrains

I remember the 36-in. bandsaw in the first shop where I worked. I was impressed by its sheer size; it stood 8 ft. tall. But most of all, I remember the raw power. It was equipped with a 7½-hp direct-drive motor, and the saw seemed unstoppable.

That bandsaw was produced for industrial use at a time when woodworking machines always seemed to have more than enough power. Today the trend seems to be to manufacture woodwork-

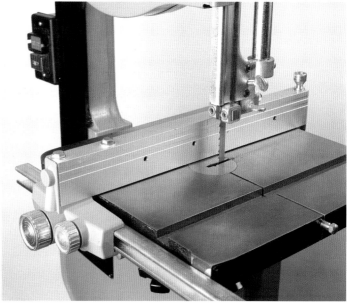

This fence easily adjusts and locks in place for secure ripping. The two bolts near the front allow you to set the fence so that it cuts a true parallel line. (Photo by Scott Phillips.)

ing machines with motors that meet minimum horsepower requirements. Many bandsaws have enough power for everyday applications, but when you raise the upper guide to the maximum height, you almost have to coax the blade through the cut.

Bandsaw motors range from the diminutive ⅕-hp motors found on some benchtop saws to the 10-hp motors on large industrial machines. Some consumer bandsaws in the 14-in. category come equipped with a 1-hp motor that often strains to get the job done, especially if you add a riser block. I know of one woodworker with a 14-in. bandsaw equipped with a riser block who is on his third motor. He began with the standard ½-hp motor and worked his way through successively larger motors. The 1-hp motor he has now seems up to the job: It's lasted eight years.

Bandsaw motors are mounted in one of three ways: directly to the shaft of the lower wheel, below the saw in a steel cabinet or stand, or mounted to the back of the bandsaw frame.

Direct-drive motors

The most basic method of turning the wheels on a bandsaw is with a direct-drive motor. Connecting the motor directly to the drive wheel is the most efficient method of turning the wheels. This method is used both on the smallest benchtop saws and on the largest industrial saws. There is no loss of power through heat and vibration, and this drive system doesn't suffer from belt slippage, out-of-round pulleys, or other similar problems that can sometimes plague belt-drive bandsaws. The fact that industrial bandsaws use direct-drive motors is one reason why they have such tremendous power and torque.

However, direct-drive bandsaws do have one potential drawback. If the motor ever fails, you're usually stuck buying a new motor from the saw's manufacturer. This is because direct-drive motors have mounts and drive connections that are unique to the machine for which they were designed. A stock motor from a supplier simply won't fit.

Motors mounted below the saw

The most common method of bandsaw motor mounting is underneath the saw in the cabinet or base that supports the saw. The motor mounts on a sheet-metal bracket that adjusts to tension the belt. The belt transfers power to the lower wheel of the bandsaw by pulleys. When the pulleys are true and balanced, this design works just fine. Unfortunately, many saws come supplied with inexpensive die-cast pulleys that are not true or round, and the flimsy sheet-metal motor-mounting bracket flexes with each revolution of the out-of-round pulleys. The resulting vibrations make the saw difficult to use. Bandsaws with die-cast pulleys can be significantly improved by simply upgrading to machined pulleys.

Motors mounted to the frame

The third method of mounting the motor is to the back of the saw frame. A drive belt and pulleys are also used with this design, but the system is much more rigid and free of vibration. The face of the motor used in this system is fastened to the saw frame, and the motor shaft protrudes through a hole in the frame. The motor pulley is connected to the wheel pulley by a belt.

There are several advantages to this mounting system, which is far superior to mounting the motor in the base of the saw and makes the saw run smoothly. First, the transmission belt is much shorter, which reduces the energy lost through the vibration of a long belt. Second, face-mount motors have much more rigid mounting than motors set on a sheet-metal bracket. Finally, bandsaws that use this mounting system typically have cast-iron pulleys that have been machined true and round.

Bandsaw Blades

I t didn't take long after buying my first bandsaw for me to realize the importance of having the right bandsaw blade. It is, without a doubt, the most important part of any bandsaw. This is true regardless of whether you own an inexpensive home-shop bandsaw or the finest industrial-grade bandsaw. An average bandsaw will cut much better with a great blade, but the finest bandsaw will disappoint you if it has the wrong blade.

Because there's such a number of blade styles to choose from, selecting the right blade can at first seem confusing. But the versatility that we all desire from our bandsaws depends entirely on selecting the proper blade for the job at hand. Most of us (myself included) probably mount a 50-tooth alternate-top bevel (ATB) combo blade on our table saws and leave it there until it needs resharpening. That

one blade will effectively miter, rip, crosscut, and do just about anything else we need it to do. It doesn't work that way on the bandsaw, where the blades are much more specialized. The best blade for cutting the contours of a cabriole leg won't accurately resaw veneer.

In this chapter, I'll discuss what you need to know about putting together an arsenal of blades for your own bandsaw that's appropriate for the woodwork you intend to do. All blades share a common terminology, so start with the sidebar on p. 280 to learn the language. Many factors are involved in selecting the right blade for the job, so I'll give you some specific examples. I'll also talk about cleaning your blades to improve their performance, how to safely coil and uncoil a bandsaw blade, and finally, what's involved in welding your own blades.

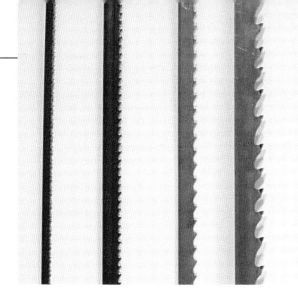

The variety of blades available is the key to the bandsaw's versatility. From left to right: ⅛ in., 18 pitch; ¼ in., 10 pitch; ¼ in., 6 pitch; ⅜ in., 3/4 pitch, carbide-tipped; ¾ in., 3 pitch; ¾ in., 2 pitch.

Bands of Steel

Woodworking tools such as sawblades, router bits, and shaper cutterheads have greatly improved over the years, and bandsaw blades are no exception. The materials and manufacturing processes used to produce bandsaw blades are extremely sophisticated. The blades available today are stronger, cut smoother, and stay sharp longer than ever before. They also cut with greater efficiency and less feed resistance.

Bandsaw blades perform a very demanding job. The back must be soft and pliable to flex around the wheels of the bandsaw several hundred revolutions each minute, yet the teeth must be hard to resist dulling while cutting. The harder and thicker the stock, the more quickly the teeth lose their edge.

To make the teeth hard and resistant to wear, manufacturers use one of three methods. In the first method, the teeth are cut into the band, set, and then hardened. This is done on carbon-steel and spring-steel blades. In the second method, a band of high-speed steel is welded to a softer back band, and the teeth are cut into the harder steel. These are called bimetal blades.

The third method is for carbide blades. Individual carbide teeth are brazed to a flexible steel band. Carbide blades are the most expensive because of the high cost of the material and the process used in making them. As you might expect, each of the three blade types has advantages and disadvantages. I'll discuss them individually.

Expect to change blades often

To get the most out of your bandsaw, you'll have to change blades often from wide to narrow or from few teeth to many. Each type of blade is best for a certain kind of cutting.

Welds

Bandsaw-blade stock is manufactured in long lengths, then individual blades are cut to length and welded together. The weld is important to blade life and performance. For best results, a weld must be strong, flexible, and smooth. A smooth weld is flush on the sides and back and free of excess flash. This allows the weld to travel through the guides without catching and breaking.

Bandsaw-Blade Terms

Bladeback: The body of the blade not including the tooth. The back of the blade must be both tough and pliable to withstand the continuous flexing as the blade runs around the wheels of the saw.

Gullet: The curved area at the base of the tooth that carries away the sawdust. The size and efficiency of the gullets decrease as the pitch is increased.

Pitch: The number of teeth per inch (tpi) as measured from the tips of the teeth. The pitch determines the feed rate at which the blade can cut and the smoothness of the sawn surface. Pitch can be either constant or variable.

Rake angle: The angle of the face of the tooth measured in respect to a line drawn perpendicular to the cutting direction. Regular and skip blades have a zero rake angle, which gives them a slow, scraping action. Hook blades have a positive rake angle, which causes them to cut more aggressively.

Set: The bending of the sawteeth to the left and right to create a kerf that is wider than the back. This prevents the back from binding in the cut. Carbide teeth are not bent; they are simply wider than the steel band to which they are brazed.

Thickness: The thickness of the steel band measured at the blade back. In general, thick blades are wider and stiffer than thin blades. Thicker blades require larger-diameter bandsaw wheels to prevent stress cracks and premature blade breakage.

Tooth: The cutting portion of the blade. Teeth must be sharp, hard, and resistant to both heat and wear.

Tooth tip: The sharp part of the tooth that shears away the wood fibers. During sawing, the tooth tip is under tremendous stress and subject to both heat and wear. The heat produced from friction during sawing can sometimes rise to 400°F on the tip of the tooth. This occurs because the wood insulates the blade during cutting.

Width: The dimension of a blade from the back of the band to the tip of the tooth. Wider blades are stiffer and resist side-to-side flexing, making them the best choice for resawing. Narrow blades can cut tighter contours.

Parts of a Bandsaw Blade

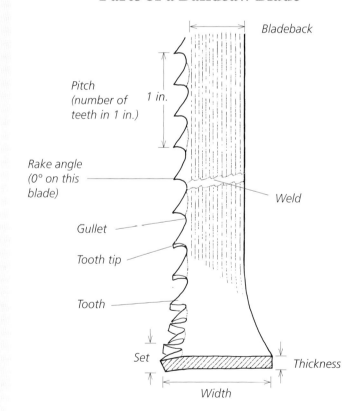

Bladeback

Pitch (number of teeth in 1 in.)

1 in.

Rake angle (0° on this blade)

Weld

Gullet

Tooth tip

Tooth

Set

Thickness

Width

Carbon steel

The most common bandsaw blades are made entirely of carbon steel. Carbon-steel blades are very popular and can be found in many forms in almost every consumer woodworking catalog. They're also the least expensive type of blade, especially when you purchase 100-ft. spools and weld or braze blades to fit your bandsaw.

Carbon-steel blades are sharp, cut well when new, and are available in a variety of widths and tooth forms. They are also inexpensive, which is probably the major reason for their popularity. The main dis-advantage to carbon-steel blades is that they dull rather quickly, particularly when used for demanding applications such as resawing.

Sawing thick hardwood stock places the greatest demands on any blade. If the tooth tip becomes too hot, it becomes soft and quickly loses both its edge and set. Once the set and sharpness are lost, the blade deflects during cutting. The result is that the expensive stock you're sawing is ruined. For these reasons, I use narrow carbon-steel bandsaw blades only for less-demanding bandsaw applications such as sawing contours.

Spring steel

Spring steel is most often associated with the cheap, stamped-out blades found on new benchtop bandsaws. Spring steel is soft and flexible, which allows it to flex around the small-diameter wheels of benchtop saws. But because spring steel is so soft, it doesn't hold an edge for very long.

Sharpness

There are certainly varying degrees of sharpness among bandsaw blades. Sharpness depends on the quality of the grinding process used, which should leave each tooth smooth and free of burrs. The type of tooth material is also a factor. The high-speed steel in a bimetal blade can be ground sharper than carbide.

More important than initial sharpness is the extent to which a blade will retain its sharpness. Because carbide is so hard, it's extremely resistant to wear. However, carbon steel is not. Carbon steel works well for general-purpose work, such as cutting contours and stock less than 2 in. thick, but it loses its edge quickly when resawing. The heat at the tooth tip soon softens it, and the edge wears away.

Several years ago, however, a unique spring-steel resaw blade was introduced into the consumer market. Instead of being stamped, the teeth on this blade are carefully ground, hardened, and polished. The teeth have a variable spacing that limits harmonic vibration. These blades cut smooth, and best of all, the kerf is a mere $\frac{1}{32}$ in., which is approximately half the kerf of a typical carbide or carbon-steel blade. This means you'll get more veneer and less waste out of each plank. Additionally, because the blade is 0.022-in.-thick spring steel it will easily flex around the medium-size wheels of consumer bandsaws. This blade is mar-keted under the trade name The Wood Slicer (see Sources on p. 379).

Bimetal

Bimetal blades are very different from carbon-steel blades and carbide-tipped blades in the way in which they are made.

Bandsaw-Blade Materials

Material	Cost	Advantages	Disadvantages	Best use
Stamped spring steel	Very inexpensive	• Very flexible for use on bandsaws with small-diameter wheels	• Stamped teeth dull very quickly	Light-duty cuts on small bandsaws
Carbon steel	Inexpensive	• Weld or braze your own • Readily available	• Dulls quickly • Cannot be sharpened	Cutting contours in relatively thin stock
Wood Slicer spring steel	Moderate	• Flexible, thin kerf • Ground teeth are polished and hardened • Variable pitch reduces vibration		Resawing
Bimetal	Moderate	• Cobalt-steel teeth don't overheat as readily as carbon-steel teeth • High recommended tension means greater beam strength		Demanding applications that generate a lot of heat such as resawing and cutting thick stock
Carbide	Moderately expensive	• Smooth cut because carbide teeth are precisely ground on all sides • Recommended tension is almost twice of that of carbon steel • Outlasts carbon-steel blades 25 to 1	• Cost • Carbide is brittle	Resawing and other demanding applications
Stellite	Very expensive	• Less brittle than carbide	• Cost • Not as hard as carbide	Resawing

Bimetal blades are actually two steel ribbons that are welded together (see the drawing at right). The back of a bimetal blade is composed of soft, flexible steel; the blade front, where the teeth are milled, is made of much harder high-speed steel.

This combination produces a relatively inexpensive blade with longer wear than ordinary carbon-steel blades. The teeth of carbon-steel blades lose their sharpness and set when overheated during resawing. However, the cobalt-steel teeth of a bimetal blade can withstand 1200°F, far more than the 400°F that damages the teeth of a carbon-steel blade.

Another advantage of a bimetal blade is the strength of its spring-steel back. The recommended tension is 25,000 psi. (Remember that greater tension increases the beam strength of a blade.) The beam strength of bimetal blades combined with their resistance to heat has endeared bimetal blades to many woodworkers.

Carbide

I'm sure that almost every woodworker is familiar with carbide. Carbide-tipped cutting tools have almost made high-speed steel tools things of the past.

A significant difference between carbide and steel blades is that each carbide tooth is individually brazed onto a strong, flexible spring-steel blade back. In fact, the recommended tension for a carbide blade is almost twice that of carbon steel, giving carbide blades much greater beam strength. The carbide teeth are precisely ground on the face, top, and both sides, which results in truer, more precise cuts.

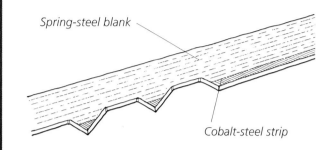

How a Bimetal Blade Is Made

A strip of cobalt steel is welded onto a spring-steel blank before the teeth are cut. When the teeth are cut, all that remains of the cobalt steel is the tooth tip.

Spring-steel blank

Cobalt-steel strip

A carbide-tipped blade is economical because it stays sharp for so long.

As you would expect, carbide bandsaw blades are significantly more expensive than ordinary carbon-steel blades. However, a carbide blade will typically outlast carbon steel 25 to 1, and carbide can be resharpened. Although more expensive initially, carbide blades are much more economical than carbon-steel blades. This is especially true for resawing.

Stellite

Stellite is the brand name of a unique type of carbide that is reportedly better suited for woodworking applications. Stellite isn't as hard as regular carbide, but it's not as brittle either. This gives Stellite the advantage of greater shock resistance. Like carbide, Stellite promises longer wear and better-quality cuts.

In many other ways, Stellite blades are a lot like carbide blades. The Stellite teeth are brazed onto the blade body, then precisely ground. And like carbide blades, Stellite blades are expensive.

Blade Width and Thickness

Thickness is related to width. Take a look at a manufacturer's blade catalog and you'll see that as blades get wider, the steel used for the blade gets thicker. This is standard industry practice, and it gives wider blades greater beam strength and stiffness. Because of the additional stiffness, wider blades need more force to reach the recommended tension, which means that they should be used only on bandsaws with frames strong enough to provide the necessary tension. Also, wide blades have a minimum wheel diameter that they can flex around without breaking.

The width of a blade relates to its beam strength. Beam strength refers to the fact that a bandsaw blade supported between two sets of guides acts like a beam when the workpiece is fed into the blade. Like a beam, the wider the blade, the stiffer it will be. Several factors can reduce the beam strength of a blade. If the blade is dull, if the workpiece is very thick, if there is insufficient tension, if the feed rate is too great, or if the blade has the wrong type of teeth for a job, the blade will be more likely to bend (see the drawing on

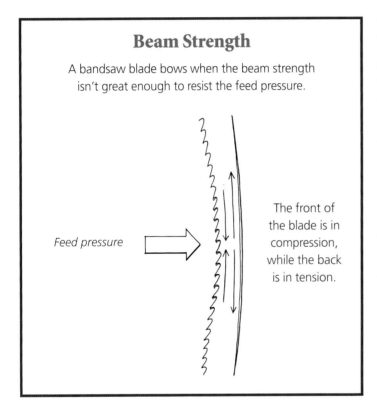

Beam Strength

A bandsaw blade bows when the beam strength isn't great enough to resist the feed pressure.

Feed pressure

The front of the blade is in compression, while the back is in tension.

Bigger isn't better

Don't try to use a blade wider or thicker than your saw can tension. Cranking up to accommodate a heavy blade can bend your saw's frame, as well as damage wheels, shafts, and bearings.

the facing page). Increasing the blade tension or blade width will increase the beam strength.

Attempting to exceed the maximum blade width for your bandsaw can wreck the saw. As you tension a blade that's too wide for the saw, the stress can distort the frame, possibly beyond repair. The excessive tension also places potentially damaging forces on the saw's wheels, shafts, and bearings.

Tooth Form

Tooth form refers to the design of the tooth and gullet, specifically the tooth size, shape, and rake angle. The three commonly known blade forms for cutting wood are the regular, skip, and hook. Another form that is gaining in popularity is the variable tooth.

Tooth form is vital
More than any other factor, the tooth form determines how well a blade will cut in a given situation.

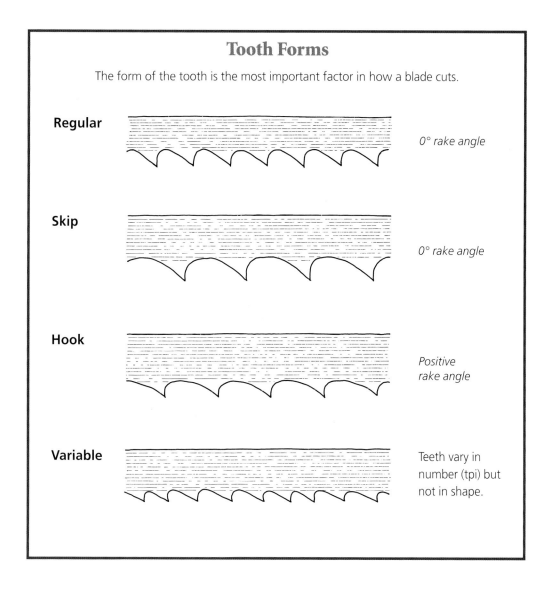

Tooth Forms

The form of the tooth is the most important factor in how a blade cuts.

Regular — 0° rake angle

Skip — 0° rake angle

Hook — Positive rake angle

Variable — Teeth vary in number (tpi) but not in shape.

Tooth Forms and Their Uses

Tooth form	Number of teeth	Rake angle	Gullet	Best uses	Limitations
Regular	Many teeth, evenly spaced	0°, scraping action cuts cleanly	Small	• Precise cutting of curves	• Gullets fill with sawdust quickly, heating blade • Requires slow feed rate
Skip	Fewer than regular; every other tooth is missing	0°, scraping action cuts cleanly	Large	• Resawing, ripping thick stock	• Doesn't cut as smoothly as regular-tooth blades
Hook	Similar to skip	Positive rake angle, aggressive cut	Large	• Aggressive blade allows a faster feed rate • Good for resawing and ripping, especially in hardwoods	• Same as skip
Variable	Both many and few in sections on the same blade; vary in size but not in shape	Can have either 0° or a positive rake angle	Like teeth: large or small, varying in size but not in shape	• Much less vibration; makes for a very smooth cut • Moderate feed rate	• Expensive

Regular tooth

The regular-tooth form, sometimes called the standard form, has evenly spaced teeth for smooth, precise cutting. Teeth and gullets are the same size, and the rake, or cutting angle, is 0°. Compared to other tooth forms, regular blades have more teeth, and the 0° cutting angle scrapes the wood surface clean. This combination of features leaves a smooth surface. Regular-tooth blades are a great choice for sawing curves.

The disadvantage of regular-tooth blades is that the gullets are too small to effectively cut thick stock. Remember that the purpose of the gullets is to haul away the sawdust from the kerf. If you attempt to cut thick stock with a regular blade, the gullets become full before the teeth exit the stock, thus cutting slows down and the teeth overheat. Obviously, regular blades are not designed for fast cutting. In fact, if you push the stock too hard in an effort to increase the cutting rate, the cut actually slows down as the gullets become packed with sawdust.

Skip tooth

As you might assess from the name, the skip form "skips" every other tooth. Skip-tooth blades have fewer teeth and larger gullets than regular-tooth blades. The large gullets can efficiently carry the sawdust away from the kerf. This makes skip-tooth blades fast cutting. Like regular-tooth blades, skip-tooth blades also have a 0° rake angle that scrapes the wood away cleanly. But because they have fewer teeth, skip-tooth blades don't cut as smoothly as regular blades.

Skip blades are best suited for resawing and ripping thick stock. They also work well for cutting softwoods. The only problem with skip-tooth blades is that the more efficient hook-tooth blade has outmoded them. Why do manufacturers still produce skip blades? One sawblade manufacturer to whom I spoke said his company still makes skip-tooth blades mainly because it's difficult to convince people to change—short of sending people a free hook blade to try.

Hook tooth

The hook tooth is really a further development of the skip tooth. The hook form has large gullets and teeth like that of skip blades, but the teeth have a positive rake angle that makes them cut more aggressively. Because of that aggressive nature, hook blades have less feed resistance than skip blades. In fact, they almost seem to feed themselves. Hook-tooth blades are a great choice for resawing and ripping thick stock.

Variable tooth

The variable-tooth blade is a hybrid among bandsaw blades. Variable-tooth blades can have regular teeth with a 0° rake angle or a more aggressive positive rake angle. But the unique feature of this type of blade is that the tooth size and spacing vary on the same blade. This means that both the teeth and gullets vary in size but not in shape. The unique design dramatically reduces vibration; the result is a quieter blade and a very smooth cut.

To understand how this works, it's helpful to think of a bandsaw blade as a string on a musical instrument (a fiddle if you like country music or a violin if you prefer classical). Both the strings on an instrument and on a bandsaw blade are under tension, but for different reasons. You want a string on an instrument to vibrate in order to produce a sound. This is called harmonic vibration. But you want to limit vibration on a bandsaw blade because vibrations create a rough

Tooth Set

Bandsaw blades designed for woodworking have an alternate set pattern. Every tooth is set in an alternating sequence.

The set creates a kerf that is wider than the blade.

surface on the stock. By varying the tooth and gullet size, you effectively limit the vibrations and create a smoother surface.

Tooth set

Tooth set is the bending of the teeth left and right to create a kerf wider than the blade body. This is important to prevent binding during cutting. There are several set patterns available, but most are designed for metal cutting. Alternate set is really the only style that is effective for woodworking blades. With alternate set, every other tooth is bent in the same direction, left, right, and so on (see the drawing at left).

Although carbide teeth are not bent, they are wider than the steel body to which they're brazed. Then they're ground to create a set pattern that helps keep the blade running true.

Pitch

Pitch is simply the number of teeth per inch (tpi) on a blade length measured from the tips of the teeth. Pitch determines two factors: the speed at which the blade will cut through the stock and the smoothness of the cut surface.

Blades with a fine pitch have more teeth per inch of blade length than those with a coarse pitch. A greater number of teeth means that each tooth is small and thus takes a small bite that leaves the surface smooth. A greater number of teeth also reduces the size of the gullets. Since small gullets can't haul away dust very quickly, fine-pitch blades cut slower and tend to get hotter than coarser blades.

The opposite is true for coarse-pitch blades. Both the teeth and the gullets are larger, so each tooth bites off a greater amount of wood, and the large gullets can easily remove the sawdust from the kerf.

Choosing a Blade

Getting the results you expect from your bandsaw greatly depends on having the best blade for the job at hand. In my own shop, I keep an assortment of blades so I'm always ready for the next woodworking project.

Thumbing through the pages of an industrial bandsaw blade catalog can seem very confusing. You should realize, though, that you can eliminate many of the blades listed simply because they are

> ### Coarser is usually better
>
> In most cutting situations, I choose coarser-pitched blades over fine. The gullets on fine-pitched blades get full of sawdust, and cutting slows dramatically. At the same time, the tips of the teeth get hot, and on a carbon-steel blade they easily become overheated and dull.

designed for cutting various metals. Rather than looking at what blades are available, I find it's much easier to narrow down the blade choices based upon the types of cuts I'll be making (see the sidebar on pp. 290–291). Below is a list of the cuts I make in my own shop:

- Curves in furniture parts such as legs, feet, and skirts. This category also includes compound curves.

- Intricate scrollwork such as the tiny curves found on mirrors and small, detailed boxes.

- Resawing 1-in.-thick soft poplar or pine into thin stock for drawer parts or other small projects.

- Ripping thick, heavy hardwood into rough sizes before milling.

- Slicing veneer from wide, highly figured hardwood stock.

- Cutting joints on furniture parts.

- Sawing small, figured logs into planks for drying.

For every job, it's important to consider the blade width, pitch, and tooth form.

Which Blade Should I Use?

Choosing a blade can be confusing until you're familiar with all the factors. Here are some examples to get you started.

This 2-pitch bimetal blade makes quick work of poplar.

Resawing 6-in.-wide poplar for drawer parts

Option 1: Carbide-tipped, 3 pitch, hook tooth.
Option 2: Bimetal, 2 pitch, hook tooth.
Comments: Poplar is soft and cuts easily. The bimetal blade would be less expensive, but the carbide blade would last much longer. For greatest beam strength, use the widest blade that your bandsaw can properly tension.

Slicing $1/16$-in. veneer from a 9-in.-wide crotch-walnut plank

Option 1: Carbide-tipped, 2/3 variable pitch, hook tooth.
Option 2: Spring steel, 3/4 variable pitch, hook tooth.
Option 3: Carbide-tipped, 3 pitch, hook tooth.
Option 4: Bimetal, 3 pitch, hook tooth.
Comments: Walnut crotch has dramatic figure and is expensive—when you can find it. I try to get as much veneer as I possibly can from a valuable plank like this. A carbon blade would be my last choice

A variable-pitch carbide-tipped blade is a great choice for accurately sawing veneer.

Ripping hardwoods on the bandsaw is easy with a $1/2$-in.-wide, 4-pitch blade.

because it dulls quickly. The variable-pitch carbide blade is very expensive, but the cut is incredibly smooth. Both of the carbide blades are stiff and require a strong frame to properly tension. The spring-steel variable-pitch blade is an excellent choice, particularly for saws with wheel diameters less than 18 in. It tensions easily since it's only 0.022 in. thick. This blade cuts incredibly smoothly, and it's relatively inexpensive compared to carbide blades—although you can't expect it to last as long. Best of all, the kerf from this blade is a slim 1/32 in., half that of the other blades in this category. You'll definitely get more veneer from this blade.

Ripping 2-in.-thick hardwood

Option 1: Carbide-tipped, 4 pitch, hook tooth, 1/2 in. wide.

Option 2: Carbon steel, 4 pitch, hook tooth, 1/2 in. or 3/4 in. wide.

Comments: If you have a 14-in. bandsaw, you'll probably get truer cuts with a 1/2-in.-wide, 0.025-in.-thick blade rather than a 3/4-in.-wide, 0.032-in.-thick blade. Your saw stands a better chance of tensioning the thinner blade.

Cutting contours in 7/8-in.-thick maple (minimum radius 9/16 in.)

Option 1: Bimetal, 10 pitch, regular tooth, 1/4 in. wide.

Option 2: Bimetal, 6 pitch, regular tooth, 1/4 in. wide.

Comments: The 10-pitch blade would create a smoother surface, thus requiring less cleanup of sawmarks.

Cutting scrolls in 1/4-in. hardwood (minimum radius 1/16 in.)

Blade: Bimetal, 24 pitch, regular tooth, 1/16 in. wide.

Comments: This tiny 1/16-in. blade is your only choice for cutting tight contours. You'll need to replace the steel guide blocks with hardwood blocks or Cool Blocks. This blade can't be used on bandsaws equipped with bearing guides.

A 1/4-in., 6-pitch blade is a good choice for cutting most contours, but a 10-pitch blade leaves a smoother surface.

A 1/16-in., 24-pitch blade cuts intricate scrolls with little or no cleanup required.

My Favorite Bandsaw Blades

Here is a list of the blades that I keep on hand.

Carbide-tipped, 2/3 pitch, variable tooth, 1¼ in.

I use this stiff blade for slicing veneer from premium, highly figured planks. Because of the 0.042-in. thickness of the blade body, you'll need at least a 24-in. bandsaw to run this blade. Its recommended tension is 25,000 psi.

If you own a 14-in. saw, a ½-in. by 0.025-in., 3-pitch, hook-tooth, carbide-tipped blade is a great choice. Most 24-in. bandsaws can tension such a wide blade. You'll be impressed with the remarkably smooth surfaces it produces. Although this blade is expensive, the carbide teeth will outlast a carbon-steel blade by 25 to 1.

Spring steel, variable tooth, ½ in.

The main advantage of this blade is the tiny $\frac{1}{32}$-in. kerf. Designed especially for resawing, this spring-steel blade is marketed under the trade name The Wood Slicer. Although it doesn't come close to the long life of a carbide-tipped blade, it cuts almost as smoothly. The thin kerf means you can squeeze every slice of veneer possible out of your next prized board.

Bimetal, 3 pitch, hook tooth, ½ in.

The high-speed steel teeth in a bimetal blade stay sharp much longer than those of carbon steel, yet the price is only two to three times higher. This blade will never approach the smoothness of a carbide blade, but I use this one as a general-purpose resawing blade and save the carbide for cutting veneer.

Carbon-steel blades, various pitches, regular tooth, ⅛ in., ¼ in., and ⅜ in.

These three blades handle all my contour cutting. I choose the pitch based upon the stock thickness.

Width is determined by the type of cut—whether you're sawing a straight line or a curve. Tooth pitch is determined by the stock thickness. Tooth form influences how aggressively or smoothly the blade will cut. I always begin by selecting the blade width.

Selecting the best width

Each blade width has a minimum radius that it can cut without binding and dragging through the kerf. Attempting to squeeze a blade through a turn that is too tight can result in a number of problems. The blade will break, the teeth will be twisted into the guides (which causes them to lose sharpness and set), or the blade will be pulled off the saw's wheels. And anytime a blade comes off the wheels while the saw is running there's a good possibility that the teeth will be damaged or the blade will bend into something that resembles modern art.

The blade-radius chart on p. 294 shows the minimum radius that each width of blade can turn. Such a chart can often be found on the box that a blade is packed in when shipped. You may find it helpful to post a copy of this chart in a conspicuous place, such as on the wheel cover of your bandsaw or on the wall where you store blades.

You may be wondering why you just can't mount a narrow blade (such as ¼ in.) on your saw and cut all curves with that. This does work—but only to a degree. Narrow blades have a tendency

Factors to Consider When Selecting a Blade

Blade thickness

Less than 0.025 in. to save material when resawing

0.025 in. for wheel diameters no less than 12 in.

0.032 in. for wheel diameters no less than 18 in.

0.035 in. for wheel diameters no less than 24 in.

Tooth material

Carbon steel is inexpensive and readily available with a variety of characteristics.
Use carbide for resawing; it has long blade life and gives the smoothest finished surface.
Use bimetal for heavy ripping.

Blade width	Best use
$\frac{1}{16}$ in. to $\frac{1}{8}$ in.	Scrolling
$\frac{3}{16}$ in. to $\frac{1}{2}$ in.	Cutting curves
$\frac{3}{8}$ in. to 1 in. and above	Resawing (base your selection on what your saw can tension)

Pitch

2/3 tpi	Resawing
3 tpi	Resawing and ripping thick stock
4 tpi	Ripping stock $1\frac{1}{2}$ in. to 3 in. thick
6 tpi	General ripping and cutting curves in stock more than 1 in. thick
10 tpi	Cutting curves in stock $\frac{3}{4}$ in. to 1 in. thick
14 tpi	Cutting curves in stock $\frac{1}{2}$ in. to $\frac{3}{4}$ in. thick
18 tpi	Scrolling in stock $\frac{3}{8}$ in. to $\frac{5}{8}$ in. thick
24 tpi	Scrolling in stock $\frac{1}{4}$ in. to $\frac{1}{2}$ in. thick

Tooth form

Regular	Curves and scrolls
Variable	Resawing veneer and other valuable stock
Hook	Ripping and resawing

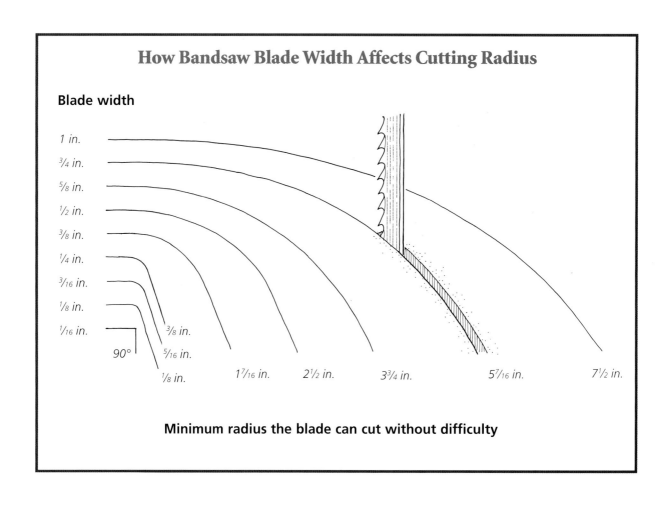

How Bandsaw Blade Width Affects Cutting Radius

Blade width

1 in.
3/4 in.
5/8 in.
1/2 in.
3/8 in.
1/4 in.
3/16 in.
1/8 in.
1/16 in.

90°

3/8 in.
5/16 in.
1/8 in.

1 7/16 in.   2 1/2 in.   3 3/4 in.   5 7/16 in.   7 1/2 in.

Minimum radius the blade can cut without difficulty

Use the widest blade

Use the widest blade possible for any job—even when cutting curves. Wider blades wander less and produce smoother curves. The limiting factor on blade width is your saw's ability to tension a blade. Many consumer-grade saws cannot tension a blade any wider than 1/2 in.

to wander. If you try to cut a large radius, such as a 36-in.-dia. tabletop for example, you'll have a hard time keeping the blades from straying from the line. You'll cut more precisely with a 1-in.-wide blade. However, with practice you'll probably cut a majority of curved work with a 1/4-in. or 3/8-in. blade.

When resawing, it's always an advantage to use the widest blade that your bandsaw can properly tension. Keep in

mind that the widest blade a saw can tension may not be as wide as the widest blade it can accept. For smaller saws, you'll most likely get better results from the next size narrower blade. Wider blades have more beam strength, but to fully create the beam strength the blade must be properly tensioned.

My own bandsaw, a 24-in. machine, can tension a 1 1/4-in. by 0.042-in. carbide blade to 25,000 psi. This blade is my best option for resawing thick, valuable stock because of its tremendous beam strength. With this blade I can easily slice 12-in.-wide boards into veneer that is consistently 1/32 in. thick.

Many of the consumer bandsaws that are mounted on a stand will accept a ¾-in. by 0.032-in. blade. This is your best choice for resawing if your saw can provide the tension it requires. If you experience blade deflection and a loss of quality in the cut with the ¾-in. blade, you'd be better off with a ½-in. by 0.025-in. blade.

Selecting the best tooth form

Tooth form affects the performance of the blade more than any other factor. A regular tooth gives the smoothest cut; a hook tooth cuts aggressively with little feed resistance; and a variable pitch cuts both smoothly and aggressively.

For cutting contours, a regular-tooth blade is often the best choice because it has the greatest number of teeth. This combined with a 0° rake angle gives you a smooth, finished surface that requires little cleanup.

A hook tooth is my choice for general resawing, such as when sawing thick planks into thin drawer parts. The coarser pitch combined with a positive cutting angle makes quick work of any hardwood.

When sawing veneer from a plank of valuable hardwood, a hook blade will do a great job, but a variable-pitch blade will leave a smoother finish. Also remember that the variable-pitch blade reduces vibration during cutting.

Selecting the proper pitch

Pitch is the number of teeth measured from tooth tip to tooth tip on 1 in. of blade length. Blades with a continuous pattern of teeth are called constant pitch.

Blades with teeth that vary in size are called variable pitch.

The major factor to consider when selecting proper tooth pitch is the thickness of the stock. In general, you want to select a blade that will have no less than 6 and no more than 12 teeth in the stock at any given time (see the drawing on p. 296). For example, if you're cutting 1-in.-thick stock, a 6-pitch blade would be a good choice, but a 14-pitch one would be too fine. However, if the stock were only ½ in. thick, a 14-pitch blade would be optimum for the stock thickness. Selecting the proper pitch is made easier by the fact that there is a limited number of pitch selections for each blade width. Although the range of available pitch is broad, from 2 tpi to 32 tpi, wide blades generally have fewer teeth and narrow blades have a greater number of teeth.

It's also important to consider how pitch will affect the life of the blade, specifically a carbon-steel blade that is easily damaged by overheating. For example, a fine-pitch blade will overheat when used on thick stock because the gullets become packed with sawdust. This causes the blade to quickly dull and lose its set. Once this occurs, the blade is worthless, so choosing the correct pitch will substantially increase blade life.

Remember that the blade pitch determines the smoothness of the cut and the speed at which the stock can be cut.

> **Try a narrower resaw blade**
>
> If you have a 14-in. bandsaw, try resawing with a ⅜-in. or ½-in. variable-pitch blade. Most saws have sufficient stiffness to tension these blades, which cut fairly aggressively and leave a wonderfully smooth surface.

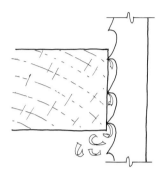
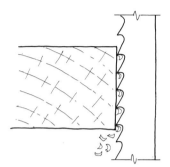
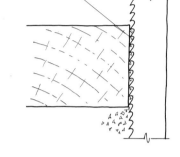
Feed slowly

When bandsawing, slower cuts are usually best, whether you're resawing or cutting contours. You'll get a cleaner cut, and you can saw closer to the line.

Speed is most important in a production setting and when ripping rough stock. However, the average woodworker normally isn't cutting enough material to be concerned about whether the blade is cutting 20 ft. per minute or 22 ft. When sawing veneer, a slow feed rate gives you a truer cut and a smoother finish with less cleanup of sawmarks—and maybe even an extra slice of veneer from your plank.

When cutting contours, you'll be able to follow the layout line more precisely if you don't hurry while cutting. The advantage is that you'll spend less time later removing bumps and irregularities where the blade didn't quite follow the line.

Sometimes smoothness and precision may not be too important. When I'm sawing a contour that will later be flush-trimmed with a router or a shaper, I'm not concerned with the surface quality from the bandsaw. In a situation such as this, I'm using the bandsaw merely to remove the excess wood before shaping.

However, when cutting fine, detailed scrollwork, I am concerned with surface quality. Some details are so fine it is difficult or impossible to smooth them afterwards with a file or other tool. In this case, I want the blade to create a smooth, finished surface, so I use a slow, steady feed so I can carefully follow the line.

You must decide which is more important to you—speed or smoothness. You can't get the best of both in the same blade. However, you can select a blade that is a good compromise.

Caring for Your Blades

The heat generated from sawing causes pitch and gum to build up on the surfaces of the teeth and in the gullets. Once the teeth and gullets become covered with gunk, the blade performs as though it were dull. Buildup can occur quickly with resinous woods like pine, but all woods contribute to the problem. The excessive heat from a blade with too fine a pitch significantly speeds up the accumulation of crud, so selecting the proper pitch helps with this problem.

Cleaning blades is easy, and for the small amount of effort it takes, you get a substantial difference in blade performance. Most woodworking stores and catalogs sell a blade-cleaning liquid. To use it, you simply remove the blade, spray it with cleaner, and wipe off the residue.

Because bandsaw-blade teeth can be easily damaged, I always store my blades on a wall-mounted rack so the teeth don't touch. Carbide teeth are brittle and especially fragile.

Have you noticed how blades are coiled into three loops when you purchase them? Coiling the blades is easy to do, and the blades take up a lot less room in your shop. There are three ways to coil a blade (see the photo essay on pp. 298–299). Try all three to find the one that you like best.

Feed resistance

Feed resistance is the amount of pressure required to push a workpiece past a saw-blade. Certain factors, such as pitch, hook angle, and blade thickness, dramatically affect the feed resistance. Because resawing thick stock is so demanding, a blade with a positive rake angle creates far less feed resistance than a blade with a rake angle of 0°.

Cleaning the pitch from this blade will dramatically improve its performance.

Coiling Blades for Storage

There are three standard ways to coil a bandsaw blade. Try each one to see which is best for you.

First Method

1 Grasp the blade with both hands in the middle of the blade (photo at right). Your palms should be facing inward, leading with your thumbs on the outside of the blade.

2 Twist the blade inward with your thumbs, and as you do so, bring your hands closer together (photo at left below).

3 As you bring your hands together, three coils will form (photo at right below).

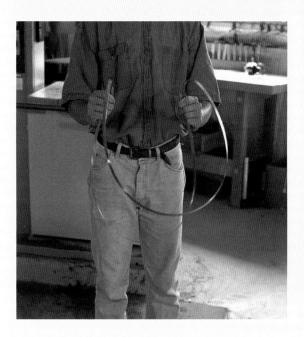

Second Method

1 Grasp the blade with both hands in the middle of the blade.

2 Twist the blade forward with your right hand and backward with your left. The blade will coil into three rings.

Third Method

1 Grasp the blade with one hand with your fingers facing toward you, and allow the blade to rest on the floor (with a wide blade, you may need to use two hands). Place your foot on the blade to hold it in place.

2 Rotate your wrist, and as you do so, push the twisting blade toward the floor. This will cause the blade to coil into three rings.

Uncoiling a large blade can be tricky. By simply grasping two of the coils and spreading them apart, the blade will naturally uncoil, but be careful. A large, coiled blade has a lot of tension in it, and if it suddenly springs open you can get a nasty cut. I recommend wearing gloves and safety glasses and holding the blade at arm's length when you uncoil it.

A resistance welder makes welding bandsaw blades almost foolproof. It's the fastest way to make your own bandsaw blades.

Making Your Own Carbon-Steel Blades

If you have the time and the inclination, you can save money by welding your own carbon-steel blades from coil stock. By purchasing the stock in 100-ft. rolls, then cutting and welding or brazing the blades yourself, you can expect to pay about half of what you normally spend on blades.

I recommend welding only carbon-steel blades that are ½ in. or less in width. The spring steel used in the bodies of bimetal and carbide blades is very difficult to weld properly. Welding them is best left to professional saw shops.

Once you've learned to weld blades, you'll find it comes in handy. If a blade breaks before it's dull, you can fix it yourself. Also, you may occasionally want to make an interior cut on stock that's too thick for a jigsaw. You can thread the blade through a hole in the stock, weld the blade ends together, and make the cut with your bandsaw.

There are two ways you can weld a blade in your own shop. You can buy a resistance welder that's similar to the one saw shops use, or you can braze the blades with a torch and silver brazing solder.

The first method, using a resistance welder, is faster but the welder is an expensive purchase. On the other hand, you can buy an inexpensive brazing kit from most woodworking-supply outfits, but brazing is time-consuming and has more of a learning curve. In the next section, I'll outline the steps involved in using both of these methods.

Resistance welding

A resistance welder uses electrical energy to create intense heat to fuse the blade ends together. The welding process leaves the joint brittle, so it must be annealed by being reheated and cooled slowly. Here's how to weld a blade with a resistance welder.

1. **Cut the blade to length.** Most bandsaws will accept blades that are 1 in. or so longer than the specified length. I always cut a new blade the maximum length the saw will accept. This gives me an extra try at welding if the first attempt fails.

2. **Check the ends of the cut for squareness.** If they are not 90°, use a grinder to make them so.

3. **Clamp the blade ends within the electrodes of the welder.** The ends of the blade should touch.

4. **Set the pressure control.** The setting is determined by the width of the blade.

5. **Press the weld button.** Hold the button until the weld is complete. During welding, the blade ends will turn bright orange and quickly return to normal color at the completion of the weld. The entire process takes three or four seconds.

6. **Annealing.** Reposition the blade at the front edge of the electrode clamp, then jog the annealing button until the steel at the weld is cherry red in color.

Safety Guidelines for Using a Resistance Welder

- Wear eye protection when welding and grinding blades.
- Don't touch the electrode jaws when welding.
- Avoid touching the blade ends. All three steps of this procedure—welding, annealing, and grinding—heat the steel enough to cause a serious burn.

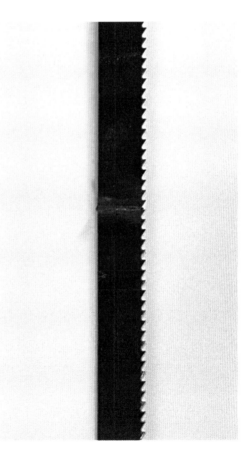

This is how the joint appears after resistance welding. The excess flash must be ground away so the blade runs smoothly over the wheels and through the guides.

Troubleshooting Welding Problems

If you've never used a resistance blade welder, then you may be one of the lucky ones who get it right the very first time. If not, I've provided a list of problems along with their solutions that you can use as a guide to get it right.

Problem	Diagnosis
There's a spark but no weld when the weld button is depressed.	• The ends of the blade are not square and even. • The pressure switch is set too low.
The joint is melted with a large gap or gaps in the weld.	• The pressure switch is set too high.
The blade easily breaks before you can even mount it on the bandsaw.	• The blade was overheated during annealing.
The blade ends are overlapped.	• The ends must be flat and straight so that they butt together perfectly when clamped in the electrode jaws.
Excessive flash on narrow blades.	• The pressure switch is set too high. • The first tooth on each end of a regular-tooth blade should be ground away before welding.

Allow a few minutes for the blade to cool naturally.

7. **Grinding the flash.** Once you've annealed the weld, grind away the flash around the joint so that the blade will run smoothly through the saw guides. Be careful not to grind the blade or teeth; grinding into the blade body weakens it. Also, grind the flash away slowly so you don't overheat the blade.

8. **Final annealing.** After grinding, anneal the blade once more, then allow the blade to cool for a few minutes before using it.

Brazing

Brazing is a much more economical option for making blades than using a resistance welder. Most woodworking-supply houses offer brazing kits that con-

To braze a blade, the ends must be held firmly in position. Apply flux to the joint before brazing.

tain a blade fixture for holding the end while brazing, a jar of flux, and silver brazing alloy for less than $50. You'll have to supply a torch that burns propane, butane, or MAPP gas. A torch with a small head makes it easier for you to avoid overheating the joint.

When properly done, a brazed joint is actually stronger than the blade itself. In fact, brazing is used for several other woodworking applications, such as joining carbide sawteeth to blade bodies and joining carbide cutting surfaces to router bits. Here are the steps I use to braze a bandsaw blade.

1. Bevel the blade ends. For greatest strength, the ends of the blade must be filed or ground to a bevel. The width of the bevel should be three times the blade thickness, and the ends of the bevel must be 90°. To ensure a uniform bevel, you'll need to clamp the blade ends. I use a piece of angle iron held in a vise and bulldog clips to hold the blade to the angle iron.

2. Clean the blade ends. Remove any trace of a burr from filing or grinding, then clean the blade ends with mineral spirits to remove any oil that may prevent the alloy from flowing. Afterwards, wipe the ends dry.

3. Clamp the blade ends in the fixture. Proper alignment is crucial for a strong braze. The bevels should overlap, and the backs should be flush.

The blade is heated with a small torch until the edges are a dull red.

4. Spread the flux. Spread the flux about ½ in. up from the blade ends. It's important to get flux on the bevels as well. To do this, I push the lower bevel downward, which allows me to get the bristles of the flux brush into the joint.

5. Brazing. This is the most difficult part of the procedure. The goal is to evenly heat the blade ends to the point that the alloy flows into the joint. The flux and the blade ends provide an indication of when you've reached the proper temperature. When the temperature is right, the flux will be clear, the blade will be almost white, and the edges will be a dull red. Next, place the end of the alloy onto the joint while continuing to apply heat with the torch. As the alloy is touched to the hot steel, it will be drawn into the joint by capillary action and create a strong bond.

7. Remove excess alloy. After allowing the blade to cool, remove any excess alloy from the joint. First, clean off the flux with a rag, then smooth the joint with a mill file, being careful not to dull the teeth.

Bandsaw Safety

The bandsaw has a reputation as being a benign machine. The back of the blade can't cut you like a circular sawblade can. More important, you won't experience violent kickbacks while using your bandsaw. But any power tool that is designed for cutting wood can quickly and easily wreak havoc with flesh and bone. I learned early in my woodworking career to treat the bandsaw with the respect that it deserves.

When I work on any machine, I follow all the safety rules. Most woodworking accidents occur because the operator did some procedure he knew he shouldn't have done. By requiring myself and my students to adhere to the rules in every situation, no matter how small the cut, I've managed to build furniture and teach a shopful of students for more than 20 years with no serious injuries.

A turning blade is an obvious safety hazard, but bandsaws also produce a more insidious hazard—dust. It's essential to protect your respiratory system from the dust, and the best way to do that is with a dust-collection system. There's no need to worry about complicated separators and ductwork: A shop vac is an adequate bandsaw dust-collection system when coupled with a mask.

Bandsaw Safety Guidelines

When it comes to bandsaw safety, you, the operator, play the critical role. I've found that by keeping my bandsaw and its guards in working order and following a few simple guidelines, bandsaw safety is virtually assured. The guidelines that I use are listed on the next two pages.

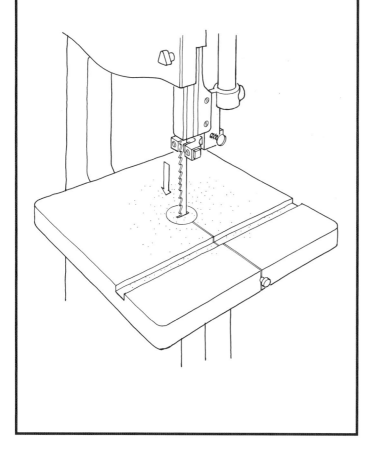
Keep your fingers out of the path of the blade. Although this may seem obvious, it's easy to allow your fingers to be in the wrong place as you are cutting contours. As you turn and rotate the workpiece to follow the layout line, you must frequently reposition your hands to keep them a safe distance from the blade's path. I never allow the sawing operation to prevent me from being aware of my hand position.

Gradually decrease the feed pressure as you approach the end of the cut. As the blade nears the edge of the workpiece, be ready for the fact that the feed resistance is dramatically reduced right at the end of the cut. If you continue pushing the workpiece with the same degree of force, you can lose control as the blade exits the kerf.

Use push sticks when ripping narrow stock or when resawing. Keep your fingers intact by keeping them a safe distance from the blade. I keep a push stick in a convenient location and use it when ripping narrow stock or when resawing. It's impossible to push the stock safely with your hands during the last few inches of resawing. The stock is often too thin for safe placement of your hands. Also, I've seen the last few inches suddenly and unexpectedly split apart when resawing. I always place a push block within easy reach, and I use it to finish the cut.

Always keep the wheel covers shut while the bandsaw is running. It may be tempting to check the tracking or guide adjustment while the saw is running, but if the tracking is way off and the blade jumps the wheels or breaks, you are unprotected.

Keep the upper guide adjusted approximately ¼ in. above the stock. One of the most common bandsaw safety mistakes is to cut a thick piece of stock and then cut a thinner piece without first lowering the guide (see the top photo on p. 308). If you don't lower the guide, a long length of blade is exposed, and it's more likely the blade will deflect while cutting, possibly ruining your cut.

Keep the blade guard in place. The guidepost has a sheet-metal guard to cover the blade. If the blade breaks, the guard is one of your major lines of defense. If you must remove the guard for blade changing, always replace it.

Disconnect the bandsaw from its power source before changing blades. I also make all tracking and guide adjustments with the power disconnected.

Always wear eye and ear protection when operating a bandsaw. Today more than ever, there's a broad selection of safety equipment from which to choose. It's easy to find eye and ear protection that's lightweight, comfortable, and effective, so make use of it.

Wear gloves when handling large blades. Long, wide blades have a lot of tension when coiled. When uncoiling a large blade (or any blade, for that matter) wear gloves and use caution.

Protect your respiratory system. The dust that's generated from the bandsaw is some of the finest from any woodworking machine. And it's the fine dust that does the most damage to your lungs. Also, fine dust stays suspended in the shop air for a long time. For these reasons, I use a dust

It's not uncommon for the last couple of inches of a board being resawn to suddenly split. A simple push block keeps your hands out of danger. Note that the hand on the board is behind the blade.

What to Do If a Blade Breaks

Ideally, blades don't break or if they do, the teeth are already worn out and it's time to throw out the blade anyway. But blades do occasionally break prematurely because of excess tension or stress from trying to push the blade through too tight a turn.

When a blade does break, it typically stays safely enclosed within the saw cabinet. When this happens, use the foot brake (if your saw has one) to stop the lower wheel. Of course, the brake doesn't stop the upper wheel unless the blade is intact, which it isn't. So for safety's sake, don't open the cabinet to install a new blade until both wheels have come to a complete stop. Otherwise the spinning top wheel could potentially send the blade or a fragment of it flying.

collector with my bandsaw, especially when resawing, which produces a huge amount of dust. Because bandsaw dust is so fine, you'll want a collector that traps fine dust and not just chips.

Keeping the upper guides about ¼ in. above the cut minimizes blade exposure.

Protect your lungs

Even the best collector can't capture 100% of the dust, so it's still a good idea to wear a high-quality dust mask.

Fitting Dust Collection to Your Bandsaw

Fine wood dust stays airborne the longest and does the most damage to your health. That's exactly the kind of dust a bandsaw produces, and lots of it, when resawing. Luckily, it's not difficult to add dust collection to your bandsaw—and you won't need an expensive collector, either. Any shop vacuum cleaner will do the job (but wear your hearing protection because the average shop vac is incredibly loud).

The most important feature of any dust-collection system is the ability to trap the fine dust particles. Many dust collectors, portable or otherwise, really only trap and hold large particles such as wood chips and shavings. The systems I've been most impressed with use a pleated filter to

Bandsaw Safety Guidelines

Here's a list of bandsaw safety guidelines. Photocopy it and hang it in your shop.

- Keep your fingers out of the path of the blade.
- Decrease the feed pressure as you near the end of a cut.
- Use push sticks when ripping or resawing.
- Keep the wheel covers shut when the saw is running.
- Keep the upper guide about ¼ in. above the workpiece.
- Keep the blade guard in place.
- Disconnect the bandsaw power source before changing blades.
- Wear eye and ear protection when bandsawing.
- Wear gloves when handling blades.
- Protect your respiratory system.

This dust collection fitting is directly beneath the table to catch the dust at the source.

trap the fine, flourlike dust. This filter resembles the filters used in your car's air and oil systems.

Unlike bandsaws made 20 years ago, most new bandsaws have a dust-collection fitting. Most are mounted directly beneath the saw's table, near the lower guide (see the bottom photo on the facing page). The idea is to catch the dust at the source before it becomes airborne. Although this fitting position works well, the momentum of the dust coming off the blade still propels some of it past the area the vacuum is able to clean.

Other manufacturers mount the fitting in the lower corner of the cabinet (see the photo below). This isn't as good as a fitting mounted nearer to the guides since few vacuums are powerful enough to pull the dust that distance. This method only catches the dust that is propelled into the lower corner of the cabinet.

In an effort to trap as much dust as possible, I've set up the bandsaw at the university where I teach with fittings in both positions: under the table and inside the cabinet. This method works the best by far. You must realize, however, that it is impossible to catch all of the dust before it enters the air, so it's still a good idea to wear a dust mask.

A second dust collection port in the lower left-hand corner of the bandsaw cabinet captures dust that gets by the first fitting.

Dust Collection for Resawing

Resawing produces an enormous quantity of very fine wood dust—the kind that is most hazardous to your health. To catch as much dust as possible, use two portable dust collectors hooked up to the bandsaw.

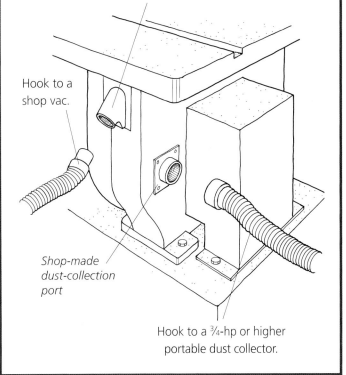

Standard dust-collection port under the table

Hook to a shop vac.

Shop-made dust-collection port

Hook to a ¾-hp or higher portable dust collector.

Tuning Your Bandsaw

Bandsaws are wonderfully versatile machines, but they still need periodic maintenance and adjustment to perform at their peak. And given the flexible nature of the bandsaw blade, you'll be spending a fair bit of time adjusting the guides, since they'll need adjusting at least every time you change the blade, maybe even more. As your saw ages, you'll be dealing with worn tires, bearings, and belts.

Vibration and tracking are common problems, especially for inexpensive consumer bandsaws. In this chapter, I'll discuss how to investigate and repair tracking and vibration problems. But if you're having a difficult time with a bandsaw you've just unpacked, I suggest you return it. These days, because of the fierce com-

petition for your woodworking dollars, it's not difficult to find a well-constructed, smooth-running bandsaw for a reasonable price. On the other hand, it may be well worth your effort to correct flaws on a used machine you picked up at a bargain price.

Many bandsaw problems such as poor tracking, frequent blade breakage, and vibration can be summed up in one word: tires. Smooth-crowned tires are a major key to bandsaw performance, but as tires age they become worn and sometimes develop cracks. Narrow blades can create grooves in your bandsaw's tires, which can make tracking difficult. Pitch, dust, and dirt can build up on tires and cause problems that are similar to those caused by wear. Fortunately, these and

By its very nature, a bandsaw blade is prone to wandering and deflection. For maximum precision, it needs the support of carefully adjusted guides.

When changing blades, open the guides so that they can't interfere with tensioning and tracking the blade.

many other bandsaw problems are not difficult to correct.

In this chapter, I'll cover a variety of techniques you can use to keep your bandsaw singing. From tire changes to guide adjustments, it's all here. So read on to discover ways to get peak performance from your bandsaw.

Changing Blades

The different blade widths, tooth forms, and pitches available for your bandsaw are what make it so versatile. As I mentioned, if you want to take full advantage of your bandsaw's versatility, you'll have to change blades often. Unfortunately, changing a blade can be a complex job, one that may seem like a chore to avoid. But with some practice, you'll find that it becomes quick and easy. The key is to follow a set of steps in a logical order. For example, you should track the blade before you adjust the guides, otherwise you'll have to adjust them a second time. Because blade tension affects tracking, you'll want to first bring the blade up to proper tension. I've listed the steps in their proper sequence in the sidebar on p. 312.

The Proper Sequence of Bandsaw-Blade Tune-Up

1. Disconnect the power.

2. Release the blade tension. I lower the upper wheel just enough to slip the blade off.

3. Set the guides so they don't interfere with the blade in any way—at the sides or at the back.

4. Install the new blade, first on the upper wheel, then around the lower wheel.

5. Apply just enough tension to take the slack out of the blade.

6. Turn one wheel a few times to move the blade to the center of the tire.

7. Tension the blade with a meter, or if using the saw's gauge, set the tension for the next widest blade.

8. Track the blade.

9. Adjust the upper and lower thrust bearings so they don't quite touch the blade.

10. Set the distance from the upper and lower guides to the blade with a scrap of paper or a dollar bill.

11. Square the table to the blade.

12. Round the back of the blade.

Expensive blades and tension

Bimetal, carbide-tipped, and spring-steel blades can be tensioned significantly tighter than carbon blades. That means they will be more rigid and less likely to deflect and wander in difficult cutting situations, making them an ideal choice for resawing.

When to reduce tension

The less likely a blade is to deflect in a certain kind of cut, the less tension you should put on the blade.

Tensioning Blades

Finding the correct blade tension always seems to be something of a mystery among woodworkers. There are all kinds of methods out there, such as plucking the blade like a guitar string until it produces a clear tone of a specific musical pitch. Although I have no doubt that this method works for a few musically inclined woodworkers, I question its practicality and accuracy for the rest of us. Other theories are even more abstract, such as the notion that you should find the tension that makes your bandsaw "comfortable." To me, this statement seems too vague.

In an effort to avoid adding to the confusion, I'm going to give you some practical ideas on tensioning blades so that you can adjust your saw for accurate cuts. But first I'd like to make some points about bandsaw blades and tension.

Finding the right tension

Bandsaw blades require tension and lots of it to consistently produce straight, uniform cuts, especially in thick or dense stock. Most blade manufacturers recommend 15,000 psi to 20,000 psi for a common carbon-steel blade.

The tension scales on most bandsaws are inaccurate. It's common for scales to indicate a tension far above the actual tension on the blade.

However, bimetal, spring-steel, and carbide-tipped blades are much stronger than carbon-steel blades, so manufacturers recommend a much higher tension: 25,000 psi to 30,000 psi. Why do bandsaw blades need so much tension? For beam strength. The tighter the blade is stretched, the more rigid it becomes and the less tendency it will have to deflect in the cut.

You only need maximum tension for the most demanding cuts, such as sawing dense hardwoods or stock of the maximum thickness that will fit under a saw's guides. In simpler circumstances, you can back off the tension a little.

All blades, regardless of width, require the same amount of tension for maximum beam strength. The variable factor is the amount of pulling force needed. For example, it takes approximately 200 lb. of force pulling on a 1/4-in.-wide by 0.025-in.-thick blade to create 25,000 psi of tension. Conversely, a 3/4-in.-wide by 0.032-in.-thick blade will require approximately 800 lb. of force to create the same 25,000 psi of tension.

Measuring tension

Bandsaw-blade tension scales are notoriously inaccurate. Tests conducted by consumer woodworking magazines have shown this, and my own tests using six different bandsaws confirmed their results. For my tests, I used a blade tension meter that clamps to the blade and gives an accurate reading on a dial indica-

A meter that clamps onto the blade is the most accurate way to tension a bandsaw blade.

Adjusting tension

You can assume the gauge on your bandsaw reads too low. Set the blade tension at the point indicated for the next wider blade.

tor (see the photo at left). The readings of all the saw tension scales that I tested, including those on the expensive floor-model saws, were lower than that indicated on the meter. Although the scales on the large machines were close to being accurate, the scales on the 14-in. saws were way off. To make matters worse, the springs used in the tension scales on bandsaws weaken with age, further reducing their accuracy.

So how do you know when blade tension is correct? The most accurate way is to check it with a tension meter such as the one I used in my tests. But tension meters are expensive—typically around $300. I know what you're thinking—is there another way? Yes, but none is as accurate as a tension meter. Other tensioning methods will work, but they're a lot like gauging air pressure in a bicycle tire simply by squeezing it.

A good place to begin is to tension the blade until the meter reads proper tension for the next wider blade. For example, if you're tensioning a ³⁄₈-in. blade, I would set the scale to ½ in. This works most of the time, since most sawing operations don't require maximum tension.

Another method is to test the tension by the amount that the blade will deflect sideways. First, I set the upper guides about 6 in. off the table. Then using a moderate amount of pressure from my index finger (obviously with the saw turned off!), I push the blade sideways. I don't want the blade to bow more than ¼ in. (see the photo on the facing page).

Of course, you'll have to develop a feel for how much pressure is moderate.

Although both of these methods work, they are imprecise. But as I stated earlier, in most situations maximum blade tension isn't necessary. I always test the blade tension with a trial piece before making cuts in an actual workpiece. If the blade wanders in the cut (assuming other factors such as blade sharpness and guide setting are correct), I'll gradually increase the blade tension.

Blade tensioning for resawing

Resawing thick, hard stock places the most demands on the blade. If the blade tension is inadequate, the blade will bow and the stock may be spoiled (see the drawing on p. 316).

I remember a situation some years ago when I attempted to resaw a wide board. It was a plank of deep red cherry—highly figured with truly awesome curly grain. I wanted to make book-matched panels for a door in a cupboard. Since I was in a hurry, I neglected the necessary precautions such as selecting a blade with the right pitch and tensioning it properly. The blade bowed badly during cutting, making one of the planks terribly thin at the end. The stock was thicker than necessary, so I was lucky enough just to squeeze out the thickness I needed from the resawn plank. But I learned my lesson: A blade needs beam strength for resawing.

Beam strength, the blade's ability to resist deflection, is achieved by combining several factors, including correct blade

If you don't have a tension meter, you can roughly tension the blade by eye. Raise the guides about 6 in. off the table and push the blade. The blade should deflect no more than ¼ in.

When the blade vibrates

The array of running gear on a bandsaw (tires, wheels, pulleys, belts, blade, etc.) can set up harmonic vibrations even when everything else is right. If that happens to you, try changing the blade tension slightly, either more or less, just enough to change the harmonic.

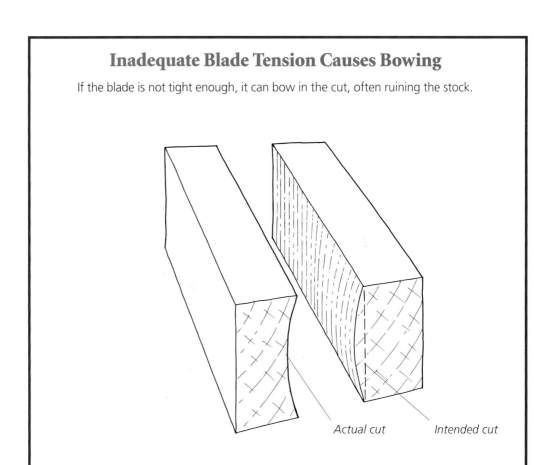

Inadequate Blade Tension Causes Bowing

If the blade is not tight enough, it can bow in the cut, often ruining the stock.

Actual cut   *Intended cut*

Don't fully compress the spring

I don't recommend completely compressing the tension spring. You might get more tension, but the spring is there to absorb minor vibration or slight bounces during cutting. The spring helps prevent the blade from breaking.

pitch, blade width, and precise guide settings. But a key factor in achieving beam strength is applying the maximum blade tension that the blade manufacturer recommends.

Some woodworkers may question whether maximum blade tension will in any way damage the saw. Based on years of experience with my 14-in. Delta bandsaw, the answer is no. But I should make it clear that I recommend using maximum blade tension only for occasional, brief periods of resawing. Otherwise, I keep the tension low for everyday sawing. I release the tension when I know I won't be using the saw for a while.

If you've purchased a bandsaw with a wheel diameter of 18 in. or more, then you're most likely planning to do serious resawing from time to time. In that case, I suggest that you also spend the money on a tension meter. Large bandsaws have frames that are capable of overtensioning a blade, which causes it to break. A tension meter is the most accurate way of setting the blade tension.

If you own one of the many consumer bandsaws with a wheel diameter of 14 in. or less, then I would use a blade no wider than ½ in. for resawing and tension it until the tension spring is nearly compressed (see the photo at right).

Tracking

Tracking a blade involves tilting the upper wheel, which causes the blade to ride in the center of the tire. If the wheels of the saw are in alignment and the tires are crowned, the blade should track entirely on its own without having to tilt the upper wheel. Then why have the tracking adjustment? It compensates for slight wheel misalignments that naturally occur when you tension a blade (see the drawing on p. 318). When the blade is tensioned, it places several hundred pounds of force on the wheels, a force that is easily enough to cause wheel misalignment on even the largest industrial bandsaws.

If you have a new bandsaw that won't track a blade, I recommend that you

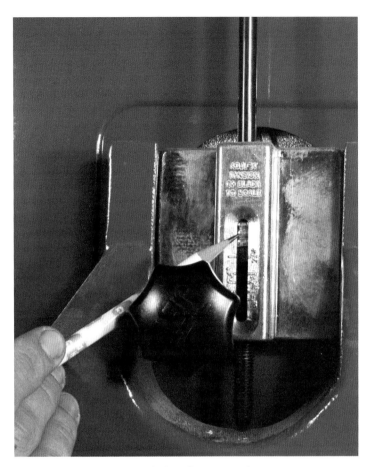

On a small consumer-grade bandsaw, I tension a ½-in. blade for resawing by almost completely compressing the tension spring.

If your bandsaw won't track

Severe misalignment is rare in bandsaws. If even careful adjustment won't keep your blades on track, it may mean that the wheels are warped or the frame is bent.

Tracking a Blade

Most bandsaws don't need a tracking adjustment until the blade is tensioned at or near the maximum. That is when the upper wheel may become misaligned so that the blade won't track on the center of the tires. You can easily correct the misalignment by carefully turning the tracking knob until the blade settles on the center of the tires.

The upper wheel tilts from side to side to keep the blade on the center of the wheel. The blade will follow the direction of the top of the wheel.

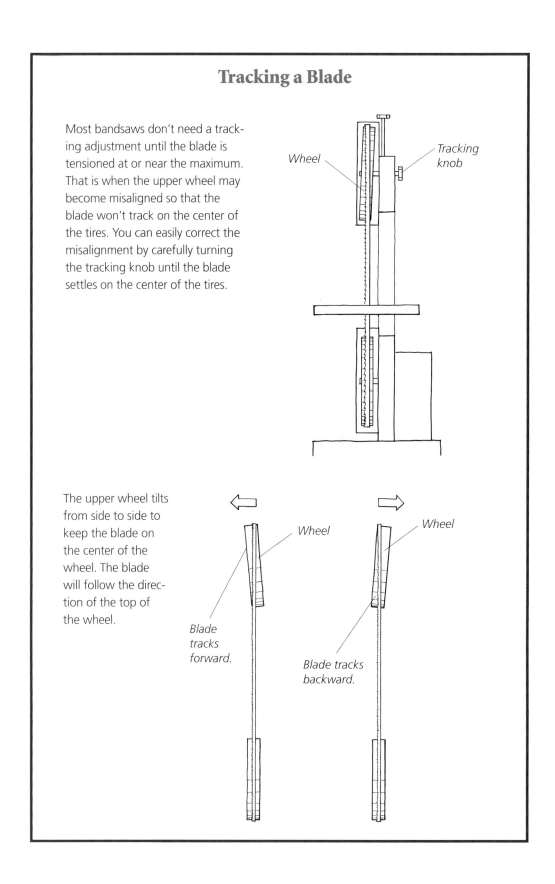

Wheel

Tracking knob

Wheel

Wheel

Blade tracks forward.

Blade tracks backward.

return the saw. If your bandsaw won't tension and track a blade, then you need a better saw.

To track a blade once it's tensioned, spin the top wheel with one hand while slowly turning the tracking knob with the other (see the photo at right). The blade will travel in the direction of the tilt. All new bandsaws have crowned tires, and the blade should track at the crown's center point. The crown on large bandsaws is very slight to give wide blades better support.

Once the blade is consistently tracking, lock the setting with the lock nut on the tracking screw, then close the covers and momentarily turn on the power for a final check of the tracking.

Adjusting the Guides

For accurate cutting, the blade needs to be fully supported at the back and at the sides both above and below the table. The goal is to set the guides so that they aren't in contact with the blade until the blade starts to wander. When the saw isn't running, set the guides right next to the blade but not touching it.

The upper and lower thrust wheels support the back of the blade to prevent feed pressure from pushing it off the saw's wheels. Set them just slightly behind the blade. They should not spin until the stock is fed into the blade.

The side blocks or bearings prevent the blade from twisting or bowing sideways. Like the thrust wheel, the side supports should contact the blade only when there

Tracking the blade is a two-handed job. Spin the upper wheel while adjusting the tracking knob until the blade rides on the center of the tire.

Adjusting the Thrust Bearings and Guides

The thrust bearings and guides surround the blade and keep it from bowing, twisting, or wandering in a cut. Adjust them so they are not touching the blade when the saw is idle but will come in contact with the blade the instant you start sawing.

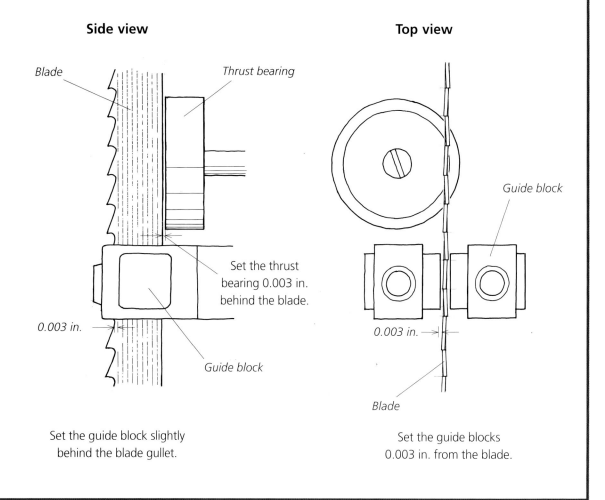

Side view

Blade

Thrust bearing

Set the thrust bearing 0.003 in. behind the blade.

0.003 in.

Guide block

Set the guide block slightly behind the blade gullet.

Top view

Guide block

0.003 in.

Blade

Set the guide blocks 0.003 in. from the blade.

is pressure from cutting. But if the side supports are set too far from the blade, the blade will wander, making it difficult to saw accurately.

To prevent damaging the teeth of the blade, set the guides. First, set the guides behind the gullets (see the drawing above). Then slip a piece of paper or a dollar bill between each guide and the blade, and bring the guide toward the blade until it barely grips the paper (see the bottom photo on p. 322). Lock the guide in place before removing the paper.

Rounding the Back of the Blade

A blade with back corners that have been slightly rounded cuts smoother, tighter curves and increases the life of your thrust bearings (see the drawing below). You can buy a special stone for honing the backs of your bandsaw blades at a woodworking specialty store. To use it, simply hold the stone on the tabletop with the blade running and bevel the back corners. Then slowly rotate the stone around the back of the blade, rounding the corners.

When the back corners of the blade have been rounded, the blades slide around tight curves more readily.

Blade not rounded

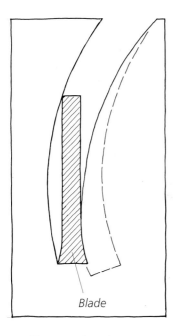

Blade

The curve is not as tight. There is a twisting force on the blade.

Blade rounded

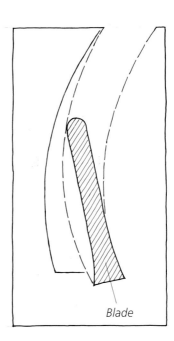

Blade

The corner of the blade does not interfere. The rounded back slides along the kerf.

Mounting a ¹⁄₁₆-in.-wide Blade

A narrow ¹⁄₁₆-in. scrolling blade has very little blade body, which makes it impossible to run with the block or bearing guides. When the blocks are set far enough back from the gullet to protect the teeth, they don't adequately support the blade.

If you have block guides, you can run a blade this narrow by replacing the steel blocks with "Cool Blocks." Cool Blocks are made from a fibrous material that is impregnated with a dry lubricant. It is soft enough to surround the blade without damage to the teeth. Instead of Cool Blocks, you can also use hardwood. I make the guide blocks for my bandsaw from scraps of maple or cherry.

Before I mount the blocks into the guide frame, I cut a very small notch into one of the blocks for the blade to ride in. Then when I mount the blocks in the guide frame, I pinch them together so that they completely surround the tiny blade.

To guide a ¹⁄₁₆-in.-wide blade, replace the steel guide blocks with shopmade wooden blocks. Cut a notch in one block, and support the blade by completely surrounding it.

You don't need a feeler gauge to set guides. Just adjust the guides so they don't quite grip a scrap of paper set between them and the blade.

Vibration Problems

Vibration is probably the most common bandsaw problem and certainly the most annoying. Because the bandsaw has so many moving parts, any number of things, such as the tires, wheels, motor, pulleys, or belt, may cause the vibration. Even a flimsy sheet-metal stand can contribute to the problem. The good news is that these problems are easy to trace, and most are easy to repair.

Tires

Bandsaw tires cushion the blade and provide traction to power the blade. With the exception of some older bandsaws, most bandsaws have crowned tires in which the middle of the tire is higher and slopes

Crowned Tires Keep the Blade on Track

The blade naturally rides on the slightly higher middle of a crowned wheel or tire.

Most new bandsaws have crowned wheels so it's unnecessary to crown the tire after installation. This wheel also has a channel to hold the tire in place.

Keep the tires clean

Clean tires make for consistent tracking and smooth performance. Pitch, dirt, and fine dust on the tires can cause the blade to bounce, wander, and vibrate. You can remove this buildup by using mineral spirits and a stiff brush. To help keep the tires clean, mount a stiff brush on the saw frame to sweep the tires as the saw is running. A dust collector also helps.

slightly toward the edges. Crowned tires make it easier to keep blades properly tracking since they naturally tend to ride on the highest point of the crown (see the drawing above). The tires on large bandsaws have relatively less crown for better support of wider blades.

Age and use cause grooves and unevenness in bandsaw tires and eventually the loss of the crown. When this occurs, you'll experience blade vibration and bouncing and difficulty in keeping the blade tracking. Fortunately, changing tires is not difficult, especially on small bandsaws.

The process involves just three steps: removing the old tire, stretching the new tire around the rim, and gluing it in place. To simplify the process further, many new

bandsaws have a channel milled into the rim of the wheel, which makes it easier to center the tire. Better yet, the surface of the channel is crowned and the tire conforms to it, making it unnecessary to crown the tire (see the photo above).

Some bandsaws have tires that simply snap into a groove that is milled into the rim of the wheel (see the drawing on p. 324). Without question, this is the easiest type to change, but it does require that you purchase a special tire from the manufacturer of your saw.

Recrowning worn tires If you're having difficulty tracking a blade (especially a narrow one), the first thing you should try is recrowning the tires. The difference

If the tires have worn slightly, you can easily reshape the crown with a sanding block while the wheels are turning (but not with the blade installed).

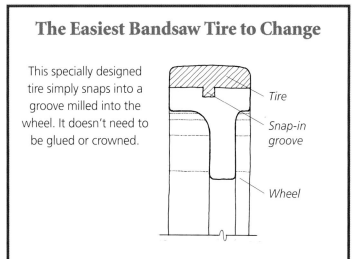

The Easiest Bandsaw Tire to Change

This specially designed tire simply snaps into a groove milled into the wheel. It doesn't need to be glued or crowned.

Tire

Snap-in groove

Wheel

Spinning the upper wheel

For recrowning, you can run the lower wheel by the motor. For the upper wheel, have a helper spin the top by holding a sanding drum chucked into a portable drill against the tire.

between the crown and the sides of the tire should be about $\frac{1}{32}$ in. If that's not enough to keep the blade on track, try $\frac{1}{16}$ in. The amount of crown required to keep the blade tracking is very small.

If the tires are thick enough, you can recrown the surface with sandpaper. I wrap the sandpaper around a wood block and gradually reshape the tire while the wheel is spinning (see the photo above). Don't attempt this with a blade on the saw! You can run the lower wheel with the motor and have a friend spin the top wheel with a sanding drum chucked into a portable drill. This method works well with tires that have slight wear, such as the loss of the crown. But if your saw's tires have severe wear or age cracks, then it's time to replace them.

Replacing tires I've done repair work on several bandsaws, each of which used a different arrangement for fastening the wheels to the shaft. If you're in doubt about the best way to remove the wheels, review the drawing in the manual for the saw (if it's available).

Once the wheel is off, lay it on a workbench, then cut the tire with a utility knife and start prying it off. If the tire isn't glued in place, it may simply fall off the rim, but most tires are glued on. If the tires were not glued on, I would still recommend gluing on the new ones.

I've found that the level of difficulty in removing a tire depends upon its age and condition. Cracked tires come off in pieces, but typically a tire peels off the rim in a long strip. You'll have to remove all traces of old tire and glue so that the new tire can seat evenly.

With all remnants of old tire and glue gone, stretch the new tires over the wheels. To ensure a tight fit, new tires are approximately 20% smaller than the wheels.

I always glue the tires in place because I've seen tires slip when resawing wide boards. When this happens, the saw will shudder violently for a brief moment. It's very annoying and nerve-racking, and it doesn't do the bandsaw a heck of a lot of good, either.

This happened recently with a friend's 14-in. bandsaw. At first we thought the drive belt was slipping, but it checked out as tight enough. Then I suspected the tires. To test the hypothesis, we marked each tire and rim with a pen before making another test cut with a slow, steady feed (see the drawing at right). The saw shuddered and squealed as before. When we opened the cover and examined the marks, they were misaligned by ½ in. on both wheels. Gluing on the tires solved the problem.

Gluing the tires in place is much easier after the tires are stretched over the wheels. Otherwise, the procedure becomes a sticky mess. I'll get back to gluing, but first I'll discuss getting the tire on the rim. Think of the tire as an oversized rubber band that you'll have to stretch around the wheel. Stretching the tires around wheels 14-in. and smaller is easy, but you'll most likely need help for anything larger. Still, the process isn't difficult—it's just more than two hands can manage.

To begin, position the wheel vertically on the floor over the tire. Next, you and a friend should each stretch the tire around the wheel in opposite directions. As the tire is stretched it will have a tendency to slip off the rim, so you should each hold the tire in position with one hand while

Removing tire adhesive

To soften tire adhesive, I use lacquer thinner. A small squeeze bottle makes it easy to get the thinner around the edge of the tire. A flat, sharp stick of wood works well as a scraper, and it doesn't damage aluminum wheels. Remember to have plenty of ventilation when using lacquer thinner. Besides being flammable, the fumes are harmful to breathe.

Check for Slipping Tires

If you suspect the tires on your bandsaw are slipping, mark the tire and rim with a felt-tip pen. Saw a test board with a slow, steady feed, then check the marks. If they're no longer lined up, the tires are slipping. Solve the problem by gluing the tires down.

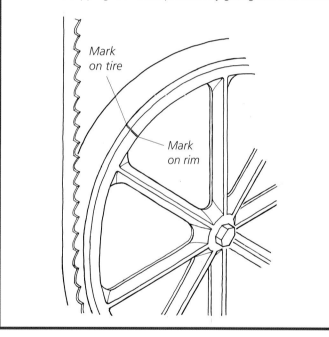

Mark on tire

Mark on rim

pulling, stretching, and positioning the tire with the other. The process takes less than two minutes.

The next step is to apply the glue. I use 3M weather-stripping adhesive. To get under the tire, insert a short length of pipe or wooden dowel between the tire

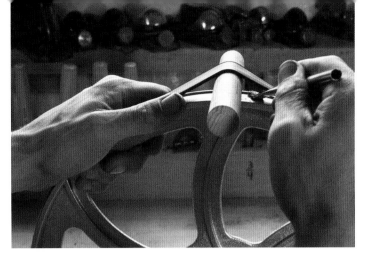

A dowel raises the tire off the rim so you can apply the glue underneath it with a small brush.

and rim. This raises the tire just enough so you can apply glue to the surfaces with a brush (see the photo above). By rolling the dowel around the rim, it's possible to apply glue to the entire perimeter. Allow the glue to set overnight.

If your wheels aren't crowned, you'll have to crown the tires once the glue is dry. Use a sanding block and sandpaper as described on pp. 323–324 for recrowning worn tires.

I've read that you should trim the tires after mounting to make them concentric, but I've never seen tire unevenness to be a problem. Not long ago, I helped a friend install tires on his old 20-in. bandsaw. Afterwards we checked tire runout with a dial indicator and found that it was within 0.010 in., which is close enough for saw smoothness and closer than I could get with any shop-built trimming jig.

Wheels

Wheels can contribute to vibration in one of several ways. The wheels could have bearing problems, they may not be round, or they could be unbalanced.

Bearings When examining wheels, the first thing to check is the bearings. Remove the blade and drive belt so they don't interfere with your inspection, then spin each wheel slowly and listen for clicking or grinding. Good bearings are smooth and quiet.

If you suspect that a bearing is worn, you can have it replaced at a local machine shop or you can do it yourself. You can remove the old bearing by resting the wheel on a workbench and knocking the bearing out with a hammer and a wood block. Then press the new bearing in place by laying a block of wood over the bearing and applying pressure with a clamp.

Roundness Old bandsaw wheels can get distorted from years of blade tension; if a new wheel is out-of-round it's because of sloppy machining. You can check for wheel roundness with a dial indicator that attaches to the frame of the saw. For an accurate reading, position the indicator tip at the edge of the machined rim of the wheel. The wheel probably won't be perfect, but if it is off by more than 0.025 in., it's enough to cause vibration.

A machine shop can true the wheel, but unless you have a large industrial bandsaw, the cost of the machining may exceed the value of the saw. Alternatively, you may be able to get a new wheel from the manufacturer.

Wheel balance To check wheel balance, spin the wheel (with the blade and drive belt removed) and allow it to coast to a stop. Mark the lowest point of the wheel

Troubleshooting Bandsaw Problems

Problem	Diagnosis	
The blade hops or bounces while running.	• Chunks of the tire are missing. • Chunks of the drive belt are missing.	• The pulleys are bent. • The blade has a sharp bend or kink.
The blade moves in and out while running.	• The blade weld is misaligned.	• There is sawdust and pitch buildup on the tires.
The blade bows during resawing and spoils the workpiece.	• The blade pitch is too fine. • There is buildup of pitch in the blade gullets.	• The blade is dull. • The feed rate is too fast.
The blade is difficult to track.	• Excess tension has distorted the frame and caused severe wheel misalignment. Decrease the blade tension.	• The tires are worn or dirty.
The sawblade wanders in the cut.	• The feed rate is too fast.	• The guides are not set closely enough.
The blade breaks prematurely.	• The weld is poor. • There is excessive tension. *Note*: This is really only a problem with large saws (20 in. and above) or very narrow blades ($1/16$ in. and $1/8$ in.).	• The wheel is too small for the blade thickness. • A turn in the stock is too tight for the blade width.
There is a ticking sound.	• There is excess flash at the weld. • There is a stress crack in the blade.	• There is a kink in the blade.
The blade dulls quickly.	• The blade was overheated (too fine a pitch).	• Incorrectly set guides pushed the set from the teeth.
There is excessive vibration.	• The tires are dirty. • The wheels are out of balance or out of round. • A cheap motor is out of balance, has a flimsy motor mount, or has loose mounting fasteners.	• The tires are extremely worn. • Cheap pulleys are out of round. • The pulleys are loose or misaligned. • The drive belt is worn. • The sheet-metal stand is flimsy.
The blade shudders when resawing.	• The drive belt slipped momentarily.	• The tires slipped momentarily.

Many bandsaw manufacturers dynamically balance the wheels of their saws. One I spoke to said that his company balances the wheels to within 0.3 grams at 700 rpm. I don't doubt this claim; the saw that I tried was very smooth indeed.

Motors

Good motors are balanced to provide a smooth, vibration-free power source. In preparation for this book, I tested several well-known brands of bandsaws. One 14-in. saw ran incredibly smoothly. When I mentioned this to the manufacturer, I learned the details about how the company achieves such smooth performance in a competitively priced saw. One of the keys was the motor, which they balanced to 0.3 grams at 1,700 rpm. I was surprised to find such attention to quality on a consumer bandsaw.

To test the motor on your saw for excessive vibration, run the motor without the drive belt and pulley. If the motor doesn't run smoothly, check the motor mount for loose fasteners. If it's well mounted, look for a replacement motor. I suggest buying a name-brand American-made motor. It's a good opportunity to increase the horsepower.

Drive pulleys

Recently, one of the bandsaws at the university where I teach began vibrating and making a terrible racket. Since this was out of character for the machine, I immediately suspected a loose pulley. On opening the stand, I discovered that the wheel pulley was indeed loose and had vibrated

and spin it several more times, each time marking the lowest point. If the wheel is out of balance, the same point will keep ending up at the bottom.

You can lighten that area of the rim by drilling shallow ⅜-in. holes in it, but be careful to avoid removing too much metal. Spin the wheel several times more. When it no longer stops at the same point, it is as close to balanced as you can get using this method.

out to the end of the wheel shaft, which caused severe drive-belt misalignment.

Vibration problems aren't typically as simple as this one, but pulleys can sometimes be the problem. When checking pulleys, look for the obvious first: looseness or misalignment (see the drawing on the facing page). Otherwise, the problem might be the pulleys themselves.

Inexpensive bandsaws generally have die-cast pulleys that are not perfectly round or the shaft hole isn't centered. You can spot pulleys that have been machined round to improve balance by the concentric rings in the surface that were created during the turning process. If your pulleys don't have those rings, replacing the pulleys will go a long way to reduce your saw's vibration.

Drive belts

I stepped into my shop one day and turned on my old Rockwell Unisaw to make a cut. The vibration was incredible, especially since this saw is normally very smooth. I pulled the power cord from the wall, crawled under the saw, and found that one of the belts in the triple-belt drive system had big chunks missing. The same thing will happen when a bandsaw's belts are worn out.

But it doesn't take a worn belt to create vibration problems. A poor-quality belt may have lumps or inconsistencies in the V-profile, which rides in the groove around the rim of the pulley.

Check the table for square against a tensioned blade.

Tables

Most bandsaws have a tilting table with an adjustable stop to accurately reset the table to 90°. To adjust the table, mount a ½-in.-wide blade, tension it, and back off the guides so that they don't interfere with the table setting. Place a reliable square on the table, and turn the stop-adjusting screw until the blade of the square is parallel to the sawblade.

Thrust-Bearing Problems

The best thrust bearing is a hardened steel disk pressed over a sealed bearing. Unfortunately, this design is used only on more expensive saws. The thrust bearing

> ### Pay attention to drive belts
>
> Drive belts are much more sophisticated than they look. An inexpensive belt is no bargain. You can buy high-quality V-belts at auto supply stores. Many woodworking specialty suppliers have link belts, which are also great for minimizing vibration.

The thrust bearing on the left is new; the one on the right is severely worn and needs replacing.

Step-Worn Guide Blocks

The bearing surfaces of guide blocks (even steel ones) become worn. Narrow blades are the worst because they wear a step into the block, which greatly decreases the block's effectiveness. All guide blocks need their bearing surfaces trued up from time to time.

Top view

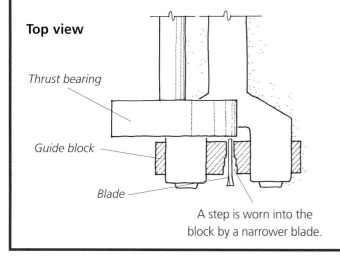

Thrust bearing

Guide block

Blade

A step is worn into the block by a narrower blade.

Keep guide blocks square

Whether you use sandpaper, a file, or a grinder to true up the face of your guide blocks, check your progress frequently with a small square.

gives more problems than the upper bearing because pitch and dust from the downward movement of the blade continually bombard it. As the pitch builds up, the bearing doesn't spin freely, so the blade wears grooves in the face of the bearing. This in turn causes the back of the blade to heat excessively, which leads to fatigue and breakage.

This whole scenario is easy to avoid by removing the lower thrust bearing occasionally and cleaning off the pitch. Even so, the lower bearing needs to be replaced more often than the upper one. This is an inexpensive part that you can find locally at a bearing or motor repair shop. I usually keep a couple of replacement bearings on hand.

Guide-Block Maintenance

If your saw has steel guide blocks, you'll need to true them up occasionally with a file or grinder. Over a long period of use, the blocks become worn, and steps form in the face of the block, which limit the effectiveness of the guide (see the drawing at left). It takes only a few minutes to reface the block.

I don't recommend replacing the steel blocks in your saw with plastic blocks. Compared to steel blocks, plastic blocks wear out very quickly and they offer no real advantages. Inexpensive carbon-steel blades may become overheated at the tooth tip during resawing, but plastic blocks won't eliminate the overheating, just as steel blocks are not the cause of it.

on most consumer bandsaws is simply a bearing mounted on a shaft, and the blade is supported on the edge of the bearing face.

The thrust bearing on the lower guide typically

Basic Bandsaw Techniques

Perhaps no other woodworking machine has greater appeal than the bandsaw. No matter what your area of woodworking interest, the bandsaw has a use. If you enjoy carving, for example, the bandsaw is indispensable for roughing out blanks. If you're a woodturner, the bandsaw is a great companion to the lathe for sizing stock for a bowl. For the furniture maker, the bandsaw is an essential tool for everything from ripping rough stock to creating curves. And because the bandsaw is relatively safe when compared to other woodworking machines, you'll find that using it can be an enjoyable experience as well.

If you're new to the bandsaw, you'll also find that the machine is easy to learn how to use. After just a few minutes of practice, most people are up to guiding the stock through the turns to make a delicate table apron or even a sculpted leg for a chair. But don't feel that the bandsaw is limited to curves. Although the bandsaw is *the* tool for creating curves, it is sometimes the safest and easiest way to rip wide boards into narrower widths.

In this chapter, I'll cover the basics of using the bandsaw for cutting curves and ripping, along with some information on removing tool marks. One word of advice before you begin: Review the safety guidelines in chapter 5 and always make safety a priority when using this versatile tool.

How to Cut Curves

No other woodworking machine can cut curves as quickly, easily, and accurately as the bandsaw. When compared to other machines designed for cutting curves,

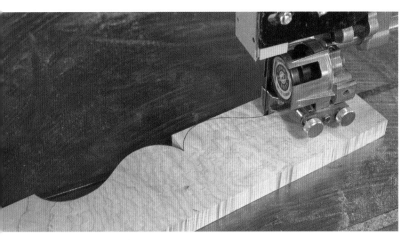

No other woodworking machine cuts curves as quickly and precisely as the bandsaw.

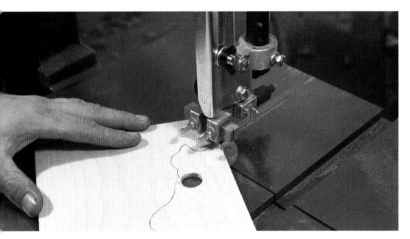

Equipped with a narrow blade, the bandsaw excels at cutting scrolls. Note the drilled hole used to make the tightest curve.

such as the scrollsaw or the jigsaw, the bandsaw has greater power and cutting depth. In many situations, the bandsaw cuts more smoothly, too. That's because a bandsaw blade continuously cuts downward but a scrollsaw blade or jigsaw blade has an erratic reciprocating movement. When equipped with the right blade, a bandsaw is much more versatile, too, since it can cut broad, shallow curves or tight, ornate scrolls.

Curved Moldings

Curved moldings, such as those in the hood of this clock, can create a dramatic effect for your work.

Curved moldings are found extensively on both furniture and architectural woodworking from the 18th and 19th centuries. Curved moldings are typically either part of a true circle, such as a molding strip on the hood of a clock, or a cyma curve, such as those seen on the pediments of casework. The curved moldings on pediments are called gooseneck moldings. They often terminate in a round carving called a rosette.

Whether or not you enjoy reproducing colonial American furniture, you may still find the bandsaw techniques for making curved moldings useful for other projects and furniture styles.

Making curved moldings involves more than just bandsawing a curve into the stock. After sawing the contour, the molding profile must be shaped on the stock with a shaper or a router. The curved stock can't be guided by a straight fence, as is normally the case when shaping moldings. Instead, the workpiece is guided by either a curved fence or a rub bearing, which is mounted on the router or shaper. Let's look at the process so that you'll have a better understanding of the steps involved in making curved moldings.

Begin by sawing only the reference surface. Rather than bandsawing both the inside and outside radii of a curved molding, bandsaw only the surface that will be molded (see the top drawing at right). This makes shaping or routing safer and more precise because the extra mass reduces vibration and provides you with a better grip and control of the stock.

Avoid short grain. Areas of short grain are weak and may break during shaping or when applying the molding. As a general rule, curved molding sections shouldn't exceed a quarter turn (90°) in order to avoid short grain. For example, use two 90° sections to produce a 180° turn (see the bottom drawing at right).

Use plywood templates. Whenever I make curved moldings, I lay out and bandsaw the curve onto ½-in. plywood for use as a template. Once made, the template serves three purposes. First, it becomes a pattern for tracing the curve to the workpiece. Second, you can quickly remove the bandsaw marks from the workpiece by securing the workpiece to the template and flush-trimming with a router. Third, the template serves as a bearing guide when shaping the molding profile.

Bandsaw the opposite radius once the shaping is complete. Take your time. The most common mistake is to saw too fast. By taking your time, you can achieve much more accurate results and avoid the tedious job of smoothing away errors with a file.

Preparing Stock for Making Curved Moldings

Molding the profile into a piece of curved stock will be much safer and more accurate if you have a substantial workpiece to run through a router or a shaper.

Extra stock provides a safe and secure grip while shaping or routing.

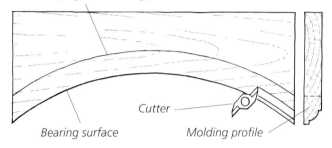

Don't bandsaw this curve until after shaping the molding profile.

Bearing surface

Cutter

Molding profile

Avoid Short Grain in Curves

When bandsawing segments of a true circle, avoid short, weak grain by using a separate plank for each quarter of the circle.

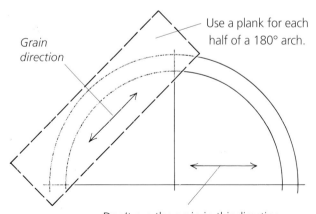

Grain direction

Use a plank for each half of a 180° arch.

Don't run the grain in this direction.

A pattern is the key to laying out great curves. I make mine out of plywood and mark all pertinent information on it for the next time I use it.

Changing the Scale of a Pattern

Although I usually draw my own designs for patterns, I sometimes use an existing design from a book or magazine. When drawn for publication, most patterns must be scaled down to fit the page. To make the design easy to enlarge, it's presented on a grid so that you can reference from the squares of the grid. To enlarge the design from the grid, you'll first have to draw a new grid with squares measuring the dimension given. Then you can re-create the curves of the design by plotting points on the grid and connecting them. This method works well, but it can be slow and tedious.

Instead, I prefer to use a photocopier. Most photocopiers can not only enlarge but can also do so in 1% increments. To use this method, I measure the squares on the copy and enlarge them until they equal the size indicated on the original drawing. Although most photocopiers will create a slight amount of distortion when enlarging, it is easy to correct when making the plywood pattern. If your pattern is large, you may want to go to a copy shop that caters to architects and engineers, where they typically have photocopy machines large enough to handle blueprints.

Once I have my enlarged drawing, I glue the paper to the plywood with rubber cement, which doesn't wrinkle paper as white or yellow glues will, and cut the pattern on a bandsaw.

Laying out curves

A good pattern is the key to bandsawing a great-looking curve. I never sketch a curve or design directly on the stock and begin sawing. Instead, I draw my design on thin plywood and cut it out for use as a pattern. This method has three distinct advantages. First, it enables me to get a better concept of the design once it is cut out on plywood. If I'm not satisfied with the outline of the curve, its scale, or its proportion, I can easily and inexpensively modify the pattern or make a new one. Second, it makes it easy to duplicate the curve, as when making four identical legs for a table or chair. Third, if the design is a complex series of twists and turns, I can get a more accurate result if I simply make a pattern for one-half of the design. By flipping the pattern over when tracing it on the workpiece, I get a perfectly symmetrical layout.

I sketch the curve on the plywood, checking, erasing, and redrawing until I'm satisfied with the design. Next, I carefully bandsaw the pattern and smooth the edges with a spindle sander and various sizes of files until they are free of lumps

The best pattern material

I like to use ¼-in. birch plywood for patterns because it is stiff and its light color enables me to see my sketch. Also, the edges of plywood won't curl or become frayed as paper or cardboard will.

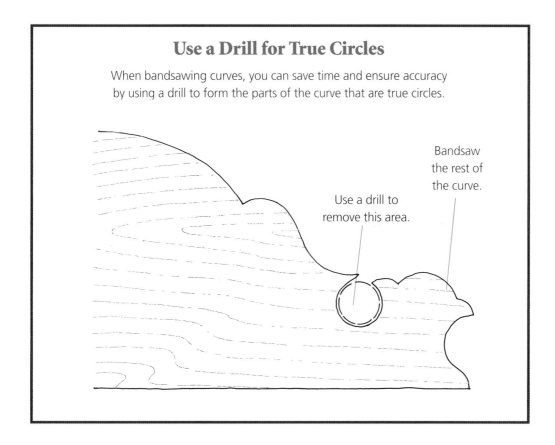

Use a Drill for True Circles

When bandsawing curves, you can save time and ensure accuracy by using a drill to form the parts of the curve that are true circles.

Bandsaw the rest of the curve.

Use a drill to remove this area.

and dead, or flat, spots. Once I'm satisfied with the pattern, I trace it onto the stock.

My plywood patterns are valuable data storage centers, too, because I write construction notes for future reference on the face of my patterns. Information such as the location of a mortise in the leg, the finished diameter of the ankle after sawing and shaping, and the required stock dimensions will be invaluable data when I want to build the same piece of furniture sometime in the future.

When laying out a complex pattern, keep your eye out for contours that are portions of true circles (see the drawing above). One way you can save a lot of

Drill first, then saw

A technique you can use to save time when sawing contours is to use a drill to contour any parts of true circles. It's faster and more precise than sawing. Always do the drilling first, then the bandsawing. Otherwise, the drill bit may wander off center and miscut the stock. You can stack several pieces and drill them together to save time.

time when sawing contours is to drill any true circles. Besides being faster than bandsawing, it's also more precise because it yields a true circle or part of a circle.

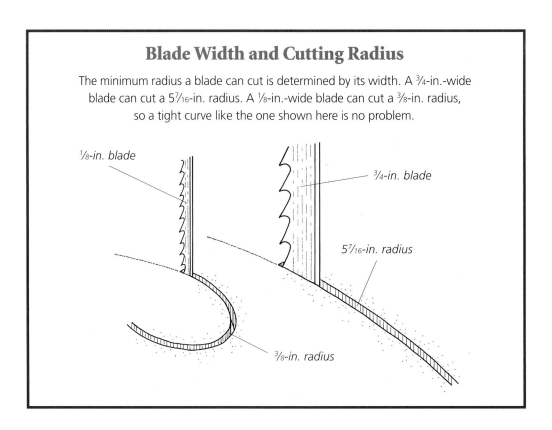

Blade Width and Cutting Radius

The minimum radius a blade can cut is determined by its width. A ¾-in.-wide blade can cut a 5⁷⁄₁₆-in. radius. A ⅛-in.-wide blade can cut a ⅜-in. radius, so a tight curve like the one shown here is no problem.

⅛-in. blade

¾-in. blade

5⁷⁄₁₆-in. radius

⅜-in. radius

Choosing a blade for cutting curves

With so many combinations of material, width, pitch, and tooth form available, choosing a blade for cutting curves can seem like a formidable task. The right blade for sawing a particular curve takes into account a number of factors, such as the radius of the curve, the size of the bandsaw, and the thickness of the stock. Let's look at some of the things you need to consider when selecting a blade for cutting curves.

Blade width The minimum radius that you can cut on your bandsaw is determined by the blade width (see the drawing above). As you follow the layout line

while cutting, you must rotate the workpiece around the blade. The narrower the blade, the tighter the radius you can cut. If you attempt to cut a curve that is too tight for the width of the blade, the blade may break or pull off the wheels.

So why not just mount a narrow blade and cut all curves with that? The difficulty is that cuts tend to wander more with narrow blades. When you're scrolling around tight curves, it's not a problem, but if you're cutting the broad curves of a chair rocker, your line will be distinctly wavy unless you are very skilled.

When you're first learning to cut curves, you'll most likely find a blade-radius chart to be helpful. It will show you the minimum radius that you can cut

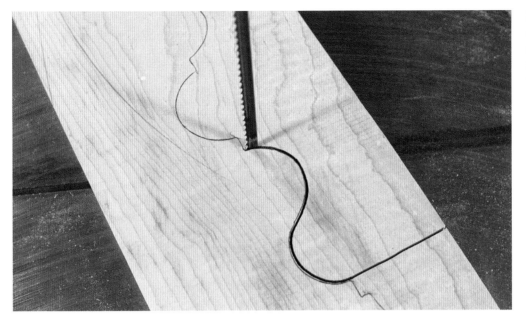

Plan your cutting sequence to avoid trapping the blade.

with the various blade widths available. There's a chart for your reference on p. 294.

Tooth form More than any other factor, tooth form determines how a blade will cut. When smoothness is a concern, the best choice is a regular-tooth blade. Because of their 0° rake angles, regular-tooth blades cut with a smooth, scraping action. In addition, they have the greatest number of teeth, which also contributes to their smooth cutting.

When the curve to be cut is broad and the stock is thick, I'll reach for a hook-tooth blade. Hook blades have positive rake angles and little feed resistance, features that make them well suited for sawing curves in thick stock. I cut all curves with either a hook-tooth blade or a regular-tooth blade.

Pitch It's best to have 6 to 12 teeth in contact with the stock at any given time. A blade on the finer end of that range will produce a smooth surface on the stock. If you go too fine and have more than 12 teeth in the stock, the gullets may become packed with sawdust and the teeth will overheat. The stock may burn, and the heat will severely shorten the life of the blade.

Cutting sequence

An important consideration when sawing contours is the sequence of the cuts. Many designs are made with a series of interconnected cuts. If you don't plan the cutting sequence, you may find yourself trapped in a corner. If you back the sawblade out of the kerf to get out of the corner, you risk pulling the blade off the wheels or breaking it.

Plan the Sequence of Cuts

When cutting a complex pattern, take the time to plan your cutting sequence to avoid trapping the blade or backing out of long curves.

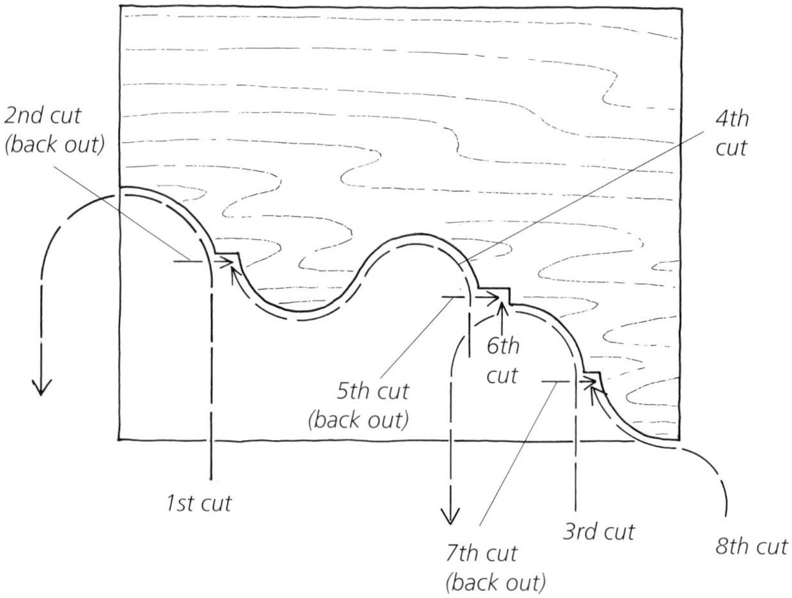

2nd cut
(back out)
4th
cut
6th
cut
5th cut
(back out)
1st cut
3rd cut
7th cut
(back out)
8th cut

If you get stuck

If you must back out of a curve, stop the saw and use a block of wood to push the blade back against the thrust bearing while you ease the workpiece around the curve and away from the blade.

To avoid such scenarios, I first make a quick analysis of the cutting sequence. The cuts I make first are those that allow me to turn and exit the stock without being trapped in an inside corner (see the drawing above). When two lines of the layout connect at an inside corner, I make the shortest, straightest cut first, then I back out and make the second cut. When backing out of a short, straight kerf, there is little risk of pulling the blade off of the wheels. When two curved cuts interconnect, I first make a straight relief cut to the inside corner. This lets me avoid backing out of a curve.

If necessary, you can relieve stress on the blade when negotiating a turn that is too tight by making a series of relief kerfs down to the line. Then you can clean up the curve by sawing a series of short straight lines around the curve as close to the line as possible (see the drawing on the facing page). This idea has been promoted to avoid changing blades,

When the Blade Is Too Wide for a Curve

If you can't change blades and you don't mind a distinctly choppy appearance,
you can use relief cuts to make a series of straight lines look somewhat like a curve.

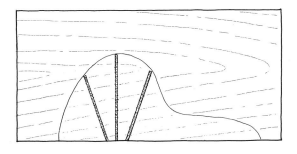

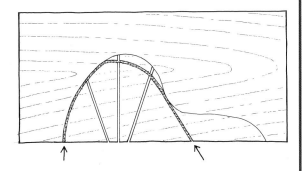

1. Make relief cuts in the tightest part of the curve.

2. Cut one side of the curve until the blade nears the line.

3. Cut the other side of the curve in the same way.

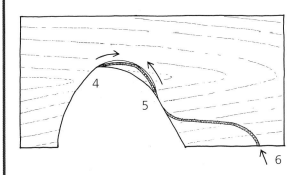

4. Move the piece so the side of the blade touches the curve near the top, then saw as close to the line as you can.

5. Saw as close to the line as you can.

6. Saw this line to complete the pattern.

The finished curve is somewhat choppy—not nearly as good as if the proper-width blade were used in the first place.

Nesting Parts to Reduce Waste

Sawing curved parts generates a lot of waste. I know this firsthand because I specialize in building 18th-century furniture such as Queen Anne and Chippendale. The chair leg in the photo at right is a good example. During the creation of the graceful curved legs for the back of a chair, several small, irregularly shaped blocks are produced. Although I often find a use for some of the larger offcuts, much of it goes into the wood stove.

To avoid generating so much waste, I nest pieces together whenever I can (see the drawing below). By selecting a board wide enough for two, three, or even four legs, I can substantially reduce the amount of waste.

By using a pattern and nesting the pieces, the rear legs of this Chippendale chair can be nested and sawn from one board to avoid waste.

You can reduce waste substantially by nesting parts together. Here, I've used a plywood pattern to draw two nested sets of Chippendale chair rear legs on one wide board.

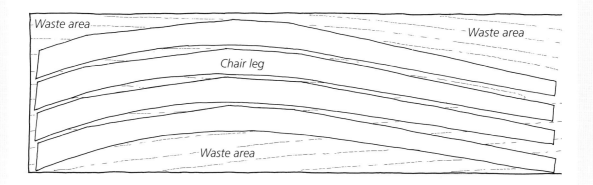

Waste area

Waste area

Chair leg

Waste area

Grasping the work on rear corners provides good control in most situations.

Grasping the work on diagonal corners provides good control and, in this case, keeps fingers out of the blade's path.

but I don't like it because it results in choppy, angular curves instead of smooth, flowing ones. It's better to take the time to change the blade if it is too wide for the radius of the curve.

Hand position

When sawing curves on your bandsaw, hand position is important both for control and for safety. Spacing your hands far apart gives the most control. Using this technique, you can use one hand to push the workpiece and the other hand to steer or guide the work. I've found that for most pieces I'm sawing, it works well to hold the rear adjacent corners (see the left photo above) or diagonal corners (see the right photo above). Either of these hand positions allows me to easily follow the twists, turns, and scrolls of even the most intricate curves.

As I follow the line, I'm also keenly aware of the position of my hands in relation to the blade. To avoid coming in contact with the blade, it's often necessary to change hand positions in the middle or near the end of the cut.

On long, narrow work such as this chair leg, you gain the most control by grasping the workpiece near the ends.

Practice

If you're inexperienced with bandsawing curves, you'll find it helpful to practice on soft, inexpensive wood such as poplar. This will give you the confidence you need to begin sawing intricate curves in more valuable stock.

When sawing long, gentle curves such as those found on a chair leg, I normally grip each end of the stock (see the photo above). Because I'm right-handed, I feel most comfortable using my right hand primarily for pushing the stock and my left hand for steering.

Stacking Multiples

You can save considerable time on sawing by stacking multiple pieces and sawing them together (see the photos on the facing page). It's important to keep the parts aligned so that they remain identical. Masking tape works well for this job. I stack the parts and bind them together tightly with a couple of layers of tape. Once the pieces are wrapped, I mark the layout on the top piece directly on the tape.

After I've completed sawing, I leave the pieces stacked while I smooth the sawmarks from the edges. It may be necessary to add another layer of tape if much of the original tape was cut when sawing.

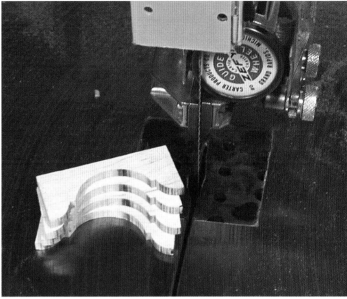

You can save time by stacking multiples and sawing them together. To keep them aligned when sawing, tape them together with masking tape.

Blade pitch for stacks

Be sure to select a blade pitch for the combined thickness of the pieces you're cutting.

Once you've tried this method a couple of times, I'm sure you'll appreciate the time it saves not only in sawing but also in layout since you won't have to draw the lines on each individual piece.

It's important to realize that there are limits to the number of pieces that you can safely and accurately stack. The higher you raise the guidepost to accommodate a tall stack, the less support the blade has from the upper guide. As a result, the blade may deflect and cause the lowest pieces in the stack to be miscut. Because you're following the layout on the top piece, you'll be unaware that the pieces underneath are being miscut. To minimize this problem, first tension the blade properly and adjust the guides. Then make a test cut to determine how tall a stack you can accurately cut through the twists and turns of your design.

Limits to stacking

For your safety, it is important for a stack to have a substantial footprint. Otherwise, the sawblade can grab it violently, causing you to lose control. Don't stack small pieces together in a tall tower. As a general rule, the height of a stack should be no more than its width.

Ripping on the Bandsaw

If you own a table saw, you may wonder why you would want to rip stock on a bandsaw. Isn't the table saw the best choice for ripping stock? Not always. A bandsaw has several definite advantages over a table saw when it comes to ripping, especially if the stock is very thick or warped.

The main advantage of ripping on a bandsaw is safety. Table saws can kick back violently, but a bandsaw can't kick back because the blade pushes the stock downward toward the table. Ripping stock that is twisted or warped in any way poses an even greater risk on the table saw because warped stock is more prone to binding the blade, which almost always results in kickback. Without a doubt, ripping on a bandsaw is safer.

Another advantage to ripping on a bandsaw is that it rips faster than a table saw and with half as much waste. The reason for this is simple: A bandsaw blade is thin, so it produces a narrow kerf. In fact, the typical bandsaw blade produces a kerf that is half that of a table-saw kerf (see the photo below). This results in less feed resistance, which makes ripping faster, especially when ripping thick hardwood. As a bonus, you'll get greater yield from your expensive stock.

Selecting a blade for ripping

Your best blade for ripping is one with a coarse pitch that places no more than six teeth in contact with the stock at one time. For example, if you're ripping 2-in.-thick stock, a 3-pitch blade would be ideal. The large gullets in a coarse-pitch blade will keep the kerf cleared of sawdust. Also, I prefer a blade with hook teeth for ripping. The aggressive cutting action of hook teeth creates very little feed resistance. In fact, hook teeth seem to almost feed themselves. To prevent blade deflection and drift, I suggest using the widest blade that will fit on your bandsaw. See chapter 6 for more information on choosing and tensioning a blade.

Freehand ripping vs. ripping with a fence

Freehand ripping simply means that you don't use a fence to guide the stock (see the photo at left on the facing page). Just mark a straight line as a guide and follow it while ripping the stock. Freehand rip-

A bandsaw kerf (left) is half the width of a table-saw kerf (right).

ping is fast because it doesn't involve setting a fence, so I often rip freehand when I've only got a couple of pieces of stock. Freehand ripping is also my choice when the stock is warped because there is no chance of it binding on a fence.

Ripping with a fence yields more consistent dimensions than ripping freehand. Whenever accuracy is required, I use a simple fence. It's also faster when there is a lot of stock to be ripped because you don't have to mark each piece with a straight line.

You may have to adjust your fence to compensate for blade drift. Blade drift simply means that the blade isn't cutting parallel to the table edge. If you attempt to rip without compensating for drift, the stock may wander from the fence, causing the stock to be cut undersized.

Many factory-made fences won't work for ripping because they are made to lock parallel to

Blade drift and narrow blades

I've noticed that blade drift is only a problem with blades that are ½ in. or less in width. In my experience, blades that are 1 in. or wider typically rip parallel to the fence.

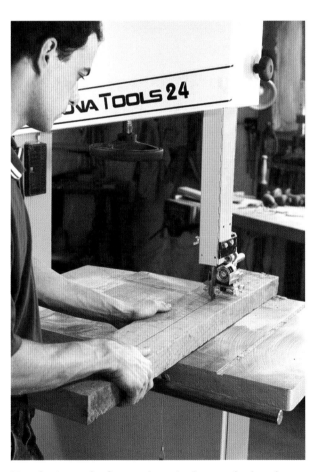

You don't need a fence when ripping on the bandsaw, just a straight line and a steady eye.

Any straight strip of wood is suitable for a fence when ripping, but you'll have to set it to take blade drift into account.

Setting the Fence for Blade Drift

The degree of drift for each blade will be a little different, so you'll have to check for drift each time you change blades. Fortunately, finding the blade-drift angle is easy.

1. Mark a line on a board parallel to an edge.

2. Rip the board free-hand about one-half its length. Follow the layout line carefully.

3. Clamp a fence to the saw table at the drift angle.

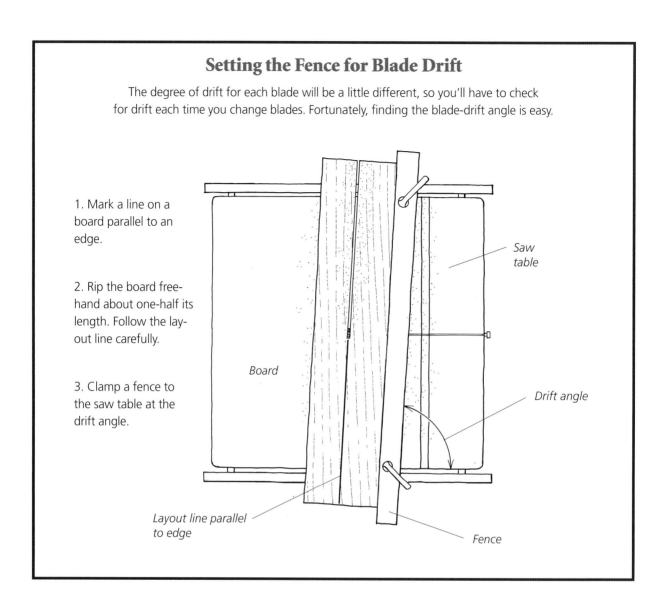

Saw table

Board

Drift angle

Layout line parallel to edge

Fence

Use a push stick

A bandsaw may be a relatively safe tool, but always use a push stick when ripping narrow stock.

the table edge. If your fence doesn't have an adjustment for drift, then you can make your own fence that clamps to the saw table. If you're in a hurry, a board with one true edge or a strip of ¾-in. plywood will suffice. Just make certain that your fence is clamped securely to the table.

Hand position

When ripping freehand, I use my right hand for pushing and both hands for guiding the stock. When ripping with a fence, I push with my right hand and hold the stock against the fence with my left hand. It's important to keep both hands a safe distance from the blade and finish the cut with a push stick.

Removing Bandsaw Marks

Unfortunately, bandsaws don't create finished surfaces, so after bandsawing, you'll have to smooth away the sawmarks from the surface. This can be done in a number of ways, such as by filing, by sanding, or even by cutting away the bandsawn surface with a router or shaper.

The more accurately you saw to the layout line, the less cleanup is required. Careless bandsawing leaves the sawn surface bumpy, and you'll have to remove more than just sawmarks. You'll have to remove enough wood to create a smooth, flowing curve. Creating the curve by hand with a file is much more labor-intensive than creating the curve on a bandsaw, so it's important to saw accurately.

Files

Small files are indispensable for removing sawmarks, especially in small, difficult-to-reach areas. Half-round files, as the name implies, are curved on one face and flat on the opposite face. Round files are available to fit the smallest of contours.

Spindle sanders

Using a spindle sander is one of the fastest and easiest ways to smooth a bandsawn contour (see the photo at left on p. 348). Most spindle sanders have at least a half dozen sanding drums of different diameters to accommodate the radius of the curve you're working.

Floor-model spindle sanders are the most powerful and come with the widest

You can avoid tedious smoothing of curved parts by sawing precisely to the layout line.

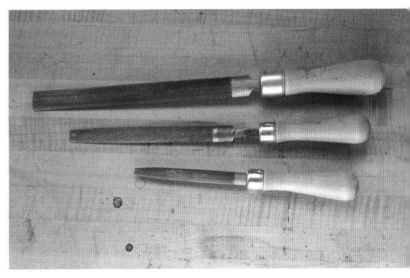

Files are indispensable tools for removing bandsaw marks. They come in a variety of shapes to suit almost any curve.

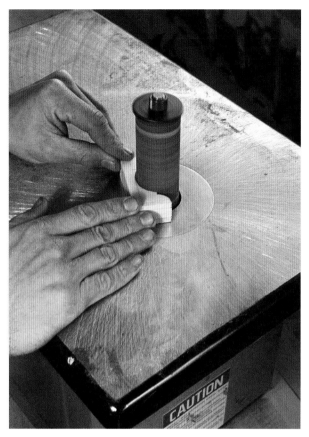

A spindle sander will make quick work of smoothing concave areas of curved work.

When the work is to be template routed, I'm not as fussy about sawing to the line.

assortment of sanding drums. On the other hand, small benchtop sanders are more affordable. The best benchtop sanders are industrial-quality machines that are powerful enough for any job.

Carving gouges and chisels

If you enjoy making reproductions of colonial American furniture, then you may wish to use carving gouges to remove the bandsaw marks from your work. Eighteenth-century craftsmen used gouges of various sizes and sweeps (radii

of the curves) to carve away sawmarks and create flowing contours on their work. Wherever gouges were used to carve away the inside edges of a chair rail or table apron, craftsmen would chamfer the edges afterwards.

As you might imagine, this can be a time-consuming method that you may wish to use only when you're attempting to strictly reproduce an antique. Although I seldom use this method, I do use ordinary flat chisels quite often to create crisp inside corners on my bandsawn work.

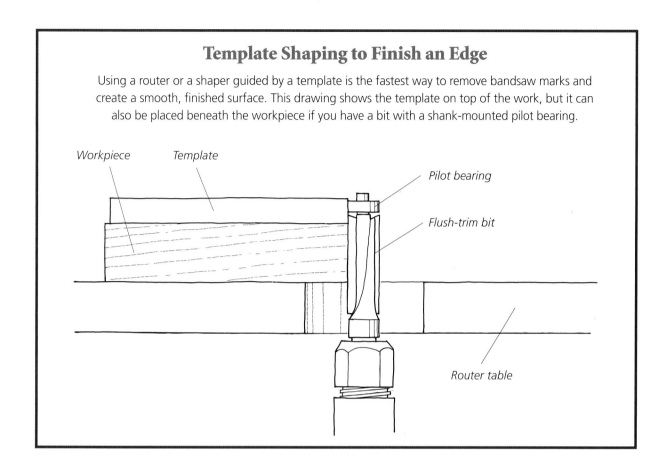

Template Shaping to Finish an Edge

Using a router or a shaper guided by a template is the fastest way to remove bandsaw marks and create a smooth, finished surface. This drawing shows the template on top of the work, but it can also be placed beneath the workpiece if you have a bit with a shank-mounted pilot bearing.

Workpiece *Template* *Pilot bearing* *Flush-trim bit* *Router table*

Template shaping

As I mentioned earlier, you generally want to follow the layout line as closely as possible when sawing contours. By carefully following the line, you can avoid the tedious cleanup associated with careless sawing. But there are times when you can saw "heavy" of the line and make the final, exact contour with a router or a shaper.

The technique is called template shaping, and it's a fast, easy way to reproduce an exact contour in any number of pieces of stock. Because a router or a shaper produces the final surface, it's not impor-

tant to saw exactly to the layout line. In this case, a bandsaw is used to remove the excess stock before making the finished cut with a router or a shaper.

To use this technique, you'll first have to make a template, which must be the exact contour that you want to reproduce. Next, secure the stock to the template with toggle clamps, brads, or double-sided tape. Before shaping, select a router bit or shaper cutter with the desired profile. The bit or cutter must have a bearing to follow the contours of the template (see the drawing above).

Using a template-guided router or shaper is the fastest way to remove bandsaw marks from curved stock.

The lower piece shows the best a router can do to shape an inside corner. I've carved the correct profile into the upper piece by hand.

Once you've got a good template, removing bandsaw marks with this method is remarkably fast and easy. As the bearing on the router or shaper follows the template, the cutter removes the bandsaw marks and creates an exact copy of the template contour on the workpiece.

I use my table-mounted router for small- and medium-size cuts, and my shaper for large, heavy cuts. Although this is a great technique, it does have a few limitations. First, neither a router nor a shaper can create sharp inside corners (see the bottom photo at left). To solve this problem, you can either soften the inside corner to accommodate the bearing diameter, or you can do what I do: Shape as much as possible, then carve inside corners by hand. The radius of a contour that you wish to shape must be no smaller than the bearing diameter. This is where a router bit has a distinct advantage over a shaper cutter; its small bearing will turn through a much tighter curve.

Removing marks on ripped boards

When ripping straight stock on a bandsaw, you'll also want to remove the bandsaw marks and create a finished surface. Either a jointer, a planer, or a handplane will work.

Advanced Bandsaw Techniques

The bandsaw is a highly versatile machine capable of much more than basic curves. For example, by cutting stock on two faces, you can create compound curves such as cabriole legs and ogee feet. You can resaw wide boards straight through or on a curve. With the right blade and a precision tune-up, your bandsaw can also cut fine joinery. You can even use a template to make multiples of a complex curved piece.

In this chapter, I'll cover these topics as well methods for slicing your own veneer. So read on to discover ways to broaden the scope of your next woodworking project.

Compound Curves

A compound curve is one that flows in two directions simultaneously. When it comes to compound curves in furniture, probably the best-known example is the cabriole leg, as shown in the photo at right on p. 352. The curves on a cabriole leg begin at the top of the leg, or knee, taper gracefully downward toward the slender ankle, then quickly broaden again at the foot. Another common example is the ogee bracket foot. I tend to talk about 18th-century furniture, which is what I specialize in building, but compound curves are also found in the stylized forms of legs used on many contemporary furniture designs.

You can use your bandsaw to make compound curves such as those found on this ogee foot. Here, the basic outline has been cut, and the operator is now sawing the curve in one of the outside edges.

The cabriole legs on this Chippendale chair are a perfect example of compound curves—they curve in two directions at the same time.

Although cutting compound curves may seem intimidating, it is easy to do with your bandsaw. It simply involves sawing curves on two adjacent surfaces.

As with all curves, begin by sketching a design on thin plywood and bandsawing the pattern. Most likely you'll have to do

some smoothing of the curves of the pattern with a file—I usually do. Next, trace the pattern outline onto two adjacent faces of the stock. After bandsawing the first face, rotate the stock 90° and saw the second face. It's that easy. Afterwards, you'll have to use hand tools to connect and blend the curves.

If you've always wanted to make furniture with compound curves, then I encourage you to give it a try. It's surprisingly easy, and it's exciting to see a straight, square blank of wood so quickly transformed. I'll now cover the process step-by-step, so read on to discover how

Take time to get the pattern right

It's important to take time to make sure that the curves of your pattern are smooth and flowing because any flaws in the pattern will be transferred to the workpiece and duplicated.

When enlarging a curve, draw it first, then glue the paper pattern directly to the plywood pattern stock before bandsawing.

you can add compound curves to your next project.

Cabriole legs

As the first example of how to make a compound curve, I'll use a cabriole leg. Legs always come in pairs, so you'll need a pattern to duplicate the curves. I like to use ¼-in. birch plywood for patterns. It's strong, stiff, and the edges don't fray and wear away as will cardboard or paper.

Drawing a curved leg is actually more difficult than sawing and sculpting it. Good proportions between the knee, ankle, and foot are critical. If this is your first time, I suggest you use a pattern. You can enlarge the drawing by redrawing the grid full size, plotting the points, and sketching in the curve, or you can have it done at a copy shop. Once you've enlarged the drawing, glue it to the ply-wood (see the photo above). I use rubber cement to prevent the paper from wrin-kling. Carefully bandsaw the pattern along the layout lines, as shown in the photo at right. After sawing, smooth the edges with a file. While filing, look for irregularities in the curve, and make sure the curve has smooth, flowing lines.

Laying out the leg When milling the stock for a cabriole leg, I size it approxi-mately ¹⁄₁₆ in. larger all around than the pattern. This allows me to easily follow the contours of the pattern when I trace

> #### Accurately sawing to the line
> Saw right next to the line so that the blade teeth touch the line but the kerf falls in the waste.

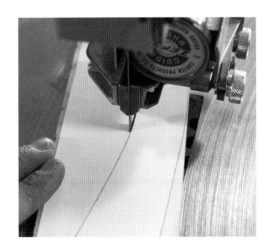

Accurate cutting reduces the amount of filing and sanding you'll do later to get the curve smooth.

Trace the cabriole leg pattern onto two adjacent faces of the leg stock back-to-back rather than knee-to-knee so you can cut the joints while the stock is still square.

around it. There's a lot of waste in a cabriole leg, so I examine the stock for minor defects, such as small knots or tearout, and locate them in the waste.

After you've traced the pattern onto the first surface, turn the leg to the adjacent surface and trace it a second time. I orient the pattern back-to-back rather than knee-to-knee. This way I can locate the area of the leg post and lay out and cut the mortise while the leg is still square.

If the leg is somewhat longer than the table on my bandsaw, I leave a couple of areas square when sawing the first face to support the leg on the table when cutting the adjacent face (see the drawing below). I'll refer to these areas as bridges. When I've finished sawing, I cut the bridges away. After sawing the first face, save the offcut at the back of the leg because it has the drawing for the adjacent face. I reattach the offcut with masking tape before sawing the adjacent face.

Bandsawing the leg Before bandsawing, make sure you have the right blade on your machine. For a typical cabriole leg, I choose a ¼-in.-wide, 6-pitch, regular-tooth blade. This narrow blade enables me to navigate the tight contour of the ankle.

Begin by making short, straight preliminary cuts for the bridges that support the second face and also at the inside corner where the knee adjoins the post (see the photo at left on the facing page). These cuts are easy to back out of, and they allow

Bridges Support the Leg while Cutting

When you are sawing a cabriole leg, bridges support the leg during the second cut. After completing the second cut, saw off the bridges.

Rotate the stock 90° to make the second cut.

Cut this line first.

Bridges

My first sawcuts are the short, straight relief cuts at the knee and bridge.

You'll have to tape this offcut back into position before sawing the second face.

you to avoid trapping the blade at the end of a long curve.

Next, start at the foot and saw the leg contours. As you approach each intersection where you made the preliminary cuts, reduce the feed pressure and ease into the junction. After sawing the contour at the back of the leg, save the offcut and tape it back into position (see the top right photo). Sawing the adjacent face is a repeat of what you've just done. When you're finished, you can saw off the existing bridges from the leg.

The sawn leg will have a graceful, curved but somewhat square appearance (see the top photo on p. 356). Use rasps

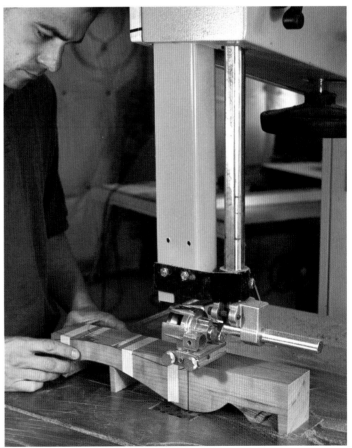

The bridges support the leg while sawing the second face.

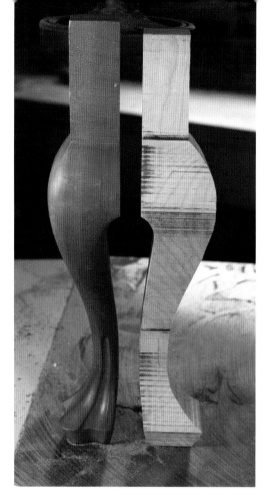

After band-sawing, use rasps and files to shape and smooth the leg.

and files to round the corners and blend the four leg surfaces.

Ogee bracket feet

Like a cabriole leg, the surfaces of an ogee foot are flowing compound curves. An ogee foot even has the classic cyma, or S, curve. It's commonly used to support casework such as chests and desks on many different styles of furniture.

But whereas a cabriole leg is sawn from a piece of solid stock, an ogee foot is sawn from two pieces joined at a right angle, typically with a miter reinforced with a spline (see the photo on the facing page).

Just as with a cabriole leg, you begin by drawing a pattern. You should realize, however, that you'll need a pattern that includes both the bracket outline and the ogee contour on the face of the foot (see the drawing on the facing page). Ogee feet come in many sizes to fit small chests to large, full-scale casework.

Cutting the joint Begin by cutting the miter joint that joins the two parts of the foot. I should mention that feet at the rear of a case have the ogee contour only at the side where it may be seen. The portion of the foot at the back of the case where it isn't usually seen is simply a square board that is fastened to the ogee half of the foot with half-blind dovetails (see the drawing on p. 358).

Before gluing the two halves of the foot together, bandsaw the bracket profile. The

Like the cabriole leg, the ogee foot has flowing curves on adjacent faces.

The two halves of a bracket foot are glued with a miter and plywood spline.

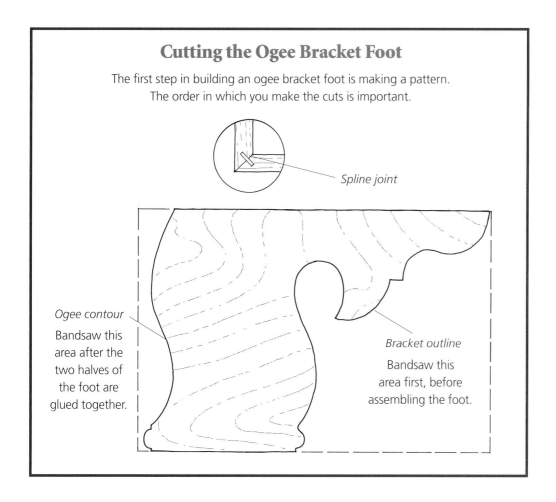

Cutting the Ogee Bracket Foot

The first step in building an ogee bracket foot is making a pattern. The order in which you make the cuts is important.

Spline joint

Ogee contour
Bandsaw this area after the two halves of the foot are glued together.

Bracket outline
Bandsaw this area first, before assembling the foot.

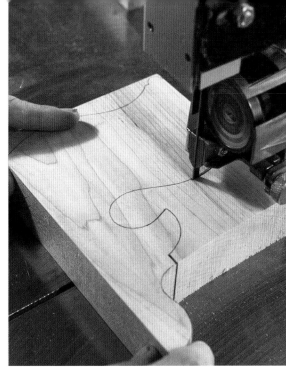
Before gluing the two halves of the foot, bandsaw the bracket outline.

Ogee Foot at the Back of the Casework

The feet at the back of the piece, which typically aren't seen, are not made with an elaborate scroll. Instead they are simple brackets fastened to the ogee half of the foot with half-blind dovetails.

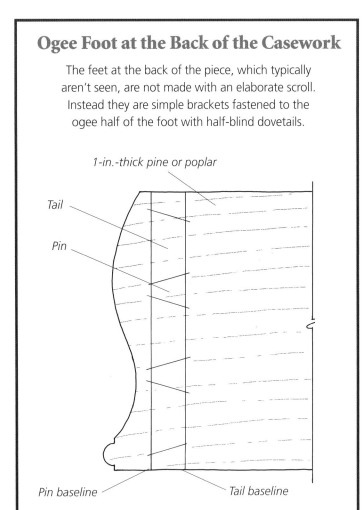

1-in.-thick pine or poplar

Tail

Pin

Pin baseline

Tail baseline

You can leave some sawmarks

It's really not necessary to smooth away all of the sawmarks inside the bracket area of the foot because they won't be seen once the finished foot is fastened to the base of the casework.

profile is often a combination of tight contours, so I use a narrow $\frac{3}{16}$-in. or $\frac{1}{8}$-in. blade. The photo on the facing page shows the proper sequence of cuts. Next, smooth the sawn surfaces with a file or a spindle sander.

Bandsawing the ogee profile Before you begin sawing, you'll need to build a stand to support the foot as it is being sawn. The stand I use is stone simple. I fasten four

boards together with dadoes, glue, and screws (see the drawing on the facing page). The stand doesn't have to be fancy—just sturdy and tall enough to suspend the foot off of the bandsaw table and position it parallel to the blade.

Now you're ready to begin sawing the foot. Secure the foot to the stand with a small clamp and adjust the upper guide no more than $\frac{1}{4}$ in. above the work for maximum safety and blade support.

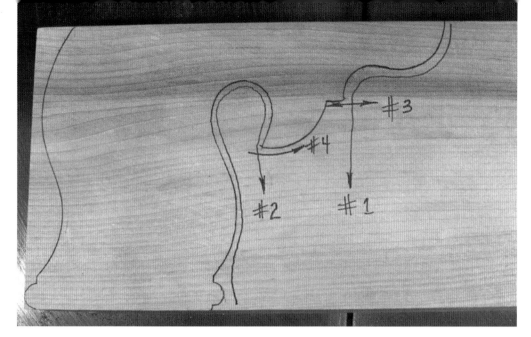

In a complex pattern such as this, it's important to plan your sequence of cuts so the blade won't get trapped.

A Stand for Bandsawing a Bracket Foot

To bandsaw an ogee contour in a bracket foot, the foot must be securely supported slightly above the table so that it is parallel to the blade.

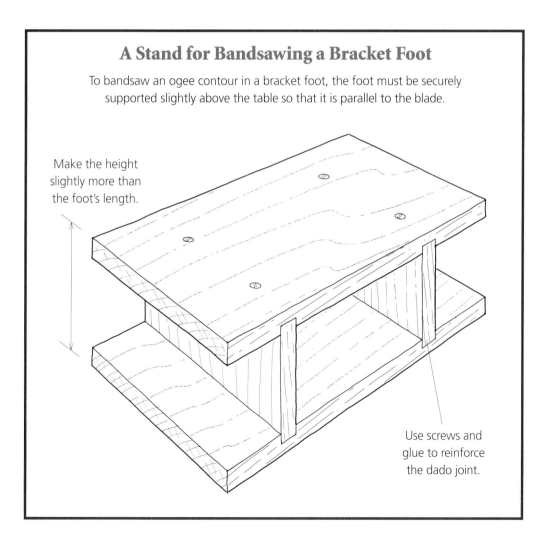

Make the height slightly more than the foot's length.

Use screws and glue to reinforce the dado joint.

The foot is supported on a simple stand for bandsawing the ogee contour into the face.

Feed slowly and cut close to the line. It will save a lot of time hand-shaping later.

The outline of the second face is revealed by the miter joint.

Blade for sawing an ogee bracket foot

A ¼-in., 4-pitch blade works well for the foot pattern I've provided. Proper tension is important to prevent the blade from deflecting and spoiling the foot.

Feed the workpiece slowly while sawing the foot, and follow the layout line as accurately as possible. This gives the foot a smooth, flowing contour and saves a lot of extra shaping by hand. When the first side is complete, reposition the foot and bandsaw the second face. You won't need to tape the offcut back in place for the layout line. You'll see that the foot contour for the second face is outlined by the miter joint (see the bottom photo on the facing page). When you're finished sawing the foot, clean it up in the usual way with files. You can also use a sharp rabbet plane for the square shoulders on either side of the bead.

Resawing

Resawing is the process of ripping a board through its thickness to make thinner boards. If you're making small boxes of any type, such as drawers, humidors, or jewelry boxes, you will need thin lumber. Rather than planing away excess thickness, you can resaw the stock and reduce your lumber expenses.

Probably the greatest benefit of resawing is that it gives you the ability to create your own veneer. With the right blade and a well-tuned bandsaw, you can create veneer as thin as $\frac{1}{16}$ in.

Using veneer is a dramatic way to decorate small boxes or to create a set of matching drawer fronts for a chest or desk. Whenever I come across a board that is highly figured, such as a walnut crotch or a slab of tight-grained curly maple, I set it aside for use as veneer. If you've never sawn your own veneer, I encourage you to give it a try. Using figured veneer is an exciting way to add visual appeal to almost any woodworking project.

Choosing a blade

More than any other bandsaw operation, resawing requires the right blade, and it must be sharp. A coarse-pitch blade is critical for sawing thin, consistently uni-

A well-tuned bandsaw can slice veneer from wide figured stock such as this walnut board.

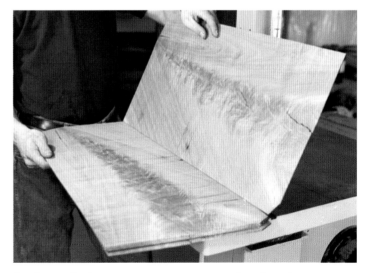

Book-matched veneer sawn on your own bandsaw is a great way to add distinction to your work.

Carbide for resawing

Although carbide-tipped band-saw blades are expensive, they are actually economical in the long run because they stay sharp so much longer than any other type of blade.

form veneer. Otherwise, the gullets pack with sawdust, and the blade bows and spoils your lumber. I prefer a variable-pitch hook-tooth blade, such as a 2/3 pitch, because it creates a smoother surface by limiting harmonic vibrations. Also, the hook-style tooth is very aggressive, which minimizes feed resistance.

For additional smoothness, it's tough to beat carbide. The carbide-tipped blades I have for my bandsaw produce a surface so smooth that very little sanding is required. This is a distinct advantage when sawing veneer.

Blade width is important, too. I recommend that you use the widest blade that your saw can properly tension. For woodworkers with a 14-in. bandsaw, that means a ½-in. blade.

Setting tension and guides

As I pointed out in chapter 4, a bandsaw blade requires 25,000 psi for maximum beam strength to resist deflection. When resawing, you definitely need this much tension. I use a tension meter to accurately tension the blade in preparation for resawing. If you have a 14-in. bandsaw and don't own a tension meter, then I recommend that you tension the blade until the tension spring is nearly compressed.

Guide adjustment is another key to produc-

Release the tension

When you're finished resawing, remember to release the blade tension. In time, high-tension settings can damage wheels, tires, bearings, and the tension spring.

ing thin, uniform sheets of veneer. You'll want to set each guide to within 0.003 in. of the blade. If you have block guides, check them for wear, and if necessary, true the faces with a file. The thrust wheel must be set close as well. I've found that guide adjustment is never more critical than with resawing. For more detail on guide adjustments, see pp. 319–322.

Using a resaw fence

Most bandsaw blades suffer from a phenomenon called drift, which means that the blades don't rip in a line that is parallel to the fence. Obviously, this can be a problem if you attempt to use your bandsaw fence to guide the stock. In my experience, the worst offenders are blades that are ½ in. wide or less. I've found that wide blades, such as 1 in. or 1¼ in., will rip parallel to the fence. So if you have a large bandsaw that can handle wide blades, you can probably use the fence that came with your saw. Otherwise, I recommend that you construct a simple plywood fence for your bandsaw so you can position it at the angle of drift (see pp. 345–346). Once the blade is tensioned and the fence is in place, make a test cut to double-check the final stock thickness.

Making the cut

Although resawing veneer takes a little practice, it's really quite easy to develop a feel for the technique. I recommend that you begin by feeding the plank very slowly, then gradually increasing the feed rate. If you're sensitive to the sounds and vibrations that the saw is producing, you'll

When bandsawing veneer, feed the stock slowly and be attentive to the sounds of your bandsaw. You'll know when you're feeding the stock too fast by the sound.

Sawing shallow kerfs first with your table saw makes resawing quick and easy, although it's not as precise as using a fence.

know when you're pushing the machine too hard. Remember to save your fingers by finishing the cut with a push stick.

Resawing without a fence

Another method for resawing on a bandsaw doesn't use a fence, but it does require a table saw. First, rip shallow kerfs on the edges of the stock with the table saw, then finish the cuts on the bandsaw—without a fence (see the right photo above). A sharp blade will have a natural tendency to follow the path of least resistance, which

is along the kerfs from the table saw. I use this method when my concern is speed rather than precision. In that case, I don't

Resaw fences are high

Height is important on a resaw fence so that wide boards are well supported. If your bandsaw came with a decent fence, consider screwing or bolting a high plywood face to it. If you're building your own fence, it's easy to make it high enough for wide boards.

want or need to take the time to set the fence and guides precisely.

Resawing on a curve

Another useful bandsaw technique to know is how to resaw a curve. Many furniture parts, such as the back of the chair on p. 352, have wide, curved parts that are relatively thin. A straight fence is useless for guiding curved stock, yet it is impossible to accurately cut such an awkward piece freehand.

The key to resawing a curve accurately is to use a point fence. This is simply a narrow piece of wood with a chamfered point that mounts to the resaw fence parallel to and right at the blade. The point fence guides the stock and positions it parallel to the blade, yet it allows you to pivot the stock to follow the contoured outline.

To use a point fence, mark the layout of the curve on the edge of the stock. Then bandsaw the first face freehand without the fence, carefully following the layout line (see the photo at left). Before sawing the second face, remove the bandsaw marks with a spokeshave to smooth the surface and create a flowing curve (see the photo at left on the facing page).

Next, lay out a parallel curved line to indicate the final thickness of the workpiece. For accurate results, I use a sharp marking gauge and follow the first curve (see the top photo at right on the facing page). Before bandsawing the second

To resaw a curve, you must first saw one face freehand. Carefully follow the layout line.

Use a sharp spokeshave to remove the bandsaw marks from the curved face and to smooth the curve.

Use a marking gauge to scribe the second face parallel to the first.

curve, fasten the point fence adjacent to the teeth of the blade at a distance equal to the final thickness.

To make the final cut, position the smooth, contoured face of the stock against the point fence and begin sawing (see the photo at right). As you saw, press the stock firmly against the fence, and pivot the stock to follow the scribed layout line from the marking gauge. Over-feeding can cause the blade to deflect, so feed the stock slowly and pay attention to the sounds and vibrations produced by your bandsaw.

Hold the workpiece firmly to the point fence and pivot it to follow the layout line to cut the second face.

Bandsaw Joinery

Because table saws are good at making accurate, square joints, it's natural that most woodworkers think first of a table saw for making joints, especially tenons. But you can also achieve surprisingly accurate work with your bandsaw. And if you don't own a table saw, then your bandsaw is certainly a good option.

For cutting joints such as dovetails and tenons on your bandsaw, you'll need a precision blade and guides to control the cut. You'll also want to review chapter 6 and make sure your saw is properly tuned. If the blade is bouncing or vibrating excessively, you can't expect to execute precise joinery. It's also vital that the table is 90° to the blade when cutting tenons and that the miter gauge is adjusted to cut square.

The best choice for a joinery blade is one that is wide with a fine pitch. The extra blade width will help to ensure that the blade cuts straight without wandering. A ½-in. blade works well for this application. The fine pitch will create the smooth surface needed for a snug fit inside the joint and a good glue bond.

When you're ready to saw, guide the stock through your bandsaw just as you would on a table saw: by using the fence and the miter gauge. To create the angles necessary for dovetails, you'll have to tilt the table to the left. I use a 15° angle for dovetails, but if your bandsaw table doesn't tilt that far, you can either use a smaller angle, such as 10°, or you can build an auxiliary angled table that clamps to your bandsaw's table (as shown in the drawing on p. 370).

Mortise-and-tenon joinery

The mortise-and-tenon joint is the strongest method for joining two pieces of wood end to edge to form a right angle. I use the mortise-and-tenon joint for making face frames on furniture and cabinets as well as for the frames on frame-

The Mortise-and-Tenon Joint

The mortise-and-tenon joint is the strongest way to join two pieces of wood at a right angle. Cut the mortise first, then the tenon to fit.

Mortise

Tenon face

Tenon shoulder

and-panel doors. I always cut the mortise first, then I cut the tenon to fit. Although I use a hollow-chisel mortising machine to cut the mortise, a plunge router also works well.

For a joint to be strong, the tenon must fit snugly inside the mortise. A standard tenon has four surfaces: two shoulders that bear against the outside of the mortise, and two tenon faces that fit within the walls of the mortise.

Cutting a tenon on the bandsaw involves sawing the shoulders first, then the two faces. Layout is critical to well-fitting joints. I use a knife and a marking gauge to incise the wood fibers for a clean cut and to help avoid confusion about which part of the stock is to be sawn away. I encourage you to take care to mill the stock precisely. Each piece must be identical in thickness, width, and length for a consistent fit of the joints.

After layout, the next step is to cut the shoulders. First, position a test piece in front of the blade for the cut. If I'm making only one or two tenons, I cut free-hand, but if I'm making several tenons, I use stops. Stops greatly increase accuracy and efficiency when cutting multiple pieces of stock. To create a fixed distance between the end of the tenon and the shoulder, use the fence as a stop. Use a second stop to control the depth of the shoulder.

Use the miter gauge to cut the tenon shoulders.

Mill all stock at once

Whenever I'm working wood to precise tolerances with a machine, I find that it's crucial to mill all the stock together along with a test piece. This helps to ensure both accuracy and consistency between all pieces of stock.

After the tenon shoulders are cut, set the fence to guide the workpiece for cutting the tenon face. This is when a test piece of stock is especially helpful. I hold the stock against the fence in front of the blade and bring the fence and test piece

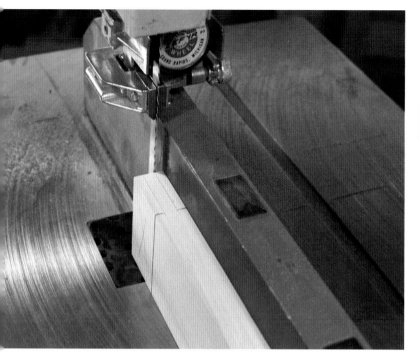

Use the layout lines as a guide when setting the fence.

Fitting the tenon

Slight fence adjustments may yield significant changes in the tenon thickness because each cut must be made on both faces of the stock to keep the tenon centered.

As you slice the face of each tenon, press the stock firmly against the fence.

A mortise-and-tenon joint is extremely strong but only when the pieces fit together snugly.

toward the blade until the teeth are right on the layout line, then I lock the fence in place. A block of wood clamped to the rear portion of the fence will act as a stop and ensure that each tenon is the same length.

Now you're ready to make the test cuts on both sides of the tenon and to test the fit within the mortise. The indication of a proper fit is when the tenon is snug within the mortise yet it doesn't require heavy blows from a mallet to assemble. If the fit isn't just right, it's easy to make adjustments by moving the fence and making more test cuts.

Dovetail joinery

No other woodworking joint denotes quality quite like the dovetail. Like the mortise-and-tenon joint, the dovetail has been around for centuries. And although faster methods of joinery have been devised, no other joint comes close to the strength of the dovetail's interlocking tails and pins.

The dovetail joint has a look of excellence when well executed, but it can be a distracting eyesore if poorly done. Unfortunately, cutting the joint by hand requires a high degree of skill and confidence. I don't think that router jigs are a viable alternative to hand-cutting dove-

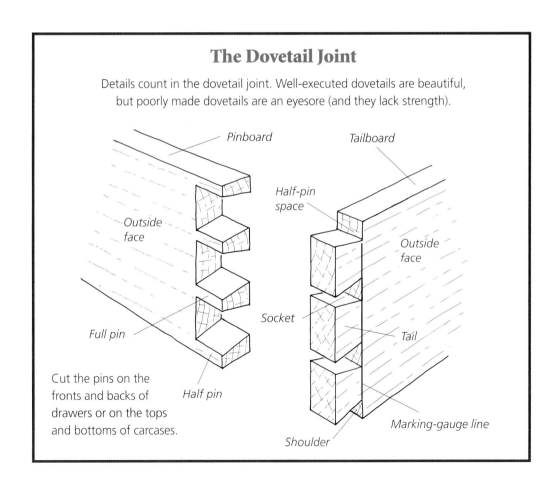

The Dovetail Joint

Details count in the dovetail joint. Well-executed dovetails are beautiful, but poorly made dovetails are an eyesore (and they lack strength).

Pinboard

Tailboard

Outside face

Half-pin space

Outside face

Full pin

Socket

Tail

Cut the pins on the fronts and backs of drawers or on the tops and bottoms of carcases.

Half pin

Marking-gauge line

Shoulder

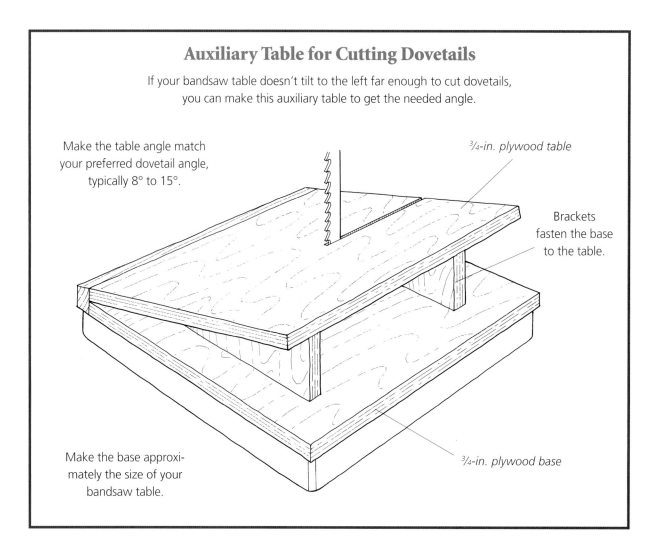

Auxiliary Table for Cutting Dovetails

If your bandsaw table doesn't tilt to the left far enough to cut dovetails, you can make this auxiliary table to get the needed angle.

Make the table angle match your preferred dovetail angle, typically 8° to 15°.

¾-in. plywood table

Brackets fasten the base to the table.

Make the base approximately the size of your bandsaw table.

¾-in. plywood base

tails because to my eye the completed joint has a machine-made, inferior look. Also, many of the router jigs I've seen cut both boards at once. They are complicated to set up, and if one of the many adjustments isn't quite right, then both the pinboard and the tailboard are spoiled.

Although I cut dovetails by hand, as a woodworking instructor I've become sympathetic to those who lack the time or patience to practice making the joint. An

excellent alternative is to cut half of the joint with a bandsaw and cut the second half by hand to fit. Most people who I introduce to this technique find that it doesn't require nearly as much time to learn, and there's very little measuring or layout involved. Also, since the pinboard is made first on the bandsaw and the tailboard is cut to match the pinboard, you don't lose all of your work if you make a mistake on one of them. Best of all, this technique yields a handmade look because you can control the size and spacing of the joint's tails and pins, which you cannot do on a router jig.

All you need to cut dovetails on a bandsaw is a saw with a table that tilts both to the right and to the left up to 15°. If your bandsaw table doesn't tilt both ways, you can still cut dovetails using the auxiliary table shown in the drawing on the facing page.

For your first set of bandsaw dovetails, I suggest you start with a simple arrangement: one full pin and two half pins. This looks good when made in fairly narrow workpieces, such as drawer sides or shallow boxes.

One way to cut dovetails on a bandsaw is to draw the pins on a board with the spacing you want and simply saw them out. Just tilt the table and adjust the fence until the blade aligns with the marks. Reset the fence for each cut, and tilt the table in the opposite direction to get the other side of the pins (see the bottom photo at right). This simple method is how I most often use a bandsaw for dovetails.

There's another method that requires very little measurement and no laying out or making marks on the end grain. It uses nothing more complicated than spacer blocks and a fence (see the drawing on pp. 372–373). The bandsaw setup takes care of everything. All you need to know is the width of your workpiece and the width of the pins, though you may find it helpful to draw the dovetails the first couple of times you make the joint.

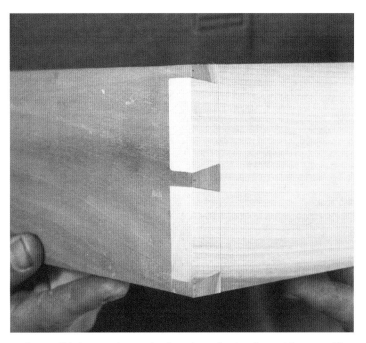

A dovetail joint made on the bandsaw is simple and fast, and it has a vibrancy lacking in those made with a router jig.

One way to cut dovetails on the bandsaw is to mark them, tilt the bandsaw fence, and simply saw the pins with the fence as a guide.

Cutting Dovetails on a Bandsaw

Bandsaw dovetails have some advantages over dovetails made with a router and jig. First, the setup is less complicated. Second, a mistake in cutting either the pins or the tails doesn't ruin both boards. The layout is easy and doesn't involve much measuring or any drawing. Perhaps most important, dovetails made on a bandsaw don't have the lifeless machine-made quality of dovetails made with a router jig.

Find the dimensions of the spacer blocks

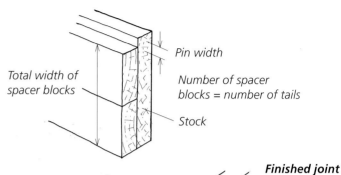

Total width of spacer blocks

Pin width

Number of spacer blocks = number of tails

Stock

Finished joint

Tails

Pins

1. Determine the width of the pin and subtract that number from the width of the stock. This gives the total width of the spacer blocks. Divide the total width of the spacer blocks by the number of tails in the joint. The result is the width of each spacer block. The number of required spacer blocks equals the number of tails.

Tilt the table and set the fence

2. Tilt the table to the right at an angle equal to the dovetail angle. Position the fence to the right of the blade by putting all the spacer blocks between the blade and the fence.

Angle of table = angle of dovetail (typically 8° to 15°)

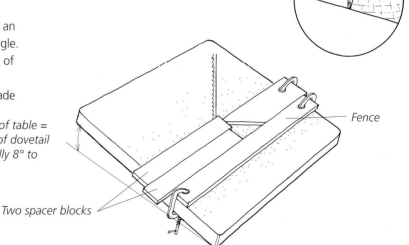

Fence

Two spacer blocks

Cut the pins

3. Remove one spacer block and cut to the scribed line.

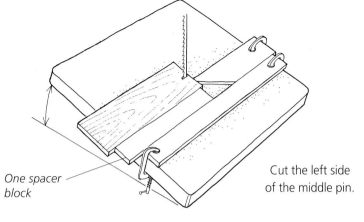

One spacer block

Cut the left side of the middle pin.

4. Remove all the spacer blocks one at a time and make a cut. Make the last cut against the fence.

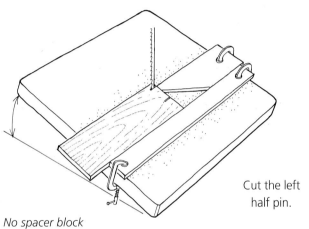

No spacer block

Cut the left half pin.

Tilt the table opposite and repeat

5. Tilt the table in the opposite direction and set the fence to the left. Remove the spacer blocks and make the cuts.

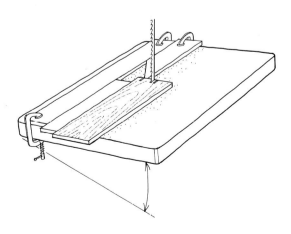

Remove most of the waste between the pins with a bandsaw, but don't try to cut to the baseline. Use a chisel to clean out the waste right along the baseline.

Let's assume you're working with a 4¾-in.-wide drawer side. First, you must decide how wide you want your pins to be. This is simply a design decision. I don't think the width of the pins is critical; you can try out various arrangements and see what you like. Let's say the pins will be ½ in. wide. Subtract the pin width from the width of the drawer side to get the total width of the spacer blocks— 4¼ in. in this case. Divide by two to get the width of each of two spacer blocks. Next,

make the spacer blocks by ripping a 2-ft.-long piece of stock to 2⅛ in. wide.

To cut the joint, take a sharp marking gauge and set it for the thickness of the stock, then run it parallel to the ends of the two workpieces. This scribed baseline prevents tearout and keeps the shoulders crisp and clean.

Position the fence by laying the spacer blocks between the fence and the blade, being careful not to bend the blade. Lock the fence and remove one of the blocks. Using the spacer block as the fence, cut the right-hand side of the middle pin. Don't cut right to the scribed line but very near. You might want to use a stop block fastened to the table or the fence to limit the length of the cut, but I typically saw it by eye. Remove the second block and cut the left-hand half pin.

To cut the other side of the dovetail, tilt the table to the left 15° and set the fence using the spacer blocks as before. Again, remove one block and cut the left-hand side of the middle pin, then remove the second block and cut the right-hand half pin. Return the table to 90° and cut out the waste by making a series of parallel cuts that leave each waste area looking like a comb. I don't attempt to saw directly on the scribed baseline. Instead, I use a mallet and a sharp chisel to chop the baseline in the traditional way (see the photo at left).

Once you've completed the pinboard, transfer the layout directly to the tailboard. Do this by positioning the end of the pinboard over the face of the tailboard. Be careful to align the pinboard on the baseline of the tailboard, and then scribe around each pin with an X-Acto knife.

The last step is to saw the tails. You can cut them in the traditional way using a dovetail saw, or you can cut them out freehand on your bandsaw with the table at 90° to the blade. Finally, chisel the waste area between the tails and assemble the joint with gentle taps from a mallet.

If you want to make more than the one full pin and two half pins in this example, simply change the number of spacer blocks. Everything else about the procedure is the same: Decide the pin width, find the total width of the spacer blocks, and divide that by the number of tails you want. The result will be the width of each spacer block. Set up the saw as before, and remove one spacer block to make the first cut. Next, remove each remaining spacer block, make a cut, and continue until you've cut the half pin. Finally, tilt the table the other way, and repeat the steps.

Scribe the tails directly from the pins and cut them freehand.

Template Sawing

The fastest way to reproduce identical parts is with a machine guided by a template. Most woodworkers are familiar with the technique as it applies to a router: A bearing, which is fastened to the end of a router bit, runs around the edge of a template fastened to the workpiece. The template is then fastened to the next workpiece, and the process is repeated. All pieces, whether there are 6 or 600, are

A template and a guide make repetitive cuts fast and easy. All you have to do is feed the stock while making sure it's pressed firmly against the guide.

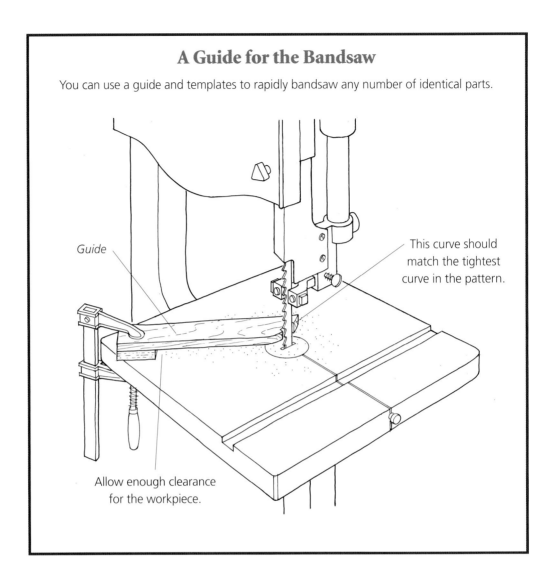

A Guide for the Bandsaw

You can use a guide and templates to rapidly bandsaw any number of identical parts.

Guide

This curve should match the tightest curve in the pattern.

Allow enough clearance for the workpiece.

exact copies because the same template is used to guide the router.

This concept can be applied to a bandsaw for reproducing curves. Rather than drawing the design on the stock and carefully sawing to the line, a template is attached to the stock and the cut is guided by a stick that is secured to the table adjacent to the blade (see the drawing above). This permits you to saw faster because you don't have to concentrate on following the layout line. Instead of following the line, you simply push the stock past the blade while maintaining contact between the template and the guide.

Bandsawing with a template is definitely a fast way to produce any number of curved parts. But the technique does have a major shortcoming: You can't saw inside corners. In fact, the technique is most beneficial for bandsawing large, sweeping curves such as chair rockers.

Also, because making an accurate template may consume a considerable amount of time, the benefit gained by sawing with a template may not outweigh the cost. Nevertheless, bandsawing with a template can be a quick, accurate method for producing large quantities of certain types of work.

For a template, you'll want to use a material that is stiff, strong, and easy to work. I've found that a high-quality plywood is ideal. Inexpensive plywood isn't suitable because it typically isn't flat and it has voids in the core between the veneer layers. Consequently, the guide will catch in the voids and spoil the workpiece.

Making a template is much like making a pattern: You simply draw the design and carefully cut it out. It's also important to sand or otherwise smooth away any irregularities. If you don't take time to smooth away errors, they will be duplicated in any work for which the template is used.

The guide is simply a stick that extends from the blade of the bandsaw to the edge of the table. The business end of the stick, near the blade, is notched to fit around the blade. It's also convex in shape to easily follow the curves of the template. The other end of the stick clamps firmly to the table edge.

With the setup complete, the actual sawing becomes the easiest part of the job. As you're sawing, always keep the template positioned against the guide.

Securing a Template

You can attach a template to your workpiece in a number of ways. My favorite method is to tack the template to the stock with small brads. If you allow the heads to protrude, it's much easier to pull the brads out again. Obviously, you don't want to use brads if the holes will show in the finished work, but typically you can position the brads in an area where they won't be seen or where the offending holes in the stock will later be removed during joinery and construction.

Another option for securing a template to a workpiece is to use double-sided tape. The cloth tape used by woodturners is strong and readily available from many woodworking-supply catalogs. I'm not a fan of this tape because the application is so slow it can often negate any benefits of template sawing.

A third option is to construct a jig that includes the template profile plus toggle clamps to secure the work. Toggle clamps are quick to operate and are ideal for most jig-clamping situations. Because constructing the jig takes time, I reserve this method for parts that I reproduce often.

Make the template a little long

I make the template approximately ½ in. longer than the stock so that the template contacts the guide before the work reaches the blade. This ensures a safe, accurate start to the cut.

Sources

Adjustable Clamp Co.
417 N. Ashland Ave.
Chicago, IL 60622-6397
(312) 666-0640
Clamps

Amana Tool® Corp.
120 Carolyn Blvd.
Farmingdale, NY 11735
(800) 445-0077
www.amanatool.com
Sawblades, router bits

Ball & Ball Hardware
463 West Lincoln Highway
Exton, PA 19341
(800) 257-3711
www.ballandball-us.com

Biesemeyer Manufacturing Corp.
216 S. Alma School Rd., Ste. 3
Mesa, AZ 85210
(800) 782-1831
www.biesemeyer.com
*Replacement rip fences, blade guards
and splitters, extension tables, sliding
crosscut sleds*

Black Diamond Guides
P.O. Box 419
Natick, MA 01760
(508) 653-4480

Blue Tornado Cyclones
P.O. Box 156
Buckner, KY 40010
(800) 292-0157
www.bluetornadocyclones.com
Dust collectors

Bridge City Tool Works, Inc.®
5820 N.E. Hassalo
Portland, OR 97213-3644
(800) 253-3332
www.bridgecitytools.com
Layout and measuring tools

Bridgewood®
Wilke Machinery Co.
3230 N. Susquehanna Trail
York, PA
(800) 235-2100
www.wilkemach.com
Table saws

Bruss Fasteners
P.O. Box 88307
Grand Rapids, MI 49518-0307
(800) 536-0009
Steel X-dowels

Carter Products Company, Inc.
437 Spring Street, NE
Grand Rapids, MI 49503
(616) 451-2928
www.carterproducts.com

CMT USA
307-F Pomona Dr.
Greensboro, NC 27407
(888) 268-2487
www.cmtusa.com
Table-saw blades, router bits

Delta Machinery
(800) 223-7278 (parts or technical
assistance)
www.deltawoodworking.com

De-Sta-Co
P.O. Box 2800
Troy, MI 48007
(810) 594-5600
Toggle clamps

DeWalt Industrial Tools
701 E. Joppa Rd., TW 425
Baltimore, MD 21286
(800) 433-9258
www.dewalt.com
*Table saws, sawblades, electric power
tools*

Eagle Tool®
2217 El Sol Ave.
Altadena, CA 91001
(626) 797-8262
www.eagle-tools.com
*Mini-Max European table saws and com-
bination machines*

Enviro Safety Products
516 E. Modoc Ave.
Visalia, CA 93292
(800) 637-6606
www.envirosafetyproducts.com
Safety supplies

Excalibur Sommerville Group
940 Brock Rd.
Pickering, ON, Canada L1W2A1
(800) 357-4118
www.excalibur-tool.com
*Replacement fences, blade covers,
rolling tables*

Fein Power Tools, Inc.
3019 W. Carson St.
Pitttsburgh, PA 15204
(412) 331-2325
Electric power tools

Felder® USA
1851 Enterprise Blvd.
West Sacramento, CA 95691
(916) 375-3190
www.felderusa.com
*European table saws and combination
machines*

Fenner Drives®
311 W. Stiegel St.
Manheim, PA 17545
(800) 243-3374
www.fennerindustrial.com
Table-saw link belts

Forrest Manufacturing Company
457 River Rd.
Clifton, NJ 07014
(800) 733-7111
Sawblades

Freud® USA
218 Seld Ave.
High Point, NC 27263
(800) 334-4107
Sawblades

Garrett Wade
161 Avenue of the Americas
New York, NY 10013
(800) 221-2942
www.garrettwade.com
*Inca European table saws,
table-saw accessories*

General® International
835, rue Cherrier
Drummondville, QB, Canada J2b 5A8
(819) 472-1161
www.general.ca
Table saws

Grizzly Industrial®
P.O. Box 2069
Bellingham, WA 98227
(800) 523-4777
www.grizzly.com
Table saws and accessories

Guhdo®-USA, Inc.
1135 JVL Industrial Blvd.
Marietta, GA 30066
(800) 544-8436
www.guhdo.com
Table-saw blades

Hammer® USA
1851 Enterprise Blvd.
West Sacramento, CA 95691
(800) 700-0071
www.hammerusa.com
*European table saws and
combination machines*

Hampton House
200 N. Brewer St.
Greenwood, IN 46142-3605
(317) 881-8601
Katie Jig

Highland Hardware
1045 North Highland Avenue, NE
Atlanta, GA 30306
(800) 241-6748
www.highland-hardware.com

Hitachi Power Tools
3950 Steve Reynolds Blvd.
Norcross, GA 30093
(800) 706-7337
Electric power tools

HTC® Products, Inc.
120 E. Hudson
P.O. Box 839
Royal Oak, MI 48068
(800) 624-2027
Replacement blade covers, fences, extension tables, tool covers, mobile bases

Incra® Tools
11050 Industrial First
North Royalton, OH 44133
(800) 752-0725
www.woodpeck.com
Replacement fences and accessories

In-Line Industries
661 S. Main St.
Webster, MA 01570
(800) 533-6709
Link belts and accessories

JDS Company
108 Leventis Dr.
Columbia, SC 29209
(800) 480-7269
Air cleaners and accessories

Jet Equipment & Tools®
P.O. Box 1937
Auburn, WA 98071
(800) 274-6848
www.jettools.com
Table saws and accessories

J&L Industrial Supply
P.O. Box 3359
Livonia, MI 48151-3359
(800) 521-9520
Machine tools

Jesada Tools, Inc.
310 Mears Blvd.
Oldsmar, FL 34677
(800) 531-5559
Router bits and accessories

JessEm Tool Co.
171 Robert St. East, Unit #8
Penetanguishene, ON L9M 1G9
Canada
(800) 436-6799
Rout-R-Lift

Jointech
11725 Warfield St.
San Antonio, TX 78216
(800) 619-1288
Joinery jigs and templates, replacement fences and accessories

JKeller & Co.
1327 I St.
Petaluma, CA 94952
(800) 995-2456
Dovetail templates

Lab Safety Supply
P.O. Box 1368
Janesville, WI 53547
(800) 356-0783
(800) 356-2501 (technical advice)
www.labsafety.com
Safety supplies

Laguna Tools
17101 Murphy Ave.
Irving, CA 92614
(800) 234-1976
www.lagunatools.com
European table saws, combination machines, rolling tables

Leigh Industries, Ltd.
P.O. Box 357
Port Coquitlan, BC U3C 4K6
Canada
(604) 464-2700
Dovetail and joinery jigs

Lenox
American Saw & Manufacturing
Company
301 Chestnut Street
East Longmeadow, MA 01028
(800) 628-3030
www.lenoxsaw.com
Blade tension meters

The L.S. Starrett Company®
121 Crescent St.
Athol, MA 01331
(978) 249-3551
www.starrett.com
Layout and measuring tools

Makita® USA
14930 Northam St.
La Miranda, CA 90638
(310) 926-8775
www.makitaope.com
Table saws

Mesa Vista Design
804 Tulip Rd.
Rio Rancho, NM 87124
(800) 475-0293
www.grip-tite.com
Safety accessories

Micro Fence
11100 Cumpton St., #35
N. Hollywood, CA 91601
(818) 766-4367
Edge circle guides, ellipse maker

Milwaukee Electric Tool
13135 W. Lisbon Rd.
Brookfield, WI 53005
(262) 781-3600
Electric power tools

Modulus 2000 Machinery Inc.
P.O. Box 206
Saint Hubert, QB
Canada J3Y 5T3
(800) 633-8587
www.modulus2000.com
*Scoring saw attachments, saw fences,
and accessories*

Mule Cabinetmaker
519 Mill St.
Lockport, NY 14095
(877) 684-7366
www.mulecab.com
Replacement fences and rolling tables

Oneida® Air Systems
1001 W. Fayette St.
Syracuse, NY 13204
(800) 732-4065
www.oneida-air.com
Dust collectors

Porter-Cable®
4825 Hwy. 45 N.
P.O. Box 2468
Jackson, TN 38302
(800) 487-8665
www.porter-cable.com
Table saws

PRC
731-C Paso Robles St.
Paso Robles, CA 93446
(800) 238-6144
Router bits

Powermatic
427 Sanford Rd.
LaVergne, TN 37086
(800) 274-6848
www.powermatic.com
Table saws

Reid Tool
2265 Black Creek Rd.
Muskegon, MI 49444-2684
(800) 253-0421
Jig hardware

Ridge Carbide
595 New York Ave.
Lyndhurst, NJ 07071
(800) 443-0992
Regrinding of router bits

Ridgid Tools
Emerson™
P.O. Box 4100
8000 W. Florissant Ave.
St. Louis, MO 63136
(800) 474-3443
www.ridgidwoodworking.com
Table saws and accessories

Rojek
7901 Industry Dr.
North Little Rock, AR 72117
(800) 787-6747
www.tech-mark.com
*European table saws and
combination machines*

Ryobi® Power Tools
5201 Pearman Dairy Rd.
Anderson, SC 29625
(800) 323-4615
www.ryobitools.com
Table saws

S-B Power Tool Co. (Bosch)
4300 W. Peterson Ave.
Chicago, IL 60646-5999
(877) 267-2499
Electric power tools

Sears Roebuck & Co.
P.O. Box 19009
Provo, UT 84605
(800) 377-7414
www.sears.com
Table saws and accessories

Shopsmith®, Inc.
3931 Image Dr.
Dayton, OH 45414
(800) 543-9396
www.shopsmith.com
Combination machines and accessories

Suffolk Machinery Corp.
12 Waverly Avenue
Patchogue, NY 11772-1902
(800) 234-7297
www.suffolkmachine.com

Tannewitz, Inc.
0-794 Chicago Drive
Jenison, MI 49428
(800) 458-0590
www.tannewitz.com

Taylor Design Group, Inc.
P.O. Box 810262
Dallas, TX 75381
(972) 418-4811
Incra jig

Tenryu® America
4301 Woodland Park Dr., Ste. 104
W. Melbourne, FL 32904
(800) 951-7297
www.tenryu.com
Sawblades

Veritas Tools, Inc.
12 East River St.
Ogdensburg, NY 13669
(800) 871-8158
Woodworking tools, router accessories

Patrick Warner
1427 Kenora St.
Escondido, CA 92027
(760) 747-2623
Acrylic offset subbases and jigs

W. L. Fuller, Inc.
P.O. Box 87677
Warwick, RI 0288
(401) 467-2900
Drilling tools

Woodhaven
501 W. 1st Ave.
Durant, IA 52747
(800) 344-6657
Router accessories

Index